Reformation

A Tudor and Stewart Genealogy

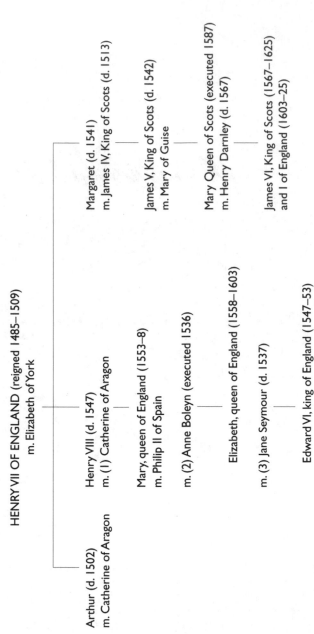

HENRY VII OF ENGLAND (reigned 1485–1509)
m. Elizabeth of York

Arthur (d. 1502)
m. Catherine of Aragon

Henry VIII (d. 1547)
m. (1) Catherine of Aragon

Mary, queen of England (1553–8)
m. Philip II of Spain

m. (2) Anne Boleyn (executed 1536)

Elizabeth, queen of England (1558–1603)

m. (3) Jane Seymour (d. 1537)

Edward VI, king of England (1547–53)

Margaret (d. 1541)
m. James IV, King of Scots (d. 1513)

James V, King of Scots (d. 1542)
m. Mary of Guise

Mary Queen of Scots (executed 1587)
m. Henry Darnley (d. 1567)

James VI, King of Scots (1567–1625)
and I of England (1603–25)

Reformation

The Dangerous Birth of the Modern World

HARRY REID

SAINT ANDREW PRESS
Edinburgh

First published in paperback in 2010 by
SAINT ANDREW PRESS
121 George Street
Edinburgh EH2 4YN

First published in hardback in 2009

ISBN 978 0 7152 0937 0

British Library Cataloguing in Publication Data
A catalogue record for this book is available from the British Library.

It is the publisher's policy to only use papers that are natural and recyclable and that have been manufactured from timber grown in renewable, properly managed forests. All of the manufacturing processes of the papers are expected to conform to the environmental regulations of the country of origin.

Typeset in Palatino by Waverley Typesetters, Warham, Norfolk
Printed and bound in the United Kingdom by Bell & Bain Ltd, Glasgow

This book is for

Julie Davidson
Laura Fiorentini
Andrew McGowan
Paul Henderson Scott
and Stuart Trotter

Contents

Quotations

All of Italy must be turned upside down, Rome as well, and then the Church must be renewed. – *Girolamo Savonarola*

Among Christians, each is the judge of the other and each is subject to the other. – *Martin Luther*

I want to talk. I want to write. But I do not want to force anyone, for faith needs to be voluntary and free, and to be received without fear. – *Martin Luther*

I cannot master myself. I want to be calm, yet I am driven into the midst of uproar. – *Martin Luther*

A simple layman armed with Scripture is to be believed above a pope. Neither the Church nor the pope can establish articles of faith. These must come from Scripture. – *Martin Luther*

Let everyone who can, smite, slay and stab, secretly or openly, remembering that nothing can be more poisonous, hurtful or devilish than a rebel. It is just as when one must kill a mad dog. – *Martin Luther*

Superstition, idolatry and hypocrisy have ample wages, but truth goes a-begging. – *Martin Luther*

A theologian is born by living, nay dying and being damned, not by thinking, reading or speculating. – *Martin Luther*

The truth is, we are beggars. – *Martin Luther*

An apostate, an open incestuous lecher, a plain limb of the devil, a manifest messenger of hell. – *St Thomas More on Martin Luther*

The blessing of a baker that knoweth the truth is as good as the blessing of our most holy father the pope. – *William Tyndale*

With kings for the most part we have no acquaintance, neither promise. They be also most commonly merciless. Moreover, if they promise, they be yet men as unconstant as are other people, and as untrue. But with God, if we have belief, we are acquainted and have an open way in unto him by the door of Christ which is never shut but through unbelief, and neither is there any porter to keep man out. – *William Tyndale*

We may allow ourselves to be surpassed by other religious orders in fasts, watchings and other austerities. But in the purity and perfection of obedience, together with the true resignation of our wills and abnegation of our judgement, I am very desirous, my dear brothers, that they who serve God in this society should be conspicuous. – *Saint Ignatius Loyola, founder of the Society of Jesus*

What seems to me white, I will believe black if the hierarchical Church so defines. – *Saint Ignatius Loyola*

Those who live in obedience must allow themselves to be led, moved about according to the will of divine providence, just like a dead body which is manipulated and moved in all directions. – *Saint Ignatius Loyola*

I suffer this day by men, not sorrowfully but with a glad heart and mind. For this cause I was sent, that I should suffer this fire for Christ's sake. Consider and behold my visage, ye shall not see me change my colour. This grim fire I fear not. And so I pray for you to do, if that any persecution come to you for the Word's sake; and not to fear them that slay the body, and afterward hath no power to slay the soul. – *Words of George Wishart before he was martyred at St Andrews in 1546*

In her heart was nothing but venom and destruction. – *John Knox on Mary Queen of Scots*

I am appointed by God to rebuke the sins and vices of all. I am not appointed to come to every man in particular to show him his offence; for that labour were infinite. – *John Knox*

To promote a woman to bear rule, superiority, dominion or empire above any realm, nation or city is repugnant to nature, contumely to God, a thing most contrarious to his received will and proved ordinance, and finally it is the subversion of good order or all equity and justice. – *John Knox*

I walk many times into the pleasant fields of the Holy Scriptures, where I pluck up the goodly green herbs of sentences, eat them by reading, chew them up by musing, and lay them at length in the seat of memory, so that I may less perceive the bitterness of this miserable life. – *Queen Elizabeth I of England*

I see many over-bold with God Almighty, making too many subtle scannings of His blessed will, as lawyers will do with human testaments. The presumption is so great, as I may not suffer it, yet mind I not hereby to animate Romanists, which what adversaries they be to mine estate is sufficiently known, nor tolerate newfangledness ... in both parts be perils. – *Queen Elizabeth I of England*

I am no lover of pompous title, but only desire that my reign may be recorded in a line or two, which shall briefly express my name, my virginity, the years of my reign, the reformation of religion under it, and my preservation of peace. – *Queen Elizabeth I of England*

You cannot name any example in any heathen author but I will better it in Scripture. – *James VI of Scotland and I of England*

No-one can be injurious to their brother or sister without wounding God himself. Were this doctrine deeply fixed in our minds, we should be more reluctant than we are to inflict injuries. – *John Calvin*

The Lord cannot endure excess, and it is absolutely necessary that it be severely punished. – *John Calvin*

If any man disapproves of us or anything we do or say, we are immediately offended without considering whether the judgement is right. If anyone examines himself, he will find this seed of pride within himself. – *John Calvin*

We know that riches and power always produce arrogance and a perverse confidence in men. Wars are not conceived in hamlets and villages, but the great cities collect the wood and kindle the fire, and the fire then spreads and sweeps over the whole land. – *John Calvin*

Social disorder is first and foremost disdain for the poor and oppression of the weak. – *John Calvin*

If you desire to have me as your pastor, correct the disorder of your lives … Re-establish pure discipline. – *John Calvin, to the Council of Geneva*

The Good Samaritan, when he came upon the man who had fallen among thieves, did not ask him to what denomination he belonged. – *Katherine Zell*

List of Popes

Innocent VIII	1484–92
Alexander VI	1492–1503
Pius III	1503
Julius II	1503–13
Leo X	1513–21
Hadrian VI	1522–3
Clement VII	1523–34
Paul III	1534–49
Julius III	1550–5
Marcellus II	1555
Paul IV	1555–9
Pius IV	1559–65
Saint Pius V	1566–72
Gregory XIII	1572–85
Sixtus V	1585–90

Key Scottish Martyrdoms

*A*BOUT twenty Scots were burned to death for heresy during the period before the Scottish Reformation finally got under way in 1559. The exact number remains unknown. The three most significant deaths are those listed below. That of the 82-year-old Walter Myln was particularly counter-productive. All three died at St Andrews.

Patrick Hamilton	February 1528
George Wishart	March 1546
Walter Myln	April 1558

The only recorded Catholic martyrdom in the Reformation era in Scotland came at the end of the period. Saint John Ogilvie was hanged (for treason) in Glasgow on 10 March 1615.

Some have claimed that the judicial execution of Mary Queen of Scots in England in 1587 made her a martyr for her faith.

1483	1485	1487	1497
Martin Luther born in Eisleben, north Germany	Henry Tudor, founder of the Tudor dynasty, crowned Henry VII of England	Henry VII wins the Battle of Stoke, securing his kingship	Girolamo Savonarola excommunicated, tortured, tried and burned to death in Florence

1527	1527	1522	1521
Leading Anabaptist Felix Manz drowned in Zurich by order of the city council Troops of Emperor Charles V sack Rome	Henry VIII seeks to annul his marriage to his first wife, Catherine of Aragon	Luther's German translation of the New Testament published, and instantly becomes a bestseller	At Worms, Emperor Charles V unsuccessfully orders Luther to recant Luther imprisoned for his own safety in Wartburg Castle

1528	1529	1533
First Scottish martyr, Patrick Hamilton, slowly burned to death at St Andrews	Huldrych Zwingli, leader of the Swiss Reformation, and Luther dispute bitterly at Marburg Henry VIII convenes his Reformation Parliament	Thomas Cranmer appointed Archbishop of Canterbury Henry VIII divorces Catherine of Aragon and marries Anne Boleyn

1559	1558	1555	1553
John Knox returns to Scotland and preaches a particularly inflammatory sermon at Perth Scotland in turmoil	Elizabeth crowned Queen of England Queen Mary's Catholic legislation repealed	Peace of Augsburg ends attempts by Emperor Charles V to reconvert Germany by conquest	Mary Tudor crowned Queen of England and embarks on the suppression of Protestantism

1559–60	1560	1562–98
Queen Elizabeth sends her navy and army north to help the Scots drive out the French and secure their Reformation	Scottish Reformation confirmed by the Scottish Parliament John Knox and his colleagues publish the *First Book of Discipline*, the seminal document of the Scottish Reformation	French Wars of Religion

1638	1603	1598
Scottish National Covenant	Union of the Crowns: James VI, King of Scots, great-grandson of Henry VII (of England) and grandson of James IV (King of Scots), becomes James I of England	Edict of Nantes grants tolerance to French Protestants outside Paris

1503
Henry VII marries
his daughter
Margaret to
James IV,
King of Scots

1509
John Calvin born
in Noyon, Picardy

Henry VII dies;
succeeded by his
second son,
Henry VIII

1513
Battle of
Flodden Field,
Scotland's
worst-ever
military defeat

1517
Luther issues his
ninety-five theses
in Wittenberg

1520
Henry VIII of England
condemns Luther and
is appointed
Defender of the Faith
by Pope Leo X

1519
Charles V elected
Holy Roman
Emperor

1518–21
Germany in
turmoil

1536
Henry VIII
executes
Anne Boleyn
(mother of
Queen Elizabeth I)

1536
First edition of
Calvin's *Institutes*
published

William Tyndale,
distinguished
translator of the Bible
into English, killed in
Antwerp

1540
Pope Paul III
sanctions the
Jesuits

1541
Calvin returns to
Geneva and begins
his long ministry
there

1552
Cranmer's *Second
Book of Common
Prayer*, the key
liturgical document
of the Anglican
Reformation,
published

1546
Luther dies

George Wishart
martyred at
St Andrews

1545
Council of Trent
opens

1564
Calvin dies in
Geneva

1567
Mary Queen of
Scots flees to
England

1577
Archbishop of
Canterbury,
Edmund Grindal,
suspended by
Queen Elizabeth for
refusing to suppress
Puritan 'prophesying'

1584
William of Orange
('William the Silent')
assassinated in the
Netherlands

1588
Spanish armada defeated by
the English, with some help
from the weather

1587
Mary Queen of Scots executed by
order of Queen Elizabeth;
England rejoices

Note on Contexts and Terms

*T*HIS book is a survey of the European Reformation of the sixteenth century and its consequences. It is not intended to be a complete history of the Reformation. What happened in countries like Norway, Sweden, Denmark, Poland, Ireland and Wales is barely touched on. The book deals mainly with Scotland, England, Germany, Switzerland, France and Italy, and to a much lesser extent Spain and its colonies in the Low Countries.

There is relatively little here about the threat of the Turks – a constant consideration for Western Europeans in that turbulent century. Suleiman the Magnificent was then the most powerful figure in the entire world, and it could be argued that the Turks saved the Reformation because the Holy Roman Emperor had to divert so much of his energy and effort to dealing with the threat from the East rather than with the Protestant revolt. And, if there is little about the Turks and the Muslim threat from the East, there is nothing at all in this book about the Eastern Orthodox Church.

Two very different places which are particularly important in our story are Wittenberg, the town in northern Germany which will always be associated with Luther, and Rome. Luther was a professor at Wittenberg's new, and very small, university. It was then a minor town of between 2,000 and 3,000 people. Its main industry was the brewing of heavy beer, a product that Luther appreciated. Rome was, by contrast, a big and important city, more like Paris. It was teeming with life, a lot of it low, though it was not quite as decadent and dirty as Paris, which in the early sixteenth century was (in some ways literally) the cesspit of Europe.

Paris was the city, ironically, where the austere and prim young Calvin studied. It was a city famous throughout Europe for its prostitutes, who sometimes picked up their clients in Notre Dame Cathedral. Rome, too, had its prostitutes, its thieves and its gangsters; but two puritanical popes in the latter part of the sixteenth century did much to clean up the city. It had suffered a grievous shock to its self-esteem during the infamous Sack of 1527.

Much of the wonderful art which today adorns Rome is associated with the Counter-Reformation that began in earnest in the mid-sixteenth century. When the young monk Luther, very much a northern provincial, was sent to Rome in 1510, he travelled in high expectation but despaired of what he found: ignorance and immorality.

The word 'Protestant' dates from the second Diet of Speyer in 1529. But I use it in its general sense, meaning an adherent of reformed Christianity as opposed to an adherent of the Roman Church, which is also referred to as the old Church or the Catholic Church. I reckon it is reasonable to talk about Luther and his followers being Protestants in 1519, ten years before the term was actually coined.

The word 'humanism' is used, not in its contemporary sense but rather to describe the loose cerebral movement that straddled the late medieval period and the age of the Reformation. Humanists then were learned men who were critical of the state of the Church yet believed that reform and criticism should be restrained. They tended to be of sceptical, urbane disposition; the greatest humanist was Erasmus of Rotterdam. Such men were too sophisticated to go along with the crudity of a bludgeoning revolutionary like Luther.

'Germany' is used to describe what is more or less the Germany of today. In the sixteenth century, it was part of the Holy Roman Empire, ruled by an elected emperor. Shortly after Luther's Reformation began, Charles V was elected emperor. He was an earnest and decent man who presided over the Diet of Worms in 1521, where Luther made his great stand. Under the Peace of Augsburg in 1555, the empire was formally divided between Roman Catholics and Lutherans.

Lutherans were, obviously enough, those Protestants who followed Luther. Later exponents of the reformed religion, such as Calvinists and Presbyterians, were generally known as belonging to the Reformed, as opposed to the Lutheran, Church. Protestantism had from the start a chronic fissile tendency.

'Presbyterian' describes a type of Reformed Church government that excludes bishops and emphasises the parity and equality of ministers. Knox's Reformation in Scotland was not firmly Presbyterian; it became properly Presbyterian in its second phase, under Andrew Melville.

Finally, the word 'Reformation' is used as a catch-all term for the reforming movement that Luther started in northern Germany in 1517. There were many separate reformations. The term 'Counter-Reformation' is used in this book to describe the impressive Catholic fightback, which, while belated, was able to take advantage of the growing division in Protestant ranks. Some historians prefer the term 'Catholic Reformation'.

The Key Players

John Calvin

Less impetuous, less exhilarating than Luther, but possessed of an orderly, lucid lawyer's mind and a strong, stern will, he masterminded the second phase of the movement that Luther so explosively began. He will always be associated with Geneva (to this day, his imprint is very clear on the old town up the hill from the lake). He was initially reluctant to undertake his ministry there, and was at times immensely unpopular with some of the citizens. But, despite appalling ill-health, he prevailed, and he created in the city state an impressive, if also repressive, democratic theocracy.

History has not been particularly generous to him; he is remembered more for the grimness of aspects of his theology and for his persistent emphasis on social discipline than for his decency and even warmth as a pastor. His teachings and his sermons are full of wisdom and sensible guidance on how to live; he was a kinder and more humane man, and far less of a fanatic, than his many detractors would have us believe, though he undoubtedly had his fierce side. Knox admired him enormously but was not greatly influenced by him.

Calvin always pined for his native France, from which he fled as a young man and to which he never managed to return.

Catherine de Medici

A scheming and duplicitous Florentine, she exercised in various roles – queen, queen mother, regent – a powerful but malign influence over the affairs of France in the latter part of the sixteenth century. A complex figure, she did at times try to pursue religious moderation and toleration, but her main drive was her dynastic ambition, and she could never resist political intrigue. She was certainly not good news for France, or for Protestantism.

She was deeply implicated in the protracted atrocity of the Massacre of St Bartholomew in 1572, during which many thousands of French Huguenots – French Protestants – were slaughtered in especially vile circumstances. Despite this, commemorative medals of celebration were struck in Rome.

William Cecil

Queen Elizabeth's chief minister. A curious mixture of boldness and caution, he lay low during the bloody reign of Mary Tudor. One of Elizabeth's first significant acts as queen was to appoint him as her principal adviser, and he rapidly embarked on an ambitious and daring pro-Protestant foreign policy.

It was Cecil who advised Elizabeth to send her army and navy north to drive the French out of Scotland. The final decision was Elizabeth's and hers alone, but it was Cecil who persuaded her, despite the many inherent risks, that it was the right thing to do.

Later, he consistently argued for the execution of Mary Queen of Scots; here, Elizabeth took much longer to heed his sage advice.

Emperor Charles V

The last Holy Roman Emperor to be crowned by the pope, he was elected emperor in 1519. His enemies were numerous and powerful – Suleiman the Magnificent, the French, the Protestants and occasionally even the papacy. He won a huge victory over the considerable Protestant forces of Germany at the battle of Mühlberg in 1547, but typically was unable to follow it up. His imperial legacy was to be the growing disunity of Christendom. Recognising this, he resigned in 1556 and split his huge territories between his two sons, the ineffective Philip of Spain and Ferdinand, who became the new emperor.

An earnest and decent man, Charles could not always control his own troops, who were sometimes little more than a feral rabble. The nadir of his imperial rule came in 1527 when his army, unpaid, leaderless and mutinous, sacked Rome in an extended and appalling orgy of rape, looting, vandalism and murder as Pope Clement VII cowered in the Castel Sant' Angelo.

Archbishop Thomas Cranmer

Cautious, diplomatic, adaptable, he was the supreme liturgist of the careful compromise that was the Anglican Reformation settlement. Unfortunately, he was executed by 'Bloody Mary' Tudor, and so he did not live to see the fruits of his life's work in the Anglican Church which Elizabeth rapidly established when she became queen a few years later.

A countryman at heart, he was also a notable secular statesman. His crowning achievement was the beautiful Anglican *Book of Common Prayer*. His mastery of English prose, and his contribution to English cultural as well as religious identity, were second only to Tyndale's.

Queen Elizabeth I of England

Wayward, vulgar, deceitful, secretive, vain, flighty, bossy, spiteful and chronically indecisive, she was frequently insufferable. One of her ministers described her as a base bastard pissing kitchen woman. She never married and was often lonely, her loneliness accentuated by her office. She was also ferociously intelligent, witty, kind, exceptionally well informed and, above all, courageous. She reigned long and well. Her mother, Anne Boleyn, was executed by her father, the monstrous Henry VIII; and generally she did not like executing people, though she knew that she had to from time to time.

In the second year of her reign, when she was just 26, she bravely decided, after long agonising, to defy the great powers of France and

Spain and send her army and navy north to help the Scots drive the French out of their country and thus secure the Scottish Reformation. This was the most important decision of her reign and probably the most important decision in Scottish history. It finally ended centuries of hostility and led to centuries of peace.

She was the supreme star in a century of glittering European monarchs, and her allure is somehow still alive to this day.

Henry VII of England

The founder of the Tudor dynasty, he was a cautious and notably pious king who slowly but surely restored peace to England, which had been ravaged for generations by the civil Wars of the Roses. Although he won his crown in battle, he was a peace-loving man, and he believed in using marriage as a means to diplomatic and political ends. Thus he, a Lancastrian, married Elizabeth of York, merging the white and red roses into a kind of peaceful pink; he married his heir Arthur to Catherine of Aragon in an attempt to secure a long-standing peace with Spain, and he married his daughter Margaret to James IV of Scotland, a visionary piece of dynastic manoeuvring that eventually, several generations later, led to the Union of the Crowns of England and Scotland.

He was an exemplary Roman Catholic and a successful king. He is the subject of the best biography in the English language, by Sir Francis Bacon; but unfortunately his thuggish younger son, who became Henry VIII, is more remembered and more celebrated.

Henry VIII of England

A wicked and duplicitous psychopath, he presided over the English Reformation, which was initially driven not by spiritual aspirations but rather by the king's complicated and tedious matrimonial difficulties. He married six times and executed two of his wives. He treated them all abominably, with the possible exception of the last, the estimable Catherine Parr.

He surrounded himself with some of the most gifted Englishmen of all time, including the four Thomases: the precocious lawyer Thomas

Cromwell, who drafted much of the far-sighted legislation that enacted the early English Reformation; Cardinal Thomas Wolsey, his first great servant; Sir Thomas More, his Lord Chancellor and the eloquent conscience of early Catholic resistance to Henry's Reformation; and Archbishop Thomas Cranmer, a liturgist of exceptional brilliance.

Cromwell and More were both executed by the tyrant; Wolsey would have been, had he not managed to die first. Cranmer, on the other hand, outlasted the old rogue. Indeed, he ministered to the bloated monster as he lay dying; and this deathbed scene has an unlikely poignancy. Henry's great achievement was to father Elizabeth, who was to become a splendid and glorious monarch.

James IV, King of Scots

Bumptious, puffed up, grandiose, he had an ambition to strut the wider European stage – and, unusually for a Scottish monarch, he almost succeeded. He could not read his times; he wanted to lead a new crusade, and he created an impressive navy, but then he led his country to its worst-ever military debacle (and there were quite a few over the years) in an inland battle. A persistent, serial womaniser, his relations with his wife Margaret Tudor were never of the best; but their marriage paved the way for the eventual Union of the Crowns.

James was dashing, generous and clever. He maintained a splendid court. Physically strong and resilient, he ruled his unruly kingdom energetically, but he was inconsistent. His relations with England were ill-judged; despite his marriage, he generally leaned towards France. In religion, he was orthodox; and, like his father-in-law Henry Tudor, he evinced no anticipation whatsoever of the tumult that was about to sweep across Europe.

He is sometimes regarded as the greatest of Scots monarchs; if that is the case, it merely shows the poverty of the general standard of Scottish kingship.

James VI, King of Scots – and King James I of England

He was desperate to become king of England from an early age, and this is perhaps why he evinced little public anger or even disapproval when Queen Elizabeth had his mother, Mary Queen of Scots, executed.

Henry VIII tried to effect the Union of the Crowns by vicious force; James, to his credit, accomplished the union peacefully, in 1603. Thereafter, he mostly ignored his northern kingdom. He was clever, and all too aware of it; he loved lecturing clerics, and he particularly liked showing off before his English Parliament, which responded by becoming ever more truculent and disputatious. He deserves credit for commissioning the Authorised Version of the Bible. He deserves less credit for the disgraceful tract he wrote against witches, which gave royal imprimatur to a frenzy of witch-hunting in Scotland.

John Knox

The guiding genius of the Scottish Reformation was a self-styled prophet, a fiery preacher, a genuine democrat and a consistent Anglophile. Indeed, he was offered an English bishopric long before he returned to his native country to mastermind what was, to some extent, a social and political as well as a religious revolution.

He learned much from Calvin during his time in Geneva, yet he was never a zealous follower of the Frenchman; for example, he was much more radical in his belief in the legitimacy of revolt against tyrants.

Knox was emphatically not the killjoy of popular caricature. Despite his ill-advised 'blast of the trumpet' against rule by women, he was always something of a ladies' man. He appreciated wine and good fellowship. His own account of the Scottish Reformation, while self-serving, is at times great fun. He was a social as well as a religious visionary, and the blueprint that he and five colleagues drew up for the new Scotland was centuries ahead of its time in its democratic integrity and its emphasis on education and social welfare.

Saint Ignatius Loyola

This Basque nobleman started as a soldier, and it was during his long agony as he recovered from a terrible wound received while defending Pamplona against the French – and two subsequent botched operations – that he discovered his inner spirituality and his need to serve Christ. His idea of service was based on supreme obedience.

Like so many of the outstanding figures of the sixteenth century, he was complex and contradictory. A tough man with an iron will, he was also highly sensitive and something of a mystic. He possessed a potent imagination. His celebrated Spiritual Exercises, still much used, rely above all on the intensive exercise of imagination.

Central to his teaching was the need for total obedience to the Church, the bride of Christ. The great order he founded, the Jesuits, were to be the shock troops of the huge fightback that is generally called the Counter-Reformation. Himself diamond-hard and ascetic, he nonetheless allowed the elite order he founded to be sinewy and subtle, to keep adjusting to the times.

Martin Luther

A stubborn man of peasant stock, and also a spiritual genius, Luther was very clever but had little subtlety and less sophistication. He was both the most influential evangelical and the most effective revolutionary in European history. A writer of superhuman productivity and a communicator of genius, he could not always control his pen. Some of what he wrote was vicious and vile. He was guilty of anti-Semitism, and at times he wrote savagely and violently in defence of the status quo. This makes his colossal contribution to the cause of change and the development of individual liberty all the more astounding. He could be boorish and foul-mouthed. He was excessively contentious and constantly divisive.

One of the multiple paradoxes of the sixteenth century was that this conservative man should have inspired momentous, continuing revolution; the movement he started in 1517 led to unimagined upheaval and the transfer of power and property on an enormous scale.

Although he resiled somewhat in his later years, the implication of his early teaching, with its supreme emphasis on faith and his notion of 'the priesthood of all believers', was that the Church was in effect redundant. All Christians were to be subject to each other, not some vast hierarchical structure. Supremely, he persuaded people to think for themselves. He ended the dark ages of the mind. He unleashed an enormous surge of popular education. He was arguably not just the greatest German, but also the greatest European.

Mary of Guise

Many people tried to rule Scotland, a turbulent and contrary nation, in the sixteenth century; Mary of Guise, a beautiful and charming French noblewoman, succeeded better than most. She was married to James V, King of Scots, from 1538 to 1542. A few years later, she came into her own. Unlike her ill-starred daughter Mary Queen of Scots, she showed sensitivity to the Scots and their affairs, and she steered a careful and skilful political course until the Scottish Reformation finally got under way. At this point, she started to panic and lost control.

She was a devout Catholic – but, unlike her namesake and contemporary in England, Mary Tudor, she did not make martyrs of Protestants. On the contrary, she actually allowed English Protestant refugees to find shelter and sanctuary in Scotland.

Mary Queen of Scots

Quite simply, the wrong queen at the wrong time. Bewitching and ardent, she sadly left the sophisticated French court; and, after a most difficult, stormy sea journey, she arrived in the bleak northern country she was to rule so disastrously – just when the weather was at its worst. John Knox, who was to harangue her with insolent but splendidly democratic confidence, noted with relish that the portents were bad from the very start.

At first, like her distinguished mother Mary of Guise, she managed to rule with some tact and sensitivity; but she simply could not understand that she had arrived in the midst of religious and social revolution.

Her taste in men was degraded; she indulged the frivolous Italian plotter David Rizzio, her so-called secretary, who was murdered by the loutish pals of her second husband, the bisexual wastrel Henry Darnley (by whom she produced the boy who was to become James VI and I). Then, when Darnley had been literally blown up (an atrocious crime in which she was surely complicit), she married the rapist, thug and sociopath Bothwell.

After unsuccessfully defying her own people, she threw herself on the mercy of Queen Elizabeth south of the Border, thus becoming history's ultimate unwanted guest. Most of England wanted her dead, particularly when she stupidly and treacherously got involved in plots against her host; yet Elizabeth defied her advisers, and it was many years until she made the fateful decision.

And so, Mary was at last executed in a forlorn Northamptonshire castle. England rejoiced; bonfires were lit, bells rang across the land, and the celebrations continued for days. As for Elizabeth, she wept uncontrollably. Then she recovered and went on to preside over the defeat of the Spanish armada.

'Bloody' Mary Tudor, Queen of England

Mary has had a bad press, not least from Protestant propagandists infuriated by her enthusiastic burning of those whom she regarded as heretics. She is still known by the unkind but valid soubriquet of 'Bloody Mary'. She executed nearly 300 Protestants, many of whom became celebrated martyrs. The policy was counter-productive, particularly because so many of those who were killed, including the leading churchmen Cranmer, Ridley, Latimer and Hooper, died so well and courageously. Although most of her subjects probably remained Catholics, Mary could not capitalise on this. Her controversial marriage to Philip II of Spain achieved little. Compared to her half-sister Elizabeth, who succeeded her, she was a poor monarch and indeed a total failure.

But she had a rotten life. She had seen her dignified mother, Catherine of Aragon, humiliated by her father, the brutish Henry VIII. She herself was declared a bastard. Her marriage to Philip was blighted by her inability to produce a child. As she was growing up, she showed a propensity to be fun-loving. She enjoyed gambling and adored fine clothes and jewellery. Slowly, grimly, dourness and duty took over.

Andrew Melville

A clever, cultured and cosmopolitan man from Angus, Melville played the part of Calvin to Knox's Luther: he organised the second phase of the Scottish Reformation and gave it intellectual solidity. Like Knox, he was a democrat and was not afraid to harangue his monarch, in this case James VI. He outdid James in debate, and also insulted him, calling him 'God's silly vassal'. He eventually paid for his impudence when James had him imprisoned in London.

A brilliant intellectual, he accomplished much at Glasgow University, of which he was principal. He was a rigorous Presbyterian, and it was mainly thanks to him that Scotland became a firmly Presbyterian nation.

Pope Paul IV

The first and lesser of the two great Counter-Reformation Puritan popes, the Neapolitan Gian Pietro Caraffa at last became pope at the grand old age of 79. Personally fearless, he was a ferocious and tyrannical figure. He despised the Council of Trent, the great engine of Catholic reform. He preferred the Inquisition and the *Index of Prohibited Books*. He detested Spaniards almost as much as he hated Protestants. He held the Holy Roman Emperor in contempt.

He was probably slightly mad. But he succeeded in cleaning Rome up, driving out prostitutes and gangsters, bandits and beggars. In his severe personal asceticism, his refusal to compromise, and his resolute war on venality, corruption and softness, he could not have been more removed from the frivolous and decadent Renaissance popes whose disgraceful, self-indulgent antics had exacerbated the crisis in the old Church at the very time when pressure for reform was stirring.

Philip II of Spain

The son of Emperor Charles V, Philip II of Spain was a poor leader and constantly betrayed his avowed cause of Catholicism. Somehow he managed to bankrupt Spain, which should have been the wealthiest power in the world. He constantly failed, not just financially but also militarily. His most celebrated defeat was by the English, when the grand armada of 1588 was scattered (with considerable help from the weather). He also managed to lose most of his Dutch colonies after years of debilitating conflict.

He was briefly married to Queen Mary Tudor of England. He never trusted his generals; and, for the most part, he was ill-served by them. He abjectly failed in his mission to stamp out heresy in Western Europe. His incompetence rendered him, paradoxically, a good friend of Protestantism.

Pope Saint Pius V

Arguably the greatest pope in a turbulent and momentous century, Michele Ghislieri was the second of the outstanding Puritan popes. A former shepherd, he was a very clean-living Dominican who steadily worked his way through various offices – including that of inquisitor general. Here he incurred the wrath of Caraffa, who thought he was too soft. Nonetheless, he carried on Caraffa's tradition of austerity and fierceness, but he mingled it with a leavening of compassion. He controversially excommunicated Queen Elizabeth of England.

He completed Caraffa's work by finally turning Rome, for most of the sixteenth century second only to Paris as a centre of decadence, into a clean and even monastic city. The later masters of the high baroque, such as Gianlorenzo Bernini, adorned Rome with gorgeous sensual art yet did not destroy the city's new spirituality.

Pius V made the eternal city a fitting place of pilgrimage. He also turned the office of pope into what it surely should be, that of a priest, a pastor and a cleric rather than a worldly potentate (despite his part in gathering the vast navy that finally defeated the Turks at Lepanto).

He has been accused of political naivety, yet he had the foresight and the wisdom to put the main decisions of the long-standing Council of Trent into effect; and this was a political as much as a spiritual process. He published the all-important catechism which codified the long work of Trent. He relied overmuch on the Inquisition, and he was not averse to using cruelty and torture when he deemed it necessary. But he cleansed Rome, he cleansed the papacy, and overall he was a good man. Arguably the most significant Catholic figure of the sixteenth century after Loyola, he was much later (in 1712) canonised.

Girolamo Savonarola

A Dominican who was a preacher of raw power, Savonarola was a terrifying enemy of frivolity, immorality, corruption, showy wealth and the abuse of clerical office. Determined to cleanse and renew the mercenary Church, he was the most notable of the 'outriders', the various anticipators of the Reformation.

For a time, he held total sway over the republic of Florence, preaching in a way that put fear into some (including Michelangelo) and inspired others. He organised the celebrated 'bonfires of the vanities'. All this was too much for the papacy; after a mockery of a trial, he was burned to death.

Suleiman the Magnificent

Ottoman sultan and warlord, his sultanate of forty-six years was crucial in that it diverted the forces that might well have otherwise crushed the Reformation. Suleiman led from the front. He was one of the most adept practitioners of the grisly art of war that the world has ever known, and he rampaged around vast tracts of Eastern Europe, posing a constant threat to the security of the West in general and the Holy Roman Empire in particular. For example, in a hard-fought battle in 1526, his cavalry utterly routed the massed armies of Hungary, leaving around 18,000 slaughtered in the field, including the king and many of his nobles.

Suleiman was even stronger in the Mediterranean, and his mastery of that sea allowed him to move with impunity through North Africa and much of the Middle East. He was indeed magnificent: he was a great legislator and a distinguished patron of the arts as well as a fearsome generalissimo. In Western Europe, popes, princes, emperors, queens and kings were all deeply afraid of him.

Five years after he died in 1566, the papacy at last managed to gather the military forces of Roman Catholic Christendom, and they defeated the Turks in the huge set-piece sea battle of Lepanto.

Suleiman's role in the history of the Reformation may be peripheral, but it is highly significant nonetheless.

William Tyndale

A scholar, linguist and translator of unsurpassed genius, his mastery of the English language was consummate. The first person to translate the Bible from the original Hebrew and Greek into English, he did so in prose which is accessible, supple, beautiful, numinous and noble. His rhythms and cadences are with us to this day. Few literary scholars manage to make a major contribution to a social, political and religious revolution, but this is precisely what Tyndale did.

His *The Obedience of a Christian Man* is one of the most underestimated books in our language. His influence on the thinking, literature and religion of English-speaking people can hardly be overstated.

Born in Gloucestershire and educated at Oxford, he travelled widely on the continent in the 1520s, staying in Hamburg and Cologne, and in Luther's Wittenberg. He was something of a loner, and valued his independence. He does not seem to have been particularly pleasant in his personal dealings. Betrayed by an Englishman called Phillips when he was living covertly in Antwerp, he was arrested by the authorities, imprisoned for heresy, and then strangled and burnt to death.

Huldrych Zwingli

A leading Swiss reformer, who dominated the important city of Zurich in the 1520s, Zwingli was highly sexed, charismatic and a theatrically powerful preacher. His short but influential career as a reformer indicated the essentially fissile nature of Protestantism; he was much alarmed by the growth of radical Anabaptism in Zurich, and he fell out with Luther in a nasty, extended spat over what happened at communion. The way the two men abused each other in a series of polemical tracts ended whatever brief hopes there had been that Protestantism might be a united movement.

Zwingli was killed in combat, wielding his battleaxe, as he fought the army of the Catholic cantons of Switzerland.

Introduction

$\mathscr{T}$HIS is an intensely dramatic story. It is the story of extraordinary courage, of martyrs, of burnings and persecution, of danger and escape, of degradation and wickedness, of superhuman heroism, of felicity and nobility, of betrayal and treachery, of the destruction of much that was precious and beautiful, of constant, unremitting and often incomprehensible change, of fervent spiritual yearning, of warfare and strife, of social renewal and visionary democratic innovation. It is in part the story of the beginning of the modern world. And that itself, paradoxically, is just the beginning of it. Most of all, this is about the Christian quest for God.

Many people still regard the European Reformation as an unmitigated disaster which led to division and secularisation. Others regard it as the most positive movement in world history, a movement that led to the opening of the minds of ordinary people and set them free from the forces of medieval darkness. Still more find in it the seeds of modern capitalism, or modern decadence, or both. The Reformation divided, and it still divides.

There is peace and piety to be found in this story, but perhaps not enough of either. One thing is clear: our story is supremely one of turbulence and uproar. Its great begetter, a beer-swilling, boorish German peasant who, in his own words, was just 'an uncivilised fellow from the backwoods', was also, despite himself, a brilliant revolutionary – possibly the most effective revolutionary in human history. This man, Martin Luther, felt himself *constantly 'impelled by God into the midst of uproar'. This is the story of the Great Uproar.*

Our story begins not with Martin Luther but with a man winning the crown of England in battle. His name was Henry Tudor. He was determined to have his royal legitimacy endorsed by the highest authority available: the pope, his 'Vicar on Earth'. When Pope Innocent VIII duly confirmed Henry Tudor as Henry VII, the rightful king of England, he was ensuring among other things that the new monarch would have the loyalty of the English clergy, of whom there were many (far too many). This was important for Henry because the senior clergy controlled much of the land of England and exercised considerable political power.

Henry VII proved to be a most pious king, though his piety was at times stagey and used for secular purposes. He went on many pilgrimages, but his principal work of devotion was the building of an extravagant and gorgeous monument to himself, the Lady Chapel at the east side of Westminster Abbey. Thousands of people visit it every week of every year; it is the most elaborate and complex part of this famous building. The chapel was to be his own resting place, the magnificent site of his tomb, as well as a shrine to his predecessor Henry VI.

Henry VII was a peace-loving man, although he won his crown in the battle at Bosworth Field in 1485. He managed to end the Wars of the Roses, the vicious dynastic squabbles that had bedevilled England for many years. But, two years later, his army had to win a hard-fought and very bloody battle to preserve his kingship. This battle is described in some detail in this book, partly because it is important to emphasise that countries like England and Scotland were not peaceful places before the Reformation.

Critics of the Reformation often insist that it led to pervasive strife and many wars. There is some truth in this – but, on the other hand, the condition of pre-Reformation Europe was hardly peaceful or stable. The worst disaster in Scottish history, the terrible military catastrophe of Flodden Field, took place in 1513, a few years before the first stirrings of religious reform were felt in Scotland. At Flodden, James IV, King of Scots, died. He was one of the most powerful and charismatic of Scotland's kings, and latterly his kingly obsession had been his desire to persuade the pope to undertake a new crusade. Rather presumptuously, James wanted to lead the navy of Venice against the Turks. The popes themselves were monarchs of a kind, ruling a large swathe of central Italy. Some of them were also warriors, notably Pope Julius II, who was however wary of James IV's grandiose plans for a new crusade.

This, then, was the late medieval world: kingship was everything. The eminent Tudor historian David Starkey has emphasised that this was indeed a king-centred world. These kings were 'the be-all and end-all of imagination and fact'.

Our story is partly about the smashing of kingly authority. The great figures in it are not kings, or queens, but men of humble birth, most notably a German, a Frenchman and a Scot: Martin Luther, John Calvin and John Knox. They created a new order (or, in some respects, a disorder) in which kingly authority was to be seriously diminished.

Even the most accomplished and glittering monarch of the sixteenth century, Queen Elizabeth of England, found that she had to endure more and more truculent and offensive challenges from religiously motivated Puritans who did not respect her office. In Scotland, Knox harangued his monarch, Mary Queen of Scots, with insolent confidence. And Mary's son James VI was lectured in a hectoring manner, and very firmly put in his place, by the first great Scots Presbyterian, Andrew Melville. The Scottish Reformation was largely driven by demotic notions. It was one of the later European reformations – after some false starts, it began properly only when John Knox returned to Scotland in 1559 – and it should be regarded as a political and social as well as a religious revolution.

The Scots reformers, led by Knox, had a visionary determination to place education at the very heart of their revolution. This education was to be democratic; the sons of the laird's servants were to receive just as good and thorough schooling as the sons of the laird.

There were many European reformations, and the first and most crucial one was German. The catch-all singular word 'Reformation' is nevertheless valid. This overall Reformation was a movement which encompassed immense national and even regional differences, and covers a series of diverse and separate reformations.

The Reformation movement – which the likes of Henry VII of England and James IV of Scotland, strong traditional Christian monarchs of the early sixteenth century, could not have dreamed of, let alone begun to understand – was unleashed by a coarse and obscure German Augustinian monk called Martin Luther. Coarse he un-doubtedly was, and remained. But the obscurity vanished almost overnight. Luther was one of the few surpassing geniuses of human history, and a writer of unparalleled power. The process which he started in 1517 gained momentum with terrifying speed. He could not control it.

A man of stupendous energy, Luther smashed his way on to the European stage and changed everything. His detractors might say he simply smashed everything to bits, though there was much that was positive and creative in his legacy. He was, however, a diligent destroyer. He shook up a continent on which the Church was the greatest landowner, where more than 10 per cent of the population were clerics, and where the pope had political as well as spiritual power and influence.

Religious life before Luther appealed to the senses rather than the mind; the people's year was punctuated by saints' days and religious holidays that brought pageantry, colour and fun into otherwise bleak and grim lives. The plague was never far away. There was much fear and much warfare; life was chancy and insecure. Amid life, death was ever-present. People spent much of their time praying for the dead.

A man who somehow combined authentic humility and explosive arrogance, Luther was never the friend of peace and quiet. For the briefest of moments, he might have been dismissed as just another

medieval prophet making lonely if eloquent criticisms of the corruption of the Church. But it rapidly became clear that he was special –
and, as a threat to the established order across Europe, toxic.

Luther must always be the first and greatest figure of the
Reformation. His crucial notion was that every individual should
have the right to read and interpret the Bible for him- or herself.
This, like the parallel notion of the priesthood of all believers, was an
incredible idea; taken to its logical conclusion, it would have destroyed
the need for any kind of Church at all: it would have made all clergy
superfluous.

Whatever his faults – and there were many, not least his detestation of Jews – Luther was the supreme exponent of reform. He was
in many ways the perfect revolutionary. This is one of his manifold
paradoxes – for, in persona and background, he was essentially
a conservative peasant, if an exceptionally clever one. A deeply
spiritual man, he always spent a lot of time praying. He was also
a journalist, a propagandist, a preacher, a pamphleteer, a writer of
tracts and hymns and polemics, and above all a brilliant translator of
the Bible. Millions of words poured from his pen in a furious torrent.
As a wordsmith, Luther was both crazed and sublime. He was one of
the most prodigious communicators in human history. And of course
he availed himself of the crucial new invention, the printing press.

This mysterious and heroic man is desperately difficult to assess
and understand even today – but it is essential to try to understand
him, for he is the key to our story.

Luther was a kind of divine disrupter. After him came John Calvin,
a colder man, the supreme organiser, a lawyer and theologian
possessed of a rigorous mind and a controlled, lucid prose style.
Towards the end of his tumultuous life, Luther became somewhat
self-indulgent; but Calvin maintained the discipline that was so
dear to his bleak soul, and drove himself to superhuman limits to
the very end. He gave Luther's erratic and shapeless Reformation
form and order. He took a great river in spate and directed it into a
more orderly channel, narrower and deeper. He created in Geneva

one of the most remarkable religious communities that has ever been known. And he in turn influenced the redoubtable Scottish reformer John Knox, who was to preside over what was probably the most complete European reformation, even though it accomplished nothing like what Knox himself hoped for.

Significantly, Luther, Calvin and Knox were all born in comparative obscurity. But they shook the established order to its foundations. They took on the great and the good of their day with a zest that was genuinely revolutionary. At the same time, their attitude to secular authority was often ambivalent.

Despite the influence and effect of these momentous reformers, kings and queens and princes and popes remained important throughout the sixteenth century. Henry VII's son Henry VIII, a duplicitous and bloodthirsty tyrant who has legitimately been compared to Stalin, nonetheless personally ushered in the English Reformation – an extraordinary process that was born not out of religious conviction but rather out of tedious matrimonial difficulties. So, in the words of Professor Andrew McGowan, the English Reformation was from the top down. The Scottish Reformation, in contrast, was against the country's monarchy, not through it. It was from the bottom up. Having said that, it is important to remember that Scotland's Reformation was achieved with the indispensable help of a foreign queen, Elizabeth of England.

The English Reformation was unique. At first a legal and political rather than a religious settlement, it was the creation of a wife-slaying despot. It became a very English compromise, a sort of ecclesiastical middle way.

There were no outstanding female reformers – but, because queens were just as important as kings, women have a large part to play in our story. Queen Elizabeth of England was one of the greatest monarchs of all time, and it was she who very bravely and provocatively, at the beginning of her long reign, sent her army and navy north to Scotland to secure the Scottish Reformation. Unfortunately, Mary Queen of Scots did not understand, and could not cope with, the early Scottish Reformation. She is sometimes presented as a tragic figure, though that is not the verdict of this book. A genuinely tragic figure was Lady Jane Grey, very briefly queen of England, who has a minor and pitiful role in our story. Then there was Mary of Guise, the mother of Mary Queen of Scots, who was to rule Scotland with some skill and sensitivity, and who altogether showed a grasp of Scottish politics (and to some extent religion) that proved to be quite beyond her daughter.

In the short term, it has to be admitted that the Reformation was not necessarily good for Europe's women. Places of refuge (and of partial freedom from male control), such as the cloister and the nunnery, were often destroyed. The clergy were allowed to marry, and many women who had been or would have been nuns became subject to male domination, which was not always benign. In some ways, women were liberated; in others, they became liable to potentially brutal domestic control, with no escape. A little later, there was to be wicked and sustained persecution of so-called witches, not least in Scotland, where King James VI lent his spurious intellectual imprimatur to the craze for witch-hunts. More of these supposed witches – most of them wholly innocent old women – were killed in Europe by Catholics than by Protestants; but, in the later stages of the Reformation, there was a terrible zeal for hunting down vulnerable old women and killing them.

Then there were the popes. Some of the Renaissance popes were disgraceful figures who took venality and immorality to obscene and barely credible levels. Some of them were warriors as much as religious leaders, notably the ever-bellicose Julius II. The most hapless popes were poor Leo X and then Clement VII. The latter simply could not deal with the blustering and bullying Henry VIII, and so he must take at least some of the blame, or credit, for the English Reformation. Clement also suffered the grotesque humiliation of the Sack of Rome in 1527, when the troops of a great Catholic potentate, the Holy Roman Emperor Charles V, breached the inadequate defences of Rome and then subjected the eternal city to a horrific orgy of slaughter and rapine. Priests were attacked with special ferocity, nuns were raped, churches were burned and the Tiber filled up with bodies. As Pope Clement and his cardinals cowered in the Castel Sant' Angelo, the Vatican itself was used a stable for the horses of looting, feral soldiers.

Lutherans gloated at these appalling scenes (the imperial army contained many German soldiers, some of whom were Lutherans), relishing the fact that they were perpetrated by the army of a great Catholic. Clement himself was never forgiven by the people of Rome for the sack – as if it was his fault. When he died, a group of citizens got hold of his corpse, mutilated it and drove a sword through his heart.

But the papacy's greatest problem was posed not by Henry VIII or by the savage rabble that was Charles V's army. The real problem was Luther. The first pope who had to deal with him, Leo X, was the wrong pope at the wrong time; he simply could not understand the scope of the challenge that the German presented.

The Catholic Church took a long time to regroup and renew. But, when the organised Catholic fightback, the Counter-Reformation, was under way, it was led by a series of quite splendid popes. Two of them were fierce puritans, men of almost superhuman austerity. The contrast with the worst of the Renaissance popes could hardly have been greater. The leading figure of fightback was, however, not a pope but a minor Spanish nobleman, Saint Ignatius Loyola, a magnificent man who equalled Luther in complexity and was almost his equal in his effect on the world.

The sixteenth century was a period of devastating and momentous change in Europe. Much of this change was intellectual and spiritual; much of it was violent and physical. And much of this was driven by people who were very complex. Some them were so complex as to be incapable of a concise summing-up.

The distinguished American scholar Richard Marius wrote of William Tyndale, perhaps the greatest writer of English that the Reformation produced – and that is high praise – in terms which suggest the essentially enigmatic nature of so many of these sixteenth-century figures. Marius concluded that Tyndale seemed to have been humourless and thoroughly unpleasant, and unable to keep a friend for long. Yet Marius also noted that he was a linguistic genius, as well as brave, constant and intelligent.

In his superb biography of Saint Thomas More, Marius judged that More would never be anything but a stranger to those who study him. He was a divided man. Of course, all human beings are to some extent complex; but, in the sixteenth century, most of the great figures had contradictory and ambiguous personalities. This makes them supremely interesting but most difficult to assess. Some of them, with their modern enthusiastic proponents and zealous detractors, divide to this day. Mary Queen of Scots is an excellent example.

This book is very much about personalities – kings, queens, popes and, above all, prophetic reformers. I strongly believe in the imprint of personality on history, though many modern historians are uneasy with this approach. But I also try, in the course of this book, to deal with the many aspects of the Reformation which transcend personality. However, before we turn to these, it is important to note that men like Luther, Calvin, Knox and Loyola were not other-worldly clerics. They knew real danger; they experienced physical terror.

Luther, fleeing for his life, had to ride fifty miles by night on an unsaddled and ill-tempered horse until he at last reached safety. On another occasion, when he was outlawed and under sentence of death, he was subjected to a false 'kidnapping' by his protector the Elector of Saxony, who then imprisoned him, for his own safety, in Wartburg Castle. Calvin had to flee from Paris in disguise; shortly afterwards, he had to leave his native France altogether, fearing for his life. Even in Geneva, the city he came to dominate, he had his enemies. Dogs were set on him; he was shot at. John Knox, as a low-born prisoner of the French, had to endure months of degrading and dangerous toil on the French galleys in the North Sea. Ignatius Loyola, who, unlike the first three, was a genuine soldier, suffered terrible wounds when he was defending the fortified walls of the city of Pamplona against the French. A cannonball smashed into him. For many months, he was in agony, not least because the subsequent surgery was botched – not once but twice.

When we come to issues rather than personalities, the most controversial and difficult is the extent to which the Reformation was a result of venality, slackness and abuse in the old Church. It is easy enough, for example, to describe with relish the depravity of the Renaissance popes. But it is also important to record that reform was already under way within the Roman Church when Luther's Reformation started, though the process was weak and piecemeal.

It is also important to remember that men like Luther and Calvin were products of the old Church that they rebelled against. The young monk Luther received from the Church a fine education that was to stand him in good stead as he tore into what had nurtured him. Calvin was educated in Paris through the good offices of the old Church; it helped that his father, the clerk to a bishop, had Church connections.

The intellectual ground which was to prove so fertile for the Reformation had been tilled in advance by men who were not by nature fierce reformers. Rather, they were inquiring, sceptical, even satirical. Most of them were humanists – and the greatest of these was Desiderius Erasmus of Rotterdam, the illegitimate son of a priest and a washerwoman, who himself became a priest – if an unusual one. He had a highly refined mind, but he was too witty, urbane and reasonable to become the booming, bruising force that Luther was. Erasmus and others like him softened up the cerebral climate, as if preparing for Luther's more crude and potent assault on the orthodoxies of the times.

Luther grew up in a provincial part of a Germany that was disunited (he was to render it even more disunited) but increasingly nationalistic, impatient with the influence of Rome. Many of the German clergy were disliked to the point of detestation. Rightly or wrongly, the Roman Church was regarded as anti-German and as being responsible for economic exploitation and political interference.

So, Luther unleashed his revolution in a Germany that was already seething with anti-Roman sentiment. There were clearly far too many clergy, and a significant proportion of them were lazy, ignorant and depraved. One of the things that Luther managed to do was to take religion from these slack priests and hand it to the people themselves.

But, having unleashed the revolt, Luther soon showed his essentially conservative credentials when he identified with the established order during the Peasants' War. He encouraged a brutal repression of the peasants. This was the time, more than any other, when he could not control his pen. Some of what he wrote was vile. He even told the secular princes that, in putting down the peasants' revolt, they could gain heaven 'more easily by bloodshed than by prayer'. This was Luther at his hellish worst, but it also indicated that here was a man with whom the German secular authorities could do business. Many of the German princes were deeply reassured by his response not just to the Peasants' War but also to the extremely radical Anabaptists.

So, in Germany, it soon became clear that the Reformation was most likely to thrive where the secular power wanted it to. Luther himself wished to make a distinction between legitimate spiritual freedom and what he regarded as mere licence or anarchy. In much of Germany, his Reformation became the device of princes and magistrates.

In a relatively brief spell at the end of the 1530s and in the early 1540s, there was a genuine chance of long-term conciliation if not absolute consensus. It seemed for a time that, if everyone could calm down, the uproar might abate and compromise could be found. Moderates on the Catholic side – numinous men like Cardinals Reginald Pole and Gasparo Contarini – could talk freely and often agree with eminently reasonable Protestant colleagues like Martin Bucer and Philip Melanchthon. These four men continued the spirit of Erasmus in a way that their wilder leaders could not. But this 'window of compromise' was soon slammed shut.

When Luther died in 1546, about three-quarters of Germany was Protestant. How was this change marked? Perhaps the most obvious manifestation was that there were far fewer clergy around. And those who were around were probably married. This was a momentous change. Also, people had been encouraged to read the Bible for themselves; before, it had been, in the words of one historian, the Church's best-kept secret. Now it had been translated by Luther into strong, vernacular German, and the printing presses had made it widely available. Partly because of this, there was a new impetus to literacy. Many monasteries and nunneries had disappeared; some had been confiscated by rapacious princes and minor landowners for their own ends; some had better fates, becoming hospitals or schools.

Norway, Sweden and Denmark were also Protestant. Then John Calvin took the Reformation to its more severe second stage, notably in Geneva, where he established what amounted to a unique theocratic republic. From there, his influence spread rapidly to his native France, to the Netherlands and, above all, to Scotland.

But, by now, the fightback, the Counter-Reformation, was well under way. The shock troops were the Jesuits; the most brutal method of recovery was through the dreaded Inquisition. At the protracted Council of Trent, in northern Italy, the Catholic Church began the tough tasks of redefining its doctrine and organising internal reform. The Reformation had made little impact in Italy and Spain; elsewhere, for example in Poland, there was a successful clawback as Protestantism became ever more fragmented and divisive.

By the end of the sixteenth century, the initial momentum was pretty well spent. Fissile movements, breakaways and extremism were to mark the progress of Protestantism, such as it was, in the seventeenth century. And today, 400 years on, the majority of European Christians are Catholic. Spectacle and hierarchy, both of which most of the early Protestants detested, are once again prevalent. Where Christianity is found, it often appeals to the senses rather than to the intellect. Unfortunately, from my point of view, most Europeans are probably neither Catholic nor Protestant. Western Europe is now the most secularised part of the entire world. If the natural condition of humanity is to be religious, this is not always apparent in today's Europe.

I have tried to write about all this turbulence, both spiritual and secular, with sensitivity and sympathy. I am a Protestant, but I have tried throughout to be fair and balanced in my treatment of the Catholic Church. The Christian religion is many things. It is obviously in essence spiritual, but it also has its social, political and cultural aspects. In writing this personal survey, my main concern has been to remind people of the colossal significance of the Reformation, for me by far the most important event – or rather, movement – in European history.

And, as a Scot, I am well aware that it played a crucial role in the distinctive development of my own small but very influential nation. Calvin and, in particular, John Knox each had a great impact on the history of Scotland, and I believe it is time that we thought more about them and that we should not be content to dismiss them in negative and glib stereotyping. They both wanted people to apply their religion to all aspects of their everyday living, which in these secular times is not an easy concept to grasp. I also believe that they believed in freedom and equality as well as discipline and control. I think we owe them both a great deal.

This introduction sets out some of the principal themes of this book and is a kind of taster for some of the many episodes and events that will be described and analysed in greater detail later. Central to it all must be the towering figure of Luther, a man who started with no specific religious or political programme but who founded the most far-reaching evangelical revival our world has ever known. Some will no doubt be appalled that God has been mentioned only twice so far and Christ not at all. But they feature in the text that follows, I can assure you.

Luther wanted to return people to God. In his attempt to achieve this, he gave huge numbers of human beings the confidence to believe that their brains were as good as anyone else's. He wanted people to read and think for themselves, to work things out with the help of the newly available Bible. In the present age, when many people are writing obituaries of the book, we should remember that Luther gave many people the special exhilaration of, for the first time, being able to handle, read and even own books. Whether his Reformation succeeded or not is a huge question, and I shall attempt an answer at the end of this book. What is certain is that Luther lit a great spiritual fire – and it is still burning today, if much less brightly.

Two Kings, Two Kingdoms, One Church

CHAPTER 1

Henry VII
of England

$\mathcal{I}$N 1485, on a battlefield in the English Midlands, Henry Tudor, heavily outnumbered by the forces of the desperate King Richard III, managed to defeat the tyrant. Richard at least ended his dishonourable life by fighting heroically. His crown fell from his head as he was slain, and landed in a thorn bush. It was recovered and placed on the new king's head. Thus commenced 118 years of Tudor rule. So, the story was romantic and in contrast to the essentially dour nature of Henry's reign.

The Battle of Bosworth, in the East Midlands, lasted two hours or so and was not very bloody by the standards of the time. Only a few hundred died. The most notable of the fallen was of course King Richard III, the 'crookback', England's most vilified monarch. Richard was almost certainly responsible for the murders of Henry VI and the two young princes – the sons of Edward IV – in the Tower of London. Tudor propagandists blackened his name with relish, as did Shakespeare in his melodrama *Richard III*. Many schoolchildren in the mid-1950s were taken to see the movie of Shakespeare's play, in which Laurence Olivier directed himself. They were mesmerised by Olivier's over-the-top performance as the evil king.

Shakespeare would have found it much more difficult to write a melodrama about Henry VII. He co-wrote, with John Fletcher, a play about the monstrous Henry VIII, Henry VII's son and successor; but, understandably, he ignored Henry VII himself, who was not the stuff of drama. Henry VII was a very good king, but there was nothing flamboyant about him. In character, he was much more akin to his granddaughter, Queen Elizabeth, justly the most celebrated of all English monarchs, than to the larger-than-life and brutish figure who was his son, Henry VIII. Although Henry VII gave his kingdom the priceless benefit of stability, history has not been kind to him. This is strange, for two reasons. First, his achievements were considerable. Second, he was the subject of a celebrated biography written in a few weeks in 1621 by the philosopher, lawyer and essayist Sir Francis Bacon.

Here is Bacon's account of the aftermath of the Battle of Bosworth:

> The King immediately after the victory, as one that had been bred under a devout mother and was in his nature a great observer of religious forms, caused Te Deum to be solemnly sung in the presence of the whole army upon the place, and was himself with general applause and great cries of joy, in a kind of military election or recognition, saluted king.
>
> Meanwhile the body of Richard after many indignities and reproaches was obscurely buried. For although the King of his nobleness gave charge to the friars of Leicester to see an honourable internment to be given to it, yet the religious people themselves (not being free of the humours of the vulgar) neglected it, wherein nevertheless they did not then incur any man's blame or censure.

Straight away, Bacon is establishing the new king's piety (and also the laziness of the friars of Leicester).

Henry was a very religious man. He was obsessively concerned with his life beyond death, to the extent that his will and testament requested 10,000 masses for his soul. He was exceedingly loyal to the Roman Catholic Church. He founded two new Franciscan houses. He also founded the somewhat over-the-top Lady Chapel at Westminster Abbey. He was a faithful and constant pilgrim, not least to the shrine of St Thomas à Becket at Canterbury. In all this, he was much influenced by his mother, the devotedly religious Lady Margaret Beaufort.

There is no suggestion whatsoever that Henry, in his personal religious life, in any way anticipated the turbulence that was about to sweep across Europe like some particularly wild hurricane. There was about him, in his personality and in his rule, not the merest hint of the coming Reformation. He sought, and received, papal sanction for his reign. He ignored the growing humanism that was becoming fashionable among the intellectual classes. Conscious of his shaky claim to the throne – and, in the early years of his reign, his shaky hold on the throne – he knew that it was not in his interests to alienate the very powerful Church. And so, he appeared to take the Church at face value. As he became more confident, he used it, but he did not wish to reform it. He was relaxed with the clerical establishment, not least because he deployed it to his own ends.

He had his rapacious side, and he always coveted the colossal revenues of the Church. So, his piety developed its pragmatic, even cynical, aspect. He used his patronage over episcopal appointments to choose men more notable for their administrative competence than for any spiritual zest. And he moved bishops around as if they were on a chess board – because, when a bishopric was vacant, the considerable diocesan revenues went to the crown, and an incoming bishop also had to pay dues to the king. Revenue was almost as important to Henry as religion. As he became increasingly decrepit and concerned for his own soul, he relied sincerely and devotedly on the Church's intercession.

Henry was relaxed about the occasional Lollard being executed for heresy. Lollardy was a small but persistent underground religious movement, more extensive in England than in Scotland. The Lollards were followers of John Wycliffe, an Oxford professor who had been the most notable English heretic of the fourteenth century. Wycliffe and his colleagues were eventually removed from the university. They were conscious of, and angered by, the contrast between the obvious wealth and power of the Church and the inner world of grace as revealed in the Bible.

The early Lollards translated key biblical passages into English, and these heretical papers were passed from generation to generation. What had begun among the intellectual classes persisted more among millers, weavers or artisans – not members of the underclass, but not people of influence either. The Lollards continued to stress biblical authority, and they disputed the status of the pope. In his constant but discreet suppression of Lollardy, Henry once again evinced pragmatism as well as loyalty to the Catholic Church – for Lollardy was obviously subversive. To be lenient with Lollards would be to encourage other dissidents.

In political terms, Henry's seizure of the English throne was the beginning of the end of years of debilitating division between two great dynastic houses, the Lancastrians and the Yorkists. The division manifested itself in constant feuding and fighting, the so-called Wars of the Roses (the phrase was invented many years later by none other than Sir Walter Scott). The Lancastrian rose was red, the Yorkist rose white. The Lancastrians and the Yorkists each had legitimate claims to the monarchy going back over 100 years.

Henry Tudor had spent the first fourteen years of his life in Wales. His father was half-Welsh, half-French. His mother Margaret was wholly English. By a series of accidents, Henry became, when barely a teenager, the only male claimant on the Lancastrian side at a time when the Yorkists were in the ascendancy. In 1471, for his own safety, he was taken to France by his uncle, Jasper, Earl of Pembroke. Here he stayed in reasonably comfortable exile, mainly in Brittany.

Henry's window of opportunity opened with the patently illegal accession of Richard III in 1482. But it was the murder of the two young princes that changed everything. The Yorkists now had no obvious successor to Richard III. This was the moment for which his Uncle Jasper had patiently prepared Henry. He knew that he was now the leading claimant to the English crown. His claim was endorsed by the king of France. His invasion of England in 1485 was the one really bold act in the life of this cautious man. His small fleet, organised and commanded by Jasper, left Honfleur on 1 August.

Henry landed in Wales, near Milford Haven. The invasion force was not large. There were a few hundred Lancastrian exiles, a significant detachment of French soldiers, and a smaller contingent of Scots, led by Bernard Stewart. The happy band, flying the flag of the Red Dragon and encountering no resistance, but gathering few supporters (though Welsh historians were later to claim that those days in the summer of 1485 were among the most glorious in Welsh history), stuck to the coast at first, moving northwards. Then they struck eastwards through the mountains and crossed the border into England near Shrewsbury. The crucial and inevitable encounter with Richard's forces came, as we have seen, much further east, at Bosworth Field near Leicester, on 22 August.

As soon as he became king, Henry set about ending the tiresome dynastic feuding which was sapping England, a reasonably prosperous country of just over two million souls. Henry married Elizabeth of York in 1486. The Roses were joined: red and white merged into a kind of pragmatic pink. The couple's first son was christened Arthur. Henry, despite his lack of showmanship, was an accomplished propagandist, an early master of spin. The idea was to invoke the glorious (and legendary) beginnings of the English royal line.

Henry's method of ending the years of strife was not so much by the expedient of marriage, useful though that was, or by brutal repression, which was contrary to his nature, but rather by the judicious deployment of that greatest of human qualities, mercy. By the standards of his time, Henry was to prove a clement king, although there were pragmatic exceptions, as with the Lollards. His compassion was frequently evident, and a good example was the way he treated the man who posed the first serious threat to his rule.

After so many years of civil war, Henry's own royal line was not yet secure. The crisis came as soon as 1487, when an insignificant lad called Lambert Simnel suddenly presented an extreme danger to the new but precarious stability of the kingdom. The chief troublemaker was the Earl of Lincoln, who had, like Henry, a flimsy claim to the throne. Lincoln had been – or pretended to be – one of Henry's leading aristocratic supporters in the aftermath of Bosworth in 1485; but, at Easter in 1487, when the pious Henry was on a pilgrimage to Walsingham in East Anglia, Lincoln started raising mercenaries in Flanders.

Lincoln moved on to Dublin, where many Yorkists were exiled, and took up Simnel (in reality the son of a cobbler from Oxford), who was now presented as the Earl of Warwick. This was ridiculous; it was well known that the real Earl of Warwick, who was the son of Edward IV's brother, and had a more valid claim to the throne than either Henry or Lincoln, was imprisoned in the Tower of London. Henry had him taken from the Tower and paraded through London to St Paul's Cathedral; but this did not deflect the mischief-makers in Ireland. In a brazen and absurd ceremony in Dublin, the impostor Simnel was 'crowned' (with a bejewelled wreath appropriated from a statue of the Virgin Mary), and a so-called 'coronation sermon' was preached by the Bishop of Meath. Simnel was presented to the people of Dublin as King Edward VI, and a feast was held in his honour at the castle.

Then Lincoln led the dupe Simnel and his army, including a force of hardened mercenaries led by Martin Schwartz, a German soldier of fortune, and many Irishmen, across the Irish Sea. They landed near Barrow in Lancashire – but the men of Lancashire unsurprisingly refused to join the Yorkist army. Nonetheless, after not even two years, Henry's kingship was in genuine peril. The 'Tudor dynasty' could have lasted less than two years.

Henry, always cautious but capable of decisive action when necessary, did not panic. Realising that a major military confrontation was now inevitable, he worked with speed and flair to organise his supporters. He gathered an army of about 15,000 men. Most of these troops were well armed and equipped; and, unlike the rebels – still no more than a conglomeration of brave but ill-disciplined and unarmoured Irishmen, continental mercenaries and relatively few English soldiers – they had the advantage of not being a multinational force. In addition, Henry, himself relatively inexperienced in battle, had a competent commander, the Earl of Oxford. Yet the morale of the royal army seems to have been brittle, and there were desertions as the crucial engagement approached.

In mid-June, Lincoln led his rebel army across the River Trent at Fiskerton Ford, a few miles south-west of Newark. That night, they settled on a broad ridge, high above the Trent to the west. The long straight Roman road known as the Fosse Way was on the other side, down to the east. The little village of East Stoke lay in lower ground a few hundred yards off towards Newark. Henry's army, meanwhile, was camped on flat land at Syerston (now an airfield) a mile or so to the south.

The battle – involving about 25,000 troops – that ensued the next day is in many ways of greater significance than the Battle of Bosworth. It is generally known as the Battle of Stoke – and that has caused confusion over the years. Even the authoritative *Brewer's Royalty* claims that it took place at Stoke on Trent, which is in the Potteries, many miles further west.

How the fighting developed is still a matter of dispute. But it is clear that the Yorkists, though outnumbered, were deployed in a strong position. Lincoln's early attacks on Henry's advance troops inflicted heavy casualties, and the royal ranks did not hold. Some of Henry's men fled, and at this point a rout seemed likely. Henry's best troops arrived as reinforcements, just in time. On the Yorkist side, the German and Swiss mercenaries maintained their discipline, but the Irish – who were poorly prepared for battle – broke and fled down through steeply wooded slopes towards the River Trent, pursued by royal troops. Hundreds of them were viciously hacked to death in the woods at the bottom of the decline between the high ground and the river, known to this day as the 'Red Gutter'.

It was all over by noon. The royal army lost about 2,000 men and the rebels many more. The king had prevailed; his throne was secure for the time being. What the Yorkists would have done next if they had won must obviously remain a matter of conjecture; Simnel was hardly a credible figure, despite constant coaching from Richard

Symonds, the priest who had 'discovered' him in Oxford. Lincoln would presumably have disposed of Simnel pretty quickly and pursued his own claim to the throne.

A defeat for Henry would have ended his kingship. He was, naturally enough, delighted. He knighted no fewer than fifty-two of his supporters. And, in victory, he showed mercy. Lincoln and Martin Schwartz were both killed in the battle, but the impostor Simnel was captured alive. Henry gave him a menial job in the royal kitchens. Later, he was promoted to falconer. He outlived Henry.

Symonds was imprisoned, but many of those who had supported the insurrection escaped even this punishment. The troublemaking Bishop of Meath was given a full pardon. Henry always showed craft and calculation in his dealings with bishops, and Meath became one of his most steadfast supporters. Many of the other leading rebels were fined. Gathering wealth was more to Henry's taste than bloody revenge. In this, as in much else, he was very different from his son Henry VIII, who had a bloodlust and revelled in cruel reprisals.

Today, the area where this crucial battle was fought is bereft of signposts, let alone a 'visitor centre'. It is nonetheless possible to circumnavigate the general area of the fighting, starting off from the village of East Stoke, which straddles the busy and dead straight A46 (formerly the Fosse Way). You walk a few hundred yards westwards down Church Lane towards the tiny and almost hidden church of St Oswald. Then you turn south-westwards along a rough bridlepath that takes you to the bottom of the high wooded bank which tumbles down to the infamous Red Gutter. As you look up to your left, you can easily enough imagine the ill-trained and ill-equipped Irish fleeing in utter terror down to the Red Gutter, where so many of them were killed. Those who survived rushed over the fields towards the supposed safety of the River Trent. If you keep alongside the wood, you come to one of the many bends in the river, which flows very fast hereabouts – so quickly that it is not navigable. If any of the escaping Irish troops managed to swim over to what appeared to be the other side, they would have been trapped, for it is in fact a narrow wooded island. The broader, more slow-flowing main branch of the river is on the far side of this island.

After looking back towards the Red Gutter – today the scene is utterly peaceful – and musing on the mayhem, the noise, the stench and the sheer horror of the battle's aftermath, I turned and saw that I was being observed by a man leaning on his 4 × 4 vehicle further along the river bank. He must have driven down Trent Lane, the off-road track that leads to the river from the A46, which was my intended route back. As I approached him, he eyed me suspiciously – he told me he thought I might be an angler without a permit – but, when I explained my interest in the battle, he at once became friendly. 'Ah yes, the last battle of the Wars of the Roses', he said. He assured me that the story of how the Trent was red with blood that day had been passed from generation to generation over the centuries.

I told him of my proposed route and how the final part would entail a walk along the busy A46. He helpfully informed me that there was a faint track leading off to the left at the top of Trent Lane, not marked on the Ordnance Survey map. This would take me along the broad ridge where the battle had been fought, high above the A46. He instructed me simply to bear left when I reached the top of the hill; I could not miss the junction. He was absolutely right. But, before I set off along the unmapped track, I turned and looked back over the Trent towards Southwell. I was only about 70 metres above the river, but the view was magnificent and I could make out the high moors of the Peak District in the far distance.

I followed the rough track between large fields. Away down to the right was the busy A46, but I could barely hear the traffic. Eventually, the track led into the narrow Humber Lane, a right of way that takes you back to East Stoke. The entire perambulation takes little more than an hour – a pleasant walk with extensive views from the uplands and a dark brooding sense of doom alongside the Red Gutter. It is easy enough to imagine the course of this critical but almost forgotten battle in which many thousands of men were slaughtered.

The battle secured Henry's kingship and established the Tudor dynasty. Henry's son, Henry VIII, was to preside over the most nationalistic and the most personal of all the European reformations; it was to become known as the Henrician Reformation. One of the key men in this process was Thomas Cranmer, the long-serving Archbishop of Canterbury who was author of the *English Prayer Book*. When the Battle of Stoke was fought, Cranmer's father Thomas was the squire of Aslockton, a small community a mile or so to the south. Young Thomas was born two years later, in 1489, into an England that was already more secure and more settled than it had been for generations.

Henry VII was to be tested later in his by now well-established reign by a second and more plausible impostor, Perkin Warbeck, who claimed to be Richard Plantagenet, Duke of York, and thus another man who should have been king. Warbeck was charismatic, and he toured the courts of Europe. He also had some supporters within Henry's own ambit; Henry never quite succeeded in ridding his court of all conspirators and potential traitors. Warbeck was dangerous insofar as he could dazzle in the pretty purlieus of a royal court; but, when it came to action, he consistently failed.

He gained some support in Ireland and in France. In 1495, he sailed from Flanders with a small invasion fleet. His attempted landing in Kent met with stiff resistance, and he withdrew to regroup. He eventually found succour at the court of James IV in Scotland, but not enough to launch a full-scale invasion across the Border. James actually presented Perkin with one of his relatives, the daughter of the Earl of Huntly, as his bride. In 1497, at the head of another hastily assembled force, Perkin landed in Cornwall and managed to proceed as far as Exeter before he surrendered to the royal forces. Understandably if untypically, Henry was in no mood for clemency. Perkin Warbeck was not 'rewarded' with a job in the royal kitchens. He was executed, as was the imprisoned real Earl of Warwick – a constant but dangerous innocent in all these shenanigans.

Henry had a serious dislike of war, and he pursued peace relentlessly. He did not want to fight France or Spain. Above all, he did not want to fight Scotland. But the Scots tried his patience sorely. Between 1488 and his death in 1509, Henry had to deal with James IV of Scotland, a charismatic, ambitious, capricious and often foolish king, who was eventually to lead his country to its worst-ever disaster. Early in his reign, James wanted to strengthen the 'Auld Alliance' between Scotland and France, which was sometimes more about annoying the English than helping the French. Also, James smarted over the English possession of the disputed Border town of Berwick. So, early relations between the kings were not propitious, and James rebuffed various overtures from England. James was at his most provocative when he not only gave sanctuary to the impostor Warbeck but also welcomed him as a friend.

In 1496, James led an army over the Border. This was not a full-scale invasion, just another of many Border raids. James spent a couple of weeks rampaging around Northumberland. When Henry started to assemble an army at Newcastle, James hastily withdrew. Then Henry had to deal with a serious rebellion at the other end of his kingdom, in Cornwall. James once again moved into Northumberland, where he made more bloody mischief.

For some time, the far-sighted Henry had wanted to marry off his eldest daughter, Margaret, to James. Although James infuriated him with his escapades along the Border, Henry always kept his eye on the bigger picture. Eventually, peace negotiations were opened, with the proposed marriage at the heart of the dealing. There was a great deal of protracted haggling, not least on the question of the dowry. A so-called Treaty of Perpetual Peace was concluded between the two nations in 1502. (Hardly perpetual – for, eleven years later, England inflicted on Scotland the most grievous defeat in the nation's history.) The actual marriage took place in August 1503.

This could be regarded as the first great event in British, as opposed to English or Scottish, history. It led directly, and exactly a century later, to the Union of the Crowns, the joining of the Thistle and the Rose. Henry VII, the bride's father, with his Welsh background, his kingdom of England, and his determination to build good relations with Scotland, should be regarded as an early,

prescient exemplar of Britishness. The same could hardly be said of
James IV of Scotland.

The wedding itself was the last great set-piece ceremonial event of
pre-Reformation Scotland. The 14-year-old Margaret said goodbye to
her father, whom by all accounts she loved dearly, early in July. There
was a long and tedious progression north, via Grantham, Doncaster,
York, Durham and Berwick. Margaret met her future husband
at Dalkeith. The actual rites were conducted by the archbishops
of Glasgow and York at Holyrood Abbey. Then James hosted an
extravagant and spectacular wedding feast. Unfortunately, Margaret
was not served until the second sitting, by which time James had
already dined with the two archbishops.

James was in some ways an appalling husband. He was not
averse to parading his mistresses before his young queen. But
Margaret had her father's tenacity, and not a little pride. The
marriage was stormy, but the queen held her own. Their first son was
born in 1507, but he died before he was a year old. Five years later,
the boy who was to become James V was born. James V's grandson
James VI eventually became the first monarch of both England and
Scotland.

Thus, the marriage of Margaret and James was hugely significant;
yet it would be wrong to claim that it immediately gave the two
nations the sense of a shared destiny. That was not to come until,
in their very different ways, England and Scotland both embraced
the Reformation. It was to be Protestantism that finally brought them
together.

Henry VII, dry and sardonic, watchful and careful, was indubitably
a great man and an exemplary king. Indeed, he was probably the
greatest king England ever had. But there was nothing flashy or
inflated or obviously regal about him. He did not engage popular
attention as his son Henry VIII or his granddaughter Elizabeth did.
There was something guarded and watchful about him. His son
Henry was a brute and a rascal, duplicitous and bloodthirsty, yet his

subjects warmed to him in a way they never did to the more austere founder of the Tudor dynasty.

Henry VII had his contemplative side, and he became increasingly exercised about the future peace of his soul. In his Christianity, he could not have been more orthodox. He behaved with restraint and lived decently. In a marginally excessive tribute, his superlative biographer Sir Francis Bacon celebrated the 'divine' in him. Bacon noted that 'he had the fortune of a true Christian as well as of a great king'. Bacon further noted that he lies buried 'in one of the stateliest and daintiest monuments of Europe so that he dwells more richly dead in the moment of his tomb, than he did alive in Richmond or any of his palaces'.

Henry had given his kingdom the benefits of order and equi- librium. He constantly contended for peace, and he was consistently far sighted. The writers of history, Bacon apart, have not been keen to celebrate him. But that is perhaps a reflection of his somewhat cold, stand-offish nature rather than a considered assessment of his twenty-four years of power. As he prepared for death and looked ahead, as he must have done, this deeply religious and essentially conservative man could hardly have imagined the extraordinary convulsions that were soon to tear his kingdom – and many others in Europe – apart, all in the name of religion. The first explosion was near – but Henry died in 1509, utterly unaware of the tumults to come.

CHAPTER 2

James IV of Scotland

W HEN Henry VII won the Battle of Bosworth and became king
of England, his counterpart north of the Border was James
III of Scotland. One thing that these monarchs had in common was
their desire for good relations between their two countries.

James was a weak man. He had persistent trouble with his
nobility – particularly those in the Borders, who detested the idea
of peace with England, which became James's prime policy – and he
was deeply unpopular with his subjects. One reason for this was that
James, like Henry, was rapacious. But Henry was cunning and effective
in his rapacity. James, by contrast, was arbitrary and inconsistent. He
annexed land, he levied extraordinary taxes and – worst of all – he
debased the coinage. All this in a random manner, and in a country
that was considerably poorer than England.

Further, James conspicuously preferred the company of low-
born favourites at his court to that of his fractious and bloodthirsty
aristocracy. Foolishly, he did not make a point of travelling around his
kingdom. He spent most of his time in Edinburgh and was regarded
(somewhat unfairly) as being reclusive. And he had a problem with
his eldest son, also James, to whom he became more and more
hostile.

In his relations with the Church, James III had mixed fortunes. He was generally able to control key Church patronage, appointing some of his strongest supporters to sensitive bishoprics. Like Henry VII, he was not interested in church reform, preferring to regard the Church as a source of revenue. His wife, Queen Margaret, was a woman of such conspicuous piety that she was actually, after death, a serious candidate for canonisation. James's key clerical ally was Bishop William Elphinstone, one of the outstanding Scots of his time.

Elphinstone was born in Glasgow in 1431. He studied for several years in France, at Paris and Orléans; and, when he returned to Scotland in 1471, his rise was rapid. He became Bishop of Ross in 1481 and was transferred to Aberdeen two years later. In 1485, he represented James at the coronation of Henry VII. In 1488, he became chancellor of Scotland. He was an accomplished lawyer and diplomat, and he undertook many negotiations with England and continental countries. He founded Aberdeen University, introduced printing to Scotland in 1507, and was responsible for the Aberdeen Breviary, a new national liturgy for Scotland.

James III coveted the Church's revenues, and he interfered constantly in Church affairs, most controversially in a dispute on the management of Coldingham Priory. But he maintained reasonable relations with the papacy in Rome – and indeed, towards the end of his reign, Pope Innocent VIII granted him a special licence, involving a 'window' during which James could make his own appointments to cathedrals and monasteries. If James had had more advisers of the calibre of William Elphinstone, he might have been a more successful king. As it was, his downfall came because of his poor relationship with his eldest son, James.

When still in his early teens, the boy was cultivated by some of the leading Scottish nobles, who regarded him as a useful figurehead in their machinations against the king. The future king in turn used these nobles to further his own excessive and premature ambition; and, in 1488, he became involved with what was to prove the most serious and final rebellion of James III's unhappy reign.

Prince James left Stirling Castle with a small rebel force, mainly from the Borders. The king's supporters confronted them, and there was a skirmish near Stirling Bridge. There was a second, more serious, engagement at Sauchieburn. King James fled from the fighting – and, some distance away, he was stabbed to death, possibly by a man claiming to be a priest. The Scottish Parliament conducted an inquiry into the king's death but was only able to conclude, in the blandest of phrases, that the king 'happened to be slain'. The new king was definitely complicit in his father's death, if not directly responsible for it. In any event, he was crowned James IV at Scone on 26 June 1488.

James IV is often described as Scotland's greatest king; cynics might aver that there was not much competition. James IV was seriously, serially ambitious. He was desperate to make his mark, and not just on his own desolate kingdom on the obscure margins of north-west Europe. He wanted to lead the new navy he created – at vast expense – in a grand Christian crusade against the Turks, an idea that was impractical and did not impress those whom he would have needed as allies. (Too often, James was a fantasist, and an impetuous one at that.)

Luckily, Pope Julius II, himself the most warlike of popes, managed eventually to persuade James that his notion of a crusade was wholly inappropriate. Twenty years earlier, Pope Innocent VIII had finally decided that the idea of pushing back Islam by force should be abandoned once and for all. In fact, James was prescient, for the Turks were to become a major menace in Eastern Europe and in the Mediterranean; but his timing was awry. Politically, he was ingenuous; his greatest skill was in giving Scotland the confidence which grew from his flamboyant and energetic kingship.

James's court glittered; he was handsome and amorous, and he fathered many illegitimate children. One of these, his son Alexander, was appointed archbishop of St Andrews in 1504, when the boy was only 11. James did nothing to stem abuse in the Church; rather, he revelled in it. He attended mass frequently; his religion, like so much else about him, was showy. His guilt for his part in his father's death seems to have been genuine; he wore an iron chain round his waist to show his contrition.

He managed to enhance the international status of Scotland in a way that Henry VII never achieved for England. James was a patron of the arts, an encourager of world-class poets like Blind Harry, William Dunbar and Robert Henryson, a great builder of halls and palaces, and the creator of an impressive navy. But this last was typical: the building of splendid naval ships was an enormous extravagance and essentially frivolous, particularly as he was never able to lead his cherished crusade. All the new ships hardly helped James at the Battle of Flodden Field, several miles inland, when he and 10,000 other Scots died in the nation's most tragic misadventure.

He was a poor judge of men. One of his particular favourites was a charlatan called John Damian, a would-be scientist of doubtful provenance; he might have been French or Italian. Damian seemed for a time to regard himself as Scotland's answer to Leonardo da Vinci. Among many other claims, Damian persuaded the king that he could transmute base metal into gold – and the gullible James gave Damian considerable funds for his various experiments. The most farcical episode came when Damian, who was nothing if not brave, decided that he had learned how to fly. He took off from the heights of Stirling Castle with artificial wings made from hens' feathers. He crash-landed in a midden far below and broke his leg. His glib explanation for this debacle was that he had mistakenly used hens' feathers, which sought the midden, rather than eagles' feathers, which would have sought the sky.

Despite such preposterous performances, James appointed Damian Abbot of Tongland near Kirkcudbright. This was exactly the kind of appointment which suggested that kings of that time, as well as popes, were mired in Church corruption. After five years at the abbey, Damian had the grace to resign; but, for several years afterwards, he continued to receive a very considerable abbot's pension.

James IV was very different from his erratic and withdrawn father, James III. He was bold and confident, indubitably regal; he had enormous zest; he travelled the length and breadth of his wild and mountainous kingdom; and he dispensed justice, sometimes harshly. In his rather flashy way, he was far-sighted. He had artistic aspirations, and he understood the importance of education. In 1496, he persuaded his Parliament to pass Scotland's first obligatory education act, by which all barons and freeholders were required to send their eldest sons to grammar school until they had a reasonable grounding in subjects such as Latin, art and law. He sent two of his own illegitimate sons to study under the humanist scholar Desiderius Erasmus of Rotterdam. He was open to new ideas; though he paid too much attention to a plausible buffoon like Damian, he also could see the significance of a world-class intellectual like Erasmus.

And yet, like so many important and powerful men in the years immediately before the convulsion of the Reformation, he did not seem to be concerned from any point of view – even that of naked self-interest – about the grotesque corruption and rottenness of the Church. Rather, he connived in this corruption and rottenness. He could do so with impunity. Anticlerical dissent, protest and heresy, if not completely unknown during James's reign, certainly did not loom large. In 1494, the Archbishop of Glasgow arranged for a group of lairds to appear before the king and his great council. They were charged with holding heretical opinions. But, although they refused to recant, the matter was not regarded as serious and they were simply dismissed, their freedom intact.

Henry VII of England, always a great believer in dynastic marriages, had arranged for his first son Arthur to marry Catherine of Aragon in 1501, when both were only 15. Arthur died just four months later, and the question of whether the marriage had been consummated was later to play a key part in the English Reformation. Henry's wife Elizabeth died in the same year soon afterwards, and for a time Henry flirted with the idea of marrying Catherine himself. But he was persuaded that, in the long term, it would be better for Arthur's younger brother to do so. Young Henry, always assertive and wilful, disliked the idea, and it was not until after his father died, in 1509, that Henry – now King Henry VIII – married Catherine. Henry VIII was in time to become a key – possibly the key – figure in the English Reformation.

James established a Renaissance court that was admired well beyond Scotland; well and good. He also sought to cut a dash in the chancy theatre of European power politics; not so good. In truth, he was out of his depth. His notion of leading a new crusade was unrealistic. But his major misjudgement came because, despite his marriage into the royal house of Tudor, James IV never really lost his atavistic taste for the Auld Alliance with France.

Around 1510 and 1511, France was emerging as the most power-ful state in Europe. Pope Julius II, the warrior pope, had disdained James IV's idea of a new crusade; but now he showed his warlike side by forming a Holy League, including Spain, Venice and England. In May 1513, Henry VIII invaded France, where he soon won a victory, the so-called Battle of the Spurs. King Louis of France asked James to help him by giving the English trouble on their northern front. He sent money, arms and some of his best soldiers to Scotland. James could not resist. Despite warnings from the pope, he felt an obligation to Louis; and he probably also felt the need to show that he was as big and important a king as his brother-in-law, Henry VIII.

Louis sent money and materials to Scotland; his queen sent James a beautiful ring, telling him to take just a pace into English ground. Was this a subtle hint that James should not do more than create a minor diversion on the Border? If so, it was ignored. Henry was of course engaged with his army in France; but he was sensible enough to have maintained an army in the north. Furthermore, its commander was the Earl of Surrey, a wily military veteran who had fought his first battle before James was born. Surrey had a keener grasp of military tactics than had the impetuous James.

James mustered a huge – by Scottish standards – army of well over 25,000 men. Apologists for the reckless king of Scotland have pointed to the make-up of this army: it surely attested to James's popularity, for it included several thousand Highlanders and most of the leading Scottish nobility. It included representatives of all ranks and all parts of the kingdom. It was an authentic national force. The size and inclusive diversity of James's great army did indeed say much about his popularity; but that simply renders James's irresponsibility all the more grievous, his culpability all the more dreadful. Had he led a smaller army, less representative of his nation, the disaster would have been on a much lesser scale.

The fateful battle took place just north of Flodden Hill, a little south of the River Tweed and only a few miles into England, on 9 September 1513, the blackest date in Scotland's long and turbulent history. It was the ranks of the Scots gunners who first let their side down; for whatever reason, the English gunners were far more effective. Despite this, King James misread the way the battle was going and led an ill-judged, impetuous charge at the heart of the English ranks. The king's folly may have been glorious, but it was folly nonetheless.

Around dusk, after between three and four hours of intense fighting, as many as 10,000 Scots, the flowers of the forest, the flower of Scotland, lay dead. Among them were the king and his illegitimate son Alexander, the archbishop of St Andrews. Eleven earls and fifteen barons were also dead. The king's body was removed from the battlefield by the victors and embalmed at Berwick. Eventually, the body ended up in a monastery in Surrey where, so the story goes, some ruffians severed the king's head and played a game of football with it.

For most of his reign, James had not been able to resist the temptations of incursions into England. In this, he was no better, no more disciplined, nor more responsible, than the reckless, hooligan nobility of the Borders. Flodden was an unnecessary battle, fought for a far-off French king (who showed scant interest in helping his ally after the defeat) to no great strategic or even opportunist end. It was a misjudgement of criminal proportions. Its aftermath was devastating. Scotland, as so often before, now had an infant king. His mother Margaret was the sister of the king, Henry VIII, whose army had just inflicted this most devastating of defeats.

The feuding and anarchic squabbling began at once. The confidence and the authority drained out of the kingdom as fast as the blood had seeped from the bodies of the fallen on Flodden Field. Henry VIII received the news of Surrey's momentous victory at his camp near Tournai, in northern France. He expressed his rejoicing in religious mode with a mass of thanksgiving. He had led his first army to victory against the French; his old general Surrey had led his second army to victory against the Scots. He had indeed much to be thankful for.

Yet, within sixty years of the dreadful disaster that was Flodden, a young and courageous English queen, Henry VIII's daughter, newly and precariously on her throne, took the heroic and dangerous decision to send both her army and her navy north to help the Scots drive the French out of their country once and for all. In doing so, she helped the Scots to accomplish to what was in effect a revolution – a revolution that at last confirmed the Scottish Reformation and rendered Scotland a forward-looking Protestant country, just like her own.

CHAPTER 3

The State of the Pre-Reformation Church in England and Scotland

*I*T is far too neat, even simplistic, to say that the Reformation happened because the Church had become corrupt. For all that, it is as well to survey the condition of the Church in this period – the late fifteenth and early sixteenth centuries – because its condition was not good. The Roman Catholic Church, for most of the fifteenth century, was recovering from the 'great Schism' of 1378–1417, the serious split when rival popes in Avignon and Rome contended for authority. The papacy recovered, and consolidated in Rome. Popes towards the end of the fifteenth century were undoubtedly corrupt, but the corruption was widely accepted and indeed endorsed. There was surprisingly little indignation about the many abuses of Church power.

The 'Renaissance popes' were in effect monarchs, competing and intriguing with the other city states and kingdoms of Italy, and trying to play their part in the power politics of Europe. Leading cardinals became courtiers. The papacy was not as wealthy as is sometimes thought; its revenue was about half of that of Venice, for example. Unlike most monarchies, the papacy was not hereditary. And tenure was generally brief; in the 100 years between 1455 and 1555, there were fifteen different popes. The lack of continuity and consistency was a major problem.

The degraded papacy reached its nadir with the Borgia Pope Alexander VI (1492–1503), who brazenly paraded his young and frankly sexy mistress around the Vatican and was reputed to have poisoned several of his cardinals. He fathered at least nine illegitimate children by three different women. He also presided over an ever more incompetent Curia – the papacy's great administrative office – where posts were bought and appointments were rarely made on merit. The jobs proliferated but the efficiency diminished. Alexander granted his son Cesare no fewer than four bishoprics when he reached the age of 18.

Despite the constant nepotism and occasional murderous violence, there was one considerable positive. The achievement of the Renaissance popes lay in their patronage of the arts. They began the reinvention of Rome, which had declined to a relatively un-distinguished obscurity, as the epicentre of the Italian Renaissance. Today's Rome – arguably the most splendidly adorned city in the world – is a glorious monument to their legacy. The popes' aesthetic taste was as refined as their lives were gross, and they could certainly spot up-and-coming artists of genius. Julius II, although best known as the 'warrior pope', famed for leading his troops in his suit of shining silver armour, also laid the foundation stone of the new St Peter's and persuaded Michelangelo to paint the ceiling of the Sistine Chapel. He was the patron of, among others, Raphael and Leonardo.

The most pressing challenge to the Church was intellectual, and it came from humanist scholars like Desiderius Erasmus in Rotterdam and John Colet in London. But, because they were eminently reasonable men, they did not represent real danger to the established order. They were scholars, not agitators. Erasmus

preferred gentle satire to bitter polemics. Colet, the son of a Lord
Mayor of London, studied at Oxford and then travelled widely on
the continent (including Florence, where he heard a certain Girolamo
Savonarola preach). When he became dean of St Paul's Cathedral
back in London, he emerged as a potential reformer. He believed –
and said publicly – that heretics were not as dangerous to the Church
as the corrupt and even evil lives of so many priests.

This indeed was the Church's main problem in the early years
of the sixteenth century. There was still widespread respect for the
Church as an institution, for its liturgy and its doctrine. There was
no obvious public desire for the Bible to be translated and made
into the stupendously popular book it was shortly to become. But
there was widespread disrespect – even contempt – for the clergy,
from the papacy downwards. Yet the Church did not appear
vulnerable. It was not so weak as to be seriously shaken by the words
of men like Colet and Erasmus. Powerful monarchs like James IV
in Scotland and Henry VII in England were, in their very different
ways, pious and essentially conventional men. They used the Church
to further their own ends, but they also had sincere personal respect
for it.

There was a kind of conspiracy of mutual convenience. These two
kings, like many others, were relaxed about exploiting the Church's
resources as best they could; at the same time, they were concerned
about their souls. So, these were not the kind of men to lead a
revolution against the Church. Heresy – serious religious dissidence
– was not for them. Nor was it for most of their subjects.

The growth of Renaissance humanism had for some time been subtly
undermining the papacy, but in a cerebral, unthreatening way. The
Italian scholar Lorenzo Valla, who fortunately enjoyed the protection
of King Alfonso of Aragon and Sicily, argued that the papacy was
too concerned with temporal power and was consequently directly
responsible for the widespread corruption that vitiated the Church.
Valla also exposed flaws in the Latin New Testament of the Vulgate,
used by the Church. But this was the stuff of recondite scholarship,

far above the heads of ordinary people. Men such as Valla, while they contributed to a growing intellectual scepticism about the papacy, hardly smashed the foundations – indeed, Valla himself ended up as senior secretary to Pope Nicholas V.

One man who was more in the mould of rabble-rousing revolutionary than the likes of Valla or Erasmus or Colet was Girolamo Savonarola. This prophetic figure, whose genius flared in a brilliant spurt of fiery fury in Florence at the end of the fifteenth century, blazed the trail – literally – for what was to come in the next century. A Dominican friar from Ferrara, in 1491 he started to excite Florence to an almost ecstatic fervour with his violent preaching, first at the church of San Marco, then at the cathedral. He soon held almost total sway over the city through the extraordinary power of his spoken words. Although he was kind and gentle as a confessor, when he preached, a special anger, at once divine and terrifying, overcame him. His sermons, delivered in his distinctive high-pitched tones, were long and electrifying. In some ways, the Reformation should have been his, not Luther's.

Among those who heard him preach were John Colet passing through Florence, Niccolò Machiavelli and Michelangelo. Savonarola so scared Michelangelo that the artist fled from Florence in panic after hearing one of his sermons. So, Savonarola had something of the demagogue about him. Those who listened to him were variously alarmed, horrified and inspired. Yet he managed to temper the extremism of his eloquence with spiritual nobility.

He was an early Puritan, and this was another way in which he anticipated much that was to come. He presided over somewhat stagey 'bonfires of the vanities' in which vulgar books, porno-graphy, immodest clothes, cosmetics, gambling materials, carnival masks and the like were publicly burned. His sermons, while severe and raw, were utterly inclusive in that he denounced sin with an unequivocal and far-reaching power that seemed to spare nobody. He abjured what he contemptuously called the 'prostitute Church'. Politically, he was a republican. He also claimed to be a heaven-sent prophet. And people believed him.

Needless to say, none of this resonated too well in Rome. Pope Alexander VI, a lover of the vanities if ever there was one, first tried to shut him up by promising to make him a cardinal. Savonarola, to his credit, was uninterested in such preferment. Then Alexander simply ordered Savonarola to desist. The friar responded by condemning Alexander as a servant of Satan – and turning his fearsome attention to the ostentatious corruption of the papal court. So, Alexander excommunicated him.

In some ways, most importantly in his courageous and stead-fast defiance of the papacy, Savonarola paved the way for the Reformation, although his impact was very localised. His main problem was political. Unlike his great successor Martin Luther, he had no friends in high places. He infuriated the Medici family, who wanted to regain their hold on Florence; he also alienated the powerful Franciscans. After he was excommunicated, his popular support – which had been enormous – ebbed rapidly away. His greatest modern biographer, Professor Lauro Martines, has noted that his enemies had the troops, the guns, the laws, the prisons and the gallows.

The city authorities, egged on by Pope Alexander, placed him on trial for heresy and schism. Alexander sent two emissaries north to Florence to assist with the trial. One of them, Francisco Remolins, quickly became the lead prosecutor. A friend of the pope's son Cesare Borgia, Remolins was a Church careerist with a taste for bishoprics (he held four – Palermo, Sorrento, Fermo and Albano).

Needless to say, Savonarola was found guilty. In 1498, with two associates, he was publicly hanged and then burned. Once most of their flesh had burned away, and what was left of the remains still hung from their iron collars, local boys who had watched the execution threw stones at the blackened bones. They were trying to get hold of them; they wanted to drag them round the piazza for sport. Instead, the charred remains, the embers and ashes, were swept up and dumped in a cart, taken to the River Arno and thrown into the water. The authorities, scared of martyrdom, were determined to leave no remains, no relics. Meanwhile, Remolins returned to

Rome with various gifts from the grateful Medici – including a nubile young widow.

Savonarola is remembered primarily as a public speaker of enormous power, but he left behind various writings. Ignatius Loyola, founder of the Society of Jesus, was to ban his Jesuits from reading anything by Savonarola, even though he admired some of his works. Of Savonarola's contemporaries, his most ardent disciple was Giovanni della Mirandola, a philosopher and scholar who was a precocious Renaissance humanist. When he came under Savonarola's influence, he changed his life and became a humble street evangelist.

Savonarola was very different from men like Valla or Colet because he was above all concerned to communicate directly with ordinary people – something he did superbly. In this, once again, he anticipated Luther. A man of magnetism, scope and apparently divine inspiration, he was by far the most charismatic of the various precursors of the Reformation. Yet his impact on Florence, while enormous, was short-lived; and his impact elsewhere was negligible.

The Christian Church had been essentially united in Europe for many centuries, yet there had been scattered breaks of serious anti-Church agitation. Jan Hus, a distant follower of the Oxford theologian John Wycliffe, was perhaps the most cerebral and influential dissident. Hus came from peasant stock in Bohemia and pursued an academic career as a philosopher at the University of Prague. He insisted, as Wycliffe had, that the fundamental authority for Christian belief was not the papacy but the Bible. Like the Lollards – and indeed the later Savonarola – he abhorred ecclesiastical grandeur and tilted bravely against it.

He was excommunicated in 1411 after he had denounced the sale of indulgences, which people bought in order to ensure their salvation. (Indulgences had originally been granted to those who had done exceptional work for the Church, such as the crusaders – but the medieval Church came to regard indulgences as an easy way of making money.) Hus was burned to death in 1415, and his martyrdom created a movement which was forcefully suppressed.

But the Hussites would not go away. Bohemia was wracked by the first serious, organised fighting between Christians over religion that Europe had known for many centuries. The Hussite 'wars' petered out in the 1430s – but they, too, anticipated the Reformation.

In the early sixteenth century in Germany, an eloquent nationalist historian called Jacob Wimpfeling became a scourge of clerical and papal corruption. He inveighed against the disgraceful state of the clergy, their ignorance and immorality. He objected vociferously to the pope's interference in the appointment of German bishops. Further, he warned that Hussite-style heresy could easily sweep through Germany. Not everybody admired Wimpfeling; Martin Luther described him as an old and distracted scarecrow. But the historian contributed to a growing mood of nascent nationalism, which was often linked with a dislike of the Italian papacy.

It would, however, be wrong to overemphasise the way in which prophetic figures like Wycliffe, Hus and Savonarola, and even Wimpfeling, were harbingers of the tumult to come. One of the key characteristics of the Protestant Reformation was the manner in which so many of the reformers sought, and received, the support of the worldly and the powerful – not least princes and monarchs. By contrast, the followers of Wycliffe, Hus and Savonarola identified with the losers in society – indeed, they often were the losers in society. Crucially, the key supporter of Martin Luther was a powerful, established figure who could protect him: the Elector of Saxony.

Another cautionary point: the Roman Catholic Church's worldliness, its riches and its frequent immorality did not inspire, or provoke, that much spiritual or holy anger. The power preaching of Savonarola in Florence was an exception.

There was, across Europe as the fifteenth century ended, a wide-spread spiritual malaise; and, while this was largely the fault of the Church, it is not correct to suggest that the Church had failed in one of its prime duties, which was to bring solace and consolation to people who were often devastated by plague, by war at both national and local level, by life-threatening poverty and by acute economic uncertainty. Not all the parish clergy were ignorant uncouth men unable to understand or even read the Latin of the services they took. Not all the parishes were in decay; some clergy were lively, helpful pastors whose minds were open to new forms of devotion. By no means everybody in the Church abhorred innovation and the new spirit of Renaissance humanism.

And, even in the countries and the areas where Protestantism was to spread like a bushfire, there often remained among the ordinary people a very strong attachment to the old ways – for example, the ritual of praying for the dead. Even when the clergy were weak and inadequate, the people stayed remarkably loyal. One of the paradoxes of the immediate pre-Reformation period was that virulent anticlericalism existed side by side with an accepted need for the religious service, flawed as it was, that both worldly prelates and second-rate priests were providing, as they had over many generations.

And, while the anticlericalism was growing rapidly, there was the concomitant question of who was to deal with its causes. Exactly who was to undertake serious, root-and-branch reform of the clergy? The papacy? Hardly. The cardinals, archbishops and bishops? They were too often appointed for the wrong reasons. Nepotism was widespread, as was pluralism (the holding of more than one ecclesiastical office at once). And the ablest of the bishops and cardinals were often heavily involved in secular affairs as diplomats, as advisers to kings and princes, as political fixers – or indeed as a mixture of all three.

Often, anticlericalism was rooted not in dissatisfaction with ecclesiastical performance but rather in worldly envy. The Church owned a lot of land. The laity – particularly the higher laity – coveted the huge incomes of the bigger abbeys, the grander bishoprics. In Scotland, abbots lived like lairds. In England, they behaved like country gentry, hunting and generally enjoying themselves.

Among the ranks of the grand and the powerful, occasional moves were made to introduce cautious but meaningful change within the Church. Pope Leo X convened in 1513 a five-year council (the Fifth Council of the Lateran, instituted by the warrior Pope Julius II) which came up with some modest but realistic proposals for reform. In the year the council concluded, a group of senior clergy and laymen gathered in Rome with the aim of drawing up a blueprint for regenerating the Church from within. Among them were two outstanding figures, Gian Pietro Caraffa and Gasparo Contarini. The former was, many years later, to become a fierce reforming pope (and a very unpopular one); the latter was to become by far the most impressive Catholic evangelical of his time. But their deliberations in 1517 came too late to prevent the conflagration that was already sparking.

If we return to Scotland, we can see in the career of the pluralist Andrew Forman much of what was wrong as well as some of what was right. Forman was educated at St Andrews University and worked for the Earl of Angus before entering the royal service. He represented James IV in Rome and then helped to negotiate the marriage of Margaret Tudor to James. He was appointed Bishop of Moray in 1501. James sent him south to congratulate Henry VIII on his accession in 1509. In the following year, Forman was working on the continent, trying to whip up support for James's plan for a new grand crusade led by the king himself. Forman, following James's instructions, presided over the Scottish side in the diplomatic negotiations that led to the renewal of the Auld Alliance, which led in turn to the debacle of Flodden in 1513.

Later, the eminent Scottish scholar and teacher of James VI, George Buchanan, was to blacken Forman's name, suggesting that he was a duplicitous self-serving rogue whose advice had led directly to the king's ill-fated revival of the alliance with France. It is true that Forman, an early advocate of peace with England, had changed his position to become a firm supporter of the French alliance. But James IV was a forceful king, and Forman was probably only doing his master's bidding as best he could. James's bastard son Alexander, the archbishop of St Andrews, was one of those killed at Flodden, a battle which Forman managed to avoid. Alexander's death prompted a grotesque and unseemly fight for the archbishopric involving candidates such as Forman, Elphinstone, James Beaton and John Hepburn.

Pope Leo X, showing almost unbelievable insensitivity to the demoralised and newly defeated nation, ignored these credible Scottish candidates and tried to impose his own young nephew, Cardinal Innocenzo Cibo, on St Andrews (thus also indicating that the Scottish Catholic Church at this time was hardly a national church). Eventually, Forman prevailed. He already possessed the bishopric of Moray, the archbishopric of Bourges in France, and the abbacies of Pittenweem, Dryburgh and Arbroath. He was also abbot of Cottingham in England. He had to shed these offices when he took up his post at St Andrews, though he was able to retain yet another abbacy, that of Dunfermline. He died in 1521, having begun, in a modest way, to show some signs of being a reformer, though he also wrote a tract against Luther.

The nearest English equivalent to Forman was Thomas Wolsey, the son of an Ipswich butcher, who took his MA at Oxford when he was only 15. He entered the service of Henry VII as a young man, and carried out a series of diplomatic missions for him. One of these was a notable failure. In 1508, Henry VII sent Wolsey to Scotland to negotiate with James IV on the release of the Earl of Arran, James's cousin, whom Henry was holding in detention at his court. Arran had been returning to Scotland through England after a diplomatic mission to France, where he had been negotiating a revival of the Auld Alliance. Although James IV had signed a perpetual peace with Henry, the Scottish king was always keen to reopen the old French alliance. When Wolsey arrived in Edinburgh, James – typically – was inspecting a gunpowder factory; when Wolsey eventually established contact with James, he found him inconsistent and elusive. After several meetings, Wolsey returned south, having accomplished nothing.

After Henry VII's death in 1509, Wolsey's rise was accelerated. In 1511, he became a member of Henry VIII's council, and soon its dominant figure. Wolsey was a superb administrator, and Henry VIII trusted him absolutely. Wolsey actually encouraged the king to go hunting, saying he could look after state affairs; and the king required little persuasion. Soon, in Henry's regular absence, Wolsey was in effect governing England. At the same time, his ecclesiastical rise progressed smoothly: he became abbot of St Albans, dean of Lincoln, Bishop of Lincoln and Archbishop of York. He drew the considerable revenues from these offices. He had an illegitimate son and daughter. The son was made dean of Wells Cathedral when he was still a schoolboy. Wolsey became a cardinal and the papal legate in England.

In 1513, it was Wolsey who drew up the masterplan for Henry's invasion of northern France. At the same time, he was carefully accumulating enormous wealth, which he flaunted. In 1517, the papal nuncio in London reported that he and other foreign diplomats regarded Wolsey not so much as a cardinal but as 'a second king'. Wolsey also wanted to become pope and was an official candidate in two papal elections.

Despite his role in preparing for war in 1513, Wolsey was generally a man of peace; like his first master, Henry VII, he had an innate dislike of warfare. In 1518, he presided over the negotiations which led to the Treaty of London, which appeared to unite all Christendom. But not for long. Wolsey was unable to keep in check Henry VIII's constant bellicose tendencies, and by 1522 England was once again at war with France.

Towards the end of his busy life, Forman had begun to flirt with reform. Wolsey never did so. Just before he died, at Leicester Abbey, he admitted ruefully that he had served his king much more diligently than his God. The Scot Andrew Forman and the Englishman Thomas Wolsey were both typical of a special breed of man who flourished in the immediate pre-Reformation period: they combined consummate diplomatic skills with superb administrative ability. Such men were usually pluralists, but their various ecclesiastical positions did not mean that they devoted much of their energy to Church affairs. Their first loyalty appears to be have been to themselves, not their Church; and their second loyalty was to their secular careers, and thus their secular masters. The Church generally came a poor third. Wolsey's fall came when he at last discovered that he could not serve both his pope and his king.

They were clever, flexible and urbane, but they were hardly good Christians despite their proliferation of Church responsibilities. Able and diplomatically adept as they were, they exemplified much of what was wrong in the pre-Reformation Church. A few years later, the greatest of all the early English Reformation figures, the numinous William Tyndale, was to write:

> To preach God's word is too much for half a man. And to minister a temporal kingdom is too much for half a man also. Either requireth an whole man. One therefore cannot well do both. He that avengeth himself on every trifle is not meet to preach the patience of Christ, how that man ought to forgive and to suffer all things. He that is overwhelmed with all manner riches and doth but seek more daily, is not meet to preach poverty. He that will obey no man is not meet to preach how we ought to obey all men.

The condition of the one, official, united European Church was thus exceedingly problematic. Its most able servants did not regard the service of their Church as a priority. There were constant stirrings of dissatisfaction, but these never merged into a cohesive movement; the expressions of disquiet, while sometimes strong, were sporadic and often recondite and cerebral. If someone could be found to combine this cerebral unease with an authentic populism, then the Church – and the world – might well be rocked. Savonarola nearly did so, but his exploits were confined to Florence.

There was no sense that the prevalent anticlericalism was about to explode into a great revolt by the lay people. There was much corruption and cynicism and abuse of privilege. People complained about it bitterly, yet they also tolerated it. What was about to happen was unlike, for example, the American Revolution, or the French one or the Russian one. It was a revolution all right, but it had not been anticipated. It was not picked over, discussed and predicted before it happened. One of the reasons was that the genius who precipitated it was in many ways an extraordinarily conservative man, a German peasant-scholar who most certainly did not want to break up the Church he loved. And so this huge, diffuse and ramshackle Church had held together, and it had retained much that was good. Not least among its virtues was its ability to educate. It is too often forgotten that Martin Luther, fine theologian and scholar as he was, owed much to the excellent training he received from the old Church.

The rise of humanism and secularism was meanwhile helping to create a mental climate that in turn created diversity. Power was soon to be based on more than the military prowess and ambitions of kings, which had so dominated the medieval period. In the future, wars, far too many of them, would be fought over religion as often as not. Violent and spectacular reform, when it came, would arrive not in one spectacular tempest but in a tumultuous succession of fierce squalls and storms that each bore its distinctive character. For example, the Reformation in England predated Scotland's Reformation by quite some time. And they were completely different in character, though the English helped the Scots to secure their Reformation.

But first we must turn to Germany.

PART 1

Luther

CHAPTER 4

Luther the Man

ARTIN LUTHER (1483–1546) was a colossus, a life-force, at once the perfect revolutionary and the imperfect man. They say that more books have been written about him than about anyone other than Christ. For nearly 500 years, he has invited huge claim and angry counter-claim. He must inevitably and justly dominate any book about the Reformation. The moving and tempestuous story of his life, with its fear, its darkness, its constant travails, its heroism, its hope, its brilliance, its extraordinary vitality, and at times its sheer badness, is a story of quintessential human struggle.

For some, such as the Scottish writer Thomas Carlyle, Luther was the ultimate hero; for others, even those you would expect to approve of him, he produces responses of disdain or worse. I know of one leading figure in the Church of Scotland who shudders with distaste every time his name is mentioned. There was always something vulgar about Martin Luther – a coarseness, a boorishness. He once concluded a letter to his wife: 'I got drunk like a German. God be praised.' He attacked his many enemies and critics with abuse and, at times, hysterical exaggeration. Luther was proud of the fact that he was German. While both the Christian Church and the new vogue for humanism were essentially transnational, Luther was very much a German nationalist.

If we contrast him with Desiderius Erasmus, the most fastidious intellectual of his time, we can understand at least something of Luther's essence. Erasmus, like Luther, was an especially clever man who, despite his cleverness, thought that theology, and indeed Christianity itself, should not be too complex. Both men believed that religion should be kept simple and that Jesus Christ was both human and humane. Both men were concerned about the corruption of the Church. But there were crucial differences between them. Above all, Erasmus was an eminently reasonable man; Luther was often anything but reasonable.

At first, Erasmus gave Luther cautious support, though he detested violence and force. In his own words, he was 'averse to any action which might lead to commotion and uproar', whereas commotion and uproar were Luther's constant companions. If you wanted a quiet life, you stayed well away from Martin Luther. Erasmus was a cool and detached man – yet when the break came, it was bitter. 'I shall not oppose it if they roast or boil him', wrote Erasmus, with uncharacteristic vehemence, in 1521. Three years later, the break was complete. Erasmus was appalled by Luther's brutish, wicked response to the German peasants' revolt. He desired moderate, steady change; he certainly did not want to see the Church smashed to bits. He called Luther, in a gentler and more typical phrase, 'a harsh and severe doctor'.

Erasmus died in Basle in 1536, a rather lonely man. He was rejected by many Catholics for helping to foment the Reformation, and rejected by many of the new Protestants for not joining it. By contrast, when Luther died, he was surrounded by adoring friends and colleagues and, above all, by his wife Catherine, who had come to love him so much that, even two months after his death, she still could not eat or sleep. His great friend and disciple, Philip Melanchthon, said that the world had lost not just a prophet but its father. 'We are entirely poor, wretched, forsaken orphans who have lost our dear noble man as our father', he said at Luther's funeral.

The prophetic man, the most significant figure in the extended birth of the modern world, was dead – but the debates raged on.

They still do. Has any man been so many-sided? Paradoxes abound. The man who could write with vicious venom was venerated for his kindness. The man who single-handedly unleashed an era of giddy change was deeply conservative. The man with the refined, clear intelligence could behave like the most egregious boor. His spirituality did not signify solace. He was sometimes, in his own words, 'angry with God'.

Luther's last recorded words were: 'We are all beggars.' Neither a king nor an emperor, neither a warlord nor a politician, but a rumbustious, earthy, flawed human being and above all a prophet, he had had an impact on humanity that was, and remains to this day, gargantuan. Despite his frequent crassness, he always had his sensitive, introverted side, and at the close he was humble and spiritually alone as he prepared to meet his Maker. But then this was the man who had said: 'They threaten us with death, they would do better to threaten us with life.'

Though he came from German peasant stock, Luther's background was quite comfortable. Unlike many Europeans of his time, he did not grow up amid grinding poverty. Indeed, the part of Germany where he was brought up and where he became a noted scholar and teacher was one of the more prosperous parts of early sixteenth-century Europe. Germany as a whole was comparatively affluent and confident.

Luther's grandfather was a modest farmer, a sort of senior peasant; his father Hans became a copper miner and then founded his own small business, a foundry. Martin was born on 10 November 1483. His upbringing was tough. Both his parents beat him; this was normal in those times. Life, despite the comparative prosperity, remained violent and chancy. Death was always near; the plague was a constant threat.

Martin was the eldest child. Hans soon realised that he was very clever. Rather than apprentice him, Hans decided to ensure that he had a good education. First locally in Mansfeld, then at Magdeburg forty miles to the north, then at Eisenach, Martin went to school. And then, in May 1501, he went on to university in the large Saxon town of Erfurt (population 20,000).

Although very bright, Martin took some time to flourish academically. He struggled to gain his first degree. As he studied for his second, the MA, he gradually began to fulfil his early promise. He came second out of seventeen students. At the same time, he suffered from persistent depression. One of his consolations was music, which he adored; he was to become one of the greatest hymn-writers of all time.

The next academic stage was to prepare for the law. One day, in the summer of 1505, when he was walking back to Erfurt from Mansfeld – he had been allowed home for a few days to celebrate the feast of the Visitation of the Blessed Virgin – he approached the gates of the university town with thunder booming around him. Then lightning suddenly flashed, and a bolt struck the ground beside him. He fell over, terrified and shouted: 'Beloved St Anne – I will become a monk.' (Anne was the patron saint of miners, and he had often heard his parents praying to her.)

Within a fortnight, he had cancelled his law course and joined the Augustinian friary in Erfurt. Hans Luther was furious, but to no avail. Martin had signed up for a life of chastity, prayer and – above all – obedience. By 1506, he was ready for full profession. He promised 'to live unto death without worldly possessions and in chastity'. He was to break both promises.

The friars kept a hard and rigorous house. In his theological and spiritual education, Martin saw little evidence of the degradation and corruption which were supposedly among the root causes of the Reformation. He moved on to the small town of Wittenberg, with its equally small university, which had been founded only a few years earlier by the Elector of Saxony. Wittenberg was an unsophisticated place compared with Erfurt. But Luther was to flourish there. He became a lecturer, popular with his students, and then in 1512 he became professor of Holy Scripture, succeeding a notably sensitive and supportive scholar called Johannes von Staupitz.

In the years between 1506 and 1512, Luther was undergoing a protracted personal crisis. He was excessively self-absorbed. He was introspective – and, despite his ability to relate to those whom he taught, he felt himself utterly alone. He could not find God. Indeed, he felt God had rejected him. He was in danger of slipping into a mire of self-loathing.

He was an original; he was trying to work out his own theology – but, although he was a clever man, his mind lacked the logic of his great successor Calvin. There was an imaginative imprecision about him. Indeed, as his hymns and some of his prose writings show, he had a lot of the poet in him. He thought and studied hard, but his conscience kept challenging his thought processes. He remained an earnest and scrupulous friar. Yet his mind was in constant torment.

Staupitz, who was vicar-general of the Augustinian friars in Saxony, did his best to help. He had been Luther's confessor; sometimes Luther's confessions took several hours, and even the well-disposed Staupitz became impatient. It was Staupitz who steered Luther towards St Paul.

As Luther turned more and more to the writings of Paul, and in particular the Epistle to the Romans, he slowly began to emphasise faith above all else. It was through faith that the grace of God flowed down; this simple insight at last gave him peace of mind. As he was able, with growing confidence, to work out his own theology, the torments eased and arrogance began to appear. In 1517, he wrote to a friend saying that his, Luther's, theology was becoming dominant in the university. On the other hand, the great Aristotle was going downhill! Perhaps the Greek would 'go all the way to hell'.

For some time, Luther had been vexed by a commonplace Church scam, the cynical sale of indulgences. It affronted him that ordinary decent people thought they could avoid penitence simply because they had purchased an indulgence. Pope Leo X had authorised a massive sale of indulgences across Germany, a fruitful country for this kind of fund-raising. The chief salesman was a Dominican friar, Johann Tetzel, whose pitch was crude and effective. Indeed, he was a spiritual snake-oil salesman of the worst kind. Like many high-profile salesmen, he was very well paid, with a substantial salary, generous expenses and – if he sold sufficient indulgences – huge bonuses. People listened to Tetzel. They enjoyed being frightened by him. After all, if they bought an indulgence, they would have escaped the fires of hell – or so they believed.

Meanwhile, as Luther's personal spiritual crisis eased, his career progressed. His main concern remained his academic work, but he was also in charge of the castle church in Wittenberg, where he preached every Sunday. He had a further responsibility: the running of various convents.

By 1517, Tetzel was conducting his hard sell not in Wittenberg itself, but nearby. The Elector, Frederick the Wise of Saxony, had banned Tetzel from his own territories, which included Wittenberg. But Luther became aware that some of his own congregation had crossed the River Elbe to places where they were free to purchase indulgences. He was appalled, but he was also measured. At this point, the 33-year-old Professor Luther was far from being some latter-day Savonarola, inciting the masses with his fiery preaching. He had become something of a Church careerist; the last thing he would have wanted was to tear his Church apart, though that was exactly what he was about to do.

Luther dealt with his concern about indulgences in a cautious, academic, restrained way. He was dealing with a specific abuse of the Church's power. He was not drawing up a vast programme for reform, a masterplan to modernise the Church. In late October 1517, he drafted a series of theses in which he did not neglect to argue that the pope himself was being slandered by the preaching of men like Tetzel. He sent the theses to the Archbishop of Mainz (somewhat naïvely, because Mainz had subcontracted Tetzel) and to the Bishop of Brandenburg. He also distributed them to various friends and colleagues at the university.

It was on the final day of October that one of the most famous and momentous events in human history took place. Or did it? Luther announced that he was convening a debate on his theses at the university the next day. He then pinned the ninety-five theses on the main door of the castle church. So what? This was a routine way of making an announcement, of alerting people to a forthcoming event. Luther was not trying to instigate a rebellion, far less a revolution. The theses were written in Latin, not German, and they had been penned by a loyalist who was steadily making his way in the Church.

It is not known whether or not the debate at the university took place. Indeed, it is not certain that the theses were actually pinned by Brother Martin to the door of the church. The only person to claim that they were was Philip Melanchthon, Luther's first biographer (the first of hundreds), who was not even in Wittenberg at the time. In Luther's own copious writings, there was no reference to pinning the theses to the church door.

If the theses were publicly displayed, this might well have caused a local stir. But what really mattered was that they found their way into the hands of a printer and were translated into German. This undoubtedly happened. And it probably happened without Luther's knowledge or approval. The printed theses were soon being distributed through Germany and beyond its border. Sir Thomas More was studying them in England early in 1518.

Even then, there was no great likelihood of anything other than an essentially academic controversy, albeit a bitter one. What first fired the great conflagration in the crucial year of 1518 was the sheer stupidity of two men: Tetzel himself, and then the man who was supposedly the foremost theologian in Germany (and a sometime friend of Luther's). This academic, John Eck of the University of Ingolstadt, was guilty of particularly foolish over-reaction.

Tetzel – who commanded the attention of ordinary people – ferociously denounced Luther as a heretic. He bragged that Luther would be burned to death within weeks. This was quite in keeping with his character. But he also had intellectual pretensions, and he decided to write a long series of 'counter-theses'. When they arrived in Wittenberg, Luther's students got hold of them and burned them publicly. (It was very much an era of burning, of documents and books as well as people.) Eck, supposedly more refined and intellectual, was almost as outspoken as Tetzel, calling Luther among other things rebellious, impudent, simple-minded and – most dangerously – 'a despiser of the pope'.

Luther had in fact been careful not to attack the pope directly. In any event, Leo X was not a cerebral man – he was basically a hedonist dilettante – and had no grasp of theological matters. More significantly, he had no political antennae. In December 1517, the Archbishop of Mainz forwarded Luther's theses to Rome, indicating that Leo would no doubt know how to deal with 'such error'. As it turned out, the pope had not the slightest notion of how to cope. An aged, obscure and pompous theologian – a man called Sylvester Prierias, the Commissioner of the Sacred Palace, and a Dominican – was asked to provide the public response to the insolent Augustinian. Prierias took precisely the wrong tack, blustering, abusing, threatening, ignoring the arguments in the theses and instead reiterating the claims of the infallible papacy.

Rome was reacting in the worst possible way. In Germany, Luther was now receiving fervent support from his own students and guarded support elsewhere. He was emerging as an unlikely public hero. The turning point, when Luther received the personal endorsement he probably needed to pursue his case, came in April 1518 when his own order held a meeting at Heidelberg. While the theses themselves were not debated, Luther was acclaimed. A young friar called Martin Bucer was especially impressed. Bucer was to become a leading reformer.

Luther, who five years previously had been tormented with self-doubt, struggling with his faith, was rapidly growing in confidence. His mindset was changing. He was more assured and was relishing his burgeoning celebrity. He was beginning to realise what a superb, potent writer he was. Already a popular and confident lecturer, he discovered that he could write fast and well, in both Latin and German. He became a consummate communicator; he was an enormously effective journalist and propagandist. The new printing technology was a godsend for him. His papers, tracts and pamphlets were printed and distributed to large audiences all over Germany.

I wrote above that Luther was the perfect revolutionary. This might seem peculiar, given that he did not intend to start a revolution and had no idea of where to take it once it started. But his sheer mastery of communication, allied to his uncanny ability to act as a focus for all the resentment and frustration, both spiritual and nationalistic, that had been simmering in Germany – these, along with the unstoppable force of his personality, turned him into a one-man machine ready to turn the world, or a considerable part of it, upside down. Further, he was by now well prepared for the coming battle, when he knew his life would be in danger. The Church had neither shut him up nor squashed the dissidence. In the summer of 1518, Luther received an instruction from Leo X to journey to Rome and face his accusers. At the same time, the pope instructed the head of the Augustinian order in Saxony to have Luther arrested, manacled and imprisoned.

Luther knew that it would be folly to venture outside Germany. Anywhere in Germany outside Saxony might also be problematic, but within Saxony he was probably safe – so long as he had the protection of the elector. So, Luther made a specific plea for that protection. He understood that Frederick the Wise's sympathy would be crucial; the secular ruler could, if he wished, safeguard both his life and his work.

Frederick was well disposed to Luther. Apart from anything else, Luther had put the little university of Wittenberg on the map. Frederick had founded the university, and he was gratified to find that it was now becoming famous. Furthermore, the elector was, obviously enough, a German – and German nationalism was nascent at this time. Frederick, although a good old-style Catholic (he was the proud possessor of a huge collection of relics), was by instinct unhappy with Italian clerics interfering in German affairs.

The specific political situation also favoured Luther. The Holy Roman Emperor, Maximilian, was in poor health. Everyone knew that his death was imminent. Frederick was a member of the six-man Electoral College that would shortly be choosing the next emperor. The pope was concerned that the next emperor should not be Charles (son of Philip of Burgundy and Joanna of Spain); he would have preferred just about anyone else, perhaps even Frederick himself. It would therefore not be in his interests to alienate Frederick. Luther, meanwhile, was determined that his 'case' should not be heard in Rome, where, whatever the merits of his arguments, he would be in acute danger. Pope Leo tentatively asked Frederick the Wise as 'a good son of the Church' to hand over Luther, 'a son of perdition'. Frederick did nothing.

Now the great test was approaching. Luther's first significant adversary was to be yet another Dominican – this time the general of the entire Dominican order, Tomasso de Vio, Cardinal Cajetan, who was also the papal legate in Germany. This was the man whom the pope chose to swat Luther into oblivion. Cajetan was decent and thoughtful, like Eck a distinguished theologian, but more personable. Cajetan had investigated the continuing cult of Savonarola. He was himself, in his own gentle, reasonable way, a reformer; he was a sincere enemy of corruption, and he wanted to restore moral rigour to the Church. But he had a tendency to snap under pressure, which was to prove fatal. In other circumstances, he might well have patched up what was still, just about, a little local difficulty.

Although he had only been in Germany as legate for a few months, Cajetan was well aware of the country's political and diplomatic complexities. When Frederick the Wise formally asked for Luther's case to be heard not in Rome but in the imperial free city of Augsburg, Cajetan told the pope that he should accede. And so, the first great set-piece of Luther's career, which was to transform him from obscure heretic into the most celebrated man in Europe, took place in Augsburg, a large, wealthy and sophisticated centre, full of bankers, artists, printers and immigrant workers.

Cajetan had no stomach for a major clash. He was a natural conciliator. His personal instinct was to admonish Luther for errors rather than to condemn him for heresies. Yet he soon found that he had a distaste for Luther. Indeed, at their three meetings, the two men discovered that, despite themselves, they seriously disliked each other. Cajetan was irked by Luther's eyes, constantly flashing with anger, and by his persistent pedantry. Further, Luther – always a terrible interrupter – showed Cajetan zero respect.

Cajetan had been advised not to get into a detailed argument with Luther but rather to demand a simple, straightforward recantation. If this was not delivered, the heretic was to be sent to Rome in chains. Luther was pugnacious, argumentative, truculently confident of his ability to debate any point, big or small, and utterly determined to force the cardinal to explain to him in fine detail precisely where and how he had lapsed into heresy. This was a trap for Cajetan, but he allowed himself to be dragged into it, and – clever as he was – he soon found himself outgunned and outclassed by the disputatious Augustinian. At the third and fatal meeting, Cajetan lost control. He shouted at Luther to get out.

Cajetan did not obtain his recantation; he had instead an escalating crisis. For it was Cajetan, more than anyone, who forced the issue, who concentrated Luther's mind on the crux. In the course of their three confrontations, it finally became clear to Luther that he had a simple choice. He had either to endorse the pope's absolute, unconditional authority – or to follow his convictions and accept, and publicly declare, that the pope could be wrong and that the Church did not have the ultimate authority to teach Scripture.

Luther still instinctively wanted to believe that the pope was just misguided, ill-informed, poorly advised. But he now had to face up to a stark truth: he was going to have to reject papacy and all it stood for. Once Luther had followed the logic of his own position, he found himself liberated, although paradoxically he was also in imminent danger of losing his personal freedom. He now knew that he would die rather than recant. He was free in his own mind; he was free to prosecute his own simple, crystalline case. At the end of the day, the pope did not matter. Scripture alone had authority.

The implications were colossal. For the last 500 years or so, we have been dealing with them. All sorts of things are supposed to have grown from this basic insight – individualism, capitalism, the opening of people's minds. But, for the moment, all we need to note is that Luther had been forced into a position where he had no option but to assert that the pope's authority did not exist. Furthermore, the Church was effectively redundant. All that the people needed was access to the Bible. If they had that access, they did not need priests.

Luther reduced Christianity to its very essence. The rising churchman had now declared his own Church superfluous. Man needed no intermediary between himself and God, as long as he had the Bible. Scripture alone possessed infallibility. Of course, this was far too simple. It could never be a case of all or nothing. The Church was needed. Priests were needed. Church buildings were needed. That was why the Reformation, in its purest essence, finally failed.

Luther was to have a major clash three years later at the Diet of the Holy Roman Emperor in the town of Worms. This has gone down in history as the time when he reached the point of no return. It was when he allegedly said: 'Here I stand. I can do no other', though these were not quite his actual words. Yet, almost certainly, the crucial, pivotal change came during his three disputes with Cajetan. Had Cajetan handled the impetuous academic differently, the revolution might never have happened.

After the third and final session in Augsburg had ended in disorder as a result of Cardinal Cajetan losing his temper and control of the proceedings, Luther's good friend and mentor, Staupitz, who had bravely come to offer his pupil and protégé support, slipped out of the city, fearing for his life. As for Cajetan, he knew that the pope would have wanted him to have Luther apprehended and hauled in humiliation and disgrace to Rome. But he was also well aware of Frederick the Wise's role in protecting Luther. The elector had granted Luther a formal safe conduct. Because of the delicate political situation in Germany, Cajetan was anxious to avoid a major confrontation with the elector. So, he dithered, not knowing whom to defy: the pope or the elector.

Luther took advantage of the cardinal's indecision. He was smuggled out of Augsburg in literal fly-by-night circumstances. He then undertook the most perilous physical journey of his life, on an ill-tempered and unsaddled horse, to the relative safety of Monheim, about fifty miles away. The story goes that, when he reached the town, he fell from the horse, utterly exhausted, on to a heap of straw.

By the end of October, he was back in Wittenberg, where the whole rumpus had started exactly a year earlier. From then on, everything moved at a giddy pace. Up until this point, Luther had not been directing events. He had wanted to purify his Church, no more; he had no idea that he could lead a huge popular wave of protest. Now, as he was discovering his extraordinary talent as a writer and mass communicator, he took off. Pamphlets followed each other in a kind of furious spate. Then, in 1520, he wrote his three great 'Reformation Treatises'. One of his themes was that the princes and magistrates of Germany should reform the Church. By now, he was blatantly bypassing the bishops and cardinals; he was trying to destroy the power of the pope himself. He wanted the princes to preside over a great moral cleansing: closing the brothels, controlling the usurers and so on.

1520 was altogether a momentous year. Across Germany, people would go up to strangers and ask: 'Are you for Martin?' It appeared as if the majority were uniting behind him. South of the Alps, few could comprehend what was happening. In the summer, the pope issued his bull *Exsurge Domine*, which started rather fancifully, saying that a wild boar had blundered into the vineyard. It condemned Luther as a heretic and ordered people to burn his books. And there was indeed to be burning, but not of Luther's books. Mobs were soon on the rampage, not just burning copies of the bull but also demonstrating raucously.

Luther himself, never one to resist the temptation of rousing a rabble, presided over one such burning, just outside the walls of Wittenberg, near the River Elbe. When the mob had thrown copies of the bull into the flames, they marched back to Wittenberg, led by a brass band, and found copies of books by Eck and other anti-

Luther theologians. These were taken back outside the walls, and a second bonfire consigned more printed material to ashes. Luther was no longer an obscure friar. He was the man of the moment; and he was enjoying it. It was not until the beginning of 1521 that Luther's excommunication was made formal, by another bull which significantly stated that those who protected him would themselves become heretics. This had no effect on Frederick.

The new, young and inexperienced Holy Roman Emperor, Charles V (born in 1500, elected in 1519), now had an immense problem before him. This was his great test, and he knew Pope Leo to be his enemy. He also knew that at least some of the Electoral College who had recently chosen him as emperor were sympathetic to Luther. On the other hand, he feared a huge popular uprising in Germany. There was perhaps still time to put Luther down. He was well aware that real power in Germany rested with the electors and the princes. His own base was in Spain, and to a lesser extent southern Italy.

So, Charles summoned Luther to the imperial diet, meeting in Worms. This in itself was regarded by the papacy as a provocative act. Since the Church had unequivocally denounced Luther as a heretic, all the secular authority had to do was to carry out the papal sentence. No more confrontations or hearings were necessary. Charles was having none of this. At the same time, he did not wish to deal with Luther personally. Luther's reputation was by now such that nobody on earth would have been confident in confronting him; and the German princes were starting to realise that matters were getting out of control. They reckoned there might be uprisings if Luther did not receive a personal hearing. So, Charles compromised; Luther would have his hearing, but there was to be no disputation.

On 17 April 1521, Luther appeared before the emperor, the electors, the princes and all the senior functionaries of the empire. Faced with this considerable assemblage of the great and the good, the patriotic German's confidence deserted him. Asked straightforward questions, he mumbled incoherently. He was treated with respect and given a day to recover. His prayers were answered – and, when he appeared the next day, he was a changed man, resolute and eloquent. Asked whether he was willing to recant, he replied with humility. His conscience was captive to the Word of God. He could not, he would not recant anything. 'For it is neither safe nor right to act against one's conscience. God help me.'

This was not what the emperor wanted. Luther was a man of eloquence; Charles himself now showed no mean eloquence when he reminded the people that he was descended from a long line of emperors of the noble German nation. They had been faithful, to the death, to the Church of Rome; he was resolved to follow them. A single friar who went against all the Christianity of 1,000 years and more had to be wrong. He was determined therefore to stake his life and his soul, so that the German nation was not disgraced.

Fine words – but the emperor remained in a quandary. He knew that at least some members of the Electoral College, including Frederick the Wise, were unhappy with the outcome. So, he changed tack. He convened a private meeting, which lasted several days, during which Luther was examined by a group of German theologians. They were reasonable and non-confrontational in their approach. But Luther stood firm.

Eventually, he was allowed to leave Worms with a safe conduct. Shortly afterwards, Charles issued the Edict of Worms. No-one was to assist or even communicate with Luther. If they did, they would be arrested and they would lose all their property. Luther's writings were to be burned. Luther himself was an outlaw, under sentence of death.

All this was far too late. Luther had not been, and would not be, silenced. Nor would he be killed. His steadfast protector, the Elector of Saxony, arranged for him to be 'abducted' by five horsemen in a forest near Morha as he progressed northwards with his safe conduct, though that of course was now of doubtful value. Frederick's men accomplished this phony kidnapping swiftly and competently. Luther, still clutching some books, was disguised and spirited off to the safety of Wartburg Castle, near Eisenach. This was derring-do, but the reality was that Germany was behind Luther. He might now be effectively imprisoned in a castle. But he was alive, and he was writing. The great communicator was just beginning.

Luther, usually on an emotional switchback, now became depressed. The confidence, the relish in his own celebrity, the truculence – all these evaporated into the Wartburg mist. He did not like living in what was virtual imprisonment. He fretted with his disguise. He suffered from constipation and insomnia. Ravens and magpies, flying round the battlements, disturbed him. He found himself, once again, battling with Satan. For a time, he discovered the Devil everywhere: he heard him on the roof, he heard him on the stairs; the Devil appeared as a black dog on Luther's bed.

The warden of the castle, seriously concerned for Luther's mental health, took him hunting. But Luther could see no point in pursuing a harmless little creature like a rabbit. Then, one day, a hunted hare, seeing Luther as a friend, sought sanctuary in the reformer's cloak; but the hounds appeared and bit through to their prey. Had God deserted him again? Luther missed his friends and supporters, the adulation of his students at Wittenberg. He fell into the slough.

And yet, despite all these travails, which were real enough, this amazing man did not sulk or succumb. Instead, he rallied and literally wrote himself out of depression. His productivity was awesome. During his period of detention at Wartburg, which lasted less than a year, he wrote no fewer than twelve books, as well as translating the New Testament into German. This last was a masterpiece – a true and honest translation, but presented in vibrant, demotic German prose. It was at last a book for the common people. More than 200,000 copies were to be sold over the next decade.

Luther's revolution was supremely a revolution of words. Between 1518 and 1523, the number of books published in the German language increased tenfold. This was almost entirely down to Luther. Printing presses were established all over Germany. And Luther's ideas spread not just through the printed word but also through word of mouth. People were not now simply asking strangers if they were 'for Martin'. They talked about his ideas and discussed his simple, straightforward version of Christianity.

Above all, he gave the people their Bible. At last, the Bible was becoming what it should always have been, the bedrock of Christianity.

In 1522, Frederick, by now the crucial secular figure in Luther's life, judged that it was safe to let Martin return to Wittenberg. Why was Frederick (who owned one of the largest collections of relics in Christendom) so consistently supportive of Luther? He never became a Lutheran himself, but he liked and admired the first and most influential Lutheran. His secretary and chaplain, George Spalatin, who was always sympathetic to Luther, had considerable influence over him.

Furthermore, Frederick was grateful for the fame and prestige that Luther had single-handedly gained for his little university. And maybe his 'wisdom' persuaded him that, deep down, Luther was less radical than he seemed. If so, Frederick was correct.

As soon as the returning hero was back in Wittenberg, he showed the conservative side of his nature. Luther began to take issue with the more extreme reformers. He was never a Wycliffe or a Savonarola. He had relied on the protection of Frederick; increasingly, he saw his Reformation as being linked to secular power and authority.

While he had been at Wartburg Castle, the students at Wittenberg had become over-excited. They had destroyed an altar in the Franciscan church. They had rioted during a Christmas Eve service. Luther now made it clear that he would have no truck with such behaviour – despite the fact that he had come close to inciting riots himself just a year or so earlier. Luther always detested social disorder.

In late 1523, a series of frenzied peasant risings swept across southern Germany. The peasants were relatively poor people in a wealthy country. But they had been enjoying a new-found prosperity. Their self-confidence was also growing. At least part of their new aggression could be attributed to Luther's Reformation. The peasants were inflamed not just by the acts of unjust and oppressive landlords but also by a virulent anticlericalism. They were joined by craftsmen and tradesmen; indeed, actual peasants became a minority in the revolt.

Amid the ferment was the extremist Thomas Müntzer, a wild, radical preacher much given to bloodthirsty incitement. Müntzer would have been a dangerous man in any context; in those times, he was in his element. We have noted that Luther was not as reasonable a man as Erasmus; compared to Müntzer, Luther was the very model of reasonableness.

Müntzer was a well-educated, intelligent priest who had imbibed the ideas of Hus but had gone on a wild cerebral journey which led him to believe in the necessity of revolution. He wanted the people to be free and God alone to rule over them. He was not afraid of violence; indeed, he revelled in it. He claimed that God was 'sharpening his scythe' within him, though he called himself not 'the scythe' but 'the hammer'. His sign combined a red cross with a sword. He was given to saying: 'Let not the sword of the saint get cold.' In truth, he was a maniac. He was also an outspoken enemy of Luther. Erasmus had called Luther a harsh and severe doctor; Müntzer called him 'Dr Liar'. Further, Luther was accused of being 'soft-living and spiritless'.

It is difficult to assess whether Müntzer was a marginal figure in the peasants' revolt or whether his hellfire ranting played a significant part in whipping up the discontent. What is important is his clash with Luther, for Martin now began to worry about what he had unleashed. He had no direct responsibility for the uprising; indeed, he was concerned to put it down. But the climate he had created undoubtedly encouraged the subversive, the rebellious and the fanatical. Müntzer was just the most prominent exemplar of this last category. There were many others.

The actual revolt was uncoordinated. It took the form of a series of sporadic uprisings. These were often sullied by an unusual cruelty, on a scale that became horrific, even for those violent times. Castles and monasteries alike were attacked; nuns were raped. Feral gangs of men, drunk on beer and wine they had looted, roamed around the country lanes. When the princes and magistrates regained control, the repression was brutal. About 100,000 died, leaving behind many more widows and children.

Luther, always brave, had travelled into what were combat zones, preaching against the uprisings and denouncing the deranged zealot Müntzer. Once again, his life was in danger, but now from different enemies and for different reasons. He could not control his pen. He could not stop himself writing with savagery. In 1525, he wrote a lamentable and deplorable tract, *Against the Murdering Thieving Hordes of Peasants*. His language was vile. He incited not the peasants but the princes 'to brandish their swords, to smite and slay the wicked'. This was bad enough, indeed it was unforgivable – but Luther sometimes dashed off crude polemics without much reflection. However, did there lie underneath his furious words a sinister, calculating motivation? Was Luther now fully aware that his Reformation depended on the civil authorities – that it was really a revolution not of the people but of the masters?

In any event, Luther could now be fairly branded as a counter-revolutionary, a man who wrote that you could not deal reasonably with a rebel; rather, you had to 'punch him in the face until he has a bloody nose'. So, Luther became wholly identified with the ruling class, with the princes, with the rich, the powerful and the strong. Many of the innocent survivors of the revolt did not forget. They had been taught hard lessons. Luther's Reformation was no longer for them. Some turned back to the old Church; some turned to the growing number of radical sects that the Reformation had spawned.

In those violent times, many of the new Lutheran ministers found themselves martyred when they had barely begun their ministry. In many parts of Germany, the Roman Catholic Church recovered its authority, and it was not slow in exacting reprisals. Whoever was now in control of the Reformation, it was not its begetter.

Luther himself was not to be martyred. Revolutions often devour those who start them. But Luther was to prove a great survivor. And, for some, he was also to prove a great betrayer.

CHAPTER 5

Early Reform in England

W E have seen that Luther's impact on Germany, in the years 1518–24, was colossal. His impact on England was to be less dramatic, but highly significant nonetheless, while his immediate impact on Scotland was almost negligible.

Both social instability and spiritual dissatisfaction had been widespread across Europe before Luther produced his theses in 1517. So, Luther's ideas were discussed eagerly in many countries beyond Germany – and that was about as far as it went, for the time being. This was because the powers-that-be were aware that social instability mingled with religious reform was a potent mixture. And, once Luther had challenged the old orthodoxies and directed ordinary people to draw their own conclusions from Scripture, his Reformation was unlikely to cohere as a united movement. It was bound to start breaking into sects and dissident groupings.

So, the authorities wanted to keep the desire for reform under control; and those who pushed most avidly for reform could not hold together. In some ways, it is remarkable that the Reformation ever happened.

England had a powerful but wilful king. Henry VIII was always keen, whenever possible, to play the part of the showman king.

Latterly, he became more and more erratic and violent, savagely so. But most of the English people, particularly in the south and east, stayed loyal to him. And, when this king became the supreme head of the Church, that made for a very English and altogether a very curious Reformation.

Thus, the Reformation in England cannot be discussed without first examining the career and persona of the monarch who presided over it, Henry VIII. Indeed, here we have one of history's great ironies, because Henry regarded himself, with some justification, as a great defender of the papacy and a devout and strong Catholic. Luther's impact on England might have been very different had Henry decided to embrace Lutheranism. But the king's initial response to Luther was wholly negative.

Lutheran ideas were eagerly discussed by a scattering of English intellectuals – particularly a group who met at the White Horse Tavern in Cambridge – and humanists. The leading English humanist, however, was Sir Thomas More – a man who detested Lutheranism with an almost deranged, scatological intensity.

The greatest English non-political reformer was William Tyndale, who was doggedly independent. He was, essentially, a loner. He had the protection of no king or prince; he had no devotees and followers. A brilliant scholar from Gloucestershire, Tyndale was educated at Oxford. He was arguably the finest writer of English prose there has ever been, bar none. Tyndale's great and abiding desire was to make the Bible available to all the people of England in their own language. When Luther's teachings were first discussed in England, Tyndale sought permission to produce and publish his own translation of the Bible. But he could find no-one to support him in the English Church. He left for Germany in 1524.

Henry VII's reign had been one of consolidation and stability; his son Henry VIII's was the precise opposite. One of its economic features was a vast transfer of land and wealth, almost all of it from the Church. The recipients were the crown, the aristocracy – already wealthy – and a new breed of up-and-coming gentry.

But, while the landholding of the crown, considerably enhanced by Henry VII, grew even more, the most durable consequence of Henry VIII's reign was not an extension of kingly significance but rather a shift of power from the monarch to Parliament. The process was not fully manifest for several generations, but the English Reformation was very much a political reformation, and it could be argued that the real long-term beneficiary was Parliament rather than the new Church of England. It was certainly not the monarch. This was because the Reformation was accomplished by parliamentary statute. Parliament was now on the way to becoming supreme, sovereign in a way that monarchs no longer could be, though various future monarchs failed to grasp this.

Henry VIII was born in 1491, the younger brother of Arthur, who was to die in 1502 not long after he had married Catherine of Aragon. Henry was 17 when he became king in 1509, and one of his first moves was to marry his brother's widow Catherine (after receiving a papal dispensation to do so). Catherine was six years older than he was; at first, their marriage was happy and successful.

Physically, Henry was huge. He was also a monster, ever capable of wickedness and duplicity, though these characteristics became much more obvious as he grew older. He always had large appetites, though his sexual appetite seems to be have been far from voracious, despite his six wives.

He had an insatiable hunger for hunting; he could wear out six or seven horses in the course of a day. He enjoyed jousting at tournaments. He wrote poetry and was an accomplished musician. He was clever and very competitive; he could speak several languages, and he fancied himself as a theologian. And he was obsessed with religion. One characteristic of Renaissance monarchs was that they were eager propagandists – and this was certainly true of Henry VIII. He was self-righteous, and his personal religion was tainted by a self-serving smarminess.

Thus, when his army routed the Scots at Flodden, the victory was presented as punishment to the Scots for challenging not Henry but the pope. There was, in truth, some justification for this spin, as the pope had not wanted James IV to renew the Auld Alliance with France; but it gave an early indication that Henry liked to pose as the champion of the papacy and the old Church. This neatly fitted in with the power politics of the time, because the papacy was an enemy of France, and the king of France, Francis I, was in turn Henry's great adversary.

When news of Martin Luther's teachings and exploits filtered over to England, Henry was not impressed. As a monarch, and a strong one at that, he disliked the idea of direct attack on papal authority. After the pope, who next? Kings? Kings could and did squabble constantly with popes about finance and about foreign policy; but it was not a monarch who was stirring things up in Germany. It was some vulgar, obscure friar. Henry regarded Luther as no more than a jumped-up chancer who was shaking the established order in a most dangerous way.

Further, Luther provoked Henry's religious conservatism. When Erasmus of Rotterdam met Henry in 1520, the king expressed his disapproval of Luther virulently. Encouraged by the sycophantic Wolsey, and puffed up with his own theological aspirations, Henry decided to write a book condemning Luther.

When the pope appealed to all monarchs in Christendom to burn Luther's books and to persecute Lutherans as heretics, Wolsey and Henry were eager to oblige – but not before Wolsey was appointed the permanent papal legate in England. Once this was confirmed, Wolsey proceeded to organise a spectacular anti-Luther extravaganza in London. It attracted more than 30,000 spectators – an amazing gathering at that time. As Bishop John Fisher of Rochester, who had taught the young Henry, preached a protracted sermon which was really just an anti-Luther rant, the reformer's books were thrown into a huge bonfire.

Henry was helped by Fisher and by the leading humanist thinker Sir Thomas More in researching his anti-Luther book. They may well have written parts of it. Henry was to execute both men later when they refused to renounce the papacy; but, for the time being, he was delighted with their support. He saw himself as the most cerebral of kings, a confident and leading member of Europe's intellectual elite. His book, called *The Assertion of the Seven Sacraments*, defended both indulgences and papal authority, and attacked Luther for promoting sedition.

A special luxury edition of the completed work, bound beautifully in gold cloth, was presented to the pope in October 1520 by John Clerk, Henry's ambassador in Rome. Leo X was delighted with the efforts of his 'most dear son in Christ' and immediately started to read the book, somewhat patronisingly (or sarcastically?) noting that it was a marvel that a king could have written such a tome. Although the book became an unlikely bestseller, its merits were dubious. Catholic theologians have regarded it as unimpressive, essentially assertive rather than analytical.

But the pope was in no mood to attend to the detail of the text. He was delighted that a significant king had taken the trouble to write a book defending him and his office against the upstart German. So, Henry – and his successors – were formally granted the title of *Fidei Defensor* (Defender of the Faith). Future events were to render this title utterly ridiculous, though for some reason it continued to appear on English coinage, and the marks FD or Fid Def are to be seen on newly minted British coins to this day. Luther himself replied with an offensive and outspoken broadside against Henry. Although Henry was soon to break with Rome, he never regarded Luther as anything but an enemy.

Henry VIII was thus doing fine in his role as an eager defender of the papacy. What was to change everything was the simple matter of his wife Catherine's inability to produce a male child. A daughter, Mary, had been born in 1516, but it was unclear whether the English people would accept a queen reigning over them. Henry became increasingly concerned about his lack of a male heir. He was worried about a renewal of the dynastic feuding and indeed warring that his father had managed to squash.

By the 1520s, it was clear that Catherine's childbearing days were behind her. Henry decided that he needed a divorce. But he had to move carefully. Catherine was very well connected; her nephew was none other than the Holy Roman Emperor, Charles V. The fiasco of the divorce took many twists and turns until eventually it became clear that the pope, whom Henry had so publicly endorsed, would not grant it. Part of the problem lay in Henry's theological bombast. He would not be satisfied with some fudge based on the obscurities of Catholic canon law. He looked directly to the Bible (in a way that might have pleased his adversary Luther) and found texts in the Book of Leviticus which appeared to forbid marriage to the wife of one's brother. Thus Henry could be regarded as appealing directly to the law of God rather than to the authority of the papacy; he was almost in danger of becoming a reformer himself.

Political and military events on the continent did not help Henry. In 1527, the Holy Roman Emperor's mutinous army did the unthinkable: it sacked Rome. This was an extraordinary debacle which further damaged the papacy's standing in Europe. The attack on Rome was not explicitly authorised by Charles V, whose troops had been fighting the French and a coalition of Italian states associated with the papacy. He was genuinely distressed by what happened. On the other hand, he had not seemed too concerned when his army of 25,000 men marched on Rome.

Most of the men were unpaid and wanted to damage Rome as a protest, but the protest rapidly deteriorated into a horrific orgy of violence. There were many Germans in the imperial army, and some of them were Lutherans, but the motivation does not appear to have been religious. Indeed, observers felt that Spanish and Italian soldiers committed far worse atrocities than the Germans. It was not Pope Clement VII's fault that the walls of Rome were inadequately defended; it was not his fault that the emperor could not control his feral troops. If Clement was to be blamed for anything, it was naïveté. He ingenuously thought that Rome would be secure because of its sacred role as the centre of Christianity.

The savagery visited on Rome suggested a loss of spiritual as well as physical authority. The devastation was dreadful. Churches, monasteries and nunneries were despoiled; their treasures were systematically removed. Many buildings were burned to the ground after they had been looted. Tombs were broken open in the crazed search for yet more booty. People were systematically tortured. Many women were raped, and some men were forced to eat their severed testicles. The pope found himself imprisoned in the Castel Sant' Angelo by the Tiber, and cowered there with his cardinals. His humiliation was complete. Eventually, in disguise, he was able to escape north to Orvieto. Rome was left as a kind of wilderness, an apocalyptic play area for rats and wild dogs. Thousands of bodies lay unburied on the streets or rotting in the Tiber; the stink remained for many months.

This ruination of Clement VII might, superficially, have seemed to aid Henry's cause back in England. In fact, these amazing and appalling events did nothing for Henry. If anything, the fall-out made things much worse for him. The sack made the emperor yet more powerful. Imperial spinners tried to present it as a kind of cleansing of a city that had become worldly and decadent. There was of course truth in this: Rome had been a disgrace for too long. But Charles's rabble were intent on pillaging, not cleansing. Clement, a weak and indecisive man, reacted to the debacle not by defying the emperor but by further endorsing his authority. Indeed, he was to crown Charles at Bologna – the last papal coronation of an emperor. Perversely, the emperor's authority was enhanced, just as the pope's was weakened.

So, the Sack of Rome, far from assisting Henry, made matters worse. If the divorce was granted on the grounds Henry wanted, the pope would in effect be decreeing that the emperor's own aunt – Catherine – had been living in a protracted incestuous relationship. Catherine herself was not disposed to help Henry – and Pope Clement VII, to be fair to him, felt considerable sympathy for her. The pope was aware that his predecessor had granted Henry a special dispensation to marry Catherine in the first place. He was now being told to declare that this dispensation was erroneous.

So, Pope Clement was in a wretched position. Humiliated across Europe, he did not want to make an enemy of a powerful king who had supported him. On the other hand, he was scared of the emperor and his influence and his army. At last, he came up with a tactic that would at least buy some time. A special papal court would be established in London to hear the case in full, in all its considerable complexity. The man chosen to preside over this delaying device was a world-class procrastinator, Cardinal Lorenzo Campeggio, who had an English connection – he had for long been the absentee Bishop of Salisbury.

Suffering from gout, and deliberately taking his time, Campeggio progressed at snail's pace from Rome to Lyons to Paris to Calais to Dover and at last to London. The journey took almost three months, which, even by the standards of the time, was suspiciously long. When he at last arrived in London, the cardinal declared himself too ill to attend the grand formal reception prepared for him. It was another fortnight before he decided he was well enough to meet the king. His private instructions from the pope were at no stage to give a judgement in the divorce case but rather to try to persuade Catherine and Henry of the need for reconciliation.

For weeks, Campeggio delayed and prevaricated doggedly. Bullied and harassed by both Wolsey and Henry, he would not give in to them. Another person who behaved doggedly was Catherine. With her pride and an almost sublime stubbornness, she resisted all the pressure bearing down on her.

Campeggio came up with a new plan. Catherine would 'find' religion and therefore abdicate as queen; she would remove herself to a nunnery. This cynical ploy did not allow for Catherine's insistence on being taken seriously. She sought a confession with the gout-stricken cardinal. She talked of her first marriage to Arthur, when they were both 15. He had never known her carnally. She had thus been a virgin when she married Henry. Gently but firmly, she declined the idea of spending the rest of her forlorn life in a nunnery. She then told Campeggio he could make the details of her confession public.

Wolsey was the next to try to overcome her obstinate integrity. He flattered her, he beseeched her. A delegation of English bishops came and wheedled before her; they had no more luck. Catherine has only a bit part in this story, but her strength and her modesty should be recorded. She possessed a quality which her blustering, bullying husband utterly lacked: dignity.

Henry, meanwhile, tried to increase the pressure on Campeggio. He went around telling peers, judges, bishops – more or less anyone who would listen – that it was utterly essential that he had a male heir. He feared an outbreak of anarchy on his death. Further, he had been living in adultery with Catherine for twenty years. His daughter Mary was a bastard.

At long last, on 31 May 1529, Campeggio formally opened the divorce court. But he quickly adjourned proceedings until 18 June. At this session, Catherine caused a sensation. She knelt before the king, asking him to take pity on her, a friendless foreigner in his kingdom. She was his loving wife, who had come to him a virgin. She then turned to Campeggio and asked for the case to be heard in Rome. This was dangerous. Catherine was beginning to arouse considerable sympathy, not least among the women of London. Campeggio dismissed her and decreed that the hearings would continue without her. Again the proceedings dragged on; Wolsey became ever more desperate.

Then, in July, word reached London that the pope (having finally decided that the emperor was more important than Henry) accepted that the case would have to be heard in Rome. Catherine had won, or so it seemed; and it was clear that the main loser was Wolsey. Campeggio departed for Rome and had the indignity of having his luggage searched aggressively at Dover. At least he could escape. For Wolsey, the end had indeed come. Henry turned on the man who had served him so well in everything but the 'great matter' of his divorce.

Wolsey found himself frozen out. He decided to visit his archbishopric of York, which he had hitherto ignored. So, he was in Yorkshire when the Earl of Northumberland, acting on behalf of the king, arrested him for high treason. He was ordered to return to London. Suffering from acute diarrhoea, he set off for the south very slowly. He was in desperate discomfort; he could hardly sit on his mule. He made it as far as Leicester, where he died on 29 November 1530. Among his last words was the hope that Henry would be vigilant in suppressing Lutheranism.

Wolsey's fall is remarkable only in that it took so long in coming. At the end of his career, he found his dual loyalty, at long last, in sharp focus. Circumstances meant that he could no longer manage to serve two masters, the king and the pope. His predicament, and his end, came because the interests of the man who made him, the king, conflicted with those of the pope. By 1529, it had become utterly apparent that the king was the master who mattered. When Henry turned against Wolsey, the pope could not save him. Nor did he even show any inclination to do so.

Henry had also turned against his wife – because she could not provide him with a son. But now there was a complicating factor. Henry was rapidly falling in love with one of the young ladies at his court, Anne Boleyn, the daughter of his former ambassador to France. Anne was one of those women whom nobody regarded as particularly beautiful or even pretty; at the same time, men found her very sexy. Henry certainly did. She was lively and sharp, and he was soon obsessed with her. This added to the desperation with which he now pursued his need to be rid of Catherine.

In 1529, against Wolsey's advice, Henry had convened a parliament, thinking (erroneously) that this might place more pressure on the pope. This was probably the most momentous decision of Henry's long and increasingly turbulent reign. Most parliaments were dissolved after just a few weeks. They were not exactly playthings of the monarch – but, beside the Church and the monarchy, Parliament was an institution of little significance. This was about to change – and how.

First, this parliament was to last no fewer than seven years. Second, it was to carry through a revolution. By the end of those seven years, England had broken with Rome – spectacularly. Papal authority in England had been completely repudiated. The king, the so-called 'Defender of the Faith', had become supreme head of the new Church of England. Most of the English monasteries had been dissolved. A leading churchman, Bishop Fisher, had been executed, as had the country's leading anti-Lutheran, Sir Thomas More, the Lord Chancellor. And Parliament itself had become central to the governance of the country, in a way that neither it nor the king yet understood.

CHAPTER 6

Luther's Impact on Scotland

$\mathcal{J}$AMES IV of Scotland, and Henry VII and Henry VIII of England, were each in their different ways very strong kings – and each took a keen interest in religious matters. After the debacle of Flodden, Scotland's new monarch was only a year and a half old. So, before he assumed his personal rule in 1528 at the age of 16, James V's impact on his country was negligible. This was a time of squabbling and confusion, of faction and fighting. At the epicentre of the mayhem was Margaret Tudor, James's mother, who, like many of the Tudors, could be something of a mischief-maker.

Even after he took charge, James was never particularly interested in religion. He had grown up in a Scotland that was introverted and devastated after Flodden, a Scotland that was very slow to wake up to the burgeoning Reformation and to respond to Martin Luther. On the continent and in England, Luther's ideas were discussed vigorously; he was the man of the moment. That is, of course, not to say that his ideas were eagerly embraced. As we saw in the previous chapter, in England, a group of Cambridge intellectuals did enthusiastically debate his ideas; but the response of key figures such as Henry VIII and his right-hand man, Cardinal Wolsey, was unremittingly hostile. We noted that the king wrote a book refuting Luther; we also noted that Wolsey organised a huge anti-Luther event in London which attracted an amazing crowd of almost 30,000 citizens.

Nothing at all comparable happened in Scotland as the boy-king grew to adulthood. A French Lutheran by the name of de la Tour did work briefly for the regent, the Duke of Albany, around 1523; he was later martyred in France. He is a sketchy figure. So, unfortunately, is Patrick Hamilton, Scotland's first Protestant martyr. But we do know at least something of his brief and noble life. He was the first Scot to embrace Lutheranism publicly and defiantly, though the word 'defiantly' is probably ill-used in any discussion of such a gracious and gentle human being.

Hamilton was well-born and related to the royal family. His father was Sir Patrick Hamilton of Kincavel in West Lothian. He became titular abbot of Fearn (near Tain) when he was 13, in 1517. So, Hamilton could have had an easy and well-rewarded career in the Church. This was the kind of abuse of Church positions that was provoking growing anticlericalism; it is significant that, in his brief career of teaching and preaching, Hamilton did not attack such abuses but preferred to concentrate on the issue of personal salvation. Income from the property at Fearn allowed him to study in Paris and then at Louvain. Here, he studied the work of Erasmus. He imbibed humanism and the early work of Luther. Significantly, he seems to have realised that he had to do much more than just digest their work; he decided on a mission to propagate the new ideas.

He returned to Scotland in 1523 and worked at St Andrews. Around 1526, he incurred the wrath of Archbishop James Beaton of St Andrews as he publicly expressed support for Luther and was listened to by both university scholars and the ordinary townsfolk. The next year, he left Scotland again and travelled to Wittenberg, where he met Luther, who was by now the main influence in his thinking and his faith. He also studied at the new university of Marburg. Once again, he came back to Scotland. This time, he preached Lutheranism directly and powerfully. Among those whom he persuaded were his brother (the Laird of Kincavel) and his sister.

Hamilton is supposed to have preached to the labourers in the fields around Linlithgow, and does not seem to have been in any way proud or haughty despite his aristocratic connections. But it was perhaps because of those connections, as much as the power of his teaching, that Beaton increasingly regarded him as a dangerous menace who had to be confronted. Further, the fact that he was not so much attacking the slackness of the Church and the lax lives of its priests, bishops and cardinals but was rather expounding the Lutheran doctrine of justification by faith made him, in the eyes of Beaton (a man who was well aware of what was happening elsewhere), a serious threat.

Beaton and his ilk were obviously aware of anticlericalism; indeed, it was largely a result of their pluralism, their illegitimate children, their wealth and their refusal to live a spiritual or modest life. But here was something dangerously different; here was a more direct challenge to the Church. It was about faith and individual salvation. This was explosive.

And so, early in 1528, Beaton summoned Patrick Hamilton to St Andrews; he was accused of heresy, found guilty and burned to death on 29 February at the gates of St Salvator's College. Hamilton's death was particularly cruel, even by the terrible standards of the time: the fire was not properly lit, and it was a wet day. He baked to death rather than burned; and his agony, watched by his persecutor Beaton, lasted for six hours. Hamilton, by now well prepared for martyrdom, is said to have behaved with composure and serenity, unlike those who, to the last, were baiting him and demanding that he recant. Hamilton died saying he was 'content'.

He had packed much into his short and good life. He had studied in various European centres of learning, and he had preached the new doctrines. He had married; he had persuaded a notable Scottish intellectual, Alexander Alesius, to embrace Lutheranism; and he had written a short book, *Patrick's Places*. The long agony of his death, nobly borne, did not go unnoticed. Much later, John Knox wrote: 'Almost within the whole realm, there was none found who began not to inquire: Why was master Patrick Hamilton burned?'

His personal courage and the clarity of his teaching made a considerable impact, yet it should not be exaggerated. Although there was spiritual hunger in Scotland, and widespread contempt for the corruption of the Church, Lutheranism still did not infiltrate the country. It remained confined to a few pockets in the east, and St Andrews was the only town which came close to embracing it. Some merchants were involved in bringing heretical books into east-coast seaports such as Leith, Aberdeen and Montrose. But there seemed to be surprisingly little similar material coming across the Border from England.

In 1525, the Scottish Parliament had legislated against Lutheran heresy, noting that Luther's ideas were spreading in 'divers countries' but insisting that Scotland had not embraced any such opinions. Any merchant bringing heretical books into Scottish ports would have his ship seized. This act was drawn to the attention of Pope Clement VII in Rome, who duly commended it. But he presumably regarded Scotland as a pretty remote and insignificant state; James IV, despite his ambitions, had not left a 'legacy' that placed Scotland in the forefront of European nations.

Meanwhile, William Tyndale, always the master translator, pondered on the possibility of a Bible in Scots. A St Andrews scholar called John Gau moved to Denmark, where he worked as a chaplain in Copenhagen and prepared an overtly Lutheran work called *The Right Way to the Kingdom of Heaven*. In this and other works, Gau produced the first significant corpus of Lutheran-based teaching by a Scottish writer.

In the 1530s, the Reformation at last began to stir in Scotland, and the agitation was led by lairds and noblemen. Sometimes their motivation was a simple reworking of anticlericalism; sometimes it was based – as it had been with Hamilton – on a sincere imbibing of Lutheran ideas about faith and salvation. Several of these lairds and noblemen were burned. At the same time, more and more Scots were reading English translations of the Bible and discussing them. This was a dangerous, even life-threatening, activity. The second

Scottish martyr, Henry Forrest, was burned for merely owning a New Testament in English.

Yet this activity was sporadic, occasional and almost random. Scotland was not in spiritual ferment as many other countries were. Indeed, it was some time before Scotland found another Hamilton. This man, George Wishart, was only 14 when Hamilton was martyred. The son of an Angus laird, Wishart was working as a schoolmaster in Montrose when he had a serious dispute with the Bishop of Brechin and had to flee abroad in 1535. He returned in 1543, and it was his evangelism in the mid-1540s that finally gave the nascent Scottish Reformation shape and intellectual clarity.

PART 2

The English Reformation to 1553

CHAPTER 7

A Lawyer of Genius

T HE long and momentous Reformation Parliament enacted the
legislation that separated the English Church from Rome.
Underlying this was the need for the king to obtain his divorce;
but a divorce on a much larger scale was also under way. It was a
divorce from the old Church. It was not just a case of removing the
pope's authority and making the king the official head of the English
Church. It was also a case of plundering the Church's vast resources.

Crucially, all this was carried through by statute. Parliament was
becoming the most important body in the land, though this would
not be apparent for some time. A century later, the slow-burning
implications of the change finally flared into the conflagration which
ended with an English monarch waging war on his Parliament and
paying for this impertinence with his life.

This book is about religion, not legalism; but the presiding genius
of the Reformation Parliament needs to be celebrated. Thomas
Cromwell was almost certainly the most skilful and brilliant lawyer
the British Isles have ever known. Cromwell used the law as a true
radical would, as an instrument of swift and far-reaching change.
He presided over the drafting of the crucial series of acts which
enabled the break with Rome. (In our era, when much parliamentary
draughtsmanship, north and south of the Border, is disgracefully

sloppy, it is salutary to note the constant clarity and precision of Cromwell's work.)

Cromwell carefully wrote lucid preambles to his legislation. He was creating a new framework for the state as well as a new Church. He was building, almost single-handedly, a 'sovereign empire' based on the integrity and supremacy not of the king but of English law. And the supreme enabling tool of English law was parliamentary statute.

While Cromwell invoked history, he was really destroying it. The papacy, an outside authority, had always had power in England. Cromwell got rid of this extraneous power and created the apparatus of a new, wholly independent state. Thomas Cromwell was a driven man who worked best alone; but he was good with people, both as a friend and as an employer, and he maintained a vast network of loyal agents in England and on the continent. At one point, his agent in Antwerp even tried to hire William Tyndale, of all people, as a propagandist.

Cromwell was aided by some of the younger Members of Parliament, like him lawyers – hungry, rising men who were driven by anticlericalism and a desire to end the nonsense of pluralism. But, in their haste to create a new polity, they destroyed as well as created – most notably in the case of the monasteries. In this respect, the English Reformation was different from the Scottish one which was to come a generation later. The Scottish Reformation placed much emphasis on education and social welfare. In suppressing the monasteries, indeed in smashing them to bits, Cromwell and his henchmen were destroying a vast, if ramshackle and corrupt and incompetent, system for the succour and support and occasional education of ordinary people.

It is, then, surprising that there was not even more of a popular revolt against the suppression of the monasteries, although there was to be a huge and heroic uprising in Yorkshire and the north and west – a rising that was put down by Henry VIII with a vicious mixture of treachery and cruelty that should surely blacken his name forever. This will be discussed in the next chapter.

From Henry's point of view, the most important act of the Reformation Parliament was the one that forbade any appeal to any court outside the country against any ruling made in an English court. This act, 'In Restraint of Appeal', allowed an English court to annul the king's marriage to Catherine without the worry of a consequent appeal being made to Rome. The act effectively severed the English clergy – and there were plenty of them – from the authority of Rome and its canon law. The Act for Ecclesiastical Appointments confirmed the monarch's absolute control over all clerical preferment. Another act stopped all revenue going to Rome; yet another formally created the new and separate Church of England with the monarch at its head. And the Act for the Dissolution of the Monasteries did just that.

Superficially, all this gave great power to the king, not Parliament. But, as the power was now based on statute, a trap was being set. Statute could only be overridden by a further statute. Parliament, not the king, was on the way to becoming supreme.

Henry's first and most pressing desire was to get rid of Catherine and to get Anne Boleyn into his bed not as his mistress but as the official queen of England. This was his grand obsession. Always unpredictable and opportunistic, in 1531, desperate for endorsement of his proposed divorce, he even sent an envoy to Wittenberg to seek the approval of his great enemy, Luther, for his intended course of action.

The crucial year was 1533. Anne became pregnant; Henry married her; the new Archbishop of Canterbury, Thomas Cranmer, decreed that Henry's marriage to Catherine was invalid; and, in June, Anne Boleyn became queen of England. In September, her child was born. Disastrously from Henry's point of view, it was a girl. But, if Henry was grievously displeased, many others – including the pope and the Holy Roman Emperor – were of course delighted. The baby was to grow into a very special woman who was to become England's most treasured and revered monarch. So, Henry's loss was England's gain. As so often, Henry seemed on the brink of getting what he wanted, only to have it snatched away. His behaviour became increasingly cruel and erratic.

Cromwell, the lawyer of genius, was a ruthless man. But, despite his ever-growing power, he never killed anyone if he thought he didn't need to. Henry took to killing people left, right and centre, almost as a recreation. It is impossible to defend him.

In the early part of his reign, Henry had been a stout defender of the papacy. He now turned on anyone of significance who dared to speak up for the pope. Bishop John Fisher and the intellectual anti-Lutheran Sir Thomas More, who had both served him well but could not, out of conscience, deny their ultimate allegiance to the papacy, were executed in 1535. As if to balance matters, Henry, having decided to execute the bishop and the Lord Chancellor, had fourteen obscure Protestants killed at the same time. No doubt he thought he was being even-handed. An equally grotesque exercise in supposed balance came in 1540, when he executed three Protestants and three Catholics on the same day.

We may note, at this point in discussing Cromwell's career, that 1540 was also the year in which this most brilliant and far-sighted of Henry's servants was himself beheaded, on the absurd grounds that he was a traitor. Few other statesmen have accomplished so much in so short a time. The Archbishop of Canterbury, Thomas Cranmer, noted: 'Such a servant, in wisdom, diligence, faithfulness and experience, as no prince in this realm ever had.' Did Henry appreciate his great servant? Probably not. In that bloody period, all that mattered was the caprice of the king.

After Cromwell, Henry's reign became shambolic. The kindest word to describe the last seven years of his monarchy would be 'drift'. The period was marked by increasing waywardness on the king's part, wholly unnecessary wars (including a vicious campaign in Scotland), and a dangerous vacuum as far as policymaking was concerned. Henry VIII's legacy to his people was dire.

The despot was savagely capricious. He had got rid of his first and very Catholic wife, and traded her for one who was much more sympathetic to Lutheranism. He had got rid of the pope and installed himself as the supreme head of the new Church under the guidance of a consummate organiser, Cromwell, who was very sympathetic to Lutheranism though he remained moderate in his quest for reform.

As for the king, he remained attached to the old faith. He regarded his new supremacy over the Church in England as a straightforward extension of his kingship, divinely ordained; he did not have to bow to any earthly authority, and certainly not to his Parliament. But he now had the authority to sort out problems in the Church, to reform it to his own liking.

His personal concern in religious matters was not that of dilettante; he read the Bible carefully and, as we saw in Chapter 5, was something of an amateur theologian. He was self-righteous and regarded himself as the very man to cleanse and purify the English Church. Because he mainly worked through immensely capable civil servants – Wolsey, Cromwell and, to a lesser extent, More – does not mean that he was not trying to direct policy. Sometimes he blustered and floundered, but the settlement that eventually emerged (and which his daughter Elizabeth refined but stayed true to) was probably fairly close to what he wanted.

There was a further paradox. Despite the legislative zeal of the Reformation Parliament, England remained a Catholic country. Most of the ordinary people remained Catholics. Protestantism was still generally regarded as subversive, even revolutionary. Yet here was the nation's Parliament presiding over what appeared to be a Protestant revolution. England was turning upside down. The explanation is that its reformation was mainly political, not spiritual.

The break with Rome had undoubtedly given succour to spiritual malcontents; there was a new breed of preachers and teachers who wanted to push things much further, though England did not produce anyone quite so maniacally dangerous as Thomas Müntzer, whom we met in Chapter 4. Partly to keep potential religious zealots under control, Cromwell was in 1534 appointed Vice-regent for Religion, a peculiar title which gave him charge of the new Church's spiritual organisation.

The clergy were in ferment. A meeting of Convocation, with representatives from all the dioceses, showed this. The conservatives complained bitterly of false doctrine; the reformers were pushing for a more overt Protestantism. Working with Archbishop Cranmer and Bishop Fox of Hereford, Cromwell drew up *Ten Articles* which were made binding on the clergy. These were a careful compromise that tended towards the old Church, though Cromwell's own sympathies were in the opposite direction. These Articles were issued in the name of the king as supreme head.

Cromwell, as vice-regent, followed up with a series of injunctions which were more radical – the clergy were warned away from such practices of the old faith as the cult of miracles and the cult of saints, from pilgrimages and relics – though these were all dear to the people. Not surprisingly, many of the ordinary clergy were confused. One priest angrily complained that there were many new laws, and went on to predict sarcastically that there would soon be a new God.

The vice-regent, though he personally was sympathetic to the reformers, was more concerned with maintaining stability in the country at large. He never wanted to encourage wild men, inside or outside the Church. As for Cranmer, he was always exceptionally cautious.

And what of Queen Anne Boleyn? Her fateful mistake was to fail to provide the king with a male heir. She compounded this insolence by flirting a little too brazenly with some young men in Henry's court, and, even worse, losing her temper when Henry dallied with other women. Henry, having divorced once, now had a taste for the process. In 1535, he had fallen in love with another young lady in his court, Jane Seymour. He asked the compliant Cranmer to organise his divorce from Anne. Two days after the divorce went through, she was beheaded for treason and adultery.

Cromwell was deeply involved in Anne's downfall. He had investigated her many alleged infidelities and was already cultivating the Seymour faction at court. Anne had been queen for less than three years. Henry was now obsessed with his succession. The new queen, Jane, did not take too long to produce a son – Edward – though he was sickly.

Meanwhile, Cromwell and Cranmer had more work to do. In particular, they wanted to preside over the publication of an official English Bible. This was to prove the most significant religious part of the English Reformation – and, more than anything, it was what persuaded more and more people to detach themselves from the old faith and embrace the new one – though the process took many years.

In 1537, Cromwell ordered every parish church in England to obtain a Bible in English, so that the ordinary people could read it – or have it read to them. This simple action helped to create a new literacy; people were desperate to learn to read so that they could grasp the Bible for themselves. Soon, the Bible was being discussed in taverns and homes, in the streets and in the fields. People argued with their clergy about what the words meant. This was a literary and intellectual as well as a religious breakthrough. There was a huge opening of minds.

Martin Luther had created his Reformation based on the authority of Scripture. He was passionate about people studying the Bible for themselves. Now this was happening in England as well as in Germany, though it is important to note that Bible-reading – and Protestantism generally – spread much more quickly in the south and east of the country than in the north and west.

The Bible translation that had been distributed in 1537 and 1538 was essentially William Tyndale's translation of the New Testament, along with his uncompleted translation of the Old Testament. Added on was a translation of the rest of the Old Testament by another Protestant scholar, John Rogers. It was not until 1539 that the English 'Great Bible' was officially published. This was a new translation undertaken by the scholar Miles Coverdale in Zurich, but incorporating many of the wonderful sentences, phrases, rhythms and cadences from the earlier translation by William Tyndale, who had been hunted down in Antwerp by agents of Henry and strangled to death in 1536.

Tyndale was a superb scholar: he had an extensive knowledge and understanding of several languages, including Greek, Latin, German and, of course, English. Before he went to Oxford, he had been brought up in the far west of England, near Wales; and it is not fanciful to suggest that the Welsh love of words and of singing may have influenced his mastery of language. In personality, he was evidently self-righteous and something of a prig; in his work, he was sublime. Clever scholar as he was, his concern was to give the Bible to the ordinary people. There was nothing elitist about him. He had a wonderful ear. He developed an English style that was powerful, clear and demotic.

As a translator into English, he was unsurpassed in his genius. The English language, as developed by Tyndale, achieved both a simple beauty and a sheer understandable accessibility that no art form in the entire Renaissance period could equal. No-one, not even Shakespeare, could deploy the English language to greater effect. Before Tyndale, English was a vigorous language, but with a certain coarseness. Single-handedly, Tyndale polished it and made it resplendent. Yet his English was never precious or self-consciously stylish. It was at once subtle and robust. The Bible is more than mere literature; but Tyndale's New Testament is unsurpassed in its sheer literary quality.

CHAPTER 8

Revolt and Treachery

HE suppression of the monasteries, organised and expedited by Thomas Cromwell, led directly to the great internal crisis of Henry VIII's reign. It was one of the most serious internal crises ever faced by the English state. The colossal rebellion known as the Pilgrimage of Grace was an ambitious attempt at counter-revolution and the biggest popular uprising in English history. Yet, today, it is very much the forgotten rebellion. Despite the publication in 2003 of a fine history of the Pilgrimage by Geoffrey Moorhouse, it remains an episode of almost total obscurity for many, possibly most, English people.

For a period in late 1536, almost the entire northern half of England – just about everywhere north of the River Trent – was in open revolt against the king and his chief minister Cromwell. Henry detested this huge challenge to his kingly authority. While he was determined to crush the rebels by force, his judgement was vitiated by his temper, his increasing bloodlust, and his serial indecision when under severe pressure. He spoke wildly of 'brute and beastly shires' and threatened the 'utter destruction' not just of the rebels but also of their wives and children. His generals knew better. They knew that they were utterly outnumbered. If it came to a simple trial of force, the rebels would win.

Even more alarming for the blustering king and the cannier Cromwell was the possibility of intervention from abroad. An opportunistic Scots incursion could never be discounted, but this would not pose too much of a threat. There were more dangerous possibilities. Was there an opening here for the Holy Roman Emperor, who had seen his favourite aunt, Catherine of Aragon, humiliated by Henry, and the papacy hustled out of England with apparent contempt – was there an opportunity for an imperial invasion? Probably not – but Cromwell's mind, at once crafty and far-seeing, would have ranged over many scenarios, some of them both feasible and perilous.

And, as the rebellion grew, a full-scale nationwide uprising seemed a real and present possibility. The fact that many of the northern nobility openly sided with the rebels probably scared Henry more than anything else in his long reign. The rebels deployed primarily in defence of the old faith, and in particular of the monasteries. There was also an element of conservative snobbery. A constant demand was that the king should rid himself of 'low-born' advisers. The monasteries were being destroyed by the state, and the state was being run by base, ill-born upstarts.

And indeed, the principal upstart, Thomas Cromwell, did not come from distinguished stock. He was the son of a drunken brewer and innkeeper, Walter Cromwell of Putney, who was constantly in trouble with the law. Cromwell told Thomas Cranmer that he himself had been a 'ruffian' in his youth. It was Cromwell, and his officials who 'visited' the monasteries, who were blamed for the suppression, not the king himself. Indeed, many of the rebels ingenuously believed that they were being loyal to the king: they thought that he was in the hands of wicked and devious advisers, led by the arch-enemy Cromwell. So, the rebellion was partly to liberate the monarch. How naïve, how wrong those rebels were.

Economic discontent was also in the mix: the rebels had grievances relating to taxation, particularly with regard to landholdings. Some of the anger was overtly political; small landowners, gentry and townsmen in the north were aware that they were under-represented in Parliament, which was becoming increasingly important.

Yet the essence of it all, like so much in the sixteenth century, was religious. Some of the monasteries had been well run to the last, and many of the monks were industrious and responsible. Equally, many others were venal, lazy and ignorant, and they were certainly not worth so much sacrifice, for the blood count was to be terribly high. The Pilgrimage showed that much of England in 1536 remained attached to the old religion – and people were prepared to die for it.

Monasticism was an ideal, and in England it had become grievously corrupted. Although monastic charity was still a reality in some houses, in others the monks kept their considerable riches to themselves. And while some abbeys were places of refuge and hospitality for the needy and destitute (and at times the high-born also), others ignored this function completely. Perhaps what mattered most to the ordinary people was that the monks still said prayers for the dead.

The Church owned between a quarter and a third of all land in England. This was coveted by many of the upwardly mobile laity. And Cromwell wanted at least some of the monastic revenues for the crown, because the crown's finances were in trouble. When he was working for Cardinal Wolsey, Cromwell had helped to reorganise a relatively minor suppression of some smaller houses – mainly to fund Wolsey's need for a personal legacy, in the form of the foundation of university colleges. So, he had some experience of this work.

In 1535, he organised an assessment of the entire Church property-holding in England. Cromwell was a consummate administrator, and the exercise was carried out swiftly and efficiently. It was followed up by a series of visitations to the smaller monasteries. The inspectors found many examples of 'manifest sin', 'abominable living' and so on. They did not have to fabricate evidence. They did not have to search rigorously to find examples of slackness and iniquity. The monastic ideal was not dead, but it was being systematically abused.

The first wave of suppression was managed with ruthless speed. Venerable, lovely buildings and their rich landholdings were abruptly nationalised. There was destruction of much that was old and beautiful, and there was some egregious philistinism. Libraries were destroyed, which was inexcusable. (The monasteries had maintained an educational function over the centuries.)

Indeed, the buildings and their treasures were treated worse than their occupants. Indignation, very justifiable indignation, at all this larceny and vandalism is still extant today. The distinguished Oxford historian A. L. Rowse wrote, towards the end of the twentieth century, that he supposed the Reformation was inevitable, but it was a pity that it was so drastic. He could not forgive the artistic losses: the books, the medieval manuscripts, the sculptures, all the art and beauty and historical treasure that simply disappeared. He thought that Henry – whom he called a bellicose old monster – could have saved at least some of the monasteries.

Instead, there was an orgy of pillaging and looting and plunder. This despoliation and destruction was distressing to many. It might just have been understood had it been based on genuine reforming zeal. But no – for the most part, the motivation was sheer greed. The monasteries had been a great social, as well as religious, presence, but this counted for nothing when rapacity was given free rein. Beams, lead, venerable stone – all were removed. Many private English houses and mansions that stand to this day were built in part with booty from the broken monasteries. Great bells were recast as cannon. Thus religious riches were transmuted into military ordnance. All over England, but in Yorkshire more than anywhere else, there are sad ruins that testify to the beauty and glory there must once have been.

But at least most of the suddenly redundant monks were quite well treated and given generous pensions – or, when they were of suitable quality, given parishes. Many of the nuns married. It is significant that few of the abbots, monks and nuns fled abroad. It is also significant that the abbots did not mount any concerted, organised opposition. Many of them actually acquiesced in the end of their houses, choosing to surrender all their monastic property to the crown without protest or demur.

There was redistribution of wealth on a grand scale. Cromwell and his aides undoubtedly benefited personally. So did the crown. But the crown was soon involved in more wars that it could not really afford, and so the land was sold on. Many people acquired significant landholdings. There was no sudden creation of a totally new cadre of militant landowners, as has sometimes been suggested. Rather, small landowners became bigger landowners. These were the 'new' gentry – men who were to become assertive and ambitious, and were to make their mark in Parliament. A social and economic revolution was taking place. But the backlash was to be religious.

In the summer of 1536, the king seemed to be easing out of his personal mid-life crisis. He was enjoying a series of lavish spectacles, pageants, feasts and other glittering entertainments, which had been organised to celebrate his third marriage – to Jane Seymour. His eye was not on the north. Cromwell, ever watchful and wary, knew of rumours that dissident elements in the northern nobility had been plotting and conspiring against the king for some time. Since 1485, two Tudor monarchs, father and son, had managed to make the kingdom of England stable and secure. But, even now, the threat of anarchy was never too far away.

The rebellion started in Lincolnshire. Stories had been spreading that it was not just the monasteries that were to go; even beloved parish churches were supposedly under threat. There was also talk of new and swingeing taxes on marriages and christenings and burials. Against this background of rumour, fear and uncertainty, the vicar of Louth preached a particularly wild sermon, which apparently inflamed all who heard it. Soon, most of Lincolnshire was in the hands of armed rebels. But, as a royal army marched northwards, there were promises of an amnesty, and the rebellion fizzled out as quickly as it had flared.

Yet it was almost as if this had been a deliberate diversion. A one-eyed barrister called Robert Aske had been travelling through Lincolnshire when it was in ferment, on his way home to Aughton, a tiny village a few miles south-east of York. When he arrived in the East Riding, he set about starting a local rebellion. He was extraordinarily successful. In a few days, he had a force of at least 40,000 men, and it was marching on York. Almost before anyone in the south realised it, most of the north was up in arms.

Everyone seemed involved – the nobility, the gentry, the ordinary people. Aske wanted each and every rebel to swear an oath for the maintenance of God's faith and Church, for the preservation of the king, for the purifying of the nobility of all bad blood and evil councillors, for the restitution of Christ's Church and for the suppression of heretical opinion. The militant pilgrims took as their badge the Five Wounds of Christ. They marched behind the cross. They sang a fierce, eerie song: 'Christ crucified / for thy wounds wide / us Commons guide / which pilgrims be / through God's grace / for to purchase old wealth and peace.'

As the Lincolnshire men were being disarmed, the Earl of Shrewsbury concentrated on forming a boundary along the Trent. He stationed men at all the fords and other strategic points. This suggests that there was now fear of a great march on the south. But Aske's men remained in the north. They took York, Doncaster and Pontefract; the rising spread as far west as Lancashire and as far north as Cumberland. This reflected the geographic nature of the English Reformation, which had taken root far more quickly in the south and the east – where the Tudor monarchy was stronger.

The king sent Thomas Howard, Duke of Norfolk, to Yorkshire. There, he met the leading rebels. He reported to the king that the only possible tactic was to offer a blanket pardon. Henry reluctantly pardoned everyone living north of Doncaster who had rebelled before the Eve of the Nativity of the Virgin. He then told Aske to come to London to discuss the pilgrims' grievances, and granted the pilgrims' leader a safe conduct. This was a humiliation for the puffed-up king, having to parley with and offer hospitality to a common rebel. Aske duly went south and spent Christmas at Greenwich with his king, who deployed his charm. Aske was duped. In his cunning, Henry almost grovelled: he would have his new queen crowned at

York Minster; he would convene a parliament at York that would deal with all the pilgrims' concerns.

Unfortunately for Aske, as he returned north with this supposed good news, a further rising took place around Hull. Aske condemned it and tried to put down the new rising himself. But he was now regarded as a traitor by many of the ordinary people. Meanwhile, in the far north, another rebel army was marching on Carlisle. Aske and his followers did manage to repress the second Yorkshire uprising, but it was too late. Norfolk was now returning northwards with an impressive army. People were ordered to wear the red cross of St George on a white garment; if they did not show the red cross, they would be treated as rebels.

Soon, Norfolk was moving through the rebel territory, terrorising the people. His personal instincts were for clemency, but he was an old soldier and he obeyed his commander-in-chief. He was working for a furious master whose bloodlust was up. Henry wanted vengeance – and how. Many men were hung, drawn and quartered without trial; many houses were burned. Some of the victims were hung in chains so that they were left hanging indefinitely as grisly testaments to the monarch's vicious reprisals against his own people. Then the iron ran out. Rope could of course be used – but it soon rotted, and the corpses were not left hanging for as long as Henry wanted.

Abbots and monks did not escape; many of them were hung too. One old man who had served in Henry's army against the Scots not once, not twice but three times, was executed. One night in Cumberland, over seventy of the hanging bodies were heroically removed by local women. They took the bodies to local priests and asked for decent burials. When the priests refused, the women did the burying themselves.

Even Henry could not exterminate the entire nobility and gentry of the north. He decided on a show trial in London. Among those selected for this charade were Aske, the abbots of Jervaulx and Fountains and a few carefully chosen others. The abbots were hung, drawn and quartered at Tyburn in London; Aske was taken to York and hung in chains.

While Aske had been Henry's guest at Greenwich, the king had not devoted his entire attention to him. Jane had conceived a child. Henry now wrote to Norfolk saying that, as the queen was pregnant, he did not wish to leave her. So, he would not after all travel to York and hold a parliament there.

The Pilgrimage was over. It had been defeated, not by an army but by duplicity.

The sixteenth century was a bloody and terrible century, yet it constantly produced men and women of almost superhuman courage. The leading Pilgrim of Grace was one such. We do not know much about this man, Robert Aske; but all that we do know is good. Aske presented the English state with a threat that was extremely dangerous yet was born mainly out of a simple, decent desire to prevent the destruction of a religion that was flawed yet loved.

We do not even know how old Aske was in 1536; probably in his mid-30s. His older brother John was lord of the manor of Aughton, a little community in the valley of the River Derwent in an obscure part of the East Riding. Robert Aske was a lawyer, a member of Gray's Inn in London, but he seems to have been a little disingenuous for a man of the law. He was sincere and steadfast, and obviously had considerable gifts as a leader of men.

Yet, was he not so much a leader as a man led, a man who was caught up in a rebellion and became its head almost by accident? There were plenty of wild men around Yorkshire in the 1530s. Some of them were bent on a violent revolution. It would be wrong to regard the Pilgrimage as wholly pure, as – dare I say it? – wholly gracious. It is quite possible that some of those who plundered and looted the monasteries also took part in the rebellion. Motives were mixed, complex and sometimes contradictory.

But I believe it would be wrong to suggest that Aske was a man to be intimidated or threatened. He was all too easily beguiled and deceived by the cunning of his rascal king, but that is another matter. His dying words show him to have been, as well as a man of God, a proud northerner. Like all condemned men, he was given the opportunity to make a last statement. He said he was aggrieved by two things: that Cromwell (the destroyer of the monasteries) had sworn that all northerners were traitors, and that Cromwell had promised him a pardon. He then commended his soul to God.

Today, Aughton is a peaceful, rustic place, a few miles east of the great old minefields around Selby. It is approached from the B1228, itself a quiet and minor road. Modern England is bedevilled by a surplus of signage; but, as you reach the tiny and discreet village, seemingly reluctant to join the contemporary world, you realise that Aske's church, the Church of All Saints, is even more discreet, for it is nowhere to be seen, and there are no signs pointing the way. It is hidden away beyond the end of the village, past the big house, not easy to seek or find.

Today's pilgrim, if that is the right word, has to obtain the key to the church from a house in the village, then walk right to the end of the road and through a field gate; still the church is not visible. You carry on through trees and round an overgrown ditch which must have once been the moat surrounding Aughton Hall, the home of the Askes. At last, you arrive at an unkempt, even savage graveyard, with broken headstones and gnarled hawthorn trees. In its midst stands an exquisite little Norman church, with a solid square tower at the far end, and a fine big round-headed doorway facing south. The church seems aloof and alone in this lost part of England.

To try to invoke both the beauty and splendour of the monasteries in their prime, and the bravery and resolve of the many thousands of pilgrims who died in their futile effort to save them, the obvious places to visit are the ruins of one of the lovely Yorkshire monasteries, like Fountains or Jervaulx or Gainsborough. Yet, numinous and still splendid as these ruins are, I think that the modest hidden church at Aughton, which still stands, is where best to reflect on this extraordinary extended episode of destruction and duplicity. Today, the little church is part of the Church of England. It has just fourteen members, with services on the first and third Sunday of each month. Parts of it have been rebuilt, but it must be essentially as it was more than 470 years ago. The graveyard around it is overgrown and rough; again, it cannot have changed that much.

As you stand beside the ancient church and look across the lonely fields to the Derwent (which often floods in winter) and hear distant swans honking from the marshes, you sense that this is an England that is almost lost forever, an England that can still just about evoke at least some understanding of that much older England that knew, and cared, about its religion more than anything else.

CHAPTER 9

End of the Tyrant

HE brutal and bloated figure of Henry VIII presided over the English Reformation; it was his more than anyone else's. It began when Henry wanted a divorce and managed to persuade himself that his marriage to his first wife was against the law of God. Thomas Cromwell may have been the architect of the English Reformation, but Henry was the driving force, the supreme director of the project. Thus, those who wish to praise the English Reformation must come to terms with the fact that its guiding spirit was such a heinous figure.

The doyen of Tudor historians, Sir Geoffrey Elton, wrote a celebrated study of Henry for the Historical Association. In it, he warned against succumbing to understandable revulsion against a figure who besmirched the practice of politics, pursued vendettas and showed indifference or even hatred to those whom he turned against. Elton reached this conclusion in 1962. A decade later, he hardened his view of Henry, suggesting that he and others had actually underestimated the sheer horribleness of the king.

Because he was such an ogre, there was little of genuine pathos about the decline of Henry's last years. His second great minister, Cromwell – who, like Wolsey before him, had proved a remarkably steady administrator when working for such a capricious master –

99

was executed by Henry in 1540. This is significant, because Cromwell had been giving the English Reformation substance and shape. He was both a destroyer and a creator.

Without Cromwell, the king held to his course: England had rejected the pope but had not embraced the reformers. This of course frustrated both the leading Catholics, who probably represented the majority of the English population – and the reformers, among whose number was Thomas Cranmer, the learned and cautious Archbishop of Canterbury. So, there was confusion; and it was not until Henry's daughter Elizabeth became queen, almost twenty years later, that England finally became unequivocally and permanently Protestant. But the settlement over which Elizabeth presided was in essence the one her father had wanted.

Cromwell's downfall was in part precipitated by a debacle which managed to combine an unlikely mix of high Renaissance art, bumbling diplomacy and the king's malevolent irascibility. After a decade of brilliant and superhuman service, Cromwell was beginning to tire and to lose his touch. He had a grandiose plan for a European Protestant alliance. He began with the Lutheran princedoms of Germany, and first turned his attention to the obscure new state of Cleves on the Lower Rhine. He then arranged a 'diplomatic' marriage between Anne of Cleves, sister of the state's ruler, and Henry. He assured Henry that Anne was beautiful, in her 'whole body' as well as her face, though Henry should have wondered how on earth Cromwell could make such a claim.

At this point, one of the most versatile and accomplished of sixteenth-century painters makes a brief appearance in our story. Hans Holbein the Younger was a genius from Augsburg who first arrived at Henry's court to design jewellery for Anne Boleyn, and developed, under Henry's patronage, into the greatest portrait-painter of the northern Renaissance. Holbein appreciated his place in the court. He knew that, in most parts of his native Germany, there was a growing hostility to religious art, and indeed to art in general. But now he was ordered to return to Germany. He was dispatched to

Düren to prepare a portrait of the 24-year-old Anne, whom neither Cromwell nor Henry had met.

In their superlative study of Holbein, the Swiss art historians Oskar Batschmann and Pascal Griener note that Henry first requested a portrait from Germany, but Lucas Cranach the Elder, the preferred painter, was indisposed. That was why, in 1538, Holbein was sent to Germany to prepare a portrait. Batschmann and Griener reckon that the distinguished artist found himself 'torn between the necessity of being honest, and of appeasing'. They describe how Holbein worked carefully to lavish gold on Anne's costume and how he chose a dark green background to offset her plain features. The portrait, which is now in the Louvre, shows a not unattractive woman – big-nosed, but certainly not plump. Holbein had apparently chosen appeasement. He had prepared a flattering portrait that was dishonest. Henry was deceived; he agreed to marry Anne.

When Anne arrived in England, Henry found her repulsive. Her complexion was sallow and scarred by smallpox. She was fat. She spoke a particularly guttural German; her manners were coarse. Henry was sorely disappointed. He described his new wife – for there was no going back now, he had to marry her – as a fat Flanders mare. He could never, he declared, 'be provoked to know her carnally'. The marriage lasted a few months – and, as Batschmann and Griener put it, Holbein 'seems to have lost the favour of the king'. Cromwell lost his head.

Admittedly, the quixotic king did not show his displeasure immediately; Cromwell was made Earl of Essex, and for a month or so actually seemed more in the ascendant than ever. But his bungle over Anne of Cleves had given his many enemies their chance. Henry was increasingly irascible and was willing to listen to those who told him that Cromwell was a dangerous heretic. When the end came, it was swift. The great lawyer was arrested, sent to the Tower and charged with a series of offences, including treason and heresy. He was executed on 28 July 1540; and, although on the same day the king married his fifth queen, Catherine Howard, in effect Henry was now alone.

Without Cromwell, the reign descended into something akin to chaos – though, to be fair, Henry more or less managed to keep his own version of the Reformation on track. The king had put himself in charge of all matters of doctrine, ritual, religious discipline and theology. He was trying to pursue a pragmatic course, equally disdainful of the papacy, whose authority he had usurped, and of the continental reformers, who were much too wild for his liking. His policy was essentially isolationist: if he was hostile to Rome, he was just as hostile to reformers in Germany and Switzerland whom he regarded as dangerously subversive. England, in religious terms, was to be a fortress, impervious to outside influences.

If this indicates canniness as well as parochialism, it is wrong to suggest that Henry was able to control his brutal tendencies. His policy towards Scotland in the 1540s was particularly vicious. And, if he was hard on the reformers who propagated what he regarded as heresy, he was equally hard on Catholics who challenged the royal supremacy over religious affairs. In the processes of Henry's diseased mind, he was pursuing a middle way.

A year before Cromwell's execution, Henry had required his Parliament to pass the so-called *Six Articles of Religion*. These comprised a stern attempt to end heresy. The first article insisted that Christ's body was present in consecrated bread and wine. Others endorsed private masses, confirmed confessions, prohibited priests from marrying and so on. Anyone who denied the first and most significant article was to be burned to death, even if he or she recanted at the time of trial. Already-married priests had to separate from their wives or be hanged. Anyone who tried to flee the kingdom after disobeying this draconian legislation was to be hung, drawn and quartered.

All this might seem like a violent lurch back towards official state Catholicism – and yet Cranmer, the Archbishop of Canterbury, was allowed by the king to oppose the legislation in the Lords. Henry had been becoming increasingly indecisive, even before Cromwell's execution. He veered one way and then the other, and in this fashion managed to steer an erratic middle course.

If he had not been so wrathful, so fierce, so tyrannical, he would have been a comic figure. Physically, he was grotesque. He was so obese that ropes had to be provided in his various palaces and castles to haul him around. He could no longer climb stairs unaided. He suffered from impotence, from piles, from grossly swelling ankles, from terrible headaches (possibly caused by earlier falls when jousting, which may have damaged his brain) and from a disgusting ulcer on his thigh which, when it suppurated, caused him such pain that his face blackened and his temper grew even worse, if that were possible.

After Anne of Cleves, his fifth wife was a large, sexy 19-year-old, Catherine Howard, who had a voracious sexual appetite. Catherine was blatantly unfaithful to the gross king, so she did not last long; she was beheaded.

The sixth and final wife, Catherine Parr, is most famous for having managed to outlive the old tyrant; but her real significance is that she befriended Henry's daughter by Anne Boleyn, Elizabeth. Catherine Parr had been married twice before. Her second husband had been one of the leaders of the Pilgrimage of Grace, the great Catholic uprising in the north. But Catherine's own instincts were with the reformers. She was friendly with Protestant luminaries such as Hugh Latimer and Miles Coverdale. Significantly for the future of England, she took a benign and thoughtful interest in Elizabeth's education and, crucially, ensured that she was brought up as a Protestant. Elizabeth was very bright and an excellent pupil. She was never a bigot or a fanatic like her Catholic sister Mary. Her Protestantism was judicious, moderate and cautious.

Catherine Parr was twenty-one years younger than her third husband, but she married him when she was 31 and in the prime of life – a mature, sensible woman, and probably the most intelligent and impressive of Henry's six wives. She may have lacked the dignity of Catherine of Aragon when she was humiliated again and again; she may have lacked the sharpness and the vivacity of Elizabeth's mother, Anne Boleyn. But she was that unlikely being in Tudor England – a female intellectual. And she possessed the inestimable virtues of kindness and common sense. The young Elizabeth could not have had a better substitute mother. England owes much to the comparatively unsung Catherine Parr.

Meanwhile, Henry continued to fret about heresy and was increasingly concerned about the subversive consequences of allowing everybody to read and discuss the Bible, as Tyndale and Cromwell had intended. In 1543, a repressive and laughably snobbish piece of legislation was enacted. The ridiculously titled Act for the Advancement of True Religion forbade servants, dependants, all below the rank of yeoman, and all women except those of gentle rank, from reading the Bible. The truth was there for all to see: Henry's Reformation was a state reformation, and for him it was ultimately about social and political control, not religious freedom.

Also in 1543, there was an extraordinary episode when an Italian emissary, one Gurone Bertano, discussed with the king the notion of a tentative reconciliation with the pope. The implication was that Henry would have to hand at least some of his religious authority back to the papacy. Needless to say, it did not take the king long to reject the olive branch, which was snatched back almost as soon as it was offered.

No great minister emerged – or was allowed to emerge – after the unnecessary death of Cromwell. Henry now governed through the Privy Council. But this did not prevent growing factionalism, itself the inevitable function of the loss of Cromwell. The inconsistent pursuit of a religious middle way, in that century of strong opinions, pleased no-one. The reformers were led by Cranmer, though 'led' is perhaps not the right word, so cautious was the archbishop. The Catholic faction was led by Bishop Stephen Gardiner of Winchester, who was clever and devious and never quite managed to gain the king's trust. At one point, Gardiner moved to destroy Cranmer by trying to persuade Henry that the archbishop was fostering heresy in the (always radical) county of Kent – but Henry refused to oblige the bishop. To some extent, he played the two men, the reforming archbishop and the conservative bishop, off against each other.

In 1545, in an address to Parliament, Henry presented himself as above faction, a ruler who could defend his own national religious settlement from the disputatious squabbles of bishops, preachers and the like. This was all very well; but the king was beginning to fail, and his son and heir, Edward, was a weak child. Both factions clustered round the ailing monarch in predatory fashion. The stakes were high: was England to return to Catholicism, or was it to become properly Protestant?

As the end neared, Henry seemed to tilt towards the radicals. He certainly ensured that his son was to be instructed by leading reformers; and those whom he nominated to govern in the name of his son after his death included more reformers than Catholics and more laymen than clerics. Significantly, Gardiner was not among them.

Henry died in 1547, a king determined, like his far wiser and better father before him, to die in the mercy of Christ. He wanted Cranmer with him as he died: perhaps a further indication that, towards the end, he had moved from his preferred middle way and finally sided with the reformers. As the last moments approached, he asked for a bowl of white wine, which was no doubt better than asking for someone's head. And, just before his final breaths, when he had lost the power of speech, Cranmer asked for some sign that he trusted in God, whereupon the old rogue squeezed the archbishop's hand. Henry was grotesque even after death: his hearse was of such monstrous proportions that the road between Westminster and Windsor had to be repaved to bear the burden.

He could have been a fine musician or a passable theologian. He had instead been a malevolent monarch. He had kicked the pope out of England, and he had destroyed, in the space of just four turbulent years, 800 monasteries, nunneries and friaries, many of them places of succour and education, and most of them buildings of exceptional beauty. He had executed many decent and numinous men and women. He had ushered in both a reformation and revolution, even if he did not properly understand the consequences of either. He had put down a huge rebellion in the north of his kingdom with vicious duplicity. He had waged savage war on Scotland and France, to little end.

He had gone through six wives, killing two of them along the way, and he had fathered various children. One of them, his daughter Elizabeth by his second wife, Anne Boleyn, was to prove a monarch beyond compare, and a notably sensible and moderate Protestant. She was by far the best thing Henry ever produced.

CHAPTER 10

Rebellion and Suppression

WHEN Henry VIII died at the start of 1547, his heir was his nine-year-old son Edward, a clever, priggish and not particularly healthy child. The man who rapidly took charge of the kingdom was the boy-king's uncle, the Duke of Somerset, who became Lord Protector. Somerset, who had previously been the Earl of Hertford, was a notable hammer of the Scots. He also presided over the terrible scorch-and-burn tactics of Henry VIII's 'rough wooing' of Scotland (to be discussed in Chapter 15), though he had expressed personal doubts about the savagery demanded by his king. Indeed, he had tried to persuade Henry that an essentially benign occupation of Scotland would be a more fruitful policy than one of vicious destruction.

But, at this point in his career, he was essentially a military man, and he was not disposed to disobey the orders of his monarch. An able general, affable and always quick-thinking – sometimes too much so – he was not a man for reflection. Later, when he exercised power on behalf of Edward, his statecraft was moderate and benign – except in matters of religion. His main diplomatic concern was to ensure the marriage of the young King Edward to the equally young Mary Queen of Scots. But his diplomatic skills were less well honed than his military ones. When his proposals for a marriage that would unite the two kingdoms were rejected, he turned once again to war, and humiliated the Scots at Pinkie Cleugh (see Chapter 15). But the victory was meaningless, because Somerset did not follow it up properly.

The young Scots queen was destined for France. The French interest was yet again in the ascendancy north of the Border, and the young Queen Mary was carefully removed to Paris, where she soon married the Dauphin, Francis. Thus the Auld Alliance seemed as strong as ever, and Somerset's diplomatic aspirations were in tatters.

Henry VIII, as we have noted, sought in his last years to steer a middle way in religion, rejecting the papacy and the zealots of Protestantism alike. Everything changed rapidly under Somerset. The intent was apparent as early as February 1547, when Edward was crowned. The boy was publicly told by Thomas Cranmer, the Archbishop of Canterbury, that he should ensure that idolatry was destroyed, images were removed, and – most significantly – the bishops of Rome banished. Set free by Somerset, the hitherto cautious Cranmer was now the man of the moment. He presided over a spectacular attack on the old faith.

The archbishop, egged on by Somerset, was now openly pursuing a religious policy for which Protestants had been executed by Henry VIII. Not only were public images to be removed from the churches, but private, personal images were to be destroyed as well. Funds for the maintenance and decoration of churches were to be diverted for the support of the poor. The rosary was banned, as was holy water. The Latin mass was abandoned. Priests were allowed to marry. If Catholics refused to attend the new services, they were to be imprisoned. Somerset and Cranmer moved to dissolve the chantries, the small religious and charitable houses that had been left largely unscathed during Cromwell's great assault on the monasteries in the 1530s.

All this amounted to a religious revolution. Cranmer's instructions were all-too-enthusiastically observed, if by a minority. There ensued an orgy of destruction, of crazed iconoclasm. Churches, including so many beautiful stained-glass windows, were smashed and ruthlessly, desperately plundered for their riches. The pope was compared to the Devil. Leading Catholic clerics were imprisoned. As for Mary, Henry VIII's elder daughter, and a solid Catholic – she was not imprisoned, but she was removed from the court.

Cranmer was encouraged by the continental reformer Martin Bucer, with whom he corresponded. Eventually, Bucer found refuge in England. Cranmer tried hard to persuade other leading reformers – including Calvin himself, and Zwingli's disciple Bullinger – to come to England, but they would not be persuaded. At the same time, Cranmer never became over-radical; he was still at heart a mild man, and he was always wary of the wilder Protestant sects.

Somerset and Cranmer had unleashed a self-interested anti-clericalism. But, as so often in the sixteenth century, where there was bad, good was to be found not too far way. Cranmer was working on a new English book of worship, which was published – and imposed on the people by Act of Parliament – in 1549. This was the first *Book of Common Prayer*. Carefully crafted, it had a whiff of compromise about it; the leading Catholic, Stephen Gardiner, perhaps mischievously, appeared to endorse it.

Cranmer's second *Book of Common Prayer*, a refined and revised version, was published in 1552. This was and remains one of the masterpieces of the English language, a notably beautiful religious document, which was to be treasured by many generations to come. It also reflects Cranmer's personal journey beyond Lutheranism to a position much more compatible with the theology of Zwingli. The 1552 version of the Holy Communion says: 'Take and eat this in remembrance that Christ died for thee.' In other words, the communion ceremony was the memorial of a sacrifice; the bread and wine were not Christ's body. Yet Gardiner, who believed in the real presence, had not rejected the 1549 version. Cranmer had moved some distance in three years.

The other positive aspect of the reforming fervour was that it was not accompanied by a bloodhunt. Not one Roman Catholic was put to death simply because of his or her religion during the reign of Edward VI, although plenty of Catholics who took part in rebellions against the state were slaughtered.

Henry VIII's middle way had been replaced by something much more one-sided. On the continent, Calvin and Zwingli could also be regarded as revolutionaries, but their religious experiments were largely confined to city states. In England, the experiment was national. There was still an element of the middle way, in that there was a Lutheran aspect to the politics of religion – state control, royally appointed bishops and so on. But, in the core doctrinal matters, such as the celebration of the Lord's Supper, the tilt was much more towards hardline Protestantism. Somerset and Cranmer were thus presiding over a national upheaval for which there was not obvious public support.

So, just what was going on? At this time on the continent, the Reformation was in crisis. Many thought it was failing. Yet, in England, the country's leaders were driving through their own version of the Reformation with reckless zeal. Edward, though just a boy, had something of the fanatic in him. He was a pugnacious Protestant, whereas Somerset, while undoubtedly a sincere and idealistic Protestant, was by no means a religious zealot. Indeed, on Sundays, he was far more interested in watching his stonemasons at work than in listening to sermons.

Far more significant than either Edward or Somerset was the Archbishop of Canterbury. There were greater reformers in the sixteenth century, but Thomas Cranmer was perhaps the most splendidly adaptable. He read voraciously and was always open to new ideas. He was a master of the English language – and words were crucial to the Reformation. He was a restrained and careful man, wary to the point of deviousness; yet he embarked, with considerable courage, on a long spiritual journey that took him from early hostility to Lutheranism in the 1520s, to cautious tinkering with reform, to outright evangelism.

And the man was liberated by Henry VIII's death. It sped him on his way, from his cautious Lutheranism to an almost extreme position. Working closely with Somerset, he had the confidence and the authority to rout the conservatives around him. Cranmer had been a model of reserve; suddenly he was emerging as a full-blown revolutionary.

And there was the danger. The people were not ready for this sudden and literally shattering change. They were attached to the old ways, the old liturgies. They hated to see beautiful religious artefacts being destroyed. They were used to lovely music in church, which they heard no more. In particular, they were used to praying for the dead, which was now forbidden.

Discontent was inevitable; rebellion was probable.

The most significant rebellion, known sometimes as the Western Rebellion, sometimes as the Great Prayer Book Rebellion, was largely confined to Cornwall and Devon, which were always regarded as 'difficult', independent-minded counties, teeming with troublemakers. While the rebels in the west had plenty of class grievances, they were basically protesting against the loss of their old religion. Ordinary people wanted to worship as their parents and grandparents had. Now they saw their much-loved churches being stripped and smashed up. The ancient rituals and liturgies that had hardly changed over many generations were suddenly to be replaced by austere services in English.

In June 1549, Cornish miners and farm labourers marched on Bodmin, while in Devon there was an uprising at a village called Sampford Courtenay, about twenty-five miles west of Exeter. The new prayer book was introduced into the churches on Whitsunday. The men of Sampford Courtenay were aware that revolt was already under way to the west, in Cornwall. When their priest, William Hayes, who had once been chaplain to Queen Catherine Parr, was ordered by his angry parishioners to put on his vestments and say mass instead of the new service, he complied. But this did not calm the men; rather, it fired them up. A local Justice, William Hellier, tried to restrain them. He was hacked to death and hastily buried.

In Bodmin, the rebels drew up their demands: principally a return to the old services, and the use of Latin, not English. Down the road in Devon, a similar document was produced. Then the rebels marched on Exeter, and their grievances were formally sent on to London. The sixteen demands of the combined rebels, 'The Articles of the commoners of Devonshire and Cornwall in divers camps by east and west Excettor', in their decent simplicity, make for moving reading. Here are two of them:

> Item: We will have the masse in latten, as was before, and celebrated by the pryest wythoute any man or woman communycatyng wyth hym.

> Item: We shall have every preacher in his sermon and every pryest at his masse, praye specialy by name for the soules in purgatory, as our forefathers dyd.

These two phrases, 'as was before' and 'as our forefathers did', say it all. This was a conservative movement, a revolt against change.

Somerset, Cranmer and their advisers, in London, misread the situation. They did not understand why Englishmen preferred Latin to English; they thought that the rebellion was being fomented solely by dissident priests. After various local skirmishes, the rebels, now numbering many thousands, marched round Exeter to a village called Clyst St Mary, where the local sheriff tried to reason with them. A tentative agreement was reached: if the insurgents returned home, they could practise the old religion. But it became clear that the sheriff had no real authority, and the rebels began to lay siege to Exeter in earnest. This was a tactical mistake. The Tudor state would have been in more peril had they marched on London. But, in those days, county was more important in most ordinary people's lives than country; for most of the rebels, Exeter was far enough.

Somerset, a decent man, still wanted to deal with the crisis through 'gentleness and persuasion', though the besieged citizens of Exeter were becoming desperate. Meanwhile, the general sent to deal with the rebels, Lord Russell, was afraid to engage; he stayed well clear and spent most of his time demanding reinforcements.

At long last, Russell took action. The fighting was brief but intense; about 400 of the rebels were killed, and many of the rest were put to flight. Meanwhile, Somerset had finally changed tack, sending a new general, Lord Grey, to Devon with cavalry and several hundred Italian mercenaries. After a skirmish at Clyst Heath, many of the remaining rebels were taken prisoner and then – to put it bluntly – massacred. Even then, the rebels were not finished. Those who were still besieging Exeter now came, bravely, to the fray; most of them were duly killed. Yet, even now, this very brave rising was not completely over; there was to be a final engagement back at Sampford Courtenay, where, after heavy fighting, Russell's troops – by now numbering more than 8,000 – put the last insurgents to flight.

Russell, who had unpleasantly moved from excessive caution to excessive zeal now that victory was assured, rushed into Cornwall to crush any lingering local resistance. For weeks, men were hunted across the county and then left swinging from quickly improvised gibbets. The leaders of the rebellion – those who had not been slaughtered in the various battles – were taken to London, tried at the end of 1549, and hung, drawn and quartered at Tyburn in January 1550. Once again, the Tudor state had taken vicious and condign action against essentially well-meaning and patriotic rebels. This was altogether one of the most horrendous episodes in English history.

The disruption was on a huge scale, and it affected more than just those who took part in the rebellion and their families. Some of the Protestant minority in Devon and Cornwall felt it best to flee. One such was the father of one of England's greatest heroes, Sir Francis Drake, who was born in 1542. His father Edmund, a strong Protestant, took the family from their home near Plymouth to Kent, where legend has it that young Francis was brought up on an old hulk on the River Medway. Another version of Drake's youth has it that his father was a horse thief who did indeed leave the West Country in a hurry, but simply to evade punishment. It is, however, certain that Edmund Drake detested Catholics – and eventually, in the 1560s, he became a Protestant preacher in the area of the Upchurch Marshes, south of the Medway. The Drake family history is interesting. Devon and Cornwall may have been solidly Catholic in the 1540s, but forty years later it was these two counties above all others that produced the heroic sailors who fought so valiantly for the Protestant cause against the Spanish.

I discussed the grisly events of 1549 with Professor Nicholas Orme of Exeter University, a leading expert on the religious history of Devon and Cornwall. He told me that Cranmer and Somerset had chosen the very worst time to impose the new service – Whitsuntide. This was when the people were ripe to rise, as it were. There was a kind of informal holiday period before the harvest; people were free to move around, and they had an unusual amount of time on their hands. At the same time, there was a sense of deprivation, for they were waiting for the harvest; most of last year's food had been used up. In the autumn and especially the winter, the lanes and tracks and bridleways were muddy and often well nigh impassable; movement was much easier in the summer.

Professor Orme also made the point that Henry VIII was – with due cause – much feared. Now England was being ruled by a child – and royal minorities were always acutely dangerous times when there was any pressing cause for discontent.

Further, the Tudors had been making England a more centralised state. The Prayer Book was imposed nationally. The people were told: here's this new service book – you have to use it immediately, starting this Sunday, Parliament has decreed it. This was going to cause trouble when ordinary folk were still seething after the dissolution of the religious houses, the loss of beautiful images in the churches, the vanishing of the shrines.

When I spoke with Professor Orme in Exeter, he suggested that I visit the tiny village of Morebath, on the southern fringes of Exmoor. Morebath is significant because its priest, Sir Christopher Trychay, served continuously from 1520 until 1574, right through the English Reformation. He carefully kept the parish records, which have been

REBELLION AND SUPPRESSION

used by the Cambridge scholar Eamon Duffy in a remarkable book, *The Voices of Morebath*, that records the quotidian events in those extraordinary times in what would normally have been a rustic backwater.

It is the building-up of detail that persuades you how law-abiding sheep-farming families in a remote area of north Devon could be stretched to breaking point by what seemed to them to be officious, unnecessary and even cruel change. Take the recitation of the rosary. In Henry VIII's time, this had been condemned, but only if done superstitiously or without understanding. Now, a few years later, praying upon beads was to be banned absolutely. As Professor Duffy suggests, this had been the most basic form of lay Catholic piety, represented by the beads of every matron in Morebath.

Today, the church of St George in Morebath is a most moving place, like the church of All Saints at Aughton, the home of the Askes in Yorkshire. But it is a far less austere church than Aughton's, and less obscurely situated. At St George's, there is a deep red carpet up the central aisle, and very bright stained-glass windows at either end of the nave. The chancel, like much of the rest of the church, was rebuilt in the Victorian era – and it is elaborate. Nowadays, the church is a riot of colour: even the bell-pulls in the tower are brightly coloured, and the prayer cushions are almost gaudy. It is as if, centuries on, the church itself is still engaged in rebellion against the rigorous reforms of Cranmer and Somerset.

The people of Morebath have worshipped in this beautiful building for almost 1,000 years. Morebath itself is a quiet community in pastoral, sheep-farming country; steep fields run down to the lovely valley of the River Exe to the west, and everywhere there are wooded coombes – the Devon word for a small, deep valley. Exmoor is a mile or so to the north, and sometimes red deer find their way down from the uplands to the village. In places like Morebath and Aughton, it is genuinely difficult to remember that England was ever industrialised.

Eventually, thanks to the Elizabethan settlement, which he was able to accept, Sir Christopher made the transition from Catholic priest to Protestant priest. Queen Elizabeth's Protestant Church was a more gentle, inclusive house than the militant Church of Edward VI, Somerset and Cranmer. Elizabeth herself was a wise and clement monarch whose instinct was not to persecute Catholics; as long as they obeyed the law of the land, and remained low-key, she would not regard herself as the custodian of their consciences.

Meanwhile, Professor Duffy sums up the nature of Sir Christopher's long ministry by emphasising its context.

> His traditionalism must have of course have had a doctrinal content, of the kind spelled out in the rebel demands of 1549 – loyalty to the mass, the ancient faith, the sacraments – but it was before everything else informed by the genius of place; his religion in the end was the religion of Morebath. The strength and weakness of such religion were the same – the local character of its conservatism, the binding of its practitioners to a place.

Moving back to London from Devon, we find Somerset increasingly under pressure, not least from his ambitious brother, Admiral Thomas Seymour, whom he eventually executed for treason. While the rebels of Cornwall and Devon were being suppressed, another serious disturbance had taken place in Norfolk. Called Ket's rebellion after its leader, it was caused by agrarian rather than religious grievances. It was put down with ferocity by John Dudley, Earl of Warwick, who facilely made his reputation by crushing Ket's poorly armed and ill-organised followers.

Like Somerset, Warwick rose fast; he too moved from an earldom to a dukedom, becoming the Duke of Northumberland. Unlike Somerset, he was greedy, arrogant and excessively ambitious. In some ways, he typified the upstarts who were making good with their gains from former monastic property, and through general land speculation, in the middle of the Tudor era. But Northumberland proved to be a tougher and more effective ruler than Somerset. He was also, for a time, an unlikely champion of the Scotsman John Knox.

Knox had come to Northumberland's attention when he was ministering in Berwick. Northumberland made him a royal chaplain and brought him to London to preach before the king. It seems that Northumberland wanted to promote Knox as a rival to Cranmer, and so the Scot was lined up for the bishopric of Rochester. But Knox, with his inimitable mixture of truculence, defiance, courage and sheer cussed independence, insolently questioned Northumberland about his own religious views. This was not the best way to ensure preferment. Northumberland eventually dismissed Knox because he was 'neither grateful nor pleasurable'.

After he had moved to destroy the Duke of Somerset, Northumberland continued the imposition of a yet more aggressive Protestantism. He did not get on well with Cranmer, as Somerset had; indeed, the two men squabbled frequently. But Northumberland allowed Cranmer to present a comprehensive statement of faith for the new English Church in the definitive *42 Articles* of 1553.

By this time, Somerset was dead. Northumberland had imprisoned him in the Tower of London, and then had him beheaded for treason. Somerset died with grace and dignity. One witness praised his great calmness, saying he was 'nothing at all abashed, neither with the sight of the axe, neither yet of the hangman, or of present death'. He told the great throng who came to witness his execution that, in England, the Christian religion had drawn closer to the 'form and order of the primitive church', and he asked them to continue this work. His last words were: 'Lord Jesus, save me.' The ordinary people of London, with whom he remained popular to the last, rushed forward and dipped their clothes in his blood.

To this day, Somerset is remembered north of the Border for the ferocity and cruelty with which he undertook Henry VIII's 'rough wooing'. And indeed, he should have resisted his king's orders and spent more time negotiating rather than scorching and burning. But, overall, this complex man was liberal, well-meaning and not at all self-seeking. At the same time, he lacked the political skills of Archbishop Cranmer and the hardness of his bitter rival Northumberland. The young King Edward, whom he had done his best to serve, was noticeably callous and dismissive at the time of his execution.

Edward did not have long to live. In the spring of 1553, he became seriously ill. Northumberland, who, as High Chamberlain of England, had been virtual ruler of the country for the past three years, began to panic. He knew that the next monarch would be Henry VIII's daughter Mary, a zealous adherent of the old religion who would attempt to restore Catholicism. In so doing, she would no doubt liquidate the man who had presided over the latest phase of the Protestant revolution.

Northumberland clearly had to act fast. One view is that, in desperation, he seized on the unlikely personage of Lady Jane Grey and hastily married her to his fourth son, Lord Guildford Dudley. Lady Jane would in due course be presented as an alternative queen to Mary. She was the granddaughter of Henry VII's youngest daughter Mary. As such, she did have some kind of claim to the throne, but to suggest that it was superior to that of the daughter of Henry VIII and his first wife Catherine of Aragon is ludicrous.

Recent years have seen a challenge to the version that the king, seriously ill at the age of 15, was persuaded by Northumberland to abrogate the will of Henry VIII and to declare that his two sisters, Mary and Elizabeth, were technically illegitimate and thus unable to succeed him. Edward VI's biographer, Chris Skidmore, suggests very persuasively that Edward had been planning for some time to disinherit his two sisters. He would create a new dynasty to ensure the continuation of the Protestantism in which he so fervently believed. And so, he himself eventually decided that Lady Jane, his cousin, should succeed him. He managed to gain the support of most of his senior advisers, including Cranmer, the leading members of his council, senior members of the nobility and several judges.

In early July 1553, the king was clearly dying. Mary, well informed and crafty, moved to Cambridgeshire and on to Norfolk, where she could be protected by the grand old Catholic family, the Howards. The king died, and Jane Grey was proclaimed queen in London. She was to 'reign' for only nine days. What happened next is explained in Chapter 18.

PART 3

The Splitting of the Continental Reformation

CHAPTER 11

Zwingli and Zurich

HULDRYCH ZWINGLI, the so-called Third Man of the Reformation (the first two being Luther and Calvin), was born in 1484 in the high Alpine valley of Toggenberg. His father was a farmer and a magistrate. Zwingli studied at Basel, Bern and Vienna – and, like so many of the early reformers, was much influenced by humanist teachers and writers, in particular Erasmus.

Zwingli acknowledged more of a debt to Erasmus than Luther ever did; and indeed, when he arrived (probably in 1514) at his crucial conviction that people had to place their faith in Christ and Christ only for salvation – not in the Virgin Mary or in saints – this was a direct result of his reading of works by Erasmus. Ironically, soon after this, he decided that the Bible alone had authority; and this became his watchword.

He served as parish priest in the small towns of Glarus and Einsiedeln, and also as a chaplain to Swiss mercenaries fighting for the papacy against the French. He was present at the catastrophic Swiss defeat of Marignano in which 10,000 Swiss – allegedly the best fighting men in Europe – were slaughtered by the French.

Always highly sexed, Zwingli began agitating for an end to clerical celibacy. He also developed his own theology, which was now based entirely on his reading of the Bible rather than on what the Church had taught him. At the end of 1518, he was called to the great cathedral of Zurich, the Grossmünster, as the 'people's priest'. Zurich, then and now the most significant city in Switzerland, was a prosperous, comfortable place with about 10,000 inhabitants.

At the start of his new ministry – the first day of 1519 – Zwingli announced that he was going to innovate and preach the New Testament from beginning to end, verse by verse. This was more than a break with tradition; this was revolutionary. At this point in his career, Zwingli was every bit as confident a preacher as Luther, and possibly more radical. He later claimed that he had been developing, and teaching, his theology long before he had heard of Luther, though he generously acknowledged Luther's unshakable courage in challenging the authority of the pope.

Zwingli was a superb preacher. His delivery was powerful; he had a fine voice, and he was something of an actor, using all sorts of stagey flourishes. The effect was electrifying. But Zwingli wished the Bible, not himself, to be at the centre of everything. Basing his teaching on Scripture and on nothing else, the new preacher questioned much that had been practised for centuries, including the observance of Lent, the worship of saints, the monastic life and penitential works.

There were now to be only two sacraments: baptism and communion. And communion was not to be about the physical realisation of the flesh of Christ. Rather, it was to be a cerebral event which was assisted, no more, by the partaking of bread and wine, the elements that Christ had distributed at the Last Supper. He presided over communion services in which the laity received the wine, and furthermore they received it sitting in their pews. This may not seem revolutionary to the modern mindset, but it was a hugely symbolic change.

Furthermore, the churches were to be stripped. Images, candles and even organs were destroyed. Everything was reduced to a pure simplicity so that people could concentrate on the Word without diversion. Zwingli was truly a 'clean break' man and had far less respect for the past than had the essentially conservative Luther. Indeed, Zwingli at times seems to have acted with some contempt for what had gone before him.

At the same time, as befitted a magistrate's son, he was careful to work with the civic authorities in Zurich. It was the city council which authorised the removal of all images from the walls of the cathedral. Zwingli believed strongly in the right of these city magistrates to control the lives of the citizens; they could even decide who was to be excommunicated. Thus, he kept the city council on board as he went further and faster than Luther was doing, hundreds of miles to the north. Far and fast – but, as it turned out, nothing like far enough for some radicals.

Meanwhile, Luther continued to believe in the real presence of Christ at the Eucharist. Soon, the two reformers were engaged in a disputation which was anything but seemly. Their animus against each other despoiled the early progress of the Reformation and nearly derailed it. Luther, so often a wild man with the pen, wrote that Zwingli was full of hate and wickedness, which was palpable nonsense. Zwingli countered by telling Luther that his ideas were worthy of a brothel. Luther told Zwingli that his books were hell's poison. And so it went on.

In Chapter 4, we left Luther fulminating against the peasants and taking the side of the German princes. In 1525, the year in which the princes finally triumphed, Luther had married Catherine von Bora, a former nun who had been working as a servant of the artist Lucas Cranach the Elder. He found much happiness with her. She was a strong and formidable woman, which was just as well, for Luther could not have maintained a stable or harmonious marriage with someone lacking in personality.

Catherine was an organiser. Luther was never wealthy despite his phenomenal output as a writer (from 1520 to his death in 1546, a third of all published works in German were written by him). He made no riches from these prolific endeavours. The money was made by the printers and the middlemen. Catherine was more sensible with money, and she helped the Luther household by establishing a vegetable garden and an orchard, and taking in lodgers. The Luthers had children, five of them – and Martin, perhaps recalling the excessive hardness of his own father, proved a compliant and easy-going parent. Despite these huge improvements in his life, marriage hardly seems to have calmed Luther. The angry words continued to flow from his pen, too often without any restraint or control.

The power of the princes, endorsed by Luther, was enhanced by their crushing of the peasants. It was also enhanced by, of all people, the Turks. It is too easy to forget that, at this time of the nascent Reformation, the most powerful man in the world was Suleiman the Magnificent, the supreme Ottoman warlord who had vanquished much of North Africa including Egypt, as well as Syria and Iraq and parts of Eastern Europe such as Greece. Suleiman was extra-special, and he knew it: he arrogantly told Francis I of France, himself a proud and showy monarch: 'I am the sultan of sultans, the sovereign of sovereigns, the Shadow of God upon Earth.'

Suleiman was now threatening to move into central and even Western Europe from his advanced positions in Hungary. This was alarming for Charles V, the Holy Roman Emperor; in a way, it was good news for the reformers, because Charles realised that he would in all probability need the support of Lutheran princes and their troops to hold off the invading Turks. In 1526, an imperial diet decided that each German ruler could decide which faith was to be followed in his territory. This could legitimately be interpreted as far-sighted religious toleration. It could also be regarded as a pragmatic response to the threat of the Turks, although a later diet, in 1529, rescinded this level of tolerance – at the very time that Suleiman was laying siege to Vienna.

It has been argued that Protestantism would never have survived without the Turks. What is indisputable is that Charles V saw the defence of Hungary and central Europe as a higher priority than quashing the reformers. Ottoman imperialism was probably crucial to the success of the Reformation.

In 1522, Zwingli had set out what was in effect his manifesto for a new Church in a book called *The Clarity and Certainty of the Word of God*. In it, he completely rejected the authority of the papacy and almost all Church tradition. Interestingly, the papacy did not seem too concerned about this latest challenge to its authority; some historians have suggested that this was because popes relied on Swiss mercenaries to protect them and to fight their wars. Thus the papacy had no interest in alienating the Swiss.

When he was a priest at Glarus and Einsiedeln, Zwingli had not been able to maintain his vows of celibacy. He had succumbed to the flesh, though he bizarrely suggested that this was not too serious as he had not slept with a virgin, a nun or a married woman. Now, in 1522, he married a well-born Zurich widow called Anna Reinhart. The marriage was kept secret for two years. Meanwhile, relations with Luther became even worse. Luther, himself the great heretic, now regarded Zwingli and his followers as heretics, people who were consorting with Satan. The Reformation, only a few years old, was already a fissile movement.

Philip, Prince of Hesse in western Germany, decided to act as conciliator. He convoked a peace conference at Marburg in 1529. Luther and Zwingli attended (Luther reluctantly) but spectacularly failed to find any common ground in their dispute over the Eucharist. Luther started in defiant form, writing 'This Is My Body' on a table for all to see, and refusing to accept any interpretation of the four words other than his own. He remained supremely stubborn throughout the proceedings.

Here was the greatest conundrum of the Reformation: it is all very well asserting that Scripture is supreme, as both Luther and Zwingli sincerely believed – but who is to interpret Scripture? And, if there are disagreements over interpretation, as there inevitably must be, who is to arbitrate? The Zurich solution to this was pragmatic and overtly political, though essentially imperfect: with Zwingli's approval, the city council assumed the right to interpret Scripture. But then, what if another city council, down the road, adjudicated otherwise?

At the end of the Marburg conference, Zwingli, with tears in his eyes, tried to make peace and to ensure that at least he and the begetter of the Reformation did not part in anger. Luther's response to this was delphic: 'Call upon God that you may receive understanding.' Although there had been agreement on many less important issues, all that Marburg achieved, therefore, was confirmation of the fact that the Reformation had already split into two. There was now little hope of unity among Protestants – and thus it has continued to this day.

Marburg failed on the huge question of what was actually happening at the Eucharist. It was a colossal lost opportunity. But it would be ingenuous to expect that the Reformation could have emerged as a coherent, united movement. It just might have done if its guiding spirit had been a man like Erasmus, a sceptical, inquiring, cautious man who, above all, detested commotion and division. But the eminently clever and influential Erasmus was not a natural leader.

At the heart of the early Reformation was a new, revolutionary emphasis on individual reading of the Bible and on individual response to Scripture. Individuals – and individual leaders – were obviously going to interpret Scripture differently. It is almost as if division and disunity were built into the Reformation from the beginning.

At Marburg, Zwingli was more impressive than Luther. He was always a more reasonable man, and more refined. Luther had his coarse, brutish side; he lacked elegance and finesse. Certainly, some of the new churches in the Rhineland and the Low Countries now looked towards Zurich rather than Wittenberg for guidance. It would have been interesting, had Zwingli lived long enough, to see if he could have steered the Reformation forward politically as well as spiritually.

But, in 1531, not long after Marburg, Zwingli died in action, wielding his battleaxe, at the Battle of Kappel, part of a series of minor wars between Zurich and the Catholic cantons of Switzerland. This was ironic, because Zwingli had for some time been genuinely appalled by the constant loss of brave Swiss soldiers; he had no objection to war as such, but he wanted war to be in a just cause, and he hated the idea of young Swiss men serving as mercenaries, as so many of them did, and losing their lives for mere money.

The Reformation was a revolution – and revolutions are not only created by revolutionaries. They also spawn them. The most extreme of those spawned by this particular revolution were the Anabaptists. These people, who emerged in Zurich in the 1520s, were by far the most exciting products of the early Reformation. It has become fashionable to group them together and describe them as comprising the 'Radical Reformation'. Many of them were extremists, but their ideas and beliefs – and also their fanaticism – anticipated much of what was to come in Europe over the next 400 or 500 years.

There was more than a whiff of anarchism about the Anabaptist movement. It is possibly erroneous to talk of 'leaders', just as it is wrong to suggest that there was a coherent corpus of beliefs. But, if there were early leaders, they were Conrad Grebel and Felix Manz. Grebel believed that you only entered the Church as a free agent, and the symbol of this entry was baptism. So, you should be baptised as an adult, not a baby or a child; obviously, a baby or a child could not be a free being. Anabaptists had to follow the Ten Commandments and the Sermon on the Mount with rigour; they had to act as if they were saints on earth, and they had to eschew the civil authority and have no truck with princes, magistrates, councils and such like. So much, then, for Luther and Zwingli.

Needless to say, this did not resonate too well with the civil authorities in Zurich. The Anabaptists were persecuted viciously. The most severe means of persecuting prominent Anabaptists was by drowning them in the River Limmat, which in a grisly way was no doubt regarded as an appropriate final punishment for those who believed so strongly in adult baptism. As Michael Baumann has reminded us, religious tolerance was a child not of the Reformation but of the much later Enlightenment.

Grebel and his colleague Felix Manz had much in common. Both were born in 1498, both were born into comfortable backgrounds (Grebel's father was one of Zurich's elite citizens), both were humanist scholars, both were respectable figures in the city: they were not the kind of men you would expect to be extremists. But the Zurich city council, with Zwingli's approval, decided that they were heretics. Manz, the son of a Catholic priest, and a more impressive preacher than Grebel, became the first martyr to be executed by a Protestant state.

In 1526, the city authorities had him arrested and incarcerated in the Welleberg Tower. Early the next year, he was taken to a fishing hut (which no longer exists) on a pontoon in the middle of the River Limmat, within sight of the Grossmünster. His hands were shackled, his feet were bound and he was drowned. As for Grebel, he evaded inevitable martyrdom when he succumbed to the plague.

On a visit to Zurich in 2008, I learned that the city fathers had for many years – indeed, for centuries – refused to allow any permanent commemoration of Manz's martyrdom. It was as if the bitterness of the early sixteenth century was still extant. As late as 1952, they had refused to allow even a modest plaque to be erected. Then, in 2004, they finally gave way. A plaque, discreet and hard to find, has been set in the wall of the quay on the west bank of the Limmat, near the point on the river where the fishing hut was sited. The words are in German. Here is a translation:

> From a fishing platform here in the middle of the Limmat, Felix Manz and five other Anabaptists were drowned between 1527 and 1532, during the time of the Reformation.

> The last Anabaptist to be executed in Zurich was Hans Landis in 1564.

Not the most gracious of memorials; the tone is matter-of-fact to the point of being grudging. But it is better than nothing.

The Anabaptists were greatly feared, despite their refusal to resist those who persecuted them. Indeed, they provoked more than fear; they provoked revulsion. Why? Perhaps because they were, in the early years anyway, pure. They showed up everyone else. The Reformation was in part about cleansing the Church; but were not the Luthers and the Zwinglis and their like so many compromisers, just so many more worldly conspirators against the true, godly life?

Another reason was their refusal to engage in war. The Anabaptist Michael Sattler made a point of defiantly asserting that even the Turks should not be resisted. He was thrown out of Zurich, and he toured southern Germany propagating Anabaptist ideas. He then returned to Switzerland and was eventually martyred.

A third reason was that Anabaptism seemed to offer a peculiar and potent kind of succour to those on the margins of society – to the poor, the weak, the alienated, the dispossessed, the unsuccessful and the unlovable. Were not these the very people whom Christ came to save?

Despite their contempt for the civil authorities, even Anabaptists had to confront the reality that all movements need to organise – and Anabaptism did become a movement of a kind. Thus, in 1527, Anabaptists convoked a meeting to draw up a statement (which became known as the Schleitheim articles). These dealt with both personal morality and Church governance.

The articles confirmed an almost total withdrawal from the conventions, rules and laws of the secular world. Grebel had written that Anabaptists were sheep among wolves; and the Schleitheim articles seemed to endorse this view. The implication was that reformers such as Zwingli and Luther had been feeble and half-hearted. Zwingli wasted no time in responding; he denounced Anabaptists as 'rotten'. They were disturbing 'the peace of the pious' in his beloved Zurich.

Following the by now all-too-predictable path of the Reformation, the Anabaptist movement started to splinter, and some Anabaptist sects were associated with violence while others forsook purity for political ambition. Indeed, at Münster in Westphalia, Anabaptists took control of the city council.

Anabaptists, as they were persecuted (and they usually were), moved around and were soon to be found in many parts of Germany, in Moravia and in the Netherlands. In England, Henry VIII and his leading minister Cromwell took Anabaptism seriously, in that they attacked it vigorously. In 1538, a man called Peter Tasch claimed that his Anabaptist sect was making converts in England despite persistent attempts at persecution. Anabaptists were burned to death at Smithfield in London, at Colchester, and in various other parts of south-east England where 'orthodox' Protestantism was strongest.

Perhaps the most influential Anabaptist was Menno Simons. Born in the Netherlands in 1496, he became a priest in 1524. He journeyed privately towards Anabaptism while maintaining his outward life as a priest. This duality imposed colossal strains, and eventually he became a wandering preacher, living the life of a fugitive. He was a man of both moral and physical heroism, for he was a cripple. He travelled constantly, hunted and always in danger, across vast tracts of northern Germany, preaching to covert assemblies and baptising adults in rivers, streams and lakes.

Much of the work was done under cover of darkness. He ordained pastors; many joined him. The word 'Mennonite' was used to describe his followers. But, once again, the fissile tendency was apparent; Mennonites became separate from, and despised by, other Anabaptist groupings and sects.

Zurich today is an introverted city, far less cosmopolitan than Geneva, and far less keen to enthuse to the visitor about its role in the Reformation. It would be difficult for any reasonably diligent, intelligent and curious tourist to spend even a couple of days in Geneva without becoming well aware of Calvin and his legacy. It would, I'm sure, be easy for such a person to spend a couple of weeks in Zurich without learning much of Zwingli. It is not that Zurich seems ashamed of the great reformer; it is just that it is a very discreet, private place.

At the same time, Zwingli's great twin-towered church, the Grossmünster, dominates the east bank of the River Limmat (it has an elevated site a little up from the quay) – and I know of no other religious building, whether big cathedral or tiny church, anywhere in Europe which so well expresses, in physical form, the pure quiddity of the Reformation. Built in its present form between 1100 and 1230, the Grossmünster stands on a site suffused with religious myth and legend – some of it the sort of nonsense that Zwingli and other reformers wished to expunge. Yet the stories resonate to this day, and they form an important part of Zurich's civic pride and sense of history.

One of the stories is that the city's patron saints, Felix and Regula, fled here as members of the Theban Legion in the third century. They were martyred beside the River Limmat. They then carried their decapitated heads up the little hill to where the Grossmünster now stands because they wanted to be buried there. Another story is that Charlemagne hunted a stag all the way here from Aachen in Germany, sometime in the early ninth century. When his horse reached the place of pilgrimage above the Limmat, it refused to chase the stag any more and went down on its knees. Charlemagne learned that this was where the martyrs were buried, and at once decreed that a great church was to be built on that very spot.

Today, the Grossmünster is an austere building, less immediately awe-inspiring than many of Europe's celebrated cathedrals. If you spend an hour or so in it, you do become slowly overwhelmed with a kind of spiritual power; this, surely, is how the Reformation was meant to be. There is an undoubted absence of warmth. But somehow the austerity and simplicity, at first very harsh, become not unfriendly, though there is an almost total absence of colour, apart from Giacometti's stained-glass windows (1933) which dominate the chancel at the east end of the church.

Zwingli was a much more aggressive iconoclast than Luther, and a little painting of the resurrected Christ is one of very few works of art that survived Zwingli's purges. Situated above the door to the apostles' chapel, it is unfortunately a rather grotesque depiction of Christ rising from his tomb. Indeed, I'm sure that many visitors to the Grossmünster will conclude that it's a pity that this particular painting managed to survive the iconoclastic zeal.

Outside, built into the wall of the church by the main door, is a twelve-foot-high statue of Zwingli's successor Heinrich Bullinger.

Nearby, down by the Limmat, is a huge and fierce statue of Zwingli himself, standing on an equally huge plinth, clutching his sword and gazing, as if for divine inspiration, to the splendid snow-capped peaks of the Alps far to the south.

The street named after Zwingli, the Zwinglistrasse, is in a very different part of town. It is a narrow and distinctly seedy street in the city's red-light district, just off the Langstrasse, Zurich's so-called 'street of sin' – a thoroughfare that Zurichers, despite their prudish reputation, appear curiously proud of. Lutherstrasse, though nearby, is rather more salubrious.

Altogether, Zurich does not strike the visitor as being particularly keen to promote its Reformation legacy, or indeed the memory of Zwingli and his achievements, in the way that Geneva does with Calvin. Calvin's spirit dominates the old town of Geneva, whereas Zwingli's hardly dominates any part of Zurich, apart from the magnificent Grossmünster.

CHAPTER 12

Calvin the Man

*J*OHN CALVIN was born in Noyon, a small town in Picardy, in July 1509. His father's father had been a cooper; his father, Girard, was a clerk who made a career in the Church. He served first as an episcopal secretary and then as the procurator of Noyon Cathedral. To develop his career, he became a lawyer.

The French scholar Bernard Cottret has noted that Calvin was brought up in a respectable, provincial and bourgeois milieu. But it was not in any way a privileged existence – and, from the start, John Calvin's life was very hard. His mother, Jeanne, died when he was just five years old. His father was, in the modern phrase, upwardly mobile. He sent John to be educated with the children of the aristocratic de Montmors family; and, when John was 11 or 12, Girard obtained a church benefice which would allow his son to study for a religious career in Paris.

Calvin's boyhood – his mother's early death, his father's insistence on improvement – helps to explain Calvin's driven and detached personality. He became a rather formal man, stern and anything but gregarious, though he did make friends quite easily. In Paris, Calvin stayed at first with his uncle, a locksmith. He studied Latin at the Collège de la Marche. Then he became a boarder at the College of Montaigu, where one of the star teachers was the Scottish scholar John Major. Calvin was a diligent student, and he acquired the reputation of being a snitch, an informer.

Paris at this time was a huge, teeming, licentious city, full of life, much of it low. Physically and intellectually, it was still rooted in the medieval era. Calvin was destined for a career in a Church that was hostile to new ideas, that was corrupt and led by venal men. But then Girard fell out with the cathedral chapter back home and told his son to switch from theology to the law.

This was, of course, the precise opposite of Luther's path as a student; Luther had switched from the law to theology, much to the fury of his father. It is very significant that Calvin did what his father told him to do, whereas Luther disobeyed his parent. As it happened, back in Noyon, Girard's career was juddering to a halt. He became involved in bitter quarrels with the cathedral chapter. He was excommunicated, and there was even some doubt as to whether he could be buried in consecrated ground.

The comparison with Luther is salutary. It is, however, too easy for authors of books such as this to insist on making constant comparisons between the begetter of the Reformation and the man who presided over its crucial second phase. So, I will from now on resist the temptation, apart from pointing out the most pressing similarity between them (apart from the obvious fact that they were both spiritual geniuses of the highest order): that they were both conservative revolutionaries. By that, I mean that they were both naturally conservative; they were both brought up in small provincial towns which might, not unkindly, be described as backwaters. They were both highly intelligent men who were not natural revolutionaries. Yet, potent revolutionaries they both became. And, as someone once noted, the conservative revolutionary is the most dangerous revolutionary of all.

We have noted that the Paris in which the 12-year-old Calvin, innocent and provincial, found himself was not perhaps the most suitable place for an earnest and shy adolescent. Rather, it was the most decadent and flagrantly sensual of all European cities. It was famed for its prostitutes; and men flocked to the city, not just from all over France but also from other countries, for their services.

There is something bizarre in the thought of the scholarly, serious youth arriving in the city of iniquity. Professor Andrew Hussey, in his acclaimed history of Paris, notes that a particularly shocking aspect of life in the heart of the city was the way sex and religion were intimately intertwined. Hussey describes graphically how, in the early part of the sixteenth century, prostitutes would sit in the nave of the great cathedral of Notre Dame, mingling with the faithful and whispering their prices to any likely-looking client. Hussey also notes that Paris inspired much fear in provincials, not just because of its great size but also because of its hustlers, its prostitutes – and its heretics.

Calvin, always austere, no doubt managed to keep himself away from temptation. He had to work hard, and the regime at Montaigu was exceptionally rigorous, though probably not too daunting for a driven and slightly priggish youth. Montaigu was as much a monastery as a college. The students were expected to denounce each other for any moral transgressions, so perhaps Calvin's supposed reputation as a snitch only means that he obeyed the rules.

Montaigu was situated in an area of Paris, high on the left bank near where the Pantheon is to be found today, that was notorious for two things in particular: crime and dirt. The lanes and alleys were full of thieves and violent criminals of every description; raw sewage flowed down the streets. Within the college, the students' day began at four. The first lectures were followed by mass at six, and then at last came breakfast – which was meagre and unappetising. And so it went on. The daily routine was tough and exacting. The college was presided over by one Noël Bedier, a medieval theologian of the old school, prejudiced, reactionary and unbending. He was not one to open his ears to those calling for reform. Calvin learned in an unforgiving and harsh school.

Perhaps too harsh. This was not a propitious environment for someone like young Calvin, blessed with a fine and eager mind. So, it was fortunate that Girard decided that his son should switch to the law. He was, after all, a lawyer himself – if an undistinguished one – and he was increasingly at odds with the Church authorities in Noyon. Also, the law was likely to pay better than the Church. There were, of course, very rich pickings for the lucky few in the Catholic Church; but, in general, lawyers, then as now, were likely to have more lucrative careers than priests.

So, Calvin, aged 16 or 17 – we cannot be exactly sure when he left Paris – moved to the University of Orléans, a more liberal establishment which specialised in the law. Here, he found himself in an academic environment that was less restrictive and more appropriate for his wide-ranging mind, and in a context that was less decadent than Paris. He was not completely turning away from religious education, for study of the law at Orléans included aspects of Church doctrine and Church history.

After two years at Orléans, Calvin moved on to Bourges to continue his legal studies. But, when Girard died in 1531, he switched again, this time to return to Paris, where he studied humanism at the Collège de France. Many scholars and lecturers in Paris were followers of Erasmus, but it was not clear how far they could push their new liberalism; the hold of the medieval Church remained strong.

It might seem surprising that someone who was to be a great evangelical Christian immersed himself so eagerly in the fashionable humanism of the times; but then Calvin – like so many intelligent people in the early sixteenth century – had been much influenced by Erasmus. At this time, he became friendly with the Cop family. Guillaume Cop, one of the physicians to King Francis I, was a distinguished doctor who had corresponded with Erasmus. Calvin liked his son Nicholas Cop, who was a lecturer at the college and became rector of the University of Paris in 1533.

Cop's rectorial address caused a sensation, for it referred with approval to Erasmus and – much more dangerously – to Luther. The speech was tantamount to a call for reformation of the Church. Calvin's associate Theodore Beza was later to claim that Calvin wrote Cop's address, though this has been disputed. In any event, Cop's words without doubt reflected the tendency of Calvin's thinking. He was by now convinced of the need for change.

The ecclesiastical authorities in Paris regarded the rector's address as blatantly heretical. In the uproar that ensued, Cop was deposed as rector and told he would have to justify his remarks at a trial for heresy. Cop did not wait to be tried; he fled from Paris. His friend Calvin found himself under intense suspicion. His room was searched, and some of his books were confiscated. At this time, the persecution of heretics in Paris was becoming ever more violent.

Calvin left the city and moved south, disguised as a gardener. First, he went to the Charente region, where an old college friend, Louis du Tillet, was a village priest. He then returned north to make a discreet visit to his home town of Noyon. He was moving here and there, travelling under an assumed name. It is not clear that he was in immediate physical danger – but, wisely, he was taking no risks.

Then the burnings began. One of those executed for heresy was another of Calvin's Paris friends, Etienne de la Forge. Calvin now decided to quit France altogether and fled to Basle. His friend Cop was already there, and he was in good company. Among the other residents of the free city at this time was the great Erasmus, by now old and decrepit, and Zwingli's associate Heinrich Bullinger.

When Calvin arrived in Basle, he had made not one but two journeys. As well as the physical one, he had made a religious journey. He was now a Protestant. Sometime between the autumn of 1533 and the spring of 1534, he had undergone a conversion. His own words were that 'God by a sudden conversion subdued and brought my mind to a teachable frame'.

Significantly, Calvin was now not just a Protestant; he was a Protestant who wanted to write. He had a fine mind, disciplined and orderly. He had an even more extraordinary capacity for sustained intellectual effort. He had been trained as a lawyer. And he could write with concision and clarity. Here was the man to give Protestantism the intellectual shape and organisation it desperately needed. In fact, he was to do even more than this; he was, at least in part, to invent the modern intellectual world.

In Basle, Calvin worked on his greatest and most influential book, his *Institutes of the Christian Religion*, which he completed towards the end of 1535 and had published in March 1536. The *Institutes* are arguably the most important work of Protestant theology. In the book, he attempted to train people in 'true godliness'. He also wanted to persuade influential people, not least the king of France, Francis I, that Protestantism was not seditious. He wanted to stop Protestants from being persecuted for heresy.

The first edition was quite a short book, but Calvin warmed to his task and, in 1539, brought out a much longer edition. Both these editions were written in Latin, but, also in 1539, Calvin produced another version in French. The final edition was not published for another twenty years. In this, the 1559 version, Calvin's great work had grown into a systematic theological treatise of immense importance.

Calvin was still restless. After the first edition of the *Institutes* was published, he moved to Ferrara in Italy, where a group of French Protestants had been given sanctuary by the liberal-minded Duchess of Ferrara, who kept a famous salon. Calvin did not stay with them long; he moved back to Basle and then returned briefly to France. He then decided to try to settle in Strasbourg, which he hoped might be a fitting place for the reclusive and timid scholar he thought himself to be. But, because of the ongoing war between France and the Holy Roman Empire, the obvious route was blocked, and he had to detour to Geneva. This proved to be one of the most momentous detours in history.

A Protestant preacher called Guillaume Farel was becoming the dominant figure in Geneva, which had recently formally adopted the Reformation, though it was very far from being a properly reformed community. The city had detached itself from the political power of the Duke of Savoy and the spiritual power of the pope, but had been left in something of a void. Farel had been an itinerant preacher, and his reputation was now such that he was in demand in both Bern and Geneva. He chose the latter, and quickly managed to dismantle the episcopal structure and to expel all the apparatus of popery.

But destroying was easier than building. Farel was a crude hellfire preacher; he was ambitious for himself and the city, but he was no organiser.

As for Calvin, he was in Geneva by accident. He wanted to pursue his private studies and had no desire to engage in the politics of a city state. According to his own account, he was harangued by Farel, who told him that God would curse his 'retirement' and the tranquillity he sought. Farel hectored and bullied. He told Calvin that his duty was to stay in Geneva and assist him. Calvin said that the force of Farel's insistence made him 'stricken with terror'.

At this point, we must ask why Farel, clearly a forceful personality, was so determined to detain in Geneva a man he hardly knew. The main reason must surely be that Farel had read the *Institutes* and knew that their author was the kind of man who could provide order and discipline to the ongoing work of reformation. Farel understood that the particular reformation he had started was floundering. He saw in Calvin a man who was both a lawyer and an educator; the *Institutes* had been written partly as a primer. And he believed that the needs of Geneva were of much greater importance than Calvin's selfish desire for a quiet life.

Calvin was intimidated by Farel, and intuitively felt that he could not work with him. By his own version, he had intended to spend just one night in Geneva and had been keen to maintain his anonymity. But somebody had betrayed his presence to Farel. On the other hand, Beza, Calvin's loyal lieutenant, later gave a very different version. Beza said categorically that Calvin had visited Farel voluntarily. Whatever happened, Calvin resented the way he was forced to stay in Geneva. His relationship with Farel was stormy. Calvin had intended for himself the withdrawn life of a private intellectual; Farel imposed on him a completely different vocation, that of the spiritual politician. Far from living a life of privacy, Calvin was now a public figure. Many eyes were on him constantly.

Farel's blustering intervention meant that Calvin spent the rest of his life – with one long interruption in Strasbourg – in Geneva. His extended ministry there was to be the most impressive ministry of the entire Reformation. He came to regard his work in Geneva as his duty, but he never, at any stage, found it easy.

The first twenty-seven years of his life had been characterised by a constant restlessness. He was always moving on, changing course, persuading himself that it was time to settle and then moving on again. Maybe there was something of the nomad in him, though this hardly accords with the stock notion of his personality. He had certainly convinced himself that he wanted to settle permanently in Strasbourg. But, perhaps temperamentally, he was not meant to stay permanently anywhere. He was never at ease in his long sojourn at Geneva. He pined for his native France. For the rest of his life, he hated the fact that he was in exile.

The paradox of his work in Geneva is that it was enormously successful but that it was achieved through constant frustration and pain. He was often in agony – spiritual, physical and intellectual. Calvin suffered enormously for his adopted city, for his religion and for his God. But he worked on, and he sustained. He was the most heroic of all the reformers.

In the autumn of 1536, Calvin made his name and convinced Farel of the wisdom of his choice, not in Geneva but in Lausanne, along the lake. The people of Lausanne were considering joining the Reformation, and a great public debate had been arranged. Farel, his colleague Pierre Viret and Calvin were to put the case for reform; the local clergy were to defend the status quo. Calvin made a stunning intervention during the debate, one that swung the argument and persuaded the citizens of Lausanne to join the Reformation. But, back in Geneva, the work of reform did not progress smoothly. Farel was a disputatious man and was always arguing, not just with Calvin but with everybody. Hostility to Farel grew rapidly, and he was expelled from the city in 1538. Calvin, his associate, had to leave with him.

Calvin now moved to the reformed city of Strasbourg, his original destination. He became pastor to the large French community, about 500 strong, and he also worked as a tutor, helping the lodgers in his house. He again demonstrated his gift for friendship by forming a close and affable alliance with Martin Bucer, a peace-loving former Dominican friar who had become one of the most distinguished reformers. Bucer masterminded the reformation in Strasbourg, and from him Calvin learned much about how to organise a Protestant city state.

Bucer performed a further service. He found a wife for Calvin, Idelette de Bure, the widow of an Anabaptist from Liège. Calvin, with wry self-mockery, noted that, as one who was so strongly opposed to celibacy, he should really marry. He also wanted a housekeeper and someone to look after his health, which always troubled him. There seems to have been no great romance in the relationship, which was arranged swiftly; the marriage took place just a few months after Idelette was widowed. But there was genuine companionship: Calvin described Idelette as 'his best companion'. She bore him three children, but they all died shortly after childbirth. When she died in 1549, Calvin was desolate.

Bucer also introduced Calvin to Philip Melanchthon, the most prominent and the most gracious of Luther's close followers. Calvin, a reserved man, came out of his shell during his time at Strasbourg. He was certainly not living the life of a private, reclusive scholar which had been his ideal when he had set out to Strasbourg before being diverted to Geneva. He became one of the leading figures in the city. But it was a settled city, and he could avoid disputation and conflict, which always exhausted him.

He took part in various – highly civilised – disputes and discussions which Bucer organised with Catholic theologians. He was always debating and preaching, and he thoroughly enjoyed the stimulus of discussion with Bucer and Melanchthon and many other reformers. Calvin was a man who could never be happy in the conventional sense; but, in his three years at Strasbourg, he reached a pleasing level of contentment.

Then, with a certain grim inevitability, he was pulled back to Geneva. In 1540, leading citizens of the lakeside city pleaded with him to return. Calvin was reluctant, in a slightly self-regarding way. He felt that, in Geneva, he had been mistreated and insulted. He told friends that he had been 'wretched' there, whereas he was at ease in Strasbourg, more so than at any other time in his life; and this made him contemplate his previous life in Geneva with something akin to horror. His own words were: 'There is no place under heaven I am more afraid of than Geneva.' This looked like posturing; it was certainly somewhat precious. Nevertheless, his fear of life in Geneva was genuine enough.

The Reformation was flourishing at Strasbourg, whereas it was under threat in Geneva. Two of the city's pastors had left, and its religious life was in disarray. Duty surely pointed him in the direction of Geneva. When faced with further supplications from the Geneva council, he eventually allowed himself to be persuaded. He realised that he could return on his own terms; he would be in a stronger position than before. He could enforce the discipline he was so keen on; he could control the development of a well-defined and planned reformation within a self-contained unit. So, he succumbed to the blandishments from the council, and the next year he returned, still with apprehension. He had been promised a generous stipend, casks of wine, a comfortable house and a splendid fur-lined robe.

He was to stay in Geneva for the rest of his life. During these years, from 1541 to 1564, he saved the Reformation, not just for Geneva but for all the world.

CHAPTER 13

Calvin and Geneva

$\mathcal{M}$ORE than Zwingli with Zurich, more than Luther with Wittenberg, Calvin and Geneva are inextricably linked. Calvin is not merely associated with Geneva; it became his city, the perfect city of God on earth. Yet his connection with Geneva was far from perfect. His long ministry there was often troubled. When he died in 1564, he was bitter. On his deathbed, he repined. He recalled that the citizens of Geneva had turned their dogs on him; they had even fired shots at him.

Geneva became the centre of the second, crucial, phase of the European Reformation, and it was where a unique experiment in Christian living was carried through, presided over by this austere genius who was both a tireless social organiser and an inspired preacher. In some ways, the perfect city of God was, to the modern sensibility, a horrible place, full of snoopers and officious moralists, a kind of honeypot for puritanical do-gooders. But, looking round our contemporary cities in the early twenty-first century, surveying the state they are in, are such admonitions not a little simplistic?

What Calvin created, at colossal cost to himself, may seem to the contemporary mindset something repressive and narrow; but it can, and in my view should, be regarded as a noble experiment in godliness on earth, a sustained attempt at better living. Furthermore, it was democratic, and it was, in the very best sense of a much-abused word, aspirational. Central to it was a sophisticated notion of social welfare. Its historical significance can hardly be exaggerated; it became the model for reformers everywhere.

Geneva, then and now, is a city blessed with a sublime physical situation, on the southernmost shores of one of Europe's most gorgeous stretches of water. It is surrounded by meadows and, immediately beyond, high peaks. A little to the south-east is the magnificent natural cathedral of Mont Blanc, Europe's highest mountain.

In Calvin's day, it was a middling city with a population of about 10,000 souls (that is, about one-thirtieth the size of Paris). The numbers grew by several thousand in the 1550s when word of Calvin's ministry spread, and Geneva became a sanctuary. The city was fortified, and its walls protected it against the world. The professional class lived up on the hill, around the great cathedral of St Pierre, with the poorer folk all around them on lower ground.

It was a self-contained republic once it had shaken off the sway of the Duke of Savoy. A significant town, then – not big, but sizeable enough to be cramped within its walls. A strategic town, set astride a frontier; a town that was to become a refuge for thousands fleeing persecution. A beautiful place, at the head of a vast, exquisite lake. And a place that became wholly dominated by a driven genius who was an incomer – a foreigner who did not even have a vote.

When he arrived for his second, and momentous, stay in Geneva in September 1541, the city council had given Calvin the authority to build an organised Christian community on his own blueprint. Calvin immediately set about the task with zeal, basing his plans partly on what he had seen in Bucer's Strasbourg. But Martin Bucer was a moderate, charismatic and slightly soft leader; Calvin was a man of steel, the ultimate ascetic. Calvin told the city fathers that he was going to banish crimes and debaucheries. He told them that the real enemies of the Gospel were not heretics or tyrants but just bad Christians. His simple aim was to make everyone in the city a good Christian.

His structure was based on four groups: the pastors, the doctors, the elders and the deacons. The function of the Church and its personnel was to preach the Gospel, to administer the sacraments, to teach the faith, to care for the afflicted, and – crucially – to train people in Christian living.

The pastor was to preach, and also to teach, and to help to uphold the laws of the city council. The pastors were to meet weekly and to have larger meetings quarterly for mutual examination; those guilty of serious infringements would be referred to the council. The pastors, significantly, were subject to the civil law.

The doctors were to be teachers, instructing the people in doctrine. Two professors were specifically employed to expound the Gospel; schoolmasters were to teach the young, in separate schools for boys and girls.

The elders, the most interesting group, were to be lay people chosen by the city magistrates. They were to enforce discipline. They and the pastors comprised the consistory, the key court (there were at first twelve elders and just five pastors, so the laymen were in the majority). The elders were to watch over the lives of everyone and to 'admonish in love' those who were erring or living disorderly lives.

The consistory met once a week to deal with miscreants Serious offenders were to be reported to the city council and excluded from communion, yet clemency was to be exercised as much as possible; the overall aim was always to bring sinners back to the Lord, not to punish unnecessarily. It was not until 1555 that the consistory acquired the historic right to excommunicate of its own authority. Until then, the magistrates retained this right. Excommunication was a severe punishment; it generally entailed banishment from the city.

As well as dealing with sinners, the consistory acted as a forum for reconciliation, trying to evolve disputes between citizens. In its decisions, the consistory took no account of an individual's standing. It did not distinguish between prominent citizens and those at the bottom of the social scale; all were equal before it. The deacons were to look after the poor, the needy, the old and the infirm. They organised poor relief and looked after the sick, both in and out of hospital. This seemed straightforward enough – but the council and Calvin had many disputes about the control of the deacons.

Calvin's aim was straightforward, if ambitious; he wanted to create a perfect Christian community where everyone looked after everyone else. This was obviously a decent aspiration; the all-too-apparent downside was that people's faults and sins, large and small, were to be reported and discussed publicly. But at least this applied to everybody; none was so grand or so important that he would not be subject to the community's discipline.

But Geneva became a city devoid of privacy, a city where spontaneity was curbed and excess was reviled. There was, without doubt, an element of the surveillance society; snooping must have been a part of everyday life in Calvin's Geneva. Calvin knew that such rigours would be difficult to enforce; he understood that the dutiful pastors would be abused and exposed to insult and slander. Enemies of Calvin, both at the time and later, felt that all this was too repressive. History has not been kind to Calvin, and indeed the great French novelist Balzac much later accused him of a religious terrorism which was worse than the most abominable excesses of the French Revolution.

And yet, at the heart of the structure he created was the ideal of democracy. Calvin was not an autocrat. He always believed in election rather than appointment. He always believed that those in authority should be judged and assessed by others in a formal and well-understood way. He himself always tried to be flexible, to be kind, to be understanding of human frailty and weakness. His desire was to create a true community of faith, with everyone helping each other.

He was more than a religious reformer; he reformed socially, morally, politically, culturally. He persuaded the council to legislate against adultery, prostitution, pornography, gambling, drunkenness and much else. He oversaw free schooling, and he worked to improve public hygiene and health, though good health continued to elude him personally. He helped to stimulate the city's industries, in particular the cloth industry and the nascent printing industry.

What he could not tolerate was imperfect faith. He thought there was nothing more execrable than an individual making up his mind about what he should believe. By modern lights, Calvin was an enemy of freedom. Yet he sincerely believed that he was providing perfect freedom.

What is indisputable about all this is that it became the model for many other reformers. The Reformation had burst forth in explosive, almost anarchic style. Calvin, a man who detested disorder, created order.

Human beings are messy, selfish and indulgent. They also have an inbuilt capacity to resist authority. Calvin's system certainly encountered resistance. Many of the people of Geneva felt that he was pushing them too hard. He certainly pushed himself hard. Often, he would eat just one meal a day. He suffered from many ailments, including migraines, gallstones, colic, piles and asthma. Worst of all was the gout, the pain of which was almost impossible to bear.

He slept only four hours a night; his waking hours were dominated more than anything by his colossal correspondence. He kept four secretaries continually at work with his fluent dictation. He despised flattery, and asked his friends and associates to point out his faults. He set a severe and constant example – and this annoyed weaker men.

In the late 1540s, the resistance became organised. The disaffection was partly about power: Calvin had become over-powerful. Although he was an incomer, an employee of the city state, who could be fired or driven away at a moment's notice, he had acquired enormous influence. By the sheer force of his personality, by his consistently eloquent preaching, by his scrupulous round-the-clock ministry, he had amassed immense personal authority. But, of course, some in the 'perfect city' were irked by the constant discipline, the relentless straining for purity.

Here are just two examples of what irritated people. The taverns, the drinking shops, were transformed into peculiar religious public houses. Everyone had to say grace before imbibing. There was to be a Bible on every table, and psalms were to be sung. Unsurprisingly, this experiment did not succeed, and the taverns returned to what they had been pre-Calvin. A second issue that irked the ordinary citizens was Calvin's officiousness about Christian names. He actually drew up a list of proscribed names, including Jesus. This kind of control made the citizenry restive.

There was also a racist element to the rebelliousness. Calvin seemed to favour Frenchmen. As persecution became more and more brutal in France, Geneva became a significant sanctuary. Thousands of Frenchmen fled to the city on the hill by the lake. Many of them were wealthy, capable, professional people. A new class of superior French exiles seemed to be gaining overmuch sway in the city. This exacerbated the tensions between Calvin and the council, and the opposition to Calvin coalesced into something strong and bitter. Eventually, he offered his resignation – but it was refused. The council resented him and wanted to control him; but they did not want to lose him. Unpopular as he was, he had rendered himself indispensable.

The key to his remarkable sway lay in his preaching. Although he was a severe man, his preaching style was intimate and engaging. Although his delivery was sometimes fierce and angry, the manner was less fiery than might have been expected. The sermons were always lucid and accessible to everybody. The ordinary people could understand him. He never talked down. In his preaching, as in everything else, he did not spare himself. He preached twice, sometimes three times, on Sundays and once every Monday, Wednesday and Friday.

Comparisons have been drawn with the preaching of Savonarola in Florence in the 1490s. Like Calvin, Savonarola preached with consistent power, which gave him near-mastery over a great city. But Calvin was more of an organiser than Savonarola – and, although his preaching was the very centre of his ministry, he burdened himself with an infinity of other tasks. It has been calculated that, in the decade of the 1550s, he officiated at about 300 weddings and about fifty baptisms.

Because he set such superhuman standards of commitment, not all his colleagues could keep up with him. He found some of them vain, unreliable and envious. We have seen that he was surprisingly good at friendship; but he also made enemies. John Knox, who was at Geneva in the late 1550s, was unusual in that Calvin seemed to regard him as neither a good friend nor an enemy.

Among those with whom Calvin quarrelled was Sebastian Castellio, a boorish but very clever teacher. The two men squabbled over the interpretation of Scripture. Calvin had him banished in 1544. Another enemy was his compatriot Jean Bolsec, who disliked Calvin's predestination theology and was expelled from the city in 1551. In doctrinal matters, Calvin was stubborn and a feisty fighter for what he regarded as the truth. He also had to face down many opponents on the city council, although on the whole these enemies did not want rid of Calvin; they just wanted to exercise some control over their spiritual leader.

At one point, when Calvin despaired of those around him, he asked Farel, now based in Neuchâtel, to return to Geneva. His relationship with Farel was tempestuous, but overall Calvin regarded him as a friend, and he understood that Farel would give him honest support. Farel declined, but he and Calvin corresponded amicably. The final falling-out did not come until the 69-year-old Farel married a girl aged 17. Calvin found this repugnant. But Farel continued to admire the man whom he had bullied into committing to Geneva all those years previously – and, when his young wife bore him a son, he was named after Calvin.

Calvin's dominance in the city was a fact for many years, but it was not until 1557 that the council at last agreed to endorse his missions abroad, and it was even later that Calvin became an official citizen with civic rights. In his last years, Calvin, having seen off almost all dissent, went too far. The consistory became all-powerful; the council was bypassed. Enforcement grew ever tougher; admonition 'in love' became a creed of the past, and whippings became commonplace. Banishments were frequent and perhaps came as a relief to some.

Behaviour improved, and so did public health and educational standards and church attendance – but at what cost?

Meanwhile, Calvin was ever more concerned with the world beyond his own godly community. Deep down, he much preferred sending missionaries out from Geneva to receiving refugees in. Himself an immigrant, he was conscious that a wall-enclosed city, already bursting with incomers, was not the best place to receive a further influx of immigrants, however talented. There were bound to be tensions. More importantly, he wanted to send his people out to spread his message throughout Europe. He was desperately keen to send pastors to help the Reformation where it was under threat, not least in his own homeland to the west. A vast underground network, complete with safe houses and messengers, was established across eastern France.

By the late 1550s, there were about 2,000 fully reformed congregations in France, and many of them were operating under constant threat of persecution. Calvin sent agents to help them. But his emissaries went well beyond France, indeed all over Europe, and they were assiduous in sending reports back to Geneva. In return, Calvin sent out yet more propaganda.

Calvin sometimes intervened directly in France's national politics. This, more than anything, gave rise to the myth that he was Geneva's absolute ruler, a man of equal standing with kings, queens and princes. The French Protestants, by now known as Huguenots, looked to him as their leader in exile. Calvin was willing to organise rebellious agitations in France. In 1560, he directed a plot to depose Catherine de Medici from her regency and to allow the Huguenot titular king of Navarre to become king of all France. This spectacularly misfired when Antony of Navarre, a weak man, decided to support Catherine, and the plot fizzled out.

Calvin required many printers for his evangelical propaganda. He enthusiastically encouraged the existing printers in Geneva, and the city became a major printing centre, helped by an influx of Huguenot printers from Paris. Evangelical tracts and Calvin's own works –

notably the *Institutes*, translated into French – flooded into France and further afield. One of Calvin's key allies was the printer Henri Estienne, son of the printer to King Francis I of France, who had settled in Geneva. Books and pamphlets were even smuggled into Spain, the original home of the Inquisition (the Catholic Church's most notorious method of eliminating heresy) and a country where the authorities were always on the lookout for subversive reformed literature. Because of the huge outpouring of printed material, there was a shortage of paper, and the city had to start a new industry: papermaking. It is often forgotten that Calvin made Geneva prosperous; it became a boom town.

He required more and more teachers. The academy of Geneva, founded by Calvin in 1559, was an enormous success. In 1559, there were just 160 students; five years later, there were more than 1,500. By now, the academy was a proper university, presided over by Theodore Beza, a man who was utterly loyal to Calvin but was a more affable person. Beza had taught Greek at the nearby university of Lausanne; teacher recruitment in Geneva was helped when there was a dispute at that institution, and Beza and Calvin managed to poach some of the better staff from the university along the lake.

Many of the graduates from Calvin's university became missionaries, brave and resourceful exponents of the Geneva message. Indeed, this was one of the most important aspects of Calvin's work. He was an internationalist, much concerned with outreach. The academy became a training centre for missionary reformers who moved, sometimes openly, sometimes surreptitiously, all across Europe.

Calvin's Geneva was a masterpiece of control and organisation; at the same time, it was a deeply controversial experiment. Yet there was just one episode which has produced pretty well universal condemnation, and this was the execution of one Michael Servetus. A controversial theologian and physician, he was a brilliant maverick, and he may have discovered the circulation of the blood before Harvey did. Before his arrival in Geneva, Servetus had conducted an irascible correspondence with Calvin on various theological questions. Calvin could not resist replying to all correspondents, even with all his other tasks; it might have been better if he had simply ignored the Spaniard, who was a persistent troublemaker. And Servetus certainly got under Calvin's skin; Calvin told his old colleague Farel that, if Servetus came to Geneva, he would not depart alive.

Servetus was nothing if not bold – and, when he had to flee from France, he made Geneva his destination. Immediately on arrival, he went to hear Calvin preach. This was foolhardy defiance, though perhaps Servetus, aware that Calvin was none too popular, may have ingenuously thought that the dissidents would rally round him and allow him to lead the opposition. He was recognised and arrested. At his trial, he insisted on attacking Calvin, calling him evil, a sorcerer, worthless and a twister. He was convicted of heresy and sentenced to death. Calvin asked for him to be beheaded, but Servetus was burned to death. Bizarrely, this unfortunate episode enhanced Calvin's popularity in the city. And other leading reformers backed him, men like Melanchthon and Bullinger.

Servetus was the only person executed for religious opinions during Calvin's ministry; and it was the city council, not Calvin, who condemned him. Nonetheless, his execution appalled many writers, then and now, who are otherwise disposed to defend Calvin.

Today, Geneva is perhaps the most cosmopolitan city in the world, teeming with diplomats and highly educated personnel working for the many international and humanitarian agencies that are headquartered in the city. Most of these people are very well paid; and, as you walk the streets, you are conscious of two things – a great sense of prosperity and a pervasive, glossy internationalism. It is impossible to be in Geneva for more than an hour or so and not hear several languages being spoken fluently. This contrasts with Zurich, which, although a larger city, is more provincial and introverted.

About twenty times bigger now in terms of population than it was in the sixteenth century, Geneva has spread enormously along the lake and into the surrounding meadows. Only in the upper old town, around the cathedral, is there any sense of what it must have been like in Calvin's day, although there are hardly any buildings extant from his time. In what is now the Rue Calvin, the site of Calvin's house is a government office; Calvin's residence was demolished in 1706. But there are many references to Calvin. You sense – in this part of Geneva, anyway – that the city is more proud of his memory and his legacy than Zurich is of Zwingli's.

Geneva is now more given over to money than to religion. There was only one bank in Calvin's day; now banks are everywhere, This is a place given over to big-time finance as well as to diplomacy. It is a city devoted to what Calvin and Luther would have called usury. There is even an elegant arcade called the 'Passage de la Monnaie'. Yet this might be in one way appropriate to Calvin's legacy, for there is a theory that the reformers of the sixteenth century, and Calvin in particular, unleashed capitalism or at least helped it on its way (see Chapter 29).

The great cathedral of St Pierre dominates the top of the hill, and the narrow streets and alleys and passages around it are particularly quiet on a Sunday morning. It is easy enough then to imagine this area as it must have been in Calvin's day. Though Geneva is now a predominantly Catholic city, the great cathedral remains a Protestant church. Just behind it, in the beautiful Cour St Pierre, is the Maison Maillet, a lovely seventeenth-century building that now houses the excellent International Museum of the Reformation, where the staff are helpful and friendly. In 2007, it won the Council of Europe prize for the best museum in Europe.

The museum's aim is to record what it calls 'the epic history of a movement that was born in sixteenth-century Geneva'. Calvin, often difficult and critical, would probably have approved. In the first of the eleven chambers, the Bible dominates the displays. The great Geneva Bible of 1562 is on show, complete with its promise on the front page that there are 'moste profitable annotations upon all the hard places'. In chamber ten, there are two fine statues by Paul Schoni: one of Luther, one of Calvin. Visitors carefully study the faces of the two great reformers. Calvin's face is stern, narrow and intense; Luther's is much fleshier and altogether more kindly-looking. Both men are declaiming, but Calvin looks as if he will brook no argument, while Luther looks as if he is eager to help the listener. Even in Geneva, Luther seems better liked.

A little further round by the back of the cathedral is another lovely but very austere building, the Auditoire. Built on a site where Christian worship has taken place over seventeen centuries, it was used by Calvin, and it was at his suggestion that it was given over to the exiled English congregation, to whom John Knox ministered for a time. The building was completely renovated in the 1950s with funds from the World Alliance of Reformed Churches. Today, the Auditoire is used by Geneva's Church of Scotland congregation for their services each Sunday.

Down the hill from the atmospheric old town, a little to the west and not far from the confluence of two fine rivers, the Rhone and the fast-flowing Arve, is the slightly grubby Rue des Rois. Halfway along it is the entrance to the discreet cemetery of Plain Palais. In the farthest corner from the entrance, among trees and near the boundary wall, and surrounded by more grandiose graves, is an obscure rectangle. It is surrounded by a little metal fence, less than two feet high, which guards the neatly tended grave on which, peculiarly, a thick and well-trimmed hedge grows. A tiny plaque tells the visitor that this is the grave of the French reformer Jean Calvin.

When I visited the cemetery, there were only four other visitors. They were all making for a grave near Calvin's, which turned out to be that of the twentieth-century Argentinian novelist and poet Jorge Luis Borges. While they paid homage at his grave, I stood a few yards away by Calvin's, wondering at the long struggle of this tormented man, so zealous in extirpating corruption, superstition and immorality, and still so influential in the intellectual as well as the religious life of the modern world, a man so resolute in trying to create the perfect city of God on earth. Surely no Christian pastor or minister has ever striven harder and demanded more of himself. Yet, in his lifetime, he never found peace.

I found his modest grave a more fitting place for contemplation than the somewhat showy 'reformation wall' which is over 100 metres long and dominates the north end of the Parc des Bastions in central Geneva. Built into the huge wall are four giant statues of the leading reformers especially associated with Geneva: Farel, Beza, John Knox – and, of course, Calvin. Across the park is a more fitting memorial to Calvin and his colleague and follower Beza: the University of Geneva, which Calvin founded in 1559 and Beza made into one of the cerebral powerhouses of Europe.

But neither a modest grave nor a fine university is the perfect memorial to this heroic man who drove so excruciatingly hard to create a glorious community on earth, a city community where God was worshipped not just in church but also by the way people lived, day in, day out. He failed, but it was not for want of effort.

PART 4

Scotland Pre-Reformation

CHAPTER 14

James V of Scotland

AMES V (1512–42) was an enigmatic monarch, difficult to assess. He could be vainglorious and vindictive; he was something of a showman, maintaining a lavish court; and he affected an empathy for his poorer subjects. He was given to travelling around his kingdom in disguise, listening to what the ordinary folk of Scotland had to say. Carrying out this deceit, he was one day attacked by ruffians near Cramond Brig, on the western approaches to Edinburgh, whereupon he was rescued by a farm labourer called Howieson, who cleaned his wounds. Howieson told James that his ambition was to own the farm on which he worked, Braehead (now the site of a civic dump and recycling facility). The wish was granted, on the condition that Howieson would always be prepared to wash the king's hands at Cramond Brig.

This was typical of James; there was something whimsical about him. But his personal rule was certainly more impressive than the feuding and division that preceded it. At first, he maintained an uneasy peace with his uncle Henry VIII (always a difficult policy to pursue). This was made official in a so-called treaty of perpetual peace in 1534. James was determined to maintain order in his unruly kingdom, and was impressively tough with the anarchic thugs who passed for leaders of men in the Borders. He pursued something of a vendetta against a man called Johnny Armstrong of Gilknockie, a wild but ingenuous freebooter who was eventually tricked by the duplicitous king. James arranged for a supposedly peaceful parley, to which the naïve Armstrong and his followers turned up unarmed. They were promptly arrested and hanged.

James was an exceptionally greedy king; his main interest in the Church was as a source of revenue. He understood the nature of the Reformation which was sweeping Europe well enough to work out that his orthodoxy, even as a relatively obscure monarch, would impress the pope, who at this time was grateful for support from any quarter. So, he set about exacting a high price for his continuing adherence to Rome. He gained from Pope Clement the authority to tax the Scottish prelates in swingeing style; the monies were supposedly to help him better administer the law. In other words, the pope had to pay him for his loyalty. James also wanted direct control over the Scottish Church; in this, he was not unlike Henry VIII, and there are some suggestions that he may have flirted with the notion of a Scottish version of the Henrician Reformation.

But the main point about him is that his orthodoxy, while lucrative, appears to have been sincere. He seems to have genuinely detested Lutheranism. He personally attended heresy trials, including that of Patrick Hamilton's brother. Yet there were still, in Scotland, relatively few executions for heresy. James was perfectly happy to execute people, including some of the high-born, such as the beautiful Countess of Glamis; but he did not execute many on religious grounds. James had several mistresses, and by them various illegitimate sons; these were placed as titular abbots, and the revenues from the abbeys went directly to the crown.

On the other hand, even James was aware that the level of corruption in the Church was unacceptable. In 1540, at Linlithgow Palace, he had watched an early performance of the satirical play by Sir David Lindsay, *The Three Estates*. Among other targets, Lindsay satirised the immorality and presumptuous power-plays of the clergy, particularly the senior clergy. After the performance, James lectured various Scottish bishops, telling them to reform their ways, or else he would send them to the tender care of Henry VIII in England. This was no doubt a jest, but it was a menacing one.

The following year, the Scottish Parliament passed various acts specifically endorsing the old faith and making it a capital crime to impugn the authority of the pope. At the same time, one act specifically exhorted all 'archbishops, ordinaries and every prelate and kirkman' to reform themselves 'in habit and manners to God and man'.

Despite this awareness of the need for reform, James himself was excessively influenced by David Beaton, the nephew of Archbishop Beaton who had presided over the death of Patrick Hamilton. Beaton, who was James's equivalent of Cardinal Wolsey and eventually became a cardinal himself, was not a man to fret about reforming the Church in Scotland. He was neither pious nor scrupulous. He had much grander concerns than the condition of the Church in Scotland. These were mainly diplomatic, for he maintained a remarkable range of contacts in France: he held a French bishopric in Languedoc and the ear of the French king, Francis I. He was rather bitterly known as 'the best Frenchman in Scotland'. He was determined to keep Scotland free of what he called 'the pollution of Anglican impiety'.

Beaton had personally negotiated the marriage of James to Francis's daughter Madeleine; their very showy wedding took place at Notre Dame in Paris on the first day of 1537. This was quite a coup. But Madeleine was sickly, and she died shortly after the wedding. Undaunted, Beaton turned his attention to Mary of Lorraine, a leading member of the powerful Guise family. One of her brothers was the Cardinal Duke of Lorraine, a zealous persecutor of French Protestants; another was the Duke of Guise. The Guises were the most puffed-up family in France, with influence spreading in all spheres and directions. Mary knew all about politics, intrigue and diplomacy. She was a formidable woman; and she was to play a pivotal role in Scotland's history. The marriage negotiations were complex, and the settlement was generous to both sides. The king received a lavish payout; in return, Mary was granted an exceptional collection of gifts including three castles (Stirling, Threave and Dingwall) and various earldoms and lordships, including the lordship of the Isles.

These two marriages, to Madeleine and then Mary, clearly signalled that James, and therefore Scotland, was reviving the Auld Alliance, which obviously would not please the irascible old king south of the Border. James was also making it clear that he was a strong supporter of the papacy; indeed, the pope had specifically rewarded him for his marriage to Madeleine. So much for perpetual peace with England.

Any Scottish alliance with France was bound to be a dangerous policy internally. There are always Scots on the make; and those who were around in the late 1530s and 1540s noted what happened to the monasteries in England. There was now considerable secular greed for religious property. Some Scots were looking south, at the example of Henry VIII; and their gaze was not necessarily disapproving. Indeed, it was becoming increasingly difficult for many Scots, patriotic Scots and self-serving Scots, far-sighted Scots and selfish Scots, to understand a policy that appeared to involve subservience to Catholicism, to the scheming and ambitious Beaton and to the French. To compound this, the Scottish king seemed to have little understanding of the heretical stirrings in the east of his kingdom – stirrings that appealed to at least some of his nobility.

Henry VIII was no doubt aware of these tensions, and in 1541 he decided to try to smash James's religious orthodoxy – in other words, to get him to break with Rome, just as he himself had. He invited James to a 'summit' at York, where the two kings would discuss their religious differences. But James did not travel south. After all, he was an ally of the king of France and of the pope; and he was receiving ever-growing income from the Church. What could Henry offer instead?

This was a grave misjudgement, as events in 1542 were to prove. Henry VIII was now plotting another war with France – the France with which Scotland was ever more closely linked. During the summer, the Holy Roman Empire declared war on France; Henry, sensing an opportunity to sort out the Scots while the French were diverted, began to make obvious preparations for war against his nephew in the north. After various skirmishes, a major English force under that ancient soldier the Duke of Norfolk – perhaps as many as 25,000 men – crossed the Border and wrought havoc around Kelso and Roxburgh. But Norfolk, always cautious, was running out of supplies. He withdrew. After some manoeuvring, James managed to muster a considerable if not a great army. The troops encamped in the area of Lochmaben, near Dumfries. An advance raiding party under the command of Lord Maxwell, the grandly named Warden of the West March, moved across the Border, although hereabouts the actual line of the Border was not clear.

What happened next – the Battle of Solway Moss – was not a national disaster on the scale of Flodden; it was, however, an episode of considerable ignominy, even by the standards of Scotland's debacle-littered history. Maxwell's leadership was in question; the king's favourite Oliver Sinclair was insisting that he was to take command. The ill-led Scottish force found itself probably in England but only just. More to the point, they were on totally the wrong kind of ground – marshy land by the estuary of the River Esk – as a smaller English force under Sir Thomas Wharton advanced. The Scots became trapped between the English and the estuary.

Some of Maxwell's men stood their ground and fought; some drowned; many others fled. An English witness, Sir William Musgrave, said that Maxwell and those alongside him 'fought valiantly'. The Scots casualties were not high, but the defeat was humiliating, particularly as the Scots had been confronted by a lesser English force. Some escaping Scottish soldiers were said to have given themselves up to English women working in distant fields.

There have been attempts to put a religious tinge on the fiasco. It has been suggested that a number of the Scots had Protestant sympathies and were not prepared to die in effect for France and Catholicism and the pope rather than for Scotland. Further, they would be fighting against good English Protestants. This is probably fanciful; what is inescapably true is that, just eighteen years later, a young English queen sent both her army and her navy north to help the Scots drive the French out of their country once and for all, thus securing the Scottish Reformation. But, in those intervening eighteen years, there was to be a great deal of grisly mayhem in both Scotland and England.

James V had apparently watched Scotland's latest military disaster from a distant hill before retreating north. John Knox, writing later, claimed that James consoled himself by consorting with a high-born whore. Meanwhile, James's French queen, Mary of Guise, was about to give birth. A girl was born on 8 December who was to become the most controversial monarch in Scotland's long history – a woman who divides historians and the ordinary people of Scotland to this very day.

Six days after the birth of his daughter, James died, probably of cholera, though there are those who insist that he had some kind of nervous breakdown. He was just 30. He had certainly driven himself hard and had imposed a kind of order on the wilder parts of his turbulent kingdom; but, in retrospect, his pro-French stance looks misguided, though his widow Mary of Guise was in time to prove an effective and reasonably benign ruler of Scotland. In his religious policy, he had been both rapacious and deeply conservative. No Reformation for him.

CHAPTER 15

Rough Wooing

*A*FTER the debacle of Solway Moss and the death of James V, Scotland found itself unsettled and unsafe. Henry VIII failed to take the opportunity to annex Scotland after the Scots' defeat, though he could probably have done so with relative ease – just as he could have done after Flodden twenty-nine years earlier. On the other hand, while it might be easy enough to take Scotland by military force, to keep the country subdued would be a very different matter. And the French might come to Scotland's aid, though their support could never be guaranteed.

The old king was for a time quite conciliatory. He repatriated various members of the Scottish nobility who had been captured in the aftermath of Solway Moss. They were to form a broadly Protestant and pro-England faction at the centre of Scottish affairs. In 1543, the Scottish Parliament made the Earl of Arran (who was reputedly a secret Protestant) regent and governor for the infant Queen Mary.

James IV and James V had been relatively strong monarchs. Now a baby was the successor to the throne – and a female baby at that. It had been more than 150 years since an adult had succeeded to the Scottish throne; but the situation in 1543 was unusually dangerous and problematic. Much would depend on the regent. Unfortunately, Arran was an inexperienced and irresolute man who underestimated

Scotland's still considerable capacity for Anglophobia. Arran flirted with reform, and convinced among others the young John Knox, who later wrote of Arran as being the most fervent Protestant in Europe. That seems absurd. He was very weak in the actual implementation of religious reform.

For a brief period, the Scottish Parliament veered towards Protestantism, just as Henry VIII south of the Border appeared to be veering away from it. The Parliament actually sanctioned ownership and reading of the Bible in the vernacular, which in almost all cases did not mean Scots but rather Tyndale's English translation of the New Testament. Meanwhile, Henry wanted the Scots to renounce the Auld Alliance with France once and for all, and to send the infant Queen Mary south to England for safekeeping. He also wanted Mary to be betrothed to his only son, Edward, who was only five years older than Mary. At least some of these demands were duly endorsed in the double-headed Treaty of Greenwich.

But it did not take long for the Scottish Parliament to repudiate the Greenwich agreements and to reassert the alliance with France. It could be argued that, at this point in Scotland's always complex history, the nationalist tendency tilted towards France rather than England, and thus to Catholicism rather than Protestantism. As far as Henry was concerned, the Scots were double-dealers, practitioners of a rascally duplicity.

The scrapping of the Greenwich accords rendered two prominent Catholics the most influential people in Scotland. These were Mary of Guise – the Queen Dowager, James V's widow, and mother of the infant queen – and Cardinal David Beaton of St Andrews. Beaton, who had arranged Mary's marriage to James, was briefly imprisoned by Arran. After his release, he was soon presiding over anti-heresy legislation. Where Arran was indecisive and impressionable, Beaton was tough and single-minded.

Beaton's behaviour infuriated the irascible old king in England. In Henry's eyes, it was becoming insolent and provocative. He had a point – but his over-reaction was grotesque. He decided to teach the

Scots the most brutal of lessons. The onslaught launched against Scotland in 1544 unleashed a heinous series of war crimes. This was the conflict described by first the Earl of Huntly and later Sir Walter Scott as the 'rough wooing' – though the adjective 'rough', intended to be ironic, is in the context a very sick misnomer, for Scotland was subjected to an unremittingly savage invasion.

The senior English general, the Earl of Hertford, was instructed among other things to 'sack Leith and burn and subvert it and all the rest putting man woman and child to fire and sword without exception where any resistance may be made against you'. Such 'extremities and destructions' were then to be visited on 'all towns', and Hertford was to spend a month spoiling and burning. Obviously, such tactics (which were enthusiastically carried out despite some misgivings on Hertford's part) were hardly likely to assist those Scots who were sincerely disposed to a pro-England, pro-Protestant policy.

After the initial sustained savagery, the war scaled down to the sort of intermittent Border raiding which had debilitated Anglo–Scottish relations for centuries. The Scots generally came off worse, though in 1545 they won an unlikely victory at Ancrum Moor near Jedburgh. Meanwhile, Beaton and Mary of Guise could only benefit from the devastating assault unleashed by the English king. Yet Beaton's position was not strong. What was the point of a pro-French policy if the French were either unwilling or unable to defend the Scots in their time of grave need?

Beaton exemplified the corruption of the old Church in spectacular style. He had amassed huge wealth through his various ecclesiastical positions, and he had fathered twenty illegitimate children. Such a man was unlikely to win hearts and minds in Scotland at this volatile time when reform was stirring. The English were sending the occasional Protestant preacher north to Scotland, and they were flooding the country with Protestant tracts and English Bibles.

Someone who could undoubtedly win hearts and minds was George Wishart, an eloquent and charismatic reformer who was by far the most important of the precursors of John Knox. Beaton's downfall came after he over-reached himself and presided over the arrest and killing of this exceptional man.

Beaton claimed that George Wishart was an English agent. It is true that Wishart had spent time in England; he had been arrested in Bristol after delivering a particularly radical sermon at St Nicholas Church. He was interrogated by Archbishop Thomas Cranmer, and he made a partial recantation. He then visited Zurich before returning to England. He studied at Corpus Christi College, Cambridge, and eventually returned to Scotland in 1543.

Theologically, Wishart is significant because he had moved away from Lutheranism towards a more Swiss version of reformation. He always stressed the primacy of Scripture. He is particularly important in our story because he was the first Scottish reformer who could attract big crowds. He did not, however, achieve in his lifetime the status of a national figure as Knox was to do. Wishart's preaching tours were in specific areas – mainly Ayrshire, Angus, Fife and East Lothian. He does not seem to have attracted an organised following that would have posed an immediate danger to Beaton. Yet his evangelism was popular and powerful. When he did not have access to a church, he preached in the open air. For a time, his 'bodyguard' was none other than John Knox, who walked before him carrying a great sword.

Knox had been brought up in East Lothian and had studied, probably at St Andrews. He became a Catholic priest. Then he switched to the law, becoming a notary, only to change course again, working as a tutor to the sons of lairds who were sympathetic to Protestantism. It was through these lairds that he met Wishart.

In 1546, Beaton finally moved against Wishart, who was arrested at Haddington and then subjected to a travesty of a trial for heresy at St Andrews Cathedral. Beaton could not suppress his adversary's eloquence and had to clear the 'court' before the inevitable verdict of guilty was pronounced. There was a strongly political element in the proceedings, since Wishart was reputed to have associated with

English agents. The trial was also, for Beaton, seriously counter-productive. He was seen as a bully. The excessive use of force made him appear weak rather than strong. Many Scots came to believe that it was Beaton who was the ultimate author of all the terrible travails suffered during the 'rough wooing'.

Wishart was subjected by Beaton to the kind of cruel death that Patrick Hamilton had suffered in the same town eighteen years earlier. He was semi-strangled, and then, half-dead, he was burned at the castle. Sachets of gunpowder had been inserted into his clothing to make his death even more explosively entertaining for the onlooking Beaton and his entourage of sycophantic clerics.

Wishart's martyrdom was to be explosive in more ways than one. As with Hamilton, his death was more useful to the Protestant cause than his life, though Wishart's martyrdom was on an altogether different scale. It was now clear that there could be no spiritual freedom in Scotland if men like Beaton were in power. Wishart's dignity and grace also helped the Protestant cause. According to Knox's later account, he exhorted the onlookers 'to love the word of God, your salvation, and suffer patiently, with a comfortable heart, for the word's sake, which is your undoubted salvation and everlasting comfort'. Again according to Knox, the executioner bent to his knees and asked Wishart to forgive him. Wishart called him over, kissed him, and forgave him.

The backlash against Beaton, while understandable, was itself violent and savage, and the motivation of those who stabbed him to death in St Andrews Castle three months after Wishart's death was complex. Possibly there was an element of English conspiracy in the murder, for Henry VIII regarded the cardinal as one of his most bitter enemies. The thugs who stormed St Andrews Castle at the end of May 1546 (disguised as stonemasons and building workers) were not low-born ruffians. They were, rather, the leaders of the local rural community: lairds and the sons of lairds. Several of them had personal grievances against the overweening Beaton which had to do with disputes over land and money. The murderers were hardly religious zealots; nor were they motivated by anti-French feeling.

The murder of Beaton was brutal. It may have been witnessed by his current mistress, Marion Ogilvy, who was certainly in his bed shortly before his death. (Knox was later to have some sarcastic sport with this.) The cardinal's genitals were rammed into his mouth, his body was hung by one of his feet from a high window in the castle, and then it was pickled and dumped in the castle dungeon.

There then followed one of the more peculiar episodes in Scotland's turbulent history. The hooligans who had butchered Beaton barricaded themselves into the castle, which became a sort of symbolic redoubt of the pro-English, pro-Protestant tendency. But the English showed no interest in coming to relieve the murderers, who were effectively under siege. And the siege lasted for over a year, though access to the castle was relatively easy. What transpired was a kind of absurd extended stand-off. One of those who joined the murderers was Knox. He had approved of Beaton's killing, but he can hardly have approved of the company he was now keeping, though he became a sort of unofficial chaplain to them.

Knox was by now unashamedly a Protestant, and a militant one at that. Under the powerful and charismatic influence of Wishart, he had completely shed his allegiance to the old Church. He had the status of a deacon; he was not a preacher. Nonetheless, he was persuaded to preach in St Andrews – to both the townsfolk and the scholars at the university. His sermon was a fiery rant, an unequivocal and ferociously forceful denial of the authority of the Roman Catholic Church. Aware that he was addressing, among others, learned men, Knox said that he was prepared to engage in debate, where he would produce scriptural backing for all that he had uttered. Some who heard his powerful sermon noted that Wishart himself had never spoken like this.

Meanwhile, the informal siege continued. Eventually, in the middle of 1547, the new French king, Henry II, was persuaded by Mary of Guise to end the protracted stalemate. He sent a naval expeditionary force to St Andrews. It bombarded the castle from the sea; and the murderers surrendered, a good fourteen months after the cardinal's death. The high-born killers were taken to genteel captivity in France; the more low-born hangers-on, including Knox, were sentenced to serve (for life) as galley slaves.

France was at the time a superpower. Her galleys were everywhere – in the North Sea, in the Mediterranean, in the Baltic. The galley slaves were chained, and the galley master would lash with his whip those who were not rowing strongly enough. The cannon was mounted at the bow; and, when the galleys were engaged in battle, the casualties were very high.

Luckily, for himself and for Scotland, Knox did not serve on the galleys for life. He was freed after just a year and a half. But those months took a grievous toll on his body, if not his spirit. One of Knox's finest biographers, Lord Eustace Percy, noted that 'a sedentary dominie does not find himself dumped on a rowing bench in rough company without suffering acutely'. He also notes that Knox was always modest about the torments he sustained on the galleys.

Knox's release came because of developments in both France and England. In France, the betrothal of the young Scottish Queen Mary to the heir to the French throne, a betrothal that was largely negotiated by the increasingly influential Mary of Guise, eased French anger with their Scottish prisoners; and in England, a year or so after the death of Henry VIII, there were diplomatic moves to restore some kind of political amity with France. During Knox's slavery on the galleys, the 'rough wooing' had slowly petered out, but not before the largest Scottish force mustered since Flodden had been comprehensively routed at Pinkie Cleugh, a few miles east of Edinburgh.

Henry VIII had died in January 1547; his heir and successor was his nine-year-old son Edward, a weak and ailing child. The English protector, the boy-king's uncle the Duke of Somerset, was determined that Edward should marry the young Queen of Scots. He totally failed to understand the sway that Mary of Guise now had over Scottish affairs. Like Henry, Somerset decided that force would do where diplomacy had failed. In September, Somerset led an army of 17,000 men, including 4,000 cavalry, across the Border. It engaged the (numerically far superior) Scots army on 8 September. The Scots' greater numbers counted for nothing in the face of their customary Scottish tactical ineptitude.

Pinkie Cleugh was to be yet another great set-piece battle between the Scots and the English. As usual, the Scots came off worse. Led by the ever-inept Earl of Arran, the Scots lost about 10,000 men; the English about 500. But, despite the crushing defeat, the English gained nothing in their triumph, for Mary Queen of Scots soon married the French Dauphin. Somerset had considerable military skill, but in politics he was no match for Mary of Guise.

Somerset did understand, if imperfectly, that, while it would be easy enough to keep defeating the Scots in battle, it would be less easy to gain long-term control over the turbulent northern country. Anyway, the reality was that, in the mid-sixteenth century, Scotland had become virtually a province of France. Henry VIII's vicious warmongering, Somerset's military aggression and the burgeoning diplomatic craft and cunning of Mary of Guise, by now the central figure in Scottish politics – all these ensured that the Scottish political classes were quite content to become, in effect, vassals of France.

The French king could boast that he held and possessed Scotland with the same authority that he deployed in France itself. All this could be taken to mean that Scotland was firmly tied to the old Church, and that a Scottish Reformation was further off than ever. In fact, it was only a decade away – but what a decade!

CHAPTER 16

Mary of Guise

ISTORY has not been particularly kind to Mary of Guise. She was a key player in the crucial years from 1550 to 1560, arguably the most important decade in Scotland's history. The momentous events of 1559 and 1560 should not allow us to forget that, in the preceding years, she had given Scotland a considerable measure of stability and had practised a pragmatic religious tolerance. When hundreds of Protestants were being burned to death south of the Border during the reign of 'Bloody Mary', Mary of Guise's Scotland saw only a single Protestant martyrdom, that of the 82-year-old Walter Myln.

The vicious persecution in England perhaps, with hindsight, has the effect of making Mary of Guise's rule look more benign and tolerant than it actually was. But Mary, whether she intended it or not, allowed Scotland to be softened up for its eventual Reformation. To put it another way: when John Knox returned permanently to Scotland in May 1559, he was to unleash a revolution; but the ground had been prepared, if accidentally, before his arrival. The skilful, canny and tolerant rule of Mary of Guise made his revolution possible. Over the centuries, Scotland has had many worse rulers than this beautiful and clever French noblewoman.

Mary was born in 1515, the eldest daughter of Claude, Duke of Guise. She received an intense and orthodox Catholic upbringing. Her early life was severe and ascetic; she lived in a convent and was much influenced by her grandmother, the redoubtable Philippa de Gueldres, who was sternly devout. When Mary was almost 15, everything changed. She was removed from the convent and taken to the French court, where she was to learn much about power, diplomacy and dynastic manoeuvring. She was sharp and confident, and she blossomed quickly in this new and far more worldly context. King Francis I liked her and personally arranged her first marriage to the grand chamberlain of France, the Duke of Longueville. This took place in 1534, but within three years the duke was dead.

Mary of Guise was now touted, in the dynastic manner of the times, as a possible bride for Henry VIII of England or James V of Scotland. Neither represented a particularly pleasant prospect to the young widow, but James was marginally more appealing. Mary, evincing her characteristic wit and courage, actually told Henry VIII that her neck was too small for her to marry him. And so she duly married the recently widowed King James of Scotland. As we saw in Chapter 14, the marriage negotiations were skilfully conducted by Cardinal David Beaton, and they marked the cementing of the Auld Alliance – to the immense displeasure of Henry VIII. The new queen arrived in St Andrews in the summer of 1538 and was formally crowned queen of Scotland at Holyrood the next year.

James died shortly after the debacle of Solway Moss in 1542. He left his queen, and a daughter who was just a few days old. This was the future Mary Queen of Scots. But she might also in time become the queen of Ireland, of England and of France. It was the huge dynastic potential of her daughter rather than any personal religious commitment that was to influence Mary's conduct of policy when she ruled Scotland – something she did effectively and well.

No doubt the specific interests of Scotland were well down her priorities; she was motivated first by ambition for her daughter, then by a loyalty to her country, France, then by the particular interests of the Guise family, and fourthly and less importantly by devotion to the Catholic religion. The needs of Scotland came a very poor fifth. Yet she held Scotland together in turbulent times, and her reasonable religious policy allowed Scotland's nascent Protestantism to develop slowly but steadily.

After the Scots' humiliating defeat at Pinkie Cleugh in 1547, Mary quickly ensured that the English were not able to capitalise on their victory. She masterminded the escape of her daughter Mary to France, where she was betrothed to the Dauphin. She played upon the ambitions and the fears of the anti-Catholic Scottish nobility; English soldiers remained in eastern Scotland after Pinkie, and they were hardly popular. Further, Mary arranged for Arran, the leading nobleman and Scotland's governor, to be given a French dukedom (Chatelherault), and in 1550 she led a party of Scots notables, aristocrats and others to France, where they received lavish gifts, inducements and blandishments – that is, bribes.

Arran's rule in Scotland lasted until 1554, though he had long since become little more than a puppet. Mary, having decided to return to Scotland rather than remain with her daughter at the French court, was ever more influential. Early in 1554, she was formally made regent by the Scottish Parliament. When the new queen of England, Mary Tudor, married Philip of Spain in 1554, this presented Mary of Guise with a crisis. If Mary and Philip had children, Mary of Guise's daughter could hardly be regarded as a serious claimant on the English throne. Scotland was now in danger from not just the English but the mighty Spanish too. One of Mary of Guise's tasks was to prepare Scotland against possible Spanish invasion.

On the other hand, the increasingly aggressive anti-Protestant policies of Mary Tudor meant that the pro-English, Protestant faction in the Scottish nobility had a dilemma. It was obviously not the best time to be pro-English. The English monarch was hardly likely to send an army over the Border to assist Scottish Protestants; far more likely was a Spanish incursion to extend Spanish–English imperial, Catholic rule. Mary of Guise used this change to her advantage.

She was notably tolerant to the Scots Protestants – and even the fiery preacher John Knox, whose reputation was rapidly growing on the continent, was allowed to revisit his homeland. He arrived in 1555 from Calvin's Geneva, and he used his visit to enthuse the dispersed Protestant congregations, particularly in Angus and Fife. Significantly, he made contact with leading noblemen who would be his most crucial supporters if he ever returned home for good. Knox also moved among the elite of Edinburgh society and exercised his charm on the ladies, rather as the Ayrshire poet Burns was to do over 200 years later. One of those whom he met was the wife of the dean of guild, Elizabeth Adamson, and he so impressed her that she later created a sensational scene on her deathbed when she told the priests around her to get out, calling them the 'Sergeants of Satan' and yelling that she rejected their 'abominations'.

Knox seems to have moved around the capital as something of a celebrity. He preached wherever he could, and he engaged, as ever, in vehement debate. Another whom he met was Lord James Stewart, Queen Mary's half-brother. It seems that they did not get on particularly well; but Stewart was to become a key ally of Knox's five years later. Was Knox systematically preparing the ground for his eventual permanent return? That is not certain; what is clear is that he influenced many people during the few months of his visit. What is also clear is that he enjoyed the protection of Mary of Guise.

Knox was greatly encouraged by the reforming activity he found. He wrote of the many Protestant activists whom he encountered that their 'fervency doth ravish me'. So, he must at the very least have wondered if his long-term destiny was to be in his native Scotland. He had, up until this point, thought that his mission would probably be either in England (but of course only after 'Bloody Mary' Tudor was gone) or in Geneva, where he was working well with Calvin.

The Scottish bishops demanded that Knox should answer heresy charges, but Mary of Guise allowed him to move safely back to Geneva. At this time, the Catholic Church in Scotland was well aware of its own failings and was undertaking tentative and belated reform in matters such as the education of priests. Perhaps because it was in reforming mode, it was all the more determined to stamp out heresy. But it received little support from the regent.

By this time, many French troops were now garrisoned in Scotland, partly to repel the Spanish, should they invade. They were highly unpopular. At one point, Mary had to intervene to ensure that they were properly fed. The condition of the country remained volatile and complicated, and it is to Mary of Guise's credit that she steered a steady course and kept Scotland secure and stable.

The second version of Cranmer's great Prayer Book was by now freely circulating in Scotland, as were various English translations of the Bible. Protestants were fleeing from 'Bloody Mary's' England to seek sanctuary north of the Border. Mary of Guise did not persecute them. Her main concern remained the future of her daughter; she did not wish to antagonise the senior Scottish nobility, a growing number of whom had strong Protestant sympathies. The balance with which she ruled may have been underpinned by her own dynastic ambitions, but she ran Scotland with goodwill and fairness. She could have enjoyed an easier, more comfortable life at the French court; but she remained in Scotland, determined to protect her daughter's inheritance.

Then, in 1557 and 1558, she changed course and became markedly less lenient towards the Scottish reformers. In 1558, the final Protestant martyr, Walter Myln, was burned to death at St Andrews. He had been the parish priest of Lunan, just north of Arbroath, where he was accused of heretical leanings. He fled to Germany in 1538, and only returned to Scotland in 1556 when he was 80. He was arrested for heresy at Dysart in Fife. At his trial, he refused to recant. Archbishop Hamilton of St Andrews, misguidedly and cruelly, decided to make an example of him. This was a disastrous miscalculation from the Catholic point of view. To burn a brave old man was utterly, crassly counter-productive.

Hamilton had to force his own servants to assist with the burning. The Provost of St Andrews, who should have been responsible for the arrangements, had nothing to do with them. Before he was put to the fire, Myln wanted to speak to the assembled people. He was refused permission, but the townspeople angrily demanded that he be heard. Myln told them not to be 'seduced by the lies of priests, monks, friars, abbots, bishops and the rest'. They were to depend solely on Jesus Christ and his mercy. When Myln was killed, Mary of Guise was conveniently in France, attending her daughter's wedding to the Dauphin.

Scotland was to have no martyrologist of the genius of John Foxe (though Foxe found space for Myln in his famous *Book of Martyrs*). But Knox's *History of the Reformation* emphasised the significance of martyrs such as Myln. Knox claimed that Myln's burning created 'a new fervency' among the whole people of Scotland. On the other hand, it is important to remember that Myln was the only Protestant martyr in the years of Mary of Guise's regency. While she was pursuing tolerance, Queen Mary in England was burning Protestants with relish.

One consequence of Mary of Guise's policy of tolerance had been that the Protestant minority became more assertive and more confident. At the beginning of 1559, a secretly printed sheet was nailed to the doors of the Scottish friaries. It ordered the friars to quit their quarters so that the genuinely poor could use them. (The friars were the leading opponents of Protestantism.)

It was now, shortly before Knox's permanent return, that Mary began to act against militant Protestants. She was belatedly and unwisely moving to Frenchify Scotland, to the extent that the country could hardly be regarded as an independent sovereign state. All Frenchmen were to be citizens of Scotland, and vice versa. The young queen was in France, and a secret treaty determined that, if she died childless, her realm of Scotland was to be freely donated to France. The queen was now married to the Dauphin, a dribbling wreck of a young man who was widely reputed to be impotent. This pathetic youth was due to be the next king of Scotland.

Mary of Guise had not necessarily been liked, but she had been trusted as a reasonably honest broker. In 1556, some of the more assertive lairds and nobles complained that she was not involving them in government; she preferred to rule through Frenchmen whom she trusted, while bribing and flattering the Scots aristocracy. Scotland, if not fervently pro-French, was most certainly not pro-English. Mary's main mid-term threat lay in the growing pushiness of the Protestant nobility. Nonetheless, in 1556 and 1557, there was little anticipation of the momentous events that were about to unfold.

From the 1530s, there had been the occasional convert from the Catholic clergy. There was a growing craze for clandestine Protestant gatherings where literate laymen could read out passages from English Bibles. But there were few Protestant preachers, and hardly any leaders. Towns like Brechin, Montrose and Stirling had semi-established Protestant congregations. But, overall, this was still a piecemeal movement rather than an organised Church, and to a large extent a covert one.

Thus, in much of Scotland, the practice of Protestantism remained discreet to the point of secrecy, generally behind closed doors, although Protestants were becoming more defiant in Angus and Fife. And Ayrshire, always the strongest Protestant area in the west, saw a remarkable development when the Protestant preacher Robert Acheson became the official minister of the burgh of Ayr and was in turn supported by the burgh council. And, all the time, the nature of Scotland's nascent Protestantism was slowly changing; from the early Lutheranism, it was becoming harder, more Calvinist.

The accession of the 25-year-old Elizabeth Tudor, the daughter of Henry VIII and Anne Boleyn, to the English throne in 1558 was to have enormously positive consequences for Protestants in Scotland as well as England. But, at the time, it looked as if her inheritance was so difficult that she would do well just to cling to her throne. Her reign looked likely to be troubled and short for many reasons; her hold on power appeared exceptionally precarious.

Mary of Guise hoped for the union of the French and Scottish crowns through her daughter Mary Queen of Scots, who was now 15 years old. She must have wondered: could England perhaps be added to this union? As French power grew, these were dangerous, even treacherous times, not just for England but also for all those who valued Scotland's independence. Increasingly, in the early months of 1559, Mary of Guise finally found herself defied.

The senior Protestant nobility, now calling themselves the Lords of the Congregation, were the likeliest defenders of Scotland's independence, but they were quarrelsome and lacked a natural leader. Suddenly, up and down the east coast, from Montrose through Dundee to Perth and Fife, religious reform was being more openly propagated. This was no longer clandestine activity; something seismic was stirring. But the movement remained localised and disorganised.

All that was needed was a leader. In Geneva, there was a 46-year-old Scots scholar whose resilience had been brutally tested on the French galleys, a man who was such a wonderful preacher that by his eloquence 'he could manage men's souls as he wished'. But why should this effulgent figure quit Calvin's Geneva, which he thought was 'the best school for a Christian', where his family was settled and he was among friends, and where he had much work still to do? Why should he leave such security and comparative stability to return to Scotland, still a Catholic country, where he would be met, in all likelihood, by hardship and constant danger? And indeed, if he did leave Geneva, why should he not return to England, where he had already made his name as a preacher and had been offered a bishopric? Well, there was, as we shall see in the next chapter, at least one very good reason why he should not go back to England.

John Knox made the fateful decision: he would return to his native land. He landed at Leith in early May 1559. The reformers in Scotland had found more than a mere leader. They had found a prophet.

CHAPTER 17

Knox the Man

*J*OHN KNOX has already flitted in and out of this narrative, though 'flitted' is probably not the right word for such a forceful, heavyweight figure. We encountered him, an obscure country lawyer, emerging as the sword-bearer and guard of the itinerant preacher George Wishart in the 1540s. We saw him joining the 'Castilians' at St Andrews and at the same time discovering his power to sway people by his preaching. We feared for him as he was captured by the French and put to work as a galley slave – backbreaking work in squalid and acutely dangerous conditions that would have broken far more robust and physical men. We saw him becoming something of a celebrity in Edinburgh society in the mid-1550s, when he enjoyed the informal protection of none other than Mary of Guise. And we saw him working with John Calvin, ministering to the exiled English congregation in Geneva.

Knox had been born in Haddington, probably in 1513. We do not know the exact date of his birth, nor do we know where he was educated, though he is supposed to have attended either Glasgow or, more probably, St Andrews University – or possibly both. He was ordained as a priest in the old Church by the Bishop of Dunblane. Apparently, he never took charge of a parish. Instead, he became a lawyer and a tutor to the sons of lairds and gentry in the East Lothian area. This was how he met Wishart, who was protected by some of these lairds. As Knox moved around with the charismatic preacher, he must have been impressed by the Lutheran message, though he soon moved on to a harder version of reformed religion.

After his adventures in St Andrews following the murder of Cardinal Beaton, Knox spent nineteen terrible months on the galleys. The hideous experience must have toughened him immeasurably. At one point, he was rowing off Dundee, and one of his companions looked to the shore and asked if he knew this land. By his own later account, Knox looked south to St Andrews and said:

> I know it well, for I see the steeple of the place where God first in public opened my mouth to his glory, and I am fully persuaded, how weak that ever I now appear, that I shall not depart this life till that my tongue shall glorify his Godly name in the same place.

Someone with high authority – possibly the strongly Protestant young English king, Edward VI – intervened to secure Knox's release. He quickly made his way to Edward's court, and there he became something of a star. He had now moved on from his Wishart-influenced Lutheranism. He travelled north to Berwick, a town crowded with foreign mercenaries, where he ministered successfully (according to his own account) before moving back south to Newcastle and another successful ministry. Both towns were filled with Scots exiles.

It was while he was in the far north of England that he married an Englishwoman called Marjorie Bowes, by whom he was to have two sons. He also formed a close friendship with Marjorie's mother, Elizabeth Bowes, who ironically was married to the master of Norham Castle, the most impressive of the forts along the Border that had been built in medieval times to protect the English from marauding Scots. Mrs Bowes was the mother of fifteen children and in her fifties when Knox first knew her. She seems to have been a very comely woman. She took an interest in theological matters and developed a need to discuss doctrinal points with Knox constantly, which maybe suggests that her interests were more than merely doctrinal. Certainly, their relationship has been the subject of much smutty conjecture. I shall return to this point shortly; meanwhile, we must note the progress of Knox's fast-moving career.

He returned to London to serve as one of the king's chaplains. He was offered the bishopric of Rochester, but declined. He thought that the national religious policy of Thomas Cranmer, the Archbishop of Canterbury, was insufficiently vigorous. When Mary Tudor became queen of England, he left England, suddenly the fief of the woman whom he described as the 'horrible monster jezebel', in a hurry. With his English wife and his mother-in-law, he stayed for a while across the water at Dieppe in France. Then he moved on to Frankfurt, to Zurich and at last to Geneva. But he only spent about half his 'wandering years' between 1554 and 1559 in Geneva, and his longest stay there lasted barely more than a year. As one of his better biographers, Lord Eustace Percy, notes: 'In England he had struck far deeper roots.'

In Frankfurt, he was uneasy. His time there was marked by constant squabbling with other exiles from England over liturgy. Many of these English exiles were, quite understandably, determined to use Cranmer's beautiful liturgy, which was too restrained and moderate for Knox. As far as Knox was concerned, Cranmer had started a journey but not finished it.

When he moved on to Geneva, he took one or two of the more extreme members of the English congregation at Frankfurt with him. In Geneva, he was much happier. He ministered to the growing English congregation – it numbered around 200 – and Calvin allowed him the use of the Auditoire near the cathedral. He and Calvin were never particularly close, though Knox learned much from the Frenchman and venerated the work he was doing. Knox's principal associate was Christopher Goodman, the former Professor of Divinity at Oxford University, whom he had first met at Frankfurt. Goodman was even more radical than Knox; in Geneva, he developed his theories on legitimate resistance to tyrants. Goodman was to help Knox in his revolutionary work in Scotland during the early 1560s before eventually returning to England.

When he was in Geneva, Knox wrote the *Appellation*, which in effect called the Scots to revolution. In it, he asked Scots nobles (those whom he had cultivated during his visit in 1555–6) to activate a Reformation. According to Knox's political theory, they had every right to depose a wrong-headed monarch, in this case Mary of Guise, the regent. Knox was now moving beyond mere advocacy of rebellion; he was becoming a fully fledged insurrectionary. The *Appellation* was to become a handbook of revolutionaries in France and the Netherlands, and it was still used in the next century by the English Puritans who were to behead a monarch and set up a republic.

When 'Bloody Mary' Tudor died and Elizabeth succeeded her, Knox would have loved to return to England, not Scotland. But he could not do so because of his most controversial book, the splendidly titled *First Blast of the Trumpet Against the Monstrous Regiment of Women*, which had been published in Geneva in 1558. In this fiery tract, which Calvin disapproved of, Knox argued that no female ruler should be obeyed (the word 'regiment' in this context means 'rule').

He was obviously influenced in particular by Mary Tudor, but also by Mary of Guise and her daughter Mary Queen of Scots, and by Mary of Hungary, who had been the Holy Roman Emperor's regent in the Netherlands. Given that Mary of Guise had protected him, and other Scottish Protestants, it was not a gracious book. His anger with 'Bloody Mary' was understandable, but the tone of the book was, to put it mildly, impolitic.

It was ingenuous for Knox, who usually had sensitive political antennae, not to anticipate what would happen when Elizabeth succeeded Mary. Perhaps, exiled in Geneva, he believed that Elizabeth was a compromiser, a Nicodemite. He knew she took mass even if she was privately a Protestant. Elizabeth, always well informed, was fully aware of Knox's unfortunate effusion. So, as queen of England, she was poorly disposed to Knox. After all, he had attacked not just her gender in general; he had attacked her right to be monarch and her status as a legitimate ruler. Throughout her long reign, Elizabeth was to evince a distaste for the work of first Calvin, and then Beza, in Geneva. She associated it with advocacy of resistance to legitimate rulers, though Knox and Goodman were more culpable in this respect.

Knox was a marvellous man – an eloquent preacher, a supreme visionary in an age of visionaries, a social as well as a religious prophet and an inspirational leader – but it must be said that, in his grovelling to Elizabeth when he realised his error, he debased himself. He wrote:

> Your Grace's displeasure with me, most unfairly conceived, has been a great and almost intolerable worry to my wretched heart ... my conscience bears witness that I never maliciously or on purpose offended your Grace, nor your realm ... I cannot deny writing a book against the usurped authorities and unjust regiment of Women; nor am I inclined to retract or call back any main point or proposition of the same.
>
> So far as your regiment is concerned, how could I or can I envy that which I have thirsted for and for which I give thanks unreservedly to God?

And so on. With its mixture of bluster, grovelling, defiance, hypocrisy and smarm, this is quite some passage, even by the standards of the sixteenth century; and it does Knox little credit. But, to be fair to him, he now realised that Elizabeth could be a great friend of his country; indeed, she could liberate Scotland. So, his greasy and servile manoeuvrings may surely be forgiven.

Anyway, in the early months of 1559, it became obvious that Knox would not be welcome in England. He returned instead to his native land. Perhaps he saw this as second best at the time; yet, within eighteen months, he had created a genuine revolution and a successful one – by far the most significant revolution in Scotland's long and turbulent history.

It will be apparent that the details of Knox's early life and career are somewhat sketchy. We know far more about the youth and early manhood of Luther and Calvin. Professor James McEwen, in one of his celebrated Croall Lectures, ruminated on this point. He felt that everyone who studied Knox would be struck by the mystery of the man. For he lived for twenty-five years in the full glare of the limelight, a controversial figure everywhere he went, and in Scotland a leader of momentous events. Yet we know very little about him. Further, McEwen contrasted Knox with Luther, pointing out that, while Knox told us nothing about himself, Luther told us everything. Knox was anonymous where Luther was constantly autobiographical.

The latter point is perhaps exaggerated. Knox, the historian of the Scottish Reformation in which he was the principal participant, could hardly be accused of downplaying his own role. Sometimes, his account of what happened is self-serving. Reading his history, you are occasionally reminded of Churchill's quip: 'History will be kind to me, for I intend to write it.'

It remains true, as McEwen suggests, that we never get 'inside' Knox as we can get inside Luther. However, we do at least know in some detail what transpired after he landed at Leith in May 1559. One historian has described what happened next as an earthquake. It was a very Scottish earthquake, and the man at its epicentre has been, ever since, at the epicentre of ongoing, and often nasty, controversy. The likes of Lord Eustace Percy and Roderick Graham have been very positive. One of his modern biographers, Elizabeth Whitley (wife of the much-loved minister of the High Kirk of St Giles, Dr Harry Whitley), wrote a book that was close to hagiography.

Others, such as Edwin Muir (whose study of Knox was dismissed as sheer spite by Professor McEwen), and contemporary Scots in the arts world such as the writer A. L. Kennedy and the composer James McMillan, have been withering in their denunciations of Knox. The historian John Prebble wrote in his 'personal history' of Scotland that Knox was a noisy rabble-rouser advocating wars and murder and exulting in the death of those whom he hated. Prebble claimed that Knox 'was drunk with self-righteous passion and demented by the influence he had upon the emotions of simple men'.

There is at least some truth in this – yet, overall, it is surely somewhat patronising and unfair, as the Reformation over which Knox presided was a remarkably bloodless one, and the people whom Knox most influenced were often highly intelligent and fastidious. To counterbalance Prebble, you can turn to the likes of the distinguished contemporary commentator on Scottish affairs, George Rosie, who has tried to work out why some of Scotland's modern intellectuals so detest Knox and his legacy. Surely a determined champion of education and democracy deserves a more benign treatment? Rosie reckons that the popular perception of Knox as 'a half-demented moorland preacher' owes much to the strength of the sentimental Left in Scotland. He also traces the cerebral debunking of Knox back to the Scottish Enlightenment, when 'the *philosophes* of Edinburgh and Glasgow found that his ideas did not sit well in their rational, moderate universe'. So, there had been a kind of accumulated disrespect – and Knox's most eager admirers, such as myself, will always have to accept that he remains, 450 years on, a deeply divisive figure.

A further area of contention concerns his undoubted appeal to the ladies. One of Knox's most sympathetic biographers, Stewart Lamont, is also a Church of Scotland minister. Lamont writes with sensitive perception:

> It is a fact well known to clergymen of all faiths that some middle-aged women develop a crush on their minister or priest. It is silly to pretend in the post-Freudian age that these feelings do not have a sexual component. The intrapersonal chemistry, tension, attraction, whatever we call it, often retains its magic all the more for never gaining physical expression.

Lamont is particularly concerned to rebut Robert Louis Stevenson, who somewhat lasciviously suggested, in Lamont's words, 'that the marriage to Marjorie was a device got up by Mrs Bowes to stop the tongues wagging, while at the same time enabling her to remain close to Knox'. Lamont's conclusion is that perhaps Knox went so far as to touch or embrace Mrs Bowes. But there, for this particular biographer, it seems to have ended. 'It is unlikely that the marriage with Marjorie could have survived, as it clearly did, if the *ménage à trois* had been less than innocent.'

Knox's wife Marjorie died in 1560; Mrs Bowes then stayed in England for a while but rejoined Knox in Scotland to look after his two young sons, which she did until Knox married again two years later.

Knox was not a tall man, and he seems to have been quite slight, though his shoulders were no doubt broadened by his toil on the galleys. His complexion was dark, and he had cold blue-grey eyes. He had a big mouth (some would say appropriately) – though, when he was not in the pulpit, he spoke gently and with a pronounced English accent. He had a long beard that made him conform to the stock notion of what a prophet should look like. He was, above all, a religious and political democrat. He fervently believed that all human beings, including kings and queens, princes and nobles, were subject to the same rule of God. He may well have thought that he himself had a direct line to God, and that many rulers and monarchs did not.

Although he clashed with kings and queens and wrote against the monstrous rule of women, he was not at all hostile to ordinary women. When he married for the second time, at the age of 50, his bride was just 16 (shades of Farel in Neuchâtel!). This young woman, Margaret Stewart, was the daughter of Lord Ochiltree and a distant relative of Mary Queen of Scots, who in her petty puffed-up way was furious that Knox had the gall to marry one of her relatives, however remote. Knox's two sons by Marjorie became Anglican clergymen and academics at Cambridge. Of his three daughters by Margaret, two married ministers in the new Scottish Kirk, and the other married an aristocrat.

Far from being a killjoy, Knox was charismatic and rumbustious, though it might be stretching it to call him fun-loving. Disputatious he may have been – but then many, perhaps most, Scots are disputatious. Like Calvin, he had benefited from a legal training, and much of his work had a forensic edge. He was clever, and he knew it. Despite his unfair reputation for excessive dourness, he possessed a marvellous, mischievous sense of humour, which often lightens up his own history of the Scottish Reformation. His account of the arrival of Mary Queen of Scots at Leith to begin her reign is a masterpiece of comic writing. He was fond of wine and sincerely hoped that, when he died, everybody would enjoy themselves by imbibing well. He had no objections to taverns and public houses being open on Sundays, as long as they were not open at the same time as religious services were taking place.

He did have a certain canniness which has led his many detractors to accuse him of cowardice. It is true that he allowed one of his early influences, the preacher Wishart, to persuade him not to travel to St Andrews when Wishart himself was in peril – he had been arrested and was facing certain death. If Knox had accompanied him, the same fate would almost certainly have befallen him. He did have a knack for slipping away when the heat was on, for example after the death of Queen Mary's 'secretary' Rizzio. But a coward? Hardly. He was a constant, eloquent, steadfast and brave opponent of those who he thought abused their power. And I wonder how long his detractors who have accused him of cowardice would have lasted on the French galleys, where the conditions were execrable and broke many men.

Thomas Carlyle summed him up well: he was brother to the high, brother to the low, and sincere in his sympathy with both. He was a man capable of long and lasting friendship with, for example, his mother-in-law Elizabeth Bowes, or his colleague in both Geneva and Scotland, the theologian and political theorist Professor Christopher Goodman. Both Elizabeth and Christopher were English; and Knox was a consistent Anglophile. He was never one of those Scots who nurture a glib and misguided disdain for England and the English. Rather, he loved and cherished England every bit as much as his native Scotland. As a revolutionary, he could never have accomplished his Scottish revolution without English military aid.

It is given to few to remake their country. Knox remade Scotland, for the better.

Context: Europe in the Mid-Sixteenth Century

Europe in the 1540s and 1550s should have been catching its collective breath after the cataclysmic changes of the previous thirty years, but it remained in ferment. The presiding genius of the early Reformation, its great spiritual begetter, Martin Luther, died in February 1546 in Eisleben, where he had been born, and was buried in Wittenberg, where he made his name.

By this time, the second phase of the Reformation was well under way, under the stern guidance of the Frenchman John Calvin, and the Catholic Church had at long last regrouped and was preparing its huge counter-assault at the Council of Trent. In some places, such as Scotland, a full Reformation was still to come; in others, including many parts of Germany, some of the early reforming fervour had fizzled out. The condition of Germany overall was at best confusion, and at worst turmoil.

We left Martin Luther when he was fulminating against the peasants in 1524 and 1525, marrying in 1525, and unable to make theological peace with Zwingli at Marburg in 1529. His diatribes against the peasants had been the nadir of his tempestuous career, showing him at his rebarbative worst. He mellowed slowly in the 1530s, enjoying married life and the veneration he deservedly received. Yet, by 1524, most of his great work was already done. His Reformation now required the shape, the authority and above all the organisation which he was unable to produce. These were eventually to be provided by the more clear and organised mind of Calvin.

In 1531, Luther told his students: 'We old men [he was only 48 at the time] soaked in the pestilential doctrine of the papists which we have taken into our very bones ... we cannot even today, in the great light of truth, cast that pernicious opinion out of our minds.' His point was that his young audience should have no difficulty in resisting the 'pestilence'. They were growing up in a free, enlightened age.

Well, only up to a point. Luther's Reformation did not progress smoothly in the last fifteen years of his life. From the failure of Marburg onwards, the German Reformation was mired in muddle. The word 'Protestant' had been coined at the Diet of Speyer in 1529, when there was a concerted attempt to outlaw all Lutheranism throughout the Holy Roman Empire. This prompted predictable protests from six Lutheran German princes and a further fourteen Lutheran cities, thus giving the world the terms 'Protestant' and 'Protestantism'. A year later, the Schmalkald League was formed. It was to be led by Philip of Hesse. This was a defensive grouping, prepared to protect Protestantism by military means if necessary. In the same year, the *Augsburg Confession* was drawn up. This was a conciliatory document, but it failed to produce a lasting settlement.

Shortly after Luther died in 1546, the emperor decided to try to smash the Lutheran princes once and for all. In April 1547, his general the Duke of Alba won a notable victory at Mühlberg. Philip of Hesse, the pre-eminent Protestant prince, was captured and imprisoned. But, as so often, the emperor had to contend with other rulers who were keen to challenge his authority, not least when he was victorious. Henry II of France formed a new alliance with Maurice of Saxony. Meanwhile, the Turks still threatened from the East.

Henry of France invaded western Germany, and Maurice's forces liberated much of the rest of Germany from imperial rule. Charles V had depended on Spanish troops to keep Germany subjugated, and now he realised that he simply could not prevail. He handed Germany over to his brother Ferdinand, who was to prove more conciliatory to Protestantism. Charles retired to a monastery in Spain; Ferdinand presided over peace talks at Augsburg in 1555. The outcome was a settlement of sorts, but it actually counted for little because Calvinists and Zwinglians were excluded from the negotiations. The principle of Augsburg, an accommodation between Catholics and Lutherans, was later summed up somewhat glibly in the four words *cuius regio, eius religio* (roughly meaning 'whoever is the king, his is the religion').

Really, all that Augsburg provided was the framework for Catholics and Lutherans to coexist within the Holy Roman Empire. This was a very limited version of religious toleration: geographic, pragmatic and conditional. But it was progressive by the standards of the time. At least in theory, if someone disagreed with his ruler's religion, then he had the right of free passage to another region of his choice. And, in any city state where both Protestants and Catholics were on the council, both religions were to be tolerated.

The German Reformation had been most successful in the towns and cities. Of the sixty-five imperial cities, more than fifty joined the Reformation at one point or another, if not permanently.

The Augsburg settlement's exclusion of Calvinists diminished its long-term significance. Already, the Reformation was well into its second phase, and Calvin was the key leader. Right across Europe, from Scotland in the west to Poland in the east, many of the nobility and gentry were moving towards Calvinism. In the Netherlands, where Protestantism had tended to be the preserve of working people, some of the gentry began to send their children to be educated in Geneva. In France, many of the senior aristocracy became Calvinists.

John Calvin himself, and perhaps even more his eminent assistant Theodore Beza, who headed Geneva's academy, well understood that the nobility were likely to take at least some of the people with them. One noble conversion often meant many more down the social line. Beza himself was a French nobleman from Burgundy. The motivations of many of these noblemen were mixed, to put it mildly. Some cast rapacious eyes on the remaining, and vast, wealth and landholdings of the Catholic Church. Some of them shrewdly identified Calvinism as the best means of resisting royal authority or policy (despite Calvin's own caution in this area). And, of course, some were motivated by genuine religious conviction.

Philip II of Spain attempted to crush the rise of the Calvinists in the Netherlands, Spain's turbulent satellite, with brutal ruthlessness, killing many thousands. Dutch Protestantism was formed and honed in the hardest of schools. And yet, paradoxically, the gentry and the aristocracy could also be the most bitter enemies of Calvinism, for Calvinism was ultimately democratic and socially subversive. Many Calvinist leaders, such as Knox, were radical men, dismissive of traditional power structures and the old social hierarchies. Both Calvin and Knox would use an aristocrat or indeed a monarch where necessary, but they were clear-sighted men and were no friends of the privileged.

Early in 1559, the Peace of Cateau Cambresis was negotiated. This seemed momentous at the time, because it marked the end of hostilities between France and Spain. The Valois dynasty of France and the Habsburgs of Spain and the empire had been at war, off and on, for the best part of sixty years. Philip of Spain, the husband of Queen 'Bloody Mary' Tudor of England, had been using thousands of English troops to fight the French. The peace seemed to be at once good and bad for the new queen of England, Elizabeth. Good, because it gave her scope to be independent of both Spain and France. Bad, because it opened up the possibility of a great Catholic alliance against the Protestants of Europe.

As it happened, the peace turned out to be catastrophic for France. There may have been peace with Spain, but there was to be no peace within France itself. No sooner had the peace treaty been signed than Henry II of France died of terrible wounds he suffered in a celebratory jousting tournament. State policy would now be directed by his ambitious Italian widow, Catherine de Medici, whose manoeuvring was to come perilously close to ruining France. Her intention was to preserve internal peace in France and to avoid religious conflict. She was to fail miserably.

The new French king, Francis, was a sickly, retarded youth, and he died within a year. His young widow, Mary, returned to her home in Scotland, where she had to cope with the Scottish Reformation, which was at last under way. This was a reformation that had been achieved not through the efforts of the Scottish queen, Mary, but rather through the intervention of the English queen, Elizabeth, who very bravely sent both her army and her navy north to help the Scots drive out the French once and for all. The Reformation, thus enabled, was now being led by an exceptional man, John Knox, who was to be Mary's most bitter enemy.

One of the most important consequences of the Scottish Reformation was that it ended centuries of more or less continuous enmity between Scotland and England, which had often spilled into war. For that benign development, Queen Elizabeth of England could take most of the credit. Her grandfather Henry VII, whose son Henry VIII had inflicted on the Scots their worst-ever military defeat, had always wanted perpetual peace with Scotland. He would have been proud of his granddaughter.

PART 5

Bloody England

CHAPTER 18

Jane and Mary

*O*N 10 July 1553, four days after the boy-king Edward VI died at Greenwich, Lady Jane Grey was proclaimed queen of England. The woman who should have been queen, Mary Tudor, was now in Norfolk, where the local people rallied to her. She was soon joined by many of the leading figures of East Anglia – by no means all of them Catholics. The Duke of Northumberland, who had been ruling England on behalf of Edward VI, sent ships to protect the Norfolk coast in case Mary tried to escape by sea; but the crews mutinied. In London, Bishop Nicholas Ridley preached an ill-advised sermon denouncing Mary and her sister Elizabeth as bastards. He was shouted down. Archbishop Thomas Cranmer was another who ill-advisedly backed the increasingly desperate Northumberland's manoeuvrings, though he was more diplomatic.

Bishop Hooper of Gloucester, another leading Protestant, announced that Mary was the rightful queen. He and other leaders of reform nobly stuck to the Protestant doctrine that Christians should not rebel against their legitimate monarch. Things were not going as Northumberland wished. He assembled a force and marched towards Norfolk, seeking to confront Mary and her supporters. But, in Cambridge, where he had the support of the university, he was informed that back in London the royal council had now proclaimed Mary to be queen, and that the Lord Mayor had made the proclamation publicly. Northumberland himself now, somewhat ludicrously, proclaimed Mary to be queen in the market place at Cambridge. Lady Jane had been queen for just nine days.

Mary took her time in moving to London. She did not want to enter the city in premature triumph. She appointed the veteran leader of the Catholic cause, Stephen Gardiner, the former Bishop of Winchester, as her Lord Chancellor, and pardoned all the Catholic prisoners in the Tower. She had Northumberland, Bishop Ridley, Jane Grey and various other prominent Protestants arrested and imprisoned in the Tower. Northumberland was duly executed, but Jane Grey was spared this fate – for the time being.

Bonfires of celebration were lit all over England. The Protestant cause, which had been burning brightly only weeks before, was now in ashes. The genuine acclaim for Mary, the enthusiasm with which she was endorsed across Norfolk, Suffolk, Cambridgeshire and Essex as she progressed in triumph to London, suggested that the Protestant revolution had been imposed, not nurtured.

But what of Jane Grey, the innocent girl caught up in the convoluted machinations of King Edward, Northumberland and her own husband, whom she had unwillingly married? This was an era of formidable, exceptional, headstrong women: Mary and Elizabeth Tudor, Mary Queen of Scots, Mary of Guise, Catherine de Medici. Could Jane Grey have evinced similar spirit, similar enjoyment of power?

Jane was a slight, pale girl who became queen at the age of 16. Her coronation was a drab, understated ceremony. When it concluded, two heralds and one trumpeter made a pitifully modest tour through London proclaiming the new queen. Yet Jane did show considerable spirit when she adamantly refused to make her husband king. She apparently declared: 'A duke perhaps, but a king – never.'

She 'reigned', and then she languished in the Tower until, in 1554, Queen Mary decided that she should be beheaded. If fate had been a little kinder to her, she might have been able to surprise the country of which she unexpectedly found herself the sovereign for just nine days.

Jane's successor as queen of England, Mary Tudor, is to this day often referred to as 'Bloody Mary'. The day of her death was celebrated as a national holiday for many generations. Her persecution of Protestants contrasted with the restraint shown by Edward VI, Somerset and even Northumberland – each of them committed Protestants – towards Catholics. Some of those whom Mary had executed were distinguished, numinous men who would have graced any country in any age: Cranmer, Ridley, Latimer, Hooper. Some of them were obscure but decent men whose only sin was to refuse to recant their Protestant beliefs. What is certain is that there were far, far too many of them. The case against Mary is colossal. But there are several points which should be made in her favour.

She was a capable monarch, in that she ruled with vigour and considerable courage. She was superbly self-disciplined. She would rise at dawn, say her prayers, attend mass and then work solidly for several hours until she took her first (very light) meal. At the end of the day, she would work on matters of state until well after midnight. Her austere, almost soulless approach to the work of monarchy perhaps reflected her unhappy upbringing. She was much closer to her Spanish mother, Catherine of Aragon, than to her bullying, blustering English father, Henry VIII. She saw her father treat her mother with contempt, and she witnessed him publicly rejoicing when Catherine died.

Catherine and Mary had both fought against Henry's Reformation, almost to the point of treason. They had made it clear that they wanted the Holy Roman Emperor Charles V to intervene to save the old religion in England. Mary was appalled by her father's embracing of his very personal form of Protestantism. She suffered many slights. At one point, she was made a lady-in-waiting to her infant sister Elizabeth. She saw her father systematically reduce her mother's household. Later, she was forced to sign a submission, drafted by Thomas Cromwell, in which she confessed to having disobediently offended her father. She had to recognise him as the Supreme Head of the Church in England. She was further required to reject the pope's 'pretended authority, power and jurisdiction' in England.

So, when Mary became queen, she had many scores to settle, many humiliations to avenge. Her Catholicism, always sincere, had been turned into something hard and unforgiving by her father's behaviour. As queen, she only allowed herself one indulgence, and that was her love of clothes. Even here, there was an element of statecraft, for she determined, like her father, to be a consistently regal figure. The splendour of her clothes and the exceptional quality of her jewellery were not merely measures of her vanity; they were displays of power. She was, like most of the Tudors, highly intelligent and fluent in Latin, French, Spanish and of course English. She was exceptionally generous to her servants.

She was tough; she needed to be. She constantly had to fight terrible headaches, of the kind her father had suffered; and she had bouts of extreme melancholy and depression. She knew but one way of beating these afflictions: by sheer hard work. Even the most bigoted Protestant – and plenty of bigoted Protestants have traduced her over the years – would have to admire her industry, her dedication to duty, the way she subsumed her very self in the interests, as she saw it, of her realm and, above all, her religion.

When she was young, she showed many signs of spirit – not just in her love of clothes, but also in her persistent gambling. She actually accumulated considerable debts. She enjoyed dancing and music. She was certainly not, in those days of her youth and early adulthood, regarded as any kind of religious fanatic. But the seeds of her later austerity were being sown, and her adolescence seems to have been pretty grim.

At one point, Thomas Cromwell tried to arrange a dynastic marriage with Philip of Bavaria, who was a Lutheran. Mary indicated that she did not want to join 'that kind of religion', but she agreed to meet Philip and indicated that, if her father insisted, she would marry him. It was Henry rather than his daughter who decided that the marriage should not go ahead.

Slowly, her devotion to her religion became entrenched, so that it was the defining aspect of her five-year reign. Her loyalty to her religion could hardly be called a fault. Estimates of the numbers of Protestants in England at the time of her accession vary from about 10 to 15 per cent of the population. What is indubitable is that Mary was not repressing the majority when she attacked Protestantism. Far from it.

Further, she worked through Parliament. Her father's Reformation was – largely thanks to the brilliance and vision of Thomas Cromwell – enacted through statute. Parliament was thus, if not indispensable, at least at the very centre of the nation's religious life. Mary did not like this, but she accepted it. Thus it was via Parliament that the mass was restored. It was via Parliament that previous heresy laws were restored. It was via Parliament that the Protestant legislation of Edward's reign was abolished. Significantly, however, Mary could not get her Parliament to restore papal power in England. Yet she did defy Parliament, crucially, in the matter of her marriage.

Why was her reign so disastrous? Because she misunderstood the nature of nascent English nationalism. Or, if she understood it, she was not prepared to bow to it. She wanted to return England to Rome. Her Catholicism was not like her father's – pragmatic and nationalistic and utterly hostile to the papacy. On the contrary, Mary was excessively devoted to the papacy. It is perhaps ridiculous to write of a Catholic being excessively devoted to the papacy – yet, if Mary had really wished to ensure that England continued as a Catholic country, she should have toned down her obeisance to Rome. This she simply would not do. And, as xenophobia was stalking the land, it was unfortunate enough to be the daughter of a Spaniard (Catherine of Aragon) – even worse to be the husband of a Spaniard, and the most powerful Spaniard at that.

Mary needed an heir, she needed a husband – and she chose Philip of Spain. The man she should have listened to, her Lord Chancellor, Stephen Gardiner – a loyal and devoted Catholic if ever there was one – advised her not to marry Philip; but (like the other Tudor monarchs) Mary had her stubborn streak. The marriage was driven not just by the 37-year-old Mary but also by Philip's father, the Habsburg Emperor Charles V. And so, the marriage seemed to many patriotic English folk like an insult, a ploy to make their country a Spanish colony or, even worse, an outpost of the Habsburg Empire.

Another consideration was that no foreigner had been king of England since William the Conqueror – and he, obviously, had conquered the country. Philip was to seize England simply by wedding its queen. (This was not quite true, for the marriage agreement carefully emasculated Philip's role in foreign policy. But the conspiracy theorists were encouraged by the fact that Simon Renard, the Emperor Charles's ambassador to Mary's court, was the man who arranged the marriage.)

The English Parliament was appalled by the proposed marriage, and the Speaker led a parliamentary delegation to try to talk Mary out of her folly – but to no avail. So, in July 1554, the disastrous marriage was celebrated at Winchester, in a ceremony presided over by Gardiner, who had changed tack and worked diligently to extract the best possible settlement.

Before the marriage took place, there was a rebellion, less serious than the Great Prayer Book rebellion of 1549, but possibly more dangerous because of its proximity to London. Two or three thousand men of Kent managed to penetrate London itself. They were led by Sir Thomas Wyatt, the son of the poet Thomas Wyatt, who had introduced the sonnet to England and was one of Anne Boleyn's lovers. The rebels' grievances were mixed, but among them was resentment of the very notion of a foreign king.

They did not reckon with the resolution of the queen. She rallied Londoners with a rousing speech at the Guildhall, and this helped to quell the revolt. The most alarming aspect of the uprising was that – or so it was rumoured – the rebels wanted to kill Mary and replace her with her younger sister Elizabeth. Earlier, Elizabeth, who, while not a trimmer, was always a politician, had asked Mary to arrange for her to have instruction in the Catholic faith. She attended mass from time to time. She took a prominent place at Mary's coronation. But none of this was enough to help her when she was implicated in the rebellion. So, Elizabeth, though she had had nothing to do with Wyatt and his followers, was now in peril.

She was aggressively interrogated by Stephen Gardiner. She admitted that the rebels had written to her, but she could hardly help that. No involvement was proved. Wyatt was tortured to reveal Elizabeth's alleged complicity in the revolt. Bravely, he stuck to the truth; Elizabeth had not supported it. Nonetheless, Mary placed her sister in the Tower. Renard disgracefully advised her to have Elizabeth executed. For two months, Elizabeth was in desperate danger. Then Mary relented, and her sister was removed to less ominous imprisonment at Woodstock, near Oxford.

Lord Williams of Thame, who guarded Elizabeth with 100 horse-men on the journey to Oxfordshire, showed her great kindness. He was typical of those Englishmen for whom loyalty to the monarch of the day was more important than their personal religion. He had served Henry VIII and Edward VI with equal dedication; now he was serving Mary, and at the same time he was most considerate to Elizabeth. It is important to remember that there were many such flexible men in England.

Philip and Mary met each other – as often happened in diplomatic dynastic marriages – just before the marriage day in 1554. They seemed to get on well, though Philip apparently confided to one of his servants later that Mary did not satisfy him sexually. His servants were a disdainful and gossipy squad; they thought Mary was older than they had been led to expect, a woman who liked gaudy clothes but had no class, no style. There was some Spanish–English tension at the wedding; the Spanish retinue well remembered the many snubs that had been visited on Catherine of Aragon. But Philip presented himself well and had good personal skills. More than anything, Mary hoped that her marriage to Philip would provide her with an heir – a Catholic heir, of course. In 1555, she became convinced for a time that she was pregnant; but it was not to be. No child was born.

Philip soon tired of England. He was more interested in pro-secuting his war with France, and he dragged England into it.

In 1556, Philip's armies were fighting a vicious war against the French in Italy. The pope, Paul IV, was viscerally anti-Spanish, and he excommunicated Philip. This was a grievous blow to Mary: her husband excommunicated! Because of her spouse's adventures on the continent, Mary herself had little option but to declare war on France. Philip actually took about 10,000 English troops with him when he invaded France from the Netherlands. The war did not go well; indeed, it ended in disaster when the English lost Calais, which had been their bridgehead in France for two centuries. All this made Mary unpopular, and the unpopularity was compounded as more and more heretics were burned.

Both Philip and Mary had no compunction about burning heretics. These executions were perfectly legal and constitutional. The English state had been killing heretics since the Lollards in the fifteenth century. A statute had been passed to allow such executions as early as 1401. Henry VIII had revived it when he was minded to execute Protestants; Somerset had the law repealed, but Mary had it re-enacted by Parliament, and it was restored as law at the beginning of 1555. Among the first to die was John Rogers at Smithfield in London. He was a well-known preacher who, almost twenty years earlier, had distributed English Bibles. He died with marked courage. He was followed by John Hooper at Gloucester and Roland Taylor at Hadley. Most of the burnings were in London and Kent.

The main blame for these unnecessary and counter-productive deaths lies with Stephen Gardiner; but the king and queen could easily have prevented them. It should be noted that, during Mary's reign in England, another Mary, Mary of Guise, was effectively ruling Scotland. During this time, Mary of Guise had only one Protestant burned.

Mary and Philip were far too easily persuaded by Gardiner, though Philip did express some doubts. The three of them were zealous in their desire to crush heresy; they did not understand either the steadfastness of the English Protestant minority or the anti-Spanish feeling of the English majority.

Altogether, about 300 were burned as heretics. This was not a large number if compared with what was going on in France or in the Spanish-controlled Netherlands. The Spanish, as colonialists, had a particularly brutal and arrogant style. But Mary and Philip were burning not just obscure fringe fanatics but eminent and gracious men. The policy was not only cruel; it was ridiculous.

The imperial ambassador Renard, who was no fool, understood this. Earlier, he had recommended the death of Elizabeth; he had no scruples about advocating execution, even of the highest-born. But now he was warning Philip and Mary that they were ill-serving their own cause. He urged them to desist, and advocated imprisonment or exile. If there had to be deaths, let the dying be done in private.

Instead, the burnings were very public. The people, few of whom were well disposed to Protestantism, were appalled. The victims were celebrated as martyrs; larger and larger crowds watched the deaths with sympathy, compassion and growing anger. After the deaths, people would move to the corpses and gather the ashes, which would be carefully parcelled and kept as mementos of suffering in a just cause.

Most of the 'heretics' were dignified as they faced their ordeal. A very few, like Sir John Cheke, who had tutored King Edward, recanted. Cranmer also recanted, but then he recanted his recantation. More and more, there were defiant demonstrations of support for the martyrs at the public burnings. Mary decreed that any observer of a burning who displayed sympathy for the victim was to be flogged.

In the summer of 1558, there was a full-scale riot when a Protestant was being burned at Winchester. Furious onlookers dragged the half-dead man from the flames, and the local sheriff gave in and had the man, who was called Bembridge, taken to a local prison. Mary responded to this by insisting that he should be taken back to the stake and burned properly. She had the sheriff imprisoned. Even as Mary lay dying of cancer, the burnings continued. A Catholic cleric called Harpsfield, who was an enthusiastic killer of heretics at

Canterbury when he was not working on his hagiography of Thomas More, seemed determined to burn as many as possible before the queen actually died.

Early English Protestantism had fed on a nasty anticlericalism. It had been identified with robbery, despoliation, the destruction of beauty, the crude ending of old and much-loved ways and rituals, and the greed of jumped-up and over-ambitious 'new men'. All this changed with the burnings. Protestantism now became seen as patriotic, as pro-English and anti-Spanish, as honest and decent. The consequences of the great accumulated martyrdom will be considered in the next chapter.

Mary died early on 17 November 1558. A group of privy councillors rode out to Hatfield, where the 25-year-old Elizabeth was staying. Later Protestant propaganda had it that they found her walking by oak trees in her garden, solemnly reading the Bible in Greek. Whatever, England had a new queen, and her reign was to be a golden age. Many have argued over whether this was a happy coincidence or whether Elizabeth herself could claim most of the credit. What is more important at this point in our story is to note that her situation was chancy, even perilous.

Bishop John White of Winchester delivered the eulogy at Mary's funeral. His remarks were political and insensitive, and they infuriated the new queen, who had him imprisoned. White said: 'The wolves will be coming out of Geneva and other places, and have sent their books before, full of pestilent doctrines, blasphemy and heresy to infect the people.' Among these 'wolves' were John Knox and his English colleague Christopher Goodman.

White hardly spoke for the nation. There was much joy in England. Distinguished refugees rushed home from exile; timid and cautious Protestants reappeared in public; a colossal burden of amassed expectation was placed on the slender shoulders of the new monarch. For the moment, she was joyful. She humbly thanked God for 'dealing as wonderfully and mercifully with her' as he had with Daniel, who had been delivered 'out of the den of raging lions'.

This was all very well, but her inheritance could hardly have been worse: an impossibly complex and fraught diplomatic situation, and a divided, nervous, impoverished and insecure nation. But her reign was to last nine times longer than Mary's, and her rule was to be beneficent and progressive. She was to lead England to glories it was never to know again. And her reign was to have momentous consequences for Protestantism – in Scotland as well as in England.

CHAPTER 19

Martyrs

$\mathcal{T}$HE leading martyrs of Mary's bloody reign, evangelicals such as Cranmer, Ridley, Latimer and Hooper, used to be known as the Masters of the English Reformation. When Ridley and Latimer were burned together at Oxford, Latimer famously said to his colleague: 'Be of good cheer, Master Ridley, and play the man; for we shall this day light such a candle, by God's grace, in England that as I trust shall never be put out.'

Such brave deaths; such inspirational words. They were to be the grist of John Foxe's celebrated and inspirational book, *Acts and Monuments of these later and perilous times touching Matters of the Church*, a title which understandably was compressed to the more impactful *Book of Martyrs*. Foxe had fled to Basle to escape Mary's persecution; soon after her death, he produced the first version of his work in Latin. A later, more comprehensive English edition came out in 1563. It was a masterclass in partisan historical writing, a propagandist's dream. Some of the material was unashamedly intended to whip up anti-Catholic fury, for instance the story of a young boy who was whipped to death in Bishop Bonner's prison because he dared to defend his father, who had been arrested for heresy.

Some of Foxe's work has been hotly disputed, not least by Catholic historians; but matters of detail and accuracy mattered little at the time. Indeed, in 1570, a second edition was published, with much new material. Copies of this new edition were lodged in all the English cathedrals and in many of the parish churches. During the Elizabethan wars with Spain, English sea captains had to have a copy of the book on their ships. Francis Drake, a particular enthusiast for Foxe's work, took it with him when he circumnavigated the world. He also translated passages from the book into Spanish and read them to his Spanish prisoners.

Foxe fed on the revulsion that many, probably most, English people felt for Mary's policy of burning heretics. Although he tried to exonerate Mary of full responsibility and to place the blame on various Catholic clerics such as Reginald Pole, Archbishop of Canterbury, and Edmund Bonner, Bishop of London, the effect of Foxe's work was to instil the belief in many generations that the queen's reign was a sickening bloodbath.

Foxe was not always accurate – what propagandists are? He included in his catalogue of martyrs at least two people who had not died. But, overall, he was an industrious historian as well as a master of spin. His book is possibly the most influential work of history ever to have been published in England. Reprints continued to be published through the seventeenth century.

Foxe had fled abroad during Mary's reign, but returned shortly after Elizabeth became queen. He travelled across the country, interviewing people who had witnessed the burnings and trawling through official records of trials and interrogations. He also mined the letters that some of the martyrs had written from prison while awaiting death. Foxe was careful to note the 'miraculous preservation' of Elizabeth during the killing times.

Chapter 1 of this book has an account of the Battle of Stoke in 1487, the last battle of the Wars of the Roses. Relatively brief but exceedingly bloody, it was the battle that secured the kingship of Henry VII, who had at that point ruled England for just two years.

A mile or so to the south of where the battle was fought is the little village of Aslockton. Here, two years later, the man who probably the greatest clergyman in England's history was born. Thomas Cranmer grew up in a land that was much more secure, much more stable, because it was being ruled well by Henry VII. The anarchy of the Wars of the Roses was over. It was also a land that was solidly, thoroughly Catholic.

As a member of the impoverished rural gentry, Cranmer would have had an upbringing dominated not so much by academic teaching as by the learning of country pursuits and skills. Of his schooling, little is known, other than that it was harsh. From the start, he was a countryman: as a boy, he learned to hunt with both the longbow and the crossbow, and he became an accomplished horseman. He was often to be accused of timidity, but throughout his life he was a brave and even foolhardy equestrian; no horse was too wild for him to ride.

At 14, he went to the newly founded Jesus College, Cambridge, where he took an arts degree and then became a fellow of the college. He took holy orders in 1523, lectured in divinity and examined candidates for that subject. Although Foxe suggests that he was a member of the reforming group who met at the White Horse Tavern, there is no other evidence for this. There is in fact more evidence that he was hostile to Lutheran ideas. Always cautious, it would seem that his main concern as a young man was to keep his head down.

Cranmer was thus an obscure Cambridge scholar when, in 1529, he was brought to Henry VIII's attention by none other than Stephen Gardiner. Cranmer had suggested that the difficult business of the king's divorce from Catherine of Aragon should be considered by university theologians – such as himself. This is how Foxe accounts for Cranmer's leap from the quiet life of an academic to the more dangerous life of adviser to a turbulent king. When scholars at both Cambridge and Oxford pronounced that Henry's marriage to Catherine of Aragon was indeed invalid, Cranmer found himself the coming man. Henry sent him to practise his sinewy diplomacy in

Italy, where he possibly employed bribery to persuade universities such as Ferrara and Bologna to declare in Henry's favour.

When he visited Rome, he found a useful patron, the absentee Bishop of Worcester, Jerome Ghinucci. But Cranmer's key patron was to be Henry VIII himself. The king appointed Cranmer his ambassador to the court of Charles V, the Holy Roman Emperor. Cranmer was involved in negotiations with Charles when the empire was under direct threat from Suleiman the Magnificent, who had a huge force of 200,000 Turks stationed in Hungary, ready to attack Austria. Cranmer's main task seems to have been to tell the emperor that Henry was not prepared to join him in fighting the Turks. This was useful diplomatic experience for Cranmer. He was certainly learning how to please Henry.

When he was working as ambassador to the imperial court, Cranmer spent some time in Nuremberg, one of the largest cities in the empire, and the most Lutheran. He was able to study the development of the continental Reformation in its heartland. It was when he was in Nuremberg that Cranmer met – and married – Margarete Preu, the niece of the Lutheran theologian Andreas Osiander.

The key moment in his career came in 1533 when the old Archbishop of Canterbury, William Warham, died after almost thirty years in post. Henry chose Cranmer as Warham's successor. Cranmer had been in Henry's service for a mere three years, but he had made an excellent impression. It also helped that he was, at the time of Warham's death, serving as Anne Boleyn's chaplain. By this time, Cranmer had shed the hostility to Lutheranism that had marked his early years at Cambridge. He had married the niece of a leading Lutheran; he had assisted Henry in various ways; he had shown himself to be adaptable and, above all, useful. But his real work was just beginning. He was embarking on his own spiritual journey, becoming ever more evangelical. His great mission was to provide his country with a single, simplified English liturgy, which he eventually did, triumphantly, in language that was both supple and sublime.

Because his personal beliefs changed through his life, and because he served various secular masters well, Cranmer was often accused of ambiguity and was derided as the greatest survivor in these turbulent times. But, of course, he did not survive. When Queen Mary and her advisers moved against him, Cranmer was an old man, nearer 70 than 60, and weary after long service to the crown. He had been no stranger to controversy, having annulled Henry VIII's marriages to Catherine of Aragon and Anne Boleyn, and having divorced him from Anne of Cleves. He had comforted the old tyrant at the time of his death.

The queen had some scores to settle. Not only had Cranmer played a key role in the end of her mother's marriage and helped to have her stigmatised as a bastard, he had also backed Lady Jane Grey against Mary. More importantly, he was England's guide through the middle stages of its very distinctive Reformation. He was also a considerable statesman, showing, at times, exquisite diplomatic skills. If at first he could not find the courage to resist Mary when she took her vengeance on him, he came good spectacularly at the end. His death was wonderfully, exceptionally noble in an era when fine deaths were commonplace.

There is no escaping the depth of his recantation, the scope of his confession. He beseeched the forgiveness of the pope and the pardon of the queen. He had offended against the universal Church of Christ. Such a comprehensive confession would normally have been enough, particularly for one of Cranmer's seniority, to gain clemency. But the old man now had far too many enemies in high places.

His final speech, an hour or so before he died, before a distinguished audience in Oxford, was an explosive and unexpected denial of his various recantations and confessions. Starting with orthodox prayers, and moving himself to tears when he spoke of the poor of England, starving across the country, he then denounced his own recantations. His weak voice suddenly growing louder, he declared that the pope was Christ's enemy, the Antichrist. Lord Williams – he who had taken Princess Elizabeth to her imprisonment at Woodstock – intervened, but the old man, by now infused with a seemingly divine defiance, shouted him down.

Then he was led through the streets of Oxford to the mound of wood prepared for his burning. As he stood in the first flames, Cranmer performed one of the most famous acts in English history. He said: 'For as much as my hand offended, writing contrary to my heart, my hand shall first be punished.' And he thrust his right hand, which had signed his recantations, into the heart of the fire. If this was theatre, it was sublime theatre – and that one gesture was to resonate through English life, to become embodied in the country's idea of itself, for centuries. Cranmer's final words were: 'Lord Jesus, receive my spirit. I see the heavens open and Jesus standing at the right hand of God.'

In the ashes, his heart was found, unburnt.

The beautiful probity of Cranmer's martyrdom should not detract from the more banal fact that it was a disaster for Mary and the forces of Catholicism. Mary and her advisers thought they had presided over a spectacular 'reconversion', a magnificent propaganda coup. But the elderly archbishop undertook a second reconversion. Not only did he recant his recantations; he then died at ease with himself, prepared to meet his merciful Maker. There were plenty of witnesses to the fact that he died with his Protestant integrity intact. In political terms, Mary's loss was to be her sister Elizabeth's gain.

If none of Foxe's many other martyrs could achieve the theatrical and gracious power of Cranmer's death, that does not mean they did not die well. Of the other leading evangelicals who were burned to death in Mary's reign, John Hooper, Bishop of Gloucester, was the most zealous in his drive to extirpate all the residue of the old Church. He had studied the Swiss Reformation in both Basle and Zurich, and he anticipated Puritanism in his eagerness to strip church buildings of all the trappings of Catholicism.

More celebrated were Ridley and Latimer, who died together. Nicholas Ridley, Bishop of London, was a fine theologian. Born in 1500 in Northumberland, just south of the Scottish Border, he studied in Paris and Cambridge, and served for a time as Cranmer's chaplain. He is always associated with Latimer, the man he died with, but in life he was much closer to Cranmer in both career and temperament. Like the archbishop, he was something of a politician.

Hugh Latimer, socially and theologically, was far more radical. Born in a small village just north of Leicester, he was brought up in the countryside a few miles to the south of where Cranmer grew up several years later. Latimer's year of birth is not certain; it was probably 1484 or 1485. He became an especially forceful preacher – probably the most powerful of the English Reformation. Professor Hugh Trevor-Roper wrote that, while Cranmer and Ridley were learned men, Latimer was no great scholar. 'He took his doctrinal position from Cranmer and left disputation to Ridley. He was a preacher.'

Latimer insisted that preaching the Gospel would cost him his life – and he was right. Trevor-Roper called him a 'tribune of the people'. He seems to have been something of a demagogue. He once gave up a bishopric in order to preach, and preach again. He was an egalitarian. He believed fervently in the basic equality of mankind. 'Peers of the realm', he once preached, 'must needs be … but the poorest ploughman is in Christ equal with the greatest prince.' He approved of the dissolution of the monasteries, but was indignant when the beautiful Jervaulx Abbey in Yorkshire became a royal stud farm; abbeys had been intended for the relief of the poor, not the rearing of horses. He stands out as a particularly outspoken man in an era of outspoken clerics, and it is not surprising that Henry VIII had him imprisoned twice.

When he was imprisoned a third time, by Mary, he was frail and spent, and was known as Old Father Latimer. When the end came in Oxford, it was presided over by the ubiquitous Lord Williams. Latimer and Ridley were chained together, but they had separate fires. Ridley's was ill-prepared; the flames would only reach his legs. He leapt up and down, shouting 'I cannot burn'. Eventually, a bystander sorted the fire – whereas Latimer, old and weak, burned very quickly.

On the lives of such men, and in particular on their deaths, Foxe built his potent propaganda.

On the other side, as it were, the outstanding figure was Cardinal Reginald Pole. He had the privilege of dying in his own bed – just a few hours after Queen Mary had died, which was just as well, for he would not have adjusted well to life under her successor Elizabeth. Pole cannot be excused for his part in many of the burnings that disfigured Mary's reign and gave Foxe so much material, but he was in many ways a decent man, a distinguished humanist scholar who, throughout his long career, understood the imperative of reforming the Catholic Church. Indeed, he had some views which were not dissimilar to Martin Luther's. He certainly believed in the possibility of reconciliation with Lutherans.

A man of noble birth, he was a cousin of Henry VIII, and his long career was a succession of near misses. Not only did he just miss the reign of Queen Elizabeth. Much earlier, under Henry VIII, he narrowly missed execution (his mother and his brother were killed by Henry for treason) by the simple expedient of fleeing the country. He then wrote a scholarly book attacking Henry's decision to make himself head of the English Church.

In 1536, the pope appointed him to a 'select commission' which was to review the need for reform in the Church of Rome. The report which was duly produced, the Consilium, was regarded as dangerous by the many influential conservatives in the Curia, who blocked it. A decade later, Pole was one of the three legates who presided over the early stages of the Council of Trent, the Roman Church's belated attempt to organise and implement serious reform.

Pole had very nearly become pope in 1549; he would probably have been a very good one. Instead, he was to return to England to become Mary's Archbishop of Canterbury. His instincts were both radical and conciliatory – radical, in that he believed in the importance of Scripture. He was appalled by widespread disrespect for the clergy, and wanted to improve their standards of education and behaviour. He was conciliatory in that he always believed that an accommodation with Protestantism was possible in England. This was too much for the irascible anti-Spanish Paul IV, who fell out with both Mary's husband Philip of Spain and Pole himself. Pole was summoned to Rome to answer charges of heresy. This was ironic, as by this time Pole himself was enthusiastically persecuting heretics. In the event, Mary refused to allow him to leave England.

Bishop Edmund Bonner of London was a lesser man than Pole. Reinstated to his bishopric by Mary, in 1554 he began an enthusiastic drive to get rid of heretics in his diocese. He, rather than Pole, was the cleric who was most fervent in the campaign to stamp out heresy. Bonner and Mary had maybe been over-impressed by the enthusiasm which had greeted the new queen when she arrived in London. Mary's reception was to some extent illusory; although most of the English people probably remained Catholic, despite the enthusiastic reforming of the Edwardian years, there was no popular desire for a brutal campaign against the reformers.

When Bonner moved to restore censers, vestments, crucifixes and so on to London's churches, there was resistance (not least because many of these items had been stolen and sold). And, when ordinary people, rather than Church leaders, were burned, the people became angry and resentful. Bonner understood this, but his response was merely to suggest that burning should be carried out in secret rather than publicly. He was a limited man, lacking both Pole's scholarship and his conciliatory tendencies. Crass and obese, he defended his decision to have an old heretic beaten up by saying, with impeccable if coarse logic, that it was 'good to have your bum beaten to save your body from burning'.

In 1558, the new queen quickly showed her contempt for Bonner. When he was presented to her, she turned her back on him. Bonner refused to take the oath of supremacy recognising Elizabeth as supreme governor of the Church. He was nothing if not obstinate; he continued to celebrate mass in St Paul's. Elizabeth eventually had him incarcerated in Marshalsea prison, where he remained until his death in 1569.

PART 6

The Scottish Reformation

CHAPTER 20

The
Biggest Decision
in Scottish History

THE years 1559 and 1560 were the most momentous in Scotland's history. But, before we consider the revolution that developed with growing momentum after Knox landed at Leith in May 1559, we should consider the position of the monarch to the south. England was to play a pivotal role in Scotland's revolution; indeed, it might well not have happened without the dramatic and brave intervention of Queen Elizabeth, the most celebrated monarch in England's history, and a woman to whom Scotland too owes much.

At the beginning of her reign in 1558, the 25-year-old daughter of Henry VIII and Anne Boleyn was faced with a multiplicity of problems. Her country had been ravaged by the plague and by a persecuting zealot. As well as killing hundreds of Protestants, Mary Tudor had overspent; England was almost bankrupt. Elizabeth had to sift through her many difficulties and begin to prioritise. She could not address everything at once. From the start, she displayed political skill and judgement that were exceptional. Her only serious flaw was her tendency to procrastinate.

She was lucky in that she was blessed with an adviser who combined consummate astuteness with occasional boldness: William

Cecil, who had earlier been secretary to the Duke of Somerset. Elizabeth, generally a good judge of men, said simply to Cecil, who was to be her right-hand man for decades: 'You will not be corrupted, and you will be faithful to the state.' She got that right, just as she got most things right.

As early as 1548, when Elizabeth was a 14-year-old princess facing a very uncertain future, she had reckoned that Cecil was the one man she could trust. An orderly, well-organised countryman, a committed Protestant who had nonetheless befriended Cardinal Pole, he could lie low when necessary. He had maintained discreet contact with Elizabeth during Mary's reign, but he had not caused the Catholic queen any trouble. He came from a line of minor Lincolnshire landowners. He went to Cambridge but did not take a degree, though he kept in touch with friends at the university. Thoughtful and scholarly, he consoled himself in times of trouble by reading not the Bible but Plato.

He had been an occasional adviser to Elizabeth since the death of her father. Like most of those who served the Tudors well, he was not averse to making a lot of money through the contacts and opportunities that came to him; but he remained a steady guide through all the sudden squalls of state. Elizabeth, a complex mixture of courage, vanity, shrewdness, spite and sheer genius, was never easy to work with. But Cecil was understanding and patient, though even he became frustrated because of her chronic inability to make swift decisions.

Two of the toughest decisions she had to make at the start of her reign involved religion. The first was what she was to do about her own country's religion. For thirty years, England had been swinging all over the place. Her father Henry's Reformation had been a peculiar affair; it had left England largely a Catholic country. Henry decided, very much for his own ends, to expunge the pope and make himself head of the English Church; but he did not want to destroy the Catholic religion. After his death in 1547, those who surrounded the young King Edward pushed the country into a much more aggressively Protestant position. Edward himself did not require that much pushing, for his tutors had ensured that he was wholly committed to reform.

So, England became more blatantly Protestant during the years of the mid-century. Through this period, Thomas Cranmer, the long-serving Archbishop of Canterbury, was giving what came to be called Anglicanism shape – and beauty – with his delicately balanced and persuasively worded new liturgy.

But then Edward died; and, after the farcical 'reign' of poor Jane Grey, Mary Tudor took the throne – and Protestantism was put to the fire. She forcefully returned the nation to Catholicism. Her religious policy was marked by viciousness and malice that did untold damage to her own cause. Most English people were still Catholic – and, in the north of her realm, Protestants were still few and far between. But her bloodthirsty repression created many celebrated martyrs – not least Cranmer himself – and was utterly counter-productive.

Even so, it would not be simple for her sister to swing back to Protestantism. As we have noted, Elizabeth was well aware of – and much irritated by – the subversive, even revolutionary, Protestantism that was being expounded by Goodman and Knox in Geneva. Goodman was even more radical than Knox; he reckoned that, if a man's conscience was clear, it was quite in order for him to kill a 'tyrannical' ruler. Secondly, Elizabeth had to move warily as far as the great Catholic powers of France and Spain were concerned. Both had the potential to defeat England in war. France, just across the water, was four times wealthier than England and had four times as many people. And France, threateningly, had troops stationed in Scotland to the north.

Both France and Spain were likely to be, at best, inconstant friends or, at worst, mighty and implacable enemies. But Elizabeth was to be fortunate. Ironically, this was because of the power of the teaching of John Calvin in Geneva. Calvin's emissaries ensured that there was serious religious strife in France and revolt in the Netherlands, Spain's most important colony. Elizabeth may not have liked what was emanating from Geneva, but in this sense it benefited her greatly.

France was to be mired in internal religious war for most of the rest of the century. Caught up in the nastiest of civil wars, it could hardly pose a threat to England. Spain, potentially even more dangerous than France, was diverted by the brave and heroic rebellion in the Netherlands. This did not remove the Spanish threat to England, but it complicated matters for the Spaniards. In the early months of her reign, however, Elizabeth could not predict these future developments in France and the Netherlands. She had to determine her religious policy, and quickly.

Temperamentally, Elizabeth was very different from her sister, 'Bloody Mary'. Her instinct may well have been to recover her father's compromise: keep the pope out, but allow the mass. Yet that was not a feasible option. Mary's terrible reign had hardened religious commitments: Protestants were more Protestant, Catholics were more Catholic. The country was divided, as was the whole of Europe. In Geneva, the hard-edged new version of Protestantism was being forged by Calvin; elsewhere, the Catholic Church was fighting back. Protestantism was now associated with rebellion and opposition to civil authority. Catholicism, on the other hand, was associated with strong rule by legitimate monarchs.

Elizabeth chose Protestantism. One of England's finest Tudor historians, Professor S. T. Bindoff, once went so far as to suggest that this choice mirrored the one that Britain had to make in 1940: appeasement or defiance. I think it is perhaps a little strong to liken Elizabeth's position to Churchill's; but there can be no doubt that to conciliate the great Catholic powers, and choose the old religion, would have been the easier and softer option for Elizabeth.

Once she had made her decision, Elizabeth moved with remarkable and uncharacteristic speed. The new settlement was more or less complete by the spring of 1559, just six months after she had become queen. She was now 'supreme governor' in all matters spiritual. Cranmer's revised Prayer Book of 1552 was restored, largely intact, as the official liturgy. This was established by law. Her new Archbishop of Canterbury, Matthew Parker, was not dissimilar to Cranmer: a studious man of moderation, a political cleric rather than a religious firebrand, he had kept his head down during the Marian persecution.

As many as 2,000 of the parish clergy objected to the new settlement. They lost their livings. Catholic bishops who refused to endorse the settlement were imprisoned.

The next key decision she had to make concerned Scotland. This was extremely difficult. There were French troops there – and Mary of Guise, the regent, had been pursuing an ever more overtly pro-French policy. This was aggravating the Scottish Protestant nobility, who increasingly saw Elizabeth as their means of getting rid of Mary and her French government. Elizabeth had a very simple and horrific fear: that a large French army would land in Scotland, join up with the French troops already there and march over the Border, gaining the support of Catholic magnates in northern England and that of their tenants.

A possible solution to this problem was to help the Scots drive the French out of their country once and for all. But this would almost certainly entail sending both her navy and her army north. It would be a risky and very costly policy. Most of her advisers, with the significant exception of Cecil, thought that the very last thing she needed to do, just a year or so into her reign, was to precipitate what might become a full-scale war in Scotland.

Apart from anything else, the Scottish Protestant lords were rebelling against their legitimate ruler, the regent, Mary of Guise. They might have been aristocrats, but it was quite reasonable to regard them as little more than a gang of self-serving feudal thugs who, for reasons of expediency, had joined up with some fanatical Calvinists. If she gave military succour to such rebels in another country, what precedent would she be setting?

Further, supporting the Scottish Protestants against their regent would be a clear, if technical, breach of the treaty of Cateau Cambresis. She would be smashing the newly drawn European peace. Far from easing gently into her reign and showing herself to be a conciliator and a lover of peace, she would be seen as confrontational and bellicose, a warmonger. On the other hand, if the Scots rebels failed, and the French gained total ascendancy over Scotland, she might well be faced with an imminent Franco–Scots threat to her throne. She was very well aware of the claim to her throne of Mary Queen of Scots, waiting over in Paris.

After an agonising period of wavering and wobbling, and much patient persuasion from Cecil, Elizabeth made her decision. She would help the Scots. This was probably the single most important and most beneficial decision in Scotland's entire history – and sensible Scots should have no problem with the fact that it was taken not by a Scot but by a young and untried Englishwoman.

CHAPTER 21

Opportunity Knox

$\mathscr{K}$NOX did not waste time when he arrived back in Scotland in May 1559. Within a few days, he had moved to Perth, which was typical of the towns that would have to be formally 'converted' if Scotland was to become truly Protestant. Some towns, notably Ayr and Dundee, were already officially Protestant with the sanction of the town councils. In Dundee, Paul Methven had been chosen as the Protestant minister and was able to operate with the protection of the magistrates. Perth, on the other hand, was one of many communities that was neither one thing nor the other. Lukewarm allegiance to the old Church was challenged by the presence of hardcore militant Protestants.

On 11 May 1559, at St John's Church, Knox preached an inflammatory sermon in which he denounced the mass as an abomination. The congregation was roused to a mixture of fervour and fury. A priest, showing foolhardy and ill-judged defiance, started to celebrate mass as soon as Knox had finished. An onlooking youth yelled out, understandably, that this was intolerable. The priest hit him hard, and the boy retreated and then threw a missile at his assailant. The riot that ensued was later blamed by Knox on the 'rascal multitude'. He may have aroused the people of Perth, but he was quick to distance himself from wanton violence.

And extreme violence there was, for a mob rampaged round the town, attacking the friaries and the Carthusian charterhouse. The more democratic, even egalitarian side of Protestantism was seen in the way that the copious provisions that were looted from the Catholic houses were distributed to the poor folk of Perth; the nastier, destructive side was evinced in what was tantamount to an orgy of destruction and despoliation that lasted for several days.

The regent, Mary of Guise, no longer in conciliatory mode, reacted in anger. She demanded that Perth be put to the fire, to its 'perpetual desolation'. One of the band of Protestant nobles calling themselves the Lords of the Congregation, the Earl of Glencairn, was so infuriated that he took precipitate action. He raised a troop of more than 2,000 men in Ayrshire and marched towards Perth. Meanwhile, Lord James Stewart, an illegitimate son of James V, and as such a half-brother of Mary Queen of Scots, who had got to know Knox during the reformer's visit to Scotland in 1555–6, tried to act as peacemaker. Stewart was not over-impressed by Knox, and he thought he could persuade Mary to see reason.

So, Mary of Guise was allowed to deploy 400 of her troops – significantly, Scots, not Frenchmen – in Perth, where freedom of worship was to be guaranteed. Meanwhile, Knox and his colleagues withdrew to St Andrews. Following the prediction he had made while a galley slave, Knox preached once again in the church where he had delivered his very first sermon. There were no riots in St Andrews. The magistrates supervised an orderly stripping of the churches.

Mary, who, under severe provocation, appeared to have lost her previous political skill, now over-reacted. The son of a Protestant laird was killed in Perth. This may well have been an accident, but Mary provocatively remarked that it was a pity it was the son, not the father. She also announced that she was under no obligation to keep promises made to heretics. This was too much for Lord James Stewart, who now aligned himself with Knox and the Lords of the Congregation. Over the summer, the Lords sought to strengthen the local Protestant congregations which had been springing up, in a disorganised and almost random way, in various parts of Scotland.

They marched on Edinburgh, where the friaries were attacked and stripped. Mary withdrew to Dunbar, where her French troops were ill-fed and mutinous.

Scotland was now mired in a low-key, low-grade civil war. There were armed stand-offs and many incidents, but no major set-piece battles. The Catholic population, who probably remained in the majority, were reluctant to take up arms to save the old religion. They lacked leaders, with the significant exception of the Earl of Huntly in the north. The defence of Catholicism was left to the increasingly unpopular regent. Senior Catholic clergy seemed more concerned to hide their treasures and to lie low than to rally to the cause.

Mary now saw the sporadic outbursts of militant Protestantism as a direct threat to the security of French rule in Scotland. She demanded, and received, military back-up to reinforce the French troops who had already deployed in Scotland. It was becoming clear that the Lords of the Congregation, if they were to prevail, would have to win a war against the might of France. These stakes could not have been higher; achieving Scotland's Reformation had become the same as achieving Scotland's independence.

Perhaps Knox had not planned it this way – but, within a few weeks of his return to Scotland, he was leading the charge not only for Protestantism but also for Scottish self-determination. He was helped by the increasingly wild behaviour of Mary, once so cautious and restrained. He was also helped by the behaviour of the French troops, which was sometimes barbarous. They certainly attacked civilians with brutish disregard for any diplomatic niceties.

Yet it was obvious that the Lords of the Congregation and their men were hardly strong enough to take on the armadas and the armies of France. So, where were they to turn for aid? There was only one answer to that question: the young English queen. After centuries of enmity, was Scotland at long last ready to make peace with England in return for freedom?

The most important religious development in the summer of 1559 was the arrival of Knox in Edinburgh, where he was appointed minister of St Giles' Kirk – a position he was to hold until his death thirteen years later. One of his first acts was to write to Queen Elizabeth, pledging to work for perpetual peace between England and Scotland. The two most important political developments during that fraught summer were the death of King Henry II of France and the start of negotiations between the Lords of the Congregation and Queen Elizabeth's key adviser, William Cecil.

Henry's death meant that his teenage son Francis – a non-entity – became king, and Francis's wife Mary Queen of Scots became queen of France. But the dominant Guise faction at the French court could now hardly regard the plight of one of their family, Mary, the Scottish regent, as a pressing priority. France suddenly lacked a strong monarch, and they had to consolidate their position; the country's finances, like England's, were in a parlous state; and, more worrying still, religious conflict was breaking out all over the country as Calvin's emissaries from Geneva became ever more brazen.

All this obviously worked to Scotland's advantage. Even more propitious for Scotland was the emergence of William Cecil as Queen Elizabeth's right-hand man. Cecil is perhaps the greatest English friend Scotland has ever had. Far-sighted but patient, he was personally eager for an alliance with the Scottish Protestants – but they were rebels, and he understood how cautious Elizabeth would be. He had to move warily. He kept in close contact with England's main man at Berwick, Sir John Croft, and told him to get the message to the Lords of the Congregation that England would not allow their cause to fail. He also indicated that after money would come arms, and, after arms, men.

So, money was sent to Scotland, and the Congregation started to pay their volunteers in English coin. Cecil was canny; Elizabeth knew what he was doing, but no documents or dispatches bore her incriminating signature or even her name. She kept her distance, for she was assisting rebels – and she was challenging France. Mary of Guise, who was no fool, had a network of informants. She was aware of Cecil's covert activities. She made formal complaints; in response, Elizabeth summoned the veteran French ambassador Antoine de Noailles and, deploying all her dramatic skill, protested her innocence.

Not all of those around the tyro Queen were as sympathetic to Scotland as Cecil. Her new Archbishop of Canterbury, Matthew Parker, was a cautious man. For Parker, John Knox was a dangerous and absurdly democratic demagogue. Parker knew of Elizabeth's extreme displeasure at Knox's ill-judged tract *First Blast of the Trumpet*. He said: 'God keep us from such a Visitation as Knox is attempting in Scotland, the people to be the orderers of things!'

As summer moved into autumn, the Lords of the Congregation were not doing as well as they had done in the heady days of early summer. The fight – sporadic and ill-defined as it was – with Mary of Guise was in danger of being lost. The Congregation were simply not strong enough to overcome her French troops; and there was the ever-present danger of more reinforcements coming from France. The Congregation formally removed Mary from her regency. In one sense, this was little more than a gesture; then again, it meant that the Congregation were now in effect claiming to be the provisional government of an independent Scotland. So, they began to play up the national cause; they were contending for nothing less than the liberty of Scotland. But that liberty looked ever less likely as Mary's French troops took control.

South of the Border, Cecil was worried. He kept working away at Elizabeth. Using a somewhat convoluted argument, he tried to persuade her that the Congregation were not technically rebels, as they were fighting against another subject. Mary of Guise was not the ruler, merely the absent ruler's mother. He also insisted, with considerably more pertinence, that the ever-increasing number of French troops in Scotland constituted a growing threat to English security. To protect her realm, Elizabeth needed to join forces with the Congregation. Elizabeth's response verged on the petulant. She knew that English money – her money – was already going to the Congregation; she demanded some military success to justify the subsidy.

Far from achieving military success, the Congregation proceeded to lose Edinburgh. After no more than a series of skirmishes in early November, the Lords retreated to Stirling, jeered on their way by the citizens of Edinburgh. Knox, as ever, tried to rally the Congregation. He preached a fiery and defiant sermon in Stirling, declaiming: 'I doubt not that this cause, in despite of Satan, shall prevail.'

The Congregation decided to retreat further and to regroup in Stirling a month later. Knox returned to St Andrews. It almost looked as if Mary and the French had won. What the Congregation needed to do at once was to win not a military battle but a propaganda war. They had to make it clear to the many doubters and waverers in Scotland that the French were genuine enemies and that the English were friendly neighbours. But this was only fifteen years after the worst of the 'rough wooing', and the new English queen was showing little sign of being a true friend. The cause was, however, helped by the behaviour of the French troops, some of whom behaved in a merciless and mindless manner. More and more, they were regarded as an army of occupation. Slowly, the Scottish mindset changed; the English might indeed be trustworthy friends.

As Elizabeth continued to prevaricate, Cecil, growing desperate, played his last card. He told her that, as he could not agree with her policy on Scotland, he wished to be transferred to other responsibilities. This was tantamount to a threat of resignation, and it could be regarded as insolence. But his boldness won the day – and, at long last, in December 1559, Elizabeth agreed to armed intervention north of the Border. She would allow one of her younger admirals, William Winter, to take a fleet north and to patrol the North Sea east of Berwick and Fife. It is understandable that she was desperately reluctant to make even this limited move, for in truth it was a decision of momentous magnitude. Indeed, it must have seemed to her that, in trying to assist a band of turbulent aristocrats and fanatical Protestants in a separate sovereign state, she was maybe throwing away her own crown.

Winter was to guard the approaches to the Firth of Forth, to prevent seagoing supplies and troops reaching Scotland from

France. This was, by any standards, a blockade, and it was close to a declaration of all-out war by England against France. The admiral was put in an impossible position, being told that, if captured, he was to claim that he had been over-zealous and had exceeded his orders. Above all, he was to make it abundantly clear that he had not acted on the authority of his queen.

Meanwhile, more and more English troops were mustering at Berwick. As the Congregation found their tenuous grip on Scotland continuing to weaken by the day, Cecil was eager to send a significant English force over the Border, to secure the Scottish Reformation and to drive the French out of Scotland once and for all. He half-persuaded the queen to allow a land army, led by the Duke of Norfolk, to invade Scotland from Berwick. But Elizabeth dithered; and Cecil was not yet the dominant figure in her council.

Elizabeth was right to be canny. Not only was she being asked by Cecil to take on France directly; she being asked to assist an assorted and ill-organised band of Protestants. Most of her subjects remained Catholics; her new religious settlement was not universally popular. If she invaded another country to support a minority of militant Protestants, what might happen back home? Another consideration was finance. Like her grandfather Henry VII, Elizabeth was hyper-careful with the state's finances. She regarded extravagance or unnecessary financial risk as an affront. She feared bankruptcy – and England was already barely solvent after all the misspending in Queen Mary's reign.

And, above all, there was her own temperament. This complex woman always tended to the oblique rather than the direct. She was the most able and clever of monarchs, but she hated bright light shining on to her ways of working. Although she knew that, often enough, she had to put on a spectacular public show, she personally tended to the shadowy world of intrigue rather than the glare of open and clear governance. Partly because of her insecure upbringing, partly because she was by nature devious, her preferred methods were those of stealth and subtlety. Elizabeth's sheer cunning meant that she instinctively preferred covert activity to open warfare.

Winter's fleet had sailed through appalling weather and had been constantly buffeted by December gales and squalls. Eventually, early in 1560, he sailed right up the Forth and attacked some French barques, which he drove ashore, where they were attacked and destroyed by men loyal to the Congregation. Meanwhile, the gales that had buffeted Winter's fleet had wrought havoc with a group of French supply vessels. Four ships went down, and with them as many as 2,000 men. Just as a propitious storm was later to scatter the Spanish armada, so the gales off the east coast of Scotland destroyed the French reinforcements.

If Cecil was the key man in England, then north of the Border Knox was the leader Scotland needed. The Lords of the Congregation could not muster a genuine leader among them. Lord James Stewart was fitfully impressive, and he showed courage in switching his allegiance from Mary to the Congregation. A man called Maitland of Lethington showed considerable diplomatic skills. But, for Lord Eustace Percy, writing of course with the benefit of centuries of hindsight, Maitland of Lethington was a diplomatist of 'the negative school'. He was brilliant at blocking his opponents' moves. 'But he could never win a game, for he had not a game to win.'

The country's true leader was Knox. He was more than a preacher – he was an inspiration. Charismatic, energetic, resolute and zealous, he gave the Scottish cause substance and heart. He was a visionary, in politics as well as religion; he could foresee the union of the two kingdoms, Scotland and England. Knox was not a military man – but, as he surveyed the scene towards the end of 1559, he must have wondered if the revolution was to fail before it had properly begun. In the north, the Catholic Earl of Huntly held sway. In the south, the French troops were more than a match for the volunteers who had at first supported the Congregation but were now drifting away.

But, in the depths of winter, the tide turned. Winter's good maritime work on the approaches to the Forth, and what Knox would have called God's excellent work in delivering the gales that wrecked the French reinforcements, meant that the Congregation might yet prevail. Winter was able to supply the Congregation with both arms and provisions. His support gave the rebels new heart, and they engaged the French in a series of intense skirmishes in Fife and the Lothians.

Meanwhile, Cecil knew that the Guise family were now struggling to retain their power in France. The French would be less and less keen to become involved in Scotland; they had more pressing matters to attend to at home, where their country was on the brink of civil war. Cecil's tenacious manoeuvring had finally paid off; he could now seize the momentum. In February, his emissary the Duke of Norfolk met with representatives of the Congregation at Berwick.

A treaty between Scotland and England was formally agreed. Elizabeth, having pretended to be satisfied that the Lords of the Congregation were loyal to their absent queen, made a treaty for the 'just freedom' of Scotland. Significantly, reference to religion was removed from the document. The events which led to this historic moment were partly about securing the Scottish Reformation, but Elizabeth was still keen to avoid public and formal admission of this.

In the next month, Elizabeth made a formal proclamation to the effect that, while she had no squabble with Mary Queen of Scots, she was concerned that, since the death of King Henry II, the Guise family had seized power in France and, further, were planning a full-scale invasion of Scotland. This could only threaten England's security. Elizabeth was now signalling unequivocally that Cecil had prevailed. Her army of around 10,000 men was told to march into Scotland; soon it was laying siege to Leith while Mary of Guise lay dying in Edinburgh Castle.

The French asked Philip of Spain for help in putting down this northern Protestant revolution. It is doubtful if Philip would have become involved; but, in the event, and not for the first time in the sixteenth century, the Turks came indirectly to the aid of Protestantism by diverting the military leader of Catholicism. The Turkish navy was wreaking havoc in the western Mediterranean, threatening both Spain and Italy.

The sizeable English army found the fighting in Leith much tougher than had been anticipated. The French, though under siege, fought with unexpected tenacity. The English lost many men, not just in the actual fighting but also as a result of disease; conditions in Leith were appalling. Cecil managed to persuade Elizabeth to send reinforcements. Slowly, it became clear that the French were not going to receive the reinforcements that they too required. They had lost.

Cecil now moved north himself. He was to negotiate with Mary of Guise and her various advisers, but his demands were to encompass just about everything that the Congregation and Knox wanted. All the French – not just the fighting troops but also the diplomats, advisers and officials – were to quit Scotland. Scotland's religious settlement was to be determined by the Scottish Parliament, not by the absent Queen Mary.

In May 1560, Lord James Stewart and Maitland of Lethington added to the pressure on Mary of Guise by presenting her with a list of specific grievances about French rule in Scotland. The complaints covered such matters as the raising of taxes to sustain French troops and the appointment of French soldiers to offices of the realm. Mary could counter-claim that such policies had been agreed by the Scottish Parliament; but it mattered little, for she was clearly failing. She died of the dropsy shortly before Cecil arrived in Edinburgh. She had been, as her biographer Pamela Ritchie notes, 'the acceptable face of French power in Scotland'. With her death, that power finally collapsed. Cecil well understood that her demise hardly strengthened the position of the French negotiating team. He was able to press home his advantage, and the French swiftly agreed to total capitulation.

On 6 July 1560, the Treaty of Edinburgh was signed. This was an unreserved triumph for England – and for Scotland too. The French agreed to withdraw completely from Scotland, as demanded; and they also agreed that the Scots could settle their religion as they wished. The English dropped their demand for the return of Calais by the

French – a minor sop that enabled the defeated party to save at least some face.

The Treaty of Edinburgh stands as one of the very highest points in Scotland's long history. It represented nothing less than total victory for Elizabeth, for Cecil, for the Congregation and for John Knox. It was a glorious triumph for Scottish independence and for Protestantism. It marked the end of the 'Auld Alliance' between Scotland and France and the beginning of a new, amicable relationship between the English and the Scots. The whole of Europe took notice of this extraordinary Anglo–Scottish achievement. Some have claimed that Elizabeth's victory in 1560 was even greater than the defeat of the Spanish armada twenty-eight years later. Most significantly of all, Elizabeth's success was Scotland's success. After centuries of conflict, the two nations were friends. Knox's dream of perpetual peace seemed to have been realised.

And indeed, what of John Knox? For Knox, the most splendid aspect of all this was that the Scottish Reformation was at last secured – and it had been secured, as he had always hoped, with the aid of the English. He held a thanksgiving service at St Giles', in which he eloquently pledged to keep faith with 'our confederates of England'. Never again, he suggested, would the two countries be set 'at variance or discord'.

Within a few weeks of the signing of the treaty, the Scottish Parliament was legislating to make Scotland a Protestant state. The mass was banned; anyone who attended an illegal mass was to be imprisoned, and a third-time offence was to be punished by death. The Church of Scotland was now to be governed not by a pope and bishops, not even by a monarch or a prince, but by a democratically elected Assembly.

Yet, despite all this, Knox was soon to be grievously disappointed. He was a revolutionary, and he and his colleagues quickly produced visionary blueprints for extremely radical reform. But these were rejected by his countrymen. It could be said that he had won the war but was to lose the peace. Even so, he had achieved much.

CHAPTER 22

The New Church

*I*N England, the Elizabethan Church settlement was quickly accomplished – it was pretty well complete within a year of her taking the throne in 1558. But the settlement was the culmination of thirty years of experiment, imposition and improvisation as England swung this way, then the other, then back again, before finally arriving somewhere on the moderate side of Protestantism. What came to be known as Anglicanism was undoubtedly Protestant, yet it embodied a typically English compromise – and many of its adherents who were instinctive Catholics managed to endorse it, and worship according to its (very beautiful) liturgy, without too much pain.

Evelyn Waugh, in his excellent biography of the covert Jesuit priest Edmund Campion, referred to the 'easy-going majority' on whom the success of Elizabeth's settlement depended. These people would have preferred to live under a Catholic regime but accepted the change without serious regret. Anglicanism reflected more than anything else the long work of that sublime ecclesiastical politician Thomas Cranmer. What a pity it was that he was martyred before he could see the culmination of all his work in the early years of the reign of the glittering new queen.

While England had been swinging this way and that, Scotland had stuck doggedly to the old Church. In the 1550s, more and more pockets of Scotland became frankly Protestant, but there was no organised structure and it did not amount to even a tentative reformation. The reforming impulse was localised, and it often depended simply on the local priest changing sides, or the laird changing sides – for a variety of motives.

The east coast of Scotland was, from the 1520s onwards, softened up for reform by the passage through the ports and towns of merchants and sailors who were well aware of – and in some cases locked into – the new thought that was sweeping across northern Europe. Tyndale's Bible was illegally imported into the country and was much read and discussed. Later, in the 1550s, Cranmer's prayer book also found its way into Scotland and was used by many of the nascent Protestant congregations. And there were the three terrible martyrdoms at St Andrews: the grotesquely misjudged burnings of Patrick Hamilton and then George Wishart, and finally the 82-year-old Walter Myln. These were vicious and unnecessary interventions that made many men and women think long and hard.

Meanwhile, the Catholic Church had from the late 1540s made more attempts to reform itself, but these were sporadic and the results were meagre. And, in any case, the most dangerous time for any entrenched regime or organisation is when it begins to reform itself, as the French historian de Tocqueville was to note in another context much later. Leading figures in the Catholic Church in Scotland remained blatantly corrupt and absurdly greedy, and they were linked in the public mind with a French regent who, after a period of moderate and conciliatory rule, began to lose her touch and rapidly became seriously unpopular. Her French troops did little to help her cause; slowly, the people of Scotland woke up to the fact that they were living in an occupied country.

Two imperatives began to coalesce in the minds of many Scots: the need to rebel against French oppression and the need to reform the Church both became more and more pressing. When the opportunity for reformation at last came, in 1559–60, the seeds had been well sown.

Everything happened in a confused rush. Before the Scottish Reformation could get properly under way, the preliminaries were played out against a background of war. It was a low-intensity but nonetheless cruel and debilitating war, in which the insurgents were the weak and poorly led Protestant forces of the Lords of the Congregation, who tilted against the more hardened and militarily competent French forces controlled by Mary of Guise, the regent. Latterly, the Scots were aided by the English, their new friends; and the war ended with the French vanquished and sent home to think again – and, as it happened, never to return.

It is reasonable to suggest that this was the time when, very belatedly, medieval Scotland vanished and Scotland finally entered the modern world. The new religious settlement which was quickly achieved and which marked this momentous change was accomplished with great speed – possibly too much speed. In some ways, Scotland might have benefited from something similar to the thirty years of experiment and division and changes of course which England had experienced.

On the other hand, the Scottish settlement, while not in itself particularly durable – it was to be constantly modified over the coming centuries – laid down the foundations of an extraordinarily forward-looking new state, far ahead of its time in matters such as education and welfare. In this, it reflected the vision of John Knox, who managed to fuse religious change with the introduction of moves for beneficial and far-sighted social amelioration. Thus, having been laggardly in moving out of the medieval era, the Scots rushed into the modern world with great haste.

The other significant point about the new Scottish state was that it became a good friend of England. Many generations of suspicion and bloody hostility suddenly ended; the new age was in this respect to be exactly what Knox, that persistent Anglophile, hoped for – one of more or less perpetual friendship with the great neighbour to the south. The Scottish revolution of 1559–60 paved the way for, first, the union of the crowns in 1603, and then the eventual union of the two states into a new superstate in 1707.

But that is to anticipate. In 1560, Scotland remained very much an independent country, doing things her own way; and many might argue that this was in fact a better way of preserving good long-term relations than getting so very close to England that the Scottish state would be effectively sucked into a much bigger one. In 1560, two sovereign states that had hitherto been condemned to bitter and protracted enmity resolved their differences almost overnight while yet maintaining their essential integrity as separate entities. There were powerful and immediate benefits from the new accord. England gained security on her problematic northern border and the friendship of a gutsy young Protestant state in a Europe where most of the great powers remained Catholic. Scotland gained nothing less than her freedom and the chance to start experimenting in areas such as education as well as religion. 1560 was indubitably the greatest year in Scotland's history.

And at heart of all this was the creation of Scotland's new Church. New Church? It is a matter of debate. Many senior figures in today's Church of Scotland insist that all that happened in 1560 was that the existing Church of Scotland was formally reformed. In one sense, this is absolutely right. Yet, to argue that means, for example, that the Church of Scotland had earlier made martyrs of the likes of Patrick Hamilton and George Wishart. I cannot see John Knox (or, for that matter, John Calvin) agreeing that the Church that was born in 1560, with its Geneva-influenced structure, was anything but a new Protestant Church.

The so-called Reformation Parliament met in August 1560. As well as the nobility, it was attended by more than 100 lairds, mainly from predominantly Protestant areas. It endorsed a new *Confession of Faith* for the Church of Scotland. This was the first of the three great documents of the early Scottish Reformation. It was drawn up by Knox and five other Johns – Douglas, Row, Spottiswoode, Willock and Winram.

Douglas was an academic at St Andrews; Row had studied in Italy and only joined the reformers in 1559; Spottiswoode had worked with Cranmer in England and had returned to Scotland as chaplain to the Protestant Earl of Glencairn; Willock was a former Dominican friar who had been accused of heresy by Mary of Guise and had latterly been an itinerant preacher in Ayr, Dundee, Edinburgh and elsewhere. He deputised for Knox at St Giles'. The last John, Winram, was quietly influential. He had been an academic at St Andrews, and a moderate Catholic; he had only formally joined the Reformation in 1559, thanks to the influence of Lord James Stewart.

The six Johns worked with admirable speed, drawing up the *Confession* in a mere four days. Scholars have disagreed about the quality of the *Confession* (a new translation, from the original Scots into modern English by Rev. J. Bulloch, was published in 2007 by Saint Andrew Press). One view is that it was repetitive and the work of a committee who were clearly not of one mind. The opposing view is that is a lucid, straightforward and concise piece of work.

What strikes me most about this short document is the emphasis on the supremacy of Scripture – even though Scripture is dealt with in just one paragraph (comprising the whole of chapter 19) which affirms that Scripture is sufficient to instruct and make perfect the man of God. The overall tone is one of moderate Calvinism; the authors 'abhor the blasphemy' of those who affirm that people who live by equity and justice shall be saved whatever religion they profess. But the *Confession* does not expound the full force of Calvin's 'double predestination'.

The *Confession* is undoubtedly hostile to the Roman Church, although the Scottish Reformation was to be in many ways remarkably tolerant. There was to be no explicit compulsion on any Scot to subscribe to the *Confession* unless he held office in the new Church or taught in a school. In the last week of August 1560, the Reformation Parliament explicitly removed all papal authority in Scotland and abolished the mass. Needless to say, these measures were not endorsed by the absent queen, so there was a question as to their legitimacy; the royal imprimatur did not come for another twenty-seven years, when James VI was the boy-king of Scotland.

The six Johns also worked on the second key document of the early Scottish Reformation, the *First Book of Discipline*. This was an attempt to roll out a completely new society, with very advanced notions of public welfare and education; and it is informed by – for the mid-sixteenth century – a remarkably passionate and compassionate social concern. The tone of the book is noticeably democratic. The *Book of Discipline* owed much, but by no means everything, to what Knox had learned in Geneva.

- Ministers were to be elected by their congregations.
- Elders were to assist ministers in the enforcement of discipline; deacons were to help with the finances. They were to be elected annually.
- Exhorters were to back up the ministers by preaching, but were not to administer the sacraments.
- Each parish was to have a kirk session in order, among other things, to oversee spiritual discipline.
- Superintendents, whom some have regarded as bishops by another name, were to look after large areas, comprising many parishes, and to report to the General Assembly. They were to examine the performance of ministers, to examine the church buildings, to maintain the spiritual condition of the people – and also look after the welfare of the poor and the education of the young. Initially, just five superintendents were appointed.
- A system of poor relief was to be introduced (on a scale virtually unknown elsewhere in Europe), and there was to be a school in every parish. Poor relief was to be funded partly by fines that the kirk session levied on delinquents, and partly by collections at worship.

- Every parish kirk was to provide for the poor (though the poor were often highly mobile).
- Much of this was to be paid for by the revenues and land of the old Church. The new Church was to take over the tithes and some of the land and rents of the old Church, and to redistribute the resources to the new Church.

This proved to be ingenuous. Much of the wealth and property of the old Church had somehow or other found its way to the nobles and the lairds, who were hardly likely to allow the bulk of such monies to be handed over for a radical national experiment in welfarism. And yet, what amounted to an ambitious plan to redistribute vast ecclesiastical endowments, which had been selfishly exploited by hardened men for generations, nearly succeeded.

Eventually, the new Church had to share just one third of the revenues of the old Church with none other than the Catholic monarch ('half to God, half to the devil', as Knox succinctly put it). While the new Church would be poor, with effective ministerial supply one of its biggest problems, it was remarkable just how much backing was received by the ambitious structure adumbrated in the *First Book*.

Schoolteachers were to be supervised by ministers and elders and paid from church revenues. Detailed proposals were put forward for the reform and improvement of the three Scots universities at St Andrews, Glasgow and Aberdeen. Medicine was to be added to the tertiary curriculum. The *First Book* dealt with education at length and with special enthusiasm. Learning, knowledge and wisdom were to be, in theory anyway, available to all. There were to be no burial services, though a sermon of thanksgiving for the life of the deceased was permitted. Everybody, from the highest to the lowest, was to be equally subject to spiritual discipline.

This radical blueprint was never endorsed by the Scottish Parliament, packed as it was with nobles and lairds; but succeeding General Assemblies of the new Kirk stubbornly plugged away and nearly succeeded in creating a nationwide organisation that followed the aspiration of the *First Book*. A *Second Book of Discipline* was published in 1578.

The third significant document was the *Book of Common Order*, which provided the new Church with its liturgy. This was a spare and almost austere liturgy when compared to Cranmer's glorious *Second Book of Common Prayer* of 1552 (which had been used by unofficial Protestant congregations in Scotland for several years). Given that the Scottish Reformation had been secured through the intervention of the English navy and the English army, and that this would not have happened without a courageous and historic decision by Queen Elizabeth, it might seem odd that Knox, the great Anglophile, was unwilling to accept Cranmer's liturgy.

But, ultimately, Knox's spiritual tastes owed more to Geneva than to England – and this is reflected in Knox's liturgy, which was published in 1562. The Lord's Supper was to be observed once a month; the Sunday service allowed for two sung metrical psalms, an offering for the poor, and the Apostle's Creed – as well as the confession-of-sin prayers, Scripture readings, a sermon – the centre-piece – and benediction.

The *First Book of Discipline* was clearly radical. It could be described, justly, as utopian. Its long-term influence was strong, but it was never implemented in full. It was a robust, virile manifesto for a better society. You could well argue that we are still waiting. Yet it had an immensely potent influence, not just on Scotland's religion but also on Scotland's culture and sociology. The downside was the rigorous emphasis on pervasive and sometimes oppressive social discipline; the benefits were the ameliorative emphasis on self-restraint, on self-improving, on education, on democracy, on social responsibility and on social inclusion. Scottish society was to progress from being feudal, ignorant and backward to being more cerebral and aspirational.

Even more importantly, there was to be a renewed emphasis on pastoral and spiritual care. The old Church, the most important institution in the kingdom, had simply not been providing these on anything like the scale needed. People were to be more accountable for their behaviour. Discussion, argument and reading became much more prevalent. People were working together. The Reformation is often alleged to have engendered individualism; this is only partly true.

The kirk sessions, at worst nosy and officious, at best supportive and caring, became the key influence in everyday life, just as the parish became the key geographic unit. The sessions investigated drunkenness (always a problem in Scotland) and sex offences as well as more overtly religious delinquency such as doctrinal error or breaking of the Sabbath. They administered poor relief and parish education; looked after the administration of marriage, birth, baptism and burial; maintained the kirk buildings and the graveyards; and sent commissioners to the General Assembly.

This Assembly, which met either once a year or biannually, effectively came into being because the new Church did not have the imprimatur of the nation's legitimate ruler, an absentee Catholic queen. So, the Assembly was a device to bypass the fact that the national Church was, in a technical sense, illegal. The first Assembly was held in December 1560. The commissioners were aware that their meeting had 'no earthly authority whatsoever'. They had the more important authority of God. This Assembly was attended by forty-two men, 'the humble as well as the eminent and the learned'. Later Assemblies were to become much larger and, indeed, grander occasions. (An excellent little book by B. A. Myers examines the lives of these first forty-two commissioners.)

The kirk session also called and assessed ministers. An acute problem for the new Church was a serious shortage of ministers; one of the driving forces behind the fresh emphasis on education was the need to educate a cadre of young, scholarly and resolute ministers. To deal with the shortfall, readers – in effect, untrained substitute ministers – were appointed to lead prayer and, eventually, to officiate at baptisms and marriages. The paucity of ministers was a difficulty without doubt; yet the clerk to the session was in some ways nearly as important a personage as the minister – and there was no shortage of lay clerks. Meanwhile, pastimes such as golf and dancing and drinking in taverns were not prohibited, but attendance at church took precedence on Sunday. Attendance at the Sunday service was obligatory, even for the laird. Searchers were appointed to scour the taverns and even people's homes to find truants.

The undoubted element of repressive enforcement was only part of the picture. Many people embraced the new religion with great enthusiasm. The reformers insisted that there was to be no intercessor between man and God, so the people needed to be able to read and understand the Bible. Standards of education undoubtedly improved in Scotland, although it was some time before most parishes did have the school they were supposed to have. And the family was an essential part of the social fabric that the session sought very much to maintain in good repair.

And yet – there was the hideous persecution of so-called witches, there was the officious snooping, there was intolerance, and there was the unnecessary, even crazed, destruction of lovely artefacts and buildings that were deemed to be idolatrous. There was the loss of ritual and ceremonial – a great juddering breach in a continuum that had lasted for centuries. It was emphatically not a time for people of a conservative disposition.

A comprehensive, balanced verdict on all this is almost impossible. For me, the most important aspect of the new social, as opposed to religious, ethic was the centrality of the democratic impulse. Long before Robert Burns in the late eighteenth century, Scotland, thanks to Knox and his colleagues, worked out that a man's a man for a' that.

And did life become better for the majority of Scots? I think it almost certainly did. But we cannot measure the spiritual and social well-being of the people in, say, 1570, just as we cannot measure it in, say, 1520. So, comparisons are well nigh impossible. Knox was trying to grow a godly society in imperfect soil; and, while he may not have succeeded – who could, with mere human beings? – the experiment was essentially benign, if impossibly ambitious, and it certainly is unfair to impugn it with comparisons to modern totalitarian regimes, as some have done.

In time, Scotland did become excessively puritan and repressive, but this was only a passing phase. And it is important to note that the new Church, in these fledgling years, was by no means Presbyterian. Indeed, at the Concordat of 1572, it was agreed that the new Church should officially embrace an Episcopalian structure. This new Church that was well established by the mid-1560s emphasised the prophetic; the sermon was at the heart of worship, and there were only two sacraments – baptism and the Lord's Supper (as opposed to seven previously).

The Lord's Supper was now a matter of genuine communion. The bread and wine were passed round from person to person. This was informal, almost humdrum, compared to what had gone before in the mass; yet it was also more special. The minister, where there was one, was the pivot in the parish; he was appointed not by remote ecclesiastical superiors but by his congregation.

Symbols and ceremonial were being expunged; idolatrous images (often things of beauty) were being ruthlessly destroyed or thrown away. But, in a way, this apparent philistinism helped the new emphasis on literacy and education. The appeal of religion was now to the intellect rather than the senses; the pull of the Church was cerebral rather than aesthetic. People had to read the Bible and to listen to the sermons. There was challenge as much as there was comfort and consolation. At the same time, there was practical, pastoral help for those with problems – and most people have problems at one time or another.

The introduction of the kirk session was crucial. Sins were carefully noted in the session records. Punishments varied; there were fines, of course, but there were also humiliations such as ducking. The penitents' stool and the stocks were used in some parishes. The big punishment of excommunication meant social as well as religious ostracism.

There was undoubtedly an imposed dullness in a land whose climate was uncongenial and grim anyway. They say that 'every day the Lord gives is in its own way beautiful' – but this is not always immediately apparent in Scotland. And many beautiful buildings were stripped and despoiled. Saints' days, midsummer days, even Christmas Day – these were no longer times for fun and celebration. The old Church had appealed to a superficial sensuality and to the certainties of repetition from one generation to the next, of ritual, of habit. So, a lot of continuity was lost – and continuity is a component of social cohesion.

The new Church appealed to something harder and more difficult. The clichéd criticism of pervasive dourness has at least some pertinence. And yet, all this was the making of modern Scotland. Here now was a society, however broken, that tried really hard to look after the vulnerable and the weak and the abused. The fines often went straight into the pool for poor relief. The elders always investigated the sudden deaths of young children. Single parents were usually supported rather than ostracised.

The abuse of children, the neglect of family members, the lives wrecked by alcohol – these were possibly proportionately less common than in today's Scotland. Parents who fell on bad times and found difficulty in bringing up their children were assisted by the kirk sessions. Delinquency and slackness in the clergy had been all too prevalent; this changed almost overnight.

What of the personnel of the old Church? Some, such as Archbishop Beaton of Glasgow, wasted little time in fleeing abroad. Indeed, it was the higher clergy who had most to fear from the new dispensation. Others waited to see what would happen; and quite a few of the old clergy became accepted into the new Church (in which they could marry). Some of the new ministers who had been priests possibly went along publicly with the new way but continued to say mass in private. The number of former priests who switched to the new Church is unknown but has been estimated at around 30 per cent.

The Counter-Reformation was now under way. It is surprising that more effort was not made to draw Scotland back to the old ways. Catholicism survived – mostly underground but, in some areas, like the north-east where the powerful Gordon family held sway, more openly.

The new Church did not sprout into full being overnight. Some towns, like Ayr and Dundee, were already well-established centres of Protestant fervour; but, in other communities, especially in the far north, Scotland could still hardly be regarded as a Protestant country. In the Highlands, there was a chronic shortage of new ministers who could speak Gaelic. After six or seven years, there were about 850 ministers to serve almost 1,200 parishes. The minister of the parish of Edinburgh was John Knox, the great exemplar. Not everyone – in fact, nobody – could match his standards. Yet a fast and potent process of evangelisation had taken place. In the 1570s and the 1580s, when the time came to refresh and renew the young Church, nobody could deny the essential fact: Scotland was a Protestant country.

CHAPTER 23

Mary Queen
of Scots

HE life of Mary Queen of Scots is generally presented as a tragedy. It could equally be regarded as a comedy, if a somewhat grisly one. Her story is at once a curious succession of mishaps and a series of grotesque misjudgements. It may ultimately be viewed as an extended misadventure. Whether all this gains genuinely tragic status obviously depends on your point of view. There is certainly enough 'tragic' material in the story for those of a romantic or sentimental disposition to mine indefinitely; but there is also a persistent current of absurdity.

What is beyond question – tragedy, comedy or whatever – is that Mary was bad news for Scotland. Even when she was a young child and could not make her own decisions, even before she was packed off to exile in France, she was the inadvertent cause of one of the blackest episodes in Scottish history.

The pro-English faction in Scotland had in 1543 tentatively arranged for Mary, the infant daughter of the dead James V, to be betrothed to Henry VIII's son, Edward. But, when the Scottish friends of France reversed this 'understanding', Henry's wrath was such that he inflicted on Scotland the terrible 'rough wooing' that visited horror and mayhem for several years on the people, most of whom were wholly innocent and uninvolved in any diplomatic duplicity.

This was, of course, hardly little Mary's fault – but, when she arrived in the country as queen, she soon showed that she could make plenty of lousy decisions of her own volition.

John Knox, displaying his wonderful penchant for retrospective mischief-making, claimed that he anticipated this. He described Mary's arrival in Leith in August 1561 to take up her rule thus:

> The sky itself plainly told what comfort she brought for this country, namely sorrow, pain, darkness, and all impiety. For in living memory, the skies were never darker than at her arrival ... besides the excessive wet, and the foulness of the air, the mist was so thick and so dark that no man could see another beyond the length of two pairs of boots ... God gave us that warning, but, alas, most were blind.

Knox is not as noted for his humour as he should be, but that is comic writing of the highest quality. Mary's biographer, Roderick Graham, called his excellent book *An Accidental Tragedy*. That was clever; while he tilted towards the tragic version, the word 'accidental' insinuated a certain caution.

Tall for her times, Mary was bewitching and beautiful; she was often, if not consistently, kind and gracious; she was a superb horsewoman and an enthusiastic dancer. But, in matters of the intellect, in politics and religion, she was inept and foolish. While she took herself seriously, she utterly lacked the judgement, guile and sheer diplomatic cunning which would have helped her through the Byzantine complexities of her new domain.

Her eminent adversary, John Knox, thought she was crafty, but in truth she lacked the ability to deploy the power-broking skills that her French mother, Mary of Guise, and her very clever cousin, Elizabeth of England, could summon when needed. And Mary was perhaps a colder woman than the stock notion of her allows. Graham notes in his biography that, although she enjoyed flirtation, she had no interest in sex.

In 1561, Mary departed, forever, from France, where she had had a short-lived marriage to the boy-king Francis II, a poor, sterile, stunted, dribbling, stuttering creature, before he had died aged just 15. She was a lovely young woman who was forsaking a sophisticated court for an austere land of which she knew little. Even her journey to Scotland was ill-fated. As her ship left Calais harbour, another ship sank and all hands drowned, to moans from Mary's servants that it was the worst of omens.

Mary and her retinue, complete with two French poets, arrived in the Firth of Forth during a dreadful rainstorm similar to the extended squalls which had scattered the French fleet eighteen months earlier. One of the poets, Brantôme, fancifully told sailors who were lighting braziers on deck that their work would not be necessary, as one glance from the queen's eyes would light up the whole sea. The same poet observed more prosaically and more realistically the next day that they had landed 'in an obscure country'.

The unpropitious journey was compounded by the fact that the landfall was a debacle. Due to a misunderstanding, no-one was waiting in Leith to receive the new queen. Eventually, an official welcoming party arrived and managed to muster at least some sense of occasion. Roderick Graham sardonically notes that 'it goes without saying that Mary wept at the squalor of her reception and Brantôme tells us that she felt she had exchanged paradise for Hell, though he was probably speaking for himself'.

Despite the inadequate welcome, the people of Edinburgh managed to show at least some enthusiasm. Although it is quite possible that Mary was not disposed to hear the loud singing of Protestant psalms at this particular point in her life, by the evening a group of musicians and singers had gathered outside the Palace of Holyroodhouse to give her that particular pleasure. Knox described them as an honest company who gave their salutations at the queen's window. Brantôme, needless to say, was less enthusiastic; he wrote of 'five or six hundred knaves of the town' with 'wretched fiddles'. The Frenchman thought the psalms were sung so badly and out of tune that 'nothing could be worse'.

It was Mary's misfortune (it was hardly a tragedy) that, inured in the ways of France and having soaked up the atmosphere of the lavish French court, she had arrived as the monarch of a small country which was now very much in anti-French mode and, further, was just embarking on an experiment in social democracy as well as religious reform. Little Scotland was suddenly contending for very large stakes. Mary did not understand such matters – that she had arrived at a time of potential social as well as religious revolution – but she did muster sufficient sense and sensitivity to make it clear that she would not interfere in the nation's religious affairs, so long as she could practise her Catholicism privately.

Yet she had already indirectly interfered; the fact that she had not endorsed the work of the Reformation Parliament rendered that entire Parliament's work technically invalid. The lack of royal imprimatur was one of the reasons why the reformers had set up their own General Assembly to meet in Edinburgh at the end of 1560. Further, the initial tolerance she showed to Scotland's Protestants hardly pleased the many remaining adherents of the old religion; and committed reformers remained suspicious of her. In truth, she did not have the skills to propitiate either side, and she did not have the regal strength and personality to impose herself on her country.

Despite her insistence on attending private masses, which was regarded by some as an affront to the more militant reformers, Mary's personal rule was perfectly tactful and circumspect for a time (despite Knox's insolent and officious hectoring) – until she made a heinous and inexplicable mistake. She fell in love with a man whom Roderick Graham, with commendable restraint, describes as a vicious syphilitic bisexual who treated the Scottish nobility with arrogant disdain and Mary with cruel neglect. This egregious man was tall and good-looking in a narcissistic, showy way. He was a fine dancer. Apart from these trifles, there was hardly anything to be said in his favour, but Mary fell for him nonetheless. His name was Henry Darnley. He realised that, if he married Mary, he would, as Graham puts it, 'have to breed', no matter how distasteful he found that part of his marriage.

Mary's marriage to Darnley in 1565 was contrary to the wishes of her more sensible aristocratic advisers. In England, Queen Elizabeth told her that the marriage would be 'perilous to the sincere amity' between the two queens. One person who advised her to go ahead was David Rizzio, an Italian musician and 'secretary' in her coterie, who was gaining more and more influence over her.

The consequence of this disastrous marriage was a divided Scotland. Mary's nobility had to choose for or against Darnley – and thus for or against the queen. Here was a 22-year-old experiencing her first real love affair. Mary may have been acting out a romantic role, but she was also playing with fire. Darnley was heir to the Earl of Lennox, the bitter rival of the powerful Duke of Hamilton. The senior nobility were now potentially even more split than usual. The nascent national Kirk was expressing unease, and Darnley was designated as the future king without the consent of Parliament.

For the supposed love of a pitiful, petulant poltroon, Mary was indulgently wrecking the always fragile stability of her country. The ill fated wedding took place at Holyroodhouse. Later, Darnley attended a service at St Giles', where John Knox preached a bitter sermon full of invective. Darnley stormed out in fury. Scotland was close to civil war. There was some sparring and manoeuvring, though serious conflict was avoided. But faction was back in a big way, and there were rumours that Mary was going to reinstate Catholicism as the country's official religion. Mary and Darnley had together sent an emissary to Philip II of Spain asking for help in restoring Catholicism and in supplanting Queen Elizabeth in England. (This was a reckless mixture of treason, treachery, duplicity and sheer stupidity.)

Darnley was in truth incapable of being politically dangerous, preferring to spend his time in the male brothels of Edinburgh rather than getting involved in serious intrigue, which did involve at least some brainpower. Meanwhile, Mary was told of the Catholic League being formed by France, Spain and the Holy Roman Empire. Rizzio, ever more influential, endorsed the league. Mary agreed to give her support. She was now in effect plotting against her own country.

Rizzio, a feline dandy who had scant political judgement, was however a quick and agreeable companion. Mary enjoyed playing cards with him. So, Darnley, despite his growing contempt for his now pregnant wife, became jealous of the Italian, who in turn despised him. A murder plot was hatched. Darnley and a gang of aristocratic hooligans determined to kill Rizzio. He was duly murdered in Holyroodhouse in 1566 by a drunken, high-born rabble. The Italian clutched at the heavily pregnant Mary's skirts as he was stabbed again and again, screaming desperately for her protection, which of course the queen was unable to provide. He was knifed fifty times. The corpse was then flung downstairs. Darnley justified the murder by telling Mary that 'Davie' had 'fallen into familiarity' with her. In the sixteenth century, there were many dignified and noble deaths. This death was not one of them. It was a squalid and wretched murder that besmirches Scotland to this day. It was odious and horrific, but it was not tragic.

Shortly before her child was born in 1566, Mary confided to the French ambassador that she wanted to return to France, possibly forever. Scotland would have been well rid of her. But she stayed. Her child, a boy who was to become James VI of Scotland and eventually James I of England, was born. So, Mary was correct when she told Darnley that he had fathered the prince who in due course would unite two kingdoms. It is a salutary thought that the king who was to unite the crowns of Scotland and England was the child of such appalling parents.

The murderer Darnley, smarting at his continued and wholly justifiable exclusion from power in Scotland, now belatedly attempted serious political intrigue. He corresponded with Philip of Spain and contacted dissident Catholic groups in England. Mary's heir James was meanwhile sent to Stirling Castle for safekeeping. This was one of the few sensible decisions Mary ever made. Darnley was becoming more than a murderous nuisance; he was now quite out of control and not afraid to snub the queen in public.

Mary's second marriage had been disastrous. Now her future third husband loomed in her life. If Darnley was weak and vain, this man, James Hepburn, Earl of Bothwell, was strong and reckless. Unlike Darnley, his sexual appetites were aggressively heterosexual:

he once had his way with a blacksmith's daughter in Haddington church. Bothwell was a typical Borders warlord – brutish, bloodthirsty and opportunistic. He acted first and thought later, if at all. He was every bit as contemptible as Darnley, if less of a wimp. In December 1566, Mary's son James was baptised at Stirling Castle. It was a Catholic ceremony, and so Bothwell, a Protestant, did not attend; but he organised the state banquet that followed. Darnley, suffering from syphilis, was absent.

Mary's reign was slipping into anarchy. Mayhem and confusion attended her every move. Any hopes of stability were dashed. The vision of Knox and his colleagues for a new, socially responsible and godly society were receding by the day. The country utterly lacked leadership from its high-born. Mary pardoned those who had killed Rizzio. The next person who had to be killed in this black farce was, obviously enough, Darnley. And so, in 1567, he was duly blown up in his house at Kirk o' Field (where the quadrangle of Edinburgh University currently stands). When the wreckage and Darnley's corpse were examined, it seemed that his neck had been wrung. It was pretty clear that Bothwell had organised this murder. Certainly, that was what all Scotland thought, although Bothwell was acquitted at a rigged court.

Mary's marriage in 1567 to the sociopath Bothwell (his wooing of her was notably rough and brutish) was, for most, the last straw. Protestants and Catholics alike were scandalised. Most of the Scottish nobility mobilised against their queen and her shameful spouse. Mary and Bothwell were confronted by an armed coalition of nobles at Carberry Hill, south-east of Edinburgh. Mary surrendered and negotiated a safe conduct for Bothwell – he was to die, insane, in a Danish prison. She underwent the humiliation of an enforced abdication. Her baby son was crowned, and her half-brother, the Protestant Earl of Moray, became regent. She was imprisoned in the castle on an island in Loch Leven. She escaped, only for her supporters to be defeated once again, this time at Langside, Glasgow. She was now faced with three choices.

She could rally her support – surprisingly, she still had some – in Scotland, and fight on. She could escape to France, where she was Queen Dowager. In France, she could have lived a life of luxury and ease; she might even have married for a fourth time and perhaps, at long last, married well. Or she could flee to England and place herself at the disposal of her cousin, now established as a distinguished and able monarch. But then, English Catholics regarded Mary as the legitimate queen of England (she was the granddaughter of James IV and Margaret Tudor – and, if the marriage of Henry VIII to Elizabeth's mother Anne Boleyn was invalid, as many Catholics genuinely believed, then Mary had a better claim to the English throne than Elizabeth).

So, in Protestant England, Mary, with this far-from-spurious claim to the throne, would serve as a dangerous focus for the considerable dissident Catholic interests. Her very presence in England was bound to revive Catholic expectations and to attract conspirators, internally as well as externally. There was little in Mary's character or her track record to suggest that the security of the established English queen would be her priority. Everywhere she went, Mary was bad news. Queen Elizabeth was only too well aware of this. But she was a decent woman as well as a formidable sovereign, and she could hardly turn away her relative, another anointed queen.

So, Mary chose option three and placed herself at Elizabeth's mercy. At least, in doing so, Mary was removing herself from Scotland, which had had more than enough of her. She thus spared Scotland yet more of the mayhem that now attended her every move. But, in inflicting herself on England – she was history's ultimate unwanted guest – this headstrong and selfish woman was hardly going to enhance England's already flimsy security. For England was now in constant peril, facing many powerful Catholic enemies, not least Spain and France. Mary's arrival was guaranteed to make the country significantly less stable.

And so, Mary's last years – nineteen of them – were spent in a kind of awkward regal captivity at a succession of dreary castles. She could not resist the temptation to plot and intrigue. Deep down, Elizabeth knew that she would have to execute her, for her own personal safety as well as the safety of England – but she procrastinated and agonised, agonised and procrastinated.

So, Mary lived on – and on. This was a long and weary coda to a wasted life full of ridiculous misjudgements and missed opportunities. At long last, Elizabeth signed the execution warrant. Mary, no longer beautiful but by now fat, round-shouldered and double-chinned, went to the executioner's block at Fotheringhay in Northamptonshire on a winter's morning in 1587. Church bells were rung and bonfires were lit throughout England in national celebration, but Elizabeth wept.

Perhaps Mary's best times had been spent with her first husband, the impotent and retarded Dauphin. She knew she was to be the queen of France; she knew equally that she was to marry not for love but for dynastic reasons. She could not expect any sexual fulfilment or any genuine adult companionship. The Dauphin, as Roderick Graham gently puts it, was like a younger, backward brother whom she could protect from harm. She was fond of him, showing him much affection. They had their private jokes and signals. As Graham suggests, with just a whiff of sentiment, she looked after her Dauphin 'as she had cared for her dolls and talked to her ponies'.

Did these relatively happy years cocoon her from reality and create a retarded persona; was she a woman of potential who suffered from arrested development? What we do know for sure is that, shortly after Mary and her little Frenchman married, he died. And, shortly after that, the young widow, ardent for something she could not grasp, sailed to this harsh, forbidding, desolate northern country that so many of us know and some of us manage to love. If there was indeed a tragedy, it was Scotland's, not Mary's.

PART 7

The Fightback

CHAPTER 24

The Counter-Reformation

$\mathscr{L}$UTHER, Zwingli, Calvin, Knox, Beza and their colleagues did not reform the Church into which they were born. They were far more than mere reformers; they were revolutionaries. They created a completely new system, with new churches, based on a new theology. Their revolution was a near-disaster for the Catholic Church. For a generation, the old Church struggled; it was rocked to its foundations by the unprecedented onslaught. At first complacent, then querulous and vacillating, then afraid, seriously afraid, it just could not get the fightback under way. Partly, this was the fault of two popes – Leo X (1513–21), who simply did not understand the significance of Luther in Germany, and then Clement VII (1523–34), who was weak, timorous and tired.

Then there came, almost miraculously, a succession of strong popes. These men, while very different in character, each played a key role in the outstanding movement that has been called both the Counter-Reformation and the Catholic Reformation. The first term certainly suggests a fightback; but some Catholic historians have objected to this terminology because they insist that a reform movement was already in existence before the Reformation and that it developed despite the Reformation. So, they prefer the latter term, the Catholic Reformation. But the distinguished Catholic historian

Philip Hughes declared himself perfectly happy with the usage 'Counter-Reformation' – and, if it was good enough for him, it is most certainly good enough for me.

Three things are indubitable.

First, the Reformation caused colossal problems for the old Church. It lost many millions of adherents. Second, because the Catholic Church was hierarchical, much depended on the reaction and leadership of the papacy. It is significant that the fightback started in earnest with an innovatory and tenacious pope, Paul III. And third, the Counter-Reformation was, eventually, a success. From around 1540, the Catholic Church contended consistently and heroically, despite continuing internal dissent and bickering, and despite almost insuperable political difficulties. The downside was that Western Christianity was now to be split indefinitely; and there were to be some terrible wars in the name of religion.

Paul III was followed by Julius III, Paul IV, Pius IV and Pius V, who, in their very different ways, collectively presided over an extraordinary renewal. Their Church regrouped and reformed and finally became once again the great Church that had all but disappeared. Above, all the Church revived thanks to its extraordinarily adroit new agency, the Society of Jesus, founded in 1534.

Luther, Calvin, Zwingli and Knox were all remarkable men who would have been exceptional in any age; but the founder of the Jesuits, Saint Ignatius Loyola (1491–1556), was their equal. Inigo (now universally known as Ignatius) Loyola, like Luther, was not always certain of where he was going and the consequences of what he was doing. The order he founded was not intended to fight against Protestantism. Initially, Ignatius dreamed of missionary work in the Middle and Far East. But soon his Jesuits were deployed as a weapon – a devastating weapon – against Protestantism.

Significantly, the Jesuits became experts in education, the providers of disciplined and organised teaching – in schools, in colleges, in seminaries, or as tutors and advisers to the great if not always the good. The Jesuits, while not altogether eschewing austerity, soon showed an adaptable ability to work with the powerful and the wealthy. As teachers and propagandists working for princes as well as bishops, they understood how the world worked. They were realists.

By the close of the sixteenth century, it was as if the Catholic Church had been reborn. It was once again confident and assertive. It was emphasising the old paths to God, through repentance, renunciation of sin, good living and good works. And this message was now far less vitiated by corruption and venality. The messengers were, for the most part, worthy of the message.

The renewed Church was able to reinvent the links between spirituality and sensuality. The Catholic Church could once again safely appeal to the senses through images, through architectural beauty and through artists of genius, such as Caravaggio and El Greco. This went against the reforming mindset that insisted that God was invisible.

Meanwhile, the trend in Protestantism was towards ever greater austerity, to an ever colder Puritanism, a banishing of all that appealed to the eye and the heart. There was a growing Protestant tendency to divorce the spiritual from the sensual, and a parallel Catholic tendency to link them. This was ironic, given that the two most formidable personalities among the Counter-Reformation popes, Paul IV (1555–9) and Pius IV (1559–65), were both Puritans of the most austere stamp. But it remains the case that, by the end of the sixteenth century, the Catholic Church was once again wholly at ease with artefacts of great beauty.

Above all, the Catholic Church had learned from the Protestants the importance – the absolutely central importance – of education. Parts of the old Church had always cherished education: we noted how Luther himself was a product of that educational excellence. But the Catholic Church had frequently failed in the training of its priests. This was addressed, to spectacular effect, during the Counter-Reformation. The most significant result of the protracted and at times chaotic Council of Trent (1545–63) was the formal instruction to all bishops to create seminaries for the proper and rigorous training of clergy.

The extent to which the people of Western Europe had been genuinely Christianised in the medieval era is debatable. What is not a matter for debate is that, after the Protestant Reformation and then the Catholic Reformation, education was used vigorously – through many diverse methods of teaching, including sermons, catechisms and homilies – to ensure that the mass of ordinary people were authentically Christian.

Ignatius Loyola has attracted almost as much controversy as Luther and Calvin. It is too easy to present him as an extremist, a world-rejecting ascetic, a man without imagination or vision. Partly, this is because of his obsessive emphasis on obedience to the Church. But he was in fact a man of supreme realism, a pragmatist who understood the world and its ways, a brilliant organiser rather than an unworldly zealot – and, above all, despite his realism and pragmatism, a man who was most certainly not devoid of imagination.

Quite the contrary. His celebrated *Spiritual Exercises* (1548) are supremely about the exercise of the imagination in the long process of personal regeneration. The word 'imagination' is often invoked to suggest a kind of effete dreaming. Loyola was far from effete. He wanted imagination to be a hard, steely instrument designed to make the sinner understand the horrors of hell as well as every last detail of the passion of Christ. The poor bereft human specimen had to experience every sound, smell and sight as a means to utter submission to Christ and his Church. If Calvin's mind and methods were supremely logical, Loyola's were supremely imaginative.

Loyola was a Basque of noble birth, born in his family's ancestral castle in the province of Guipuzcoa. In his youth, like so many of the great figures of the sixteenth century, he showed few signs of being exceptional. He was, as a soldier, helping to defend the town of Pamplona against a French incursion when a cannonball hit him, smashing one leg to bits and severely wounding the other one. The consequent surgery was botched; his wounded leg was wrongly set, not once but twice.

A period of extreme pain turned out to be what Loyola needed to steer him to his purpose. His long physical agony slowly transmogrified into a spiritual agony not dissimilar to that which Luther had gone through a few years earlier. As his body slowly healed, Loyola found no parallel healing in his soul. It remained in torment. He decided to become a saint. This was one of the great moments of Christian history.

Loyola saw a vision of the Madonna and her child; he now understood that he could indeed be a saint, just like Francis or Dominic. For a whole year, in a convent at Manresa, he punished himself with unremitting severity. He spent a third of each day praying; he beat himself; he left his hair and his nails uncut. But still, like Luther, he could not gain the spiritual release he so desperately sought.

Luther at last found his way forward by studying the teaching of St Paul; Loyola made his breakthrough by deciding to dedicate himself to the Christ who had suffered for him and for all humanity. Luther decided that faith was the key; for Loyola the key was obedience. Luther was unable to reconcile himself with God by leading a virtuous and faithful life; Loyola's struggles led him to a totally different understanding of God. Serving God entailed total submission to the 'Holy Mother Church'. So, Loyola steeled himself to become not only a saint but the supreme soldier, obedient and constant, serving the Church with complete and perfect discipline.

He was ready now, but the way forward was neither smooth nor easy. He went on a pilgrimage to Jerusalem; he returned to Spain and prepared for ordination, but such was his extraordinary zeal that – irony of ironies – he incurred the suspicion of the Inquisition and found himself in prison. Once released, he went to Paris, and there he chose his first disciples. In a chapel in northern Paris, Loyola and his new followers vowed to go to Palestine to convert Turks.

Remembering his terrible ordeal in Pamplona, Loyola seems to have nursed the vague idea of his followers being both missionaries and medical auxiliaries; they would work as stretcher-bearers and hospital orderlies. They convened in Venice, but a series of accidents prevented them from sailing for the Middle East. Instead, they moved south to Rome, where they regrouped as the Society of Jesus. In 1541, Pope Paul III confirmed them in the status of a religious order, with Loyola as their first leader or 'general'.

This papal recognition did not come by accident. Loyola had negotiated long and hard; he had also seen off the Inquisition. Like Calvin, when he gained control he insisted on an absolute, terrifying emphasis on discipline. His men were to be trained over a protracted period, with thoroughness and intensity. Yet, as well as strict discipline, there was a sinewy quality to the Jesuits. They quickly gained a reputation for suaveness and for skill in making crafty accommodations with the wider world. They also managed to straddle the two conflicting cultures of Spain and Italy, an achievement that was rare in the Counter-Reformation period. By any standards, they were a formidable weapon for the renewed Church. And they were dangerous, highly dangerous, foes of Protestantism.

They were prepared to advocate the murder of heretics. Whether it was (very brave) Jesuit priests organising covert subversion against Queen Elizabeth in England, or fanatics like the Jesuit-trained Spanish historian Juan Mariani declaring that it would be 'glorious' to exterminate the whole of the pestilential and pernicious race (i.e. Protestants), the Jesuits soon seemed to be everywhere, fighting their war with cunning, with guile, with fierce fervour and with persistent heroism.

Endorsing the Jesuits was the most significant thing Pope Paul III ever did. But he did much else. Feeble, exhausted and disillusioned when he became pope in 1534 at the age of 66, he somehow summoned the will to carry on for another fifteen years. This was heroic in itself; given all that he achieved, it was almost superhuman.

After many false starts, and a catalogue of disappointments that would have defeated a lesser man, Paul III at last managed in 1545 to convene his reforming council at Trent in the far north of Italy. This unlikely destination was chosen for political reasons; it was in Italy, just, but also in the Holy Roman Empire, just. Paul commissioned three senior cardinals to preside: Del Monte, who was to become Pope Julius III, Cervini, and the Englishman Reginald Pole.

Earlier, Paul had appointed a lesser reform commission and boldly packed it with men who he knew would be critical of the papacy and the cardinals. He was an unlikely reformer – an exhausted old man who, as a cardinal, had fathered several illegitimate children. He adored lavish spectacles such as carnivals, horse races and bull fights. But his hedonistic love of decadent entertainment belied his seriousness as a reformer. He plucked a layman, a distinguished humanist called Gasparo Contarini, from relative obscurity in Venice, making him a cardinal and Bishop of Belluno.

Contarini, who was born in 1480 three years before Luther, and died in 1542 four years before Luther died, was one of the great men of the sixteenth century and is not celebrated enough. A conciliator by temperament and persuasion, he was perhaps the last great Catholic figure capable of achieving genuine rapprochement with the Protestants and thus reuniting the Western Church. He represented the pope at the Colloquy of Ratisbon (also known as Regensburg) in 1541, where he almost reached an agreement with Bucer and Melanchthon on the vexed and crucial issue of justification by faith.

But the talks eventually broke down on another matter: what actually took place at communion. It must also be noted that, even if a concordat had been reached on justification, the leading enemies of conciliation – Francis I of France on the political side, and Cardinal Gian Pietro Caraffa on the spiritual side – would have worked long and hard to destroy it. Contarini, and other Catholic conciliators like the Englishman Pole, came very close to sharing Luther's belief that the sinner was saved by faith. They placed far less emphasis on good works. When Contarini died in 1542, almost immediately his great enemy, the Neapolitan Caraffa, became the second most powerful figure in Rome after the 74-year-old pope.

Caraffa was a complex man who had served a long apprenticeship as a priest in the slums of Rome. He was a genuine reformer and evangelical but also a zealot who detested heretics with a crazed anger. He had always hated Luther and all he stood for, and he saw the likes of Pole and Contarini as weak appeasers. Contarini's death was an opportunity for him, and he was quick to seize it.

Caraffa, supported by Ignatius Loyola, who had himself suffered earlier at the hands of the Inquisition, persuaded the pope to introduce the Inquisition to Rome. Caraffa's tactics were simple. Heresy had to be expunged at all costs. Brutality, torture and the most extreme repression were, as far as he was concerned, entirely appropriate. He rejected conciliation for the simple reason that it encouraged heresy. He was encouraged in this simplistic approach by the ominous conversion of prominent Catholics such as Bernardino Ochino and Peter Martyr to the Protestant cause.

Caraffa now announced that no toleration whatsoever was to be shown to any sort of heretic, and least of all to a Calvinist, adding that, if his own father had been a heretic, he would have gathered the wood to burn him. He bought a large house in Rome and turned it into a prison where heretics would be incarcerated and tortured.

Paul III's bull in July 1542, *Licet ab initio*, appointed Caraffa as an inquisitor-general and was in effect a declaration of all-out spiritual warfare on the Protestants. The Roman Inquisition had fearsome sway. People could be imprisoned on mere suspicion of heresy; all their property could be confiscated; and those judged guilty of heresy were to be executed. Only the pope himself could issue pardons.

Caraffa relished these draconian powers; they enhanced his contempt for conciliation. For Calvinists, he reserved a special, obsessive loathing which almost suggests madness. In the course of little more than a year, all hopes of a great conciliation had been dashed. The Catholic Church was now resurgent, aggressive and not too fastidious about what methods it was to use in the sustained fightback. But Paul III deserves credit for not giving in completely to the zealot Caraffa. He allowed Caraffa to repress, but he doggedly continued with the reforming process.

If the Roman Inquisition was from the start a terrifying weapon, the Council of Trent (which Caraffa deprecated) was at first almost laughable in its inadequacy. It was due to start in April 1545, but only six bishops turned up. The formal opening at last took place in December, with only four cardinals and four archbishops present – and not that many more bishops. Senior Catholic clergy from Germany were conspicuous by their absence.

The council's convener, Bishop Madruzzo of Trent, certainly knew how to entertain his guests. At the opening feast, seventy-four different dishes were served, and these were washed down with a venerable wine that was over 100 years old. Then Madruzzo's private orchestra provided musical accompaniment – and, when the banquet was at last over, he invited the various ladies present to join him in dancing. Whatever all this was signalling, it was clearly not a new asceticism. Indeed, this lavish indulgence apparently indicated a disdain for cleansing and reform; and yet, through protracted, tortuous and muddled deliberations, the council finally, eighteen years later, found its way to an impressive conclusion.

The first session ran until 1547. In January that year, it produced a formal denunciation of Luther's doctrine of justification by faith. The council specifically decreed that the impious could not be justified by faith alone. The Catholic position was now absolutely clear; but it could also be argued that the Catholic Church was now in the business of defining its doctrine in response to Luther.

The council reconvened four years later. There had been vague hopes of significant Protestant participation, but this never materialised. But there was now a realism, a recognition of why Luther's uproar had happened. Giambattista Castagna, who became (for only twelve days in 1590) Pope Urban VII, admitted openly that much of what Luther had taught was true. Indeed, Luther's admonitions, even if offensively expressed, were now regarded by some Catholics as part of a necessary process. It was almost as if the German had been God's instrument, telling the Church that it was erring and it simply had to change.

The final session, which was very well attended, took place from 1561 to 1563. The presence of many more non-Italian bishops led to nationalistic divisions and a new factionalism. There were punch-ups in the council, and street fights outside. Despite this, the session was productive and finally achieved unity on all major issues.

An extensive catechism, to be used by all parish priests in instructing their parishioners, was being drawn up as the last session drew to a close. The increasingly influential Charles Borromeo was appointed to chair the catechism committee, which then reconvened in Rome. Borromeo presided over much revising. Yet more revisions were undertaken under the supervision of two Dominicans, Thomas Manriquez and Eustace Locatelli. Finally, in 1566, the agreed version was endorsed by Pope Pius V. The Catholic Church now had an agreed and lucid statement of its doctrine for universal use. This was to be of crucial importance.

The Council of Trent concluded with the old Church more confident and more settled in its theology. There was now no chance whatsoever of reconciliation with Protestantism. On contentious issues – married clergy, justification by faith, vernacular translations of the Bible, and much more – there was to be no compromise. In some ways, this was a tragedy; but it meant that the Catholic Church was bolder and more resolute. It was better staffed, and its clergy were better trained and better educated.

One of the problems that had beset the council was the role of the papacy. Reforming popes were also keen to maintain the power of the papacy. There can be little doubt that the papacy in the late 1560s, after Trent, was far stronger than it had been in the early 1540s before Trent.

Paul III was succeeded in 1550 by Julius III, a throwback to the hedonistic Renaissance era. He was infatuated by his monkey-keeper, a youth whom he had first encountered in Parma – the unfortunately named Innocenzo. But Julius, in between guzzling onions and pandering to Innocenzo, was determined to push along the second session of the council. This duly did much work on strengthening the role of bishops and giving them powers to deal with slack or incompetent parish clergy. It condemned the various Protestant versions of the Eucharist and endorsed the practice of oral confession to priests.

When imperial politics rendered the suspension of the second session inevitable, Julius quietly set up various committees in Rome to prepare the ground for the next (and final) session, which he did not live to see. He was succeeded in 1555 by the unlucky Marcellus II, who lasted only a few weeks before dying.

Marcellus was succeeded by Caraffa. As Pope Paul IV, Caraffa's watchword was intolerance. Among the myriad institutions and people whom he could not tolerate was the Council of Trent, which was never going to meet as long as he was pope. He was a fierce, intransigent man who ruled through fear. So, he employed fear as a weapon, though he himself feared nobody. The word 'diplomacy' was not in his vocabulary. He hated Spaniards; he brought the distinguished archbishop Caranza, cardinal primate of Spain, to Rome and imprisoned him.

Caraffa was almost totalitarian in the exercise of his centralised authority. He herded Rome's Jews into the ghetto by the River Tiber and forced them to wear yellow. Prostitutes were imprisoned. Bishops lived in constant fear of imprisonment. Lazy and inefficient clergy were ruthlessly swept out of the Church. On one famous day, Caraffa rejected no fewer than fifty-eight proposed bishops.

More than anyone else, it was Caraffa who removed the last vestiges of Renaissance hedonism. Although he hated Protestants with extraordinary intensity, he shared one tendency of later sixteenth-century Protestantism – the trend to Puritanism. He loathed the idea of popes living as worldly rulers, surrounded by the gaudy trappings of power and show. He may have been excessively rigid, but he – more than any other pope of this period – left his stamp on the conduct of future popes. After Caraffa, popes were seen as priests, not princes. He purged monasteries, convents and the episcopate of the inadequate and the corrupt. No slack or decadent bishop could escape his ire. He was happy to humiliate them and, if necessary, to punish them like common criminals.

One of the long-term trends of the Catholic Church after Trent was to recover a judicious sensuality. Yet no-one hated the sensual more than Caraffa. He was suspicious of creative figures. Had he been pope for longer, he might have destroyed the Council of Trent itself – it did not meet during his papacy – as well as reversing the underlying trend to softness. He eluded true, universal greatness because of the unremitting bleakness of his vision. Nonetheless, in his courage, in his consistent defiance of anybody and everybody he disapproved of, no matter how powerful, and in his diamond-hard integrity, he was an absolutely outstanding pope. He was also, needless to say, highly unpopular. His death in 1559 was greeted with an outbreak of wild joy across Italy. Celebrating mobs marched through Rome releasing the prisoners of the Inquisition.

Caraffa will always be associated with fear. This terrifying and in some ways terrible man had, in his wrath, his harshness and his determination to cleanse the Church come what may, made the papacy an institution that invoked terror more than anything else. This had its counter-productive side: it made it easier for Protestant propagandists to condemn the pope as Antichrist – and, far from making all heretics afraid, to bear the hatred of a man like Caraffa was to at least some Protestants an inspiration.

In some ways, then, it was just as well that his successor, Pius IV, was a good-natured man, an effective if extravagant administrator, a cautious, political pope whose career had progressed in the relative safety of the Curia. His two great achievements were the reconvening of the Council of Trent and his promotion of his young nephew Charles Borromeo. This was not a corrupt display of nepotism; Borromeo was an exceptional man who, as Bishop of Milan, served for many years as the perfect model of all that a reforming prelate should be. Borromeo applied the many decisions of the final session of the Council of Trent with both sensitivity and firmness.

After Pius IV (1559–65) came a pope who has often been underestimated. Supported by Borromeo among others, Michele Ghislieri was a former shepherd. As Pius V (1566–72), he was almost as stern as the irascible Paul IV, but he had a more controlled personality, and his temper was less spectacular. He was an authentically holy man. He meditated on his knees at least twice every day. He fasted during Lent and Advent.

It was up to Pius V to ensure that the long work of the Council of Trent was translated into meaningful action with long-lasting effect. He had been an inquisitor, and he was a hard man, yet he nourished an idealised and almost romantic view of the papacy's mission. He sought to be a pastor, a rigorous and uncompromising one – but there was (although it was sometimes well hidden) compassion in the mix as well. He personally nursed the sick in the hospitals of Rome; he washed the wounds of the poor; he held lepers in his arms. He walked through Rome on his bare feet, and he confronted the hired killers who infested the city. He carried an aura of personal sanctity as well as an obvious moral severity.

He revised the *Index of Prohibited Books*; he introduced the revised missal and the great Catechism of Trent. He ensured that the new seminaries were properly staffed. As ever, there was a downside. His campaigns against witches, homosexuals and even matadors were distasteful and at times downright repellent. Like Calvin, he placed an enormous emphasis on discipline; he drove himself ludicrously hard. Not only did he live cleanly and modestly himself, but also he halved the expense of the upkeep of the papacy – a colossal achievement in just six years, although the costs of the papal court had shot up under his predecessor's generous spending. His frugality was legendary. A skinny, self-denying man, he could command an almost Churchillian rhetoric; he once declared that all he could offer were prayers, fasts, tears and the Bible. If anything, he was even more single-minded than Paul IV in his determination to expunge blasphemy, sodomy, concubinage, prostitution, drunkenness and adultery.

Indeed, he was keen to introduce the death penalty for adultery, but allowed himself to be dissuaded. He hated showy feasts and parties; he wanted weddings to be conducted in a Spartan manner. He abolished bullfighting – or at least he tried to. His favourite meal consisted of a small bowl of vegetable broth. He maintained, and occasionally participated in, the Roman Inquisition, which remained horrific in its punishments (though Pius IV had accused him of being too lenient when he was an inquisitor).

He reformed the breviary, and he excommunicated Queen Elizabeth of England (a deed for which many English historians have never forgiven him). He encouraged and nurtured the new religious orders – not just the celebrated Jesuits but also the Theatines, the Barnabites and the increasingly important Capuchins, who in France were to become great rivals of the Jesuits. His legacy was the implementation of the positive work of the Council of Trent; he was also politically adept and sure-footed as he developed the role of nuncios to practise diplomacy across Europe. But, like too many of the sixteenth-century popes, he remained pitifully ill-informed about faraway lands where Protestantism had taken hold, such as Scotland and the Scandinavian countries.

The political background to the Counter-Reformation was problematic. The fightback required funds; and most of the money came from Spain. But Italian popes, notably Paul IV, could be almost as hostile to Spain as they were to Protestantism. Spain became even more important to the work of the Counter-Reformation after the Holy Roman Empire split in 1556 with the abdication of Charles V. Neither his German territories nor his imperial title went to his son, Philip II of Spain.

Charles's brother Ferdinand took charge of the German heart of the empire, while Philip had to content himself with Spain, the

Netherlands, Milan, Naples – and the new territories in America. These new territories were providers of great wealth in the form of untold amounts of gold and silver – but, even so, Philip II, the secular leader of the Counter-Reformation, managed to bankrupt Spain. By 1574, his chief financial officer, Juan de Ovando, calculated that the king was somehow managing to spend fourteen times his annual revenue – and his annual revenue was not modest. Meanwhile, Ferdinand had died in 1564, and his son and successor Maximilian II proved to be seriously sympathetic to Protestantism. This did not help the Counter-Reformation cause in Germany.

In some ways, the abdication of Charles V in 1556 was a blessing for the popes. Charles V had wanted to control the papacy, and through the papacy the Church. He had sought to determine the course (and composition) of the Council of Trent, but the papacy wanted the council to be its creature. In the 1550s and 1560s, Rome steadily became the nucleus of a revived and refreshed Catholicism; but Charles would have been worried about Rome becoming the nucleus of anything significant. He certainly did not want the papacy to be in charge of reform; he wanted to keep overall control of the reforming process himself. So, his abdication was one of the key moments of the Counter-Reformation.

Philip II found it easier to work directly with popes in campaigns against Protestants – and against the Turks, who should never be forgotten. The pope who worked most closely with Philip was Pius V; and the two of them presided (from a distance) over the greatest of all the victories against the Turks in the momentous sea battle of Lepanto.

For many years, the Spaniards had been smarting over their inability to drive the Turks from the western Mediterranean. Spanish military and naval prestige, such as it was, suffered a grievous blow in 1570 when the king of Algiers opportunistically seized the Spanish satellite state of Tunisia. Pius V and Philip II agreed that a new crusade against the Turks was now essential.

After several months of complex negotiations, agreement was reached. A vast fleet would be assembled to smash the Turks once and for all. Spain, inevitably, was to be the paymaster, contributing at least half of the funds. It was also to contribute a considerable proportion of the troops, sailors and ships. The Venetians would contribute a third, the pope a sixth; and various other smaller Italian states would play their more minor parts. The supreme commander would be Don John of Austria, the bastard brother of Philip II. After some mishaps, a colossal Christian fleet gathered at Messina in Sicily. There were 300 ships and nearly 100,000 men, of whom more than half were oarsmen and sailors. The Muslim fleet was of roughly the same size, though the Turks had more soldiers and a much larger proportion of galleys.

In September 1571, the Christian fleet, under the dashing command of Don John – a man who was adept at holding his diverse force together – sailed east. The Ottoman leader, Ali Pasha, kept his fleet anchored off Lepanto in the Gulf of Corinth. Then, on 7 October, the two huge armadas engaged in one of the most spectacular sea battles ever fought. Don John's flagship was flanked to his left by the Venetians, with the Genoese and the papal galleys on his right. To his rear was a large reserve force of Spanish and Venetian galleys. The Christian cause that his fleet was fighting for was very apparent: on each of his ships a great crucifix was raised, and before the battle the crews knelt on the decks in prayer.

The turning point in the titanic struggle came when Ali Pasha's flagship was boarded – at the third attempt – and he was slain. His head was duly impaled on the prow of his ship, and the flag of the Christian cross was raised on his mainmast. Of the Turkish fleet of over 300 ships, over 100 were seized, and about 30,000 Turks were killed. The Christian losses were twenty ships and about 10,000 men. It was by any standards a massive victory, but it was essentially a defensive one; the Turks would be kept in check, and never again were they to attempt to dominate the entire Mediterranean. But there was to be no significant Christian expansion into the eastern Mediterranean and beyond; old dreams of recapturing Jerusalem were not revived. Lepanto was nonetheless an exceptional victory; and Pius V declared 7 October to be the day of the Feast of Our Lady of Victory. It was of course a Catholic victory, though there had been a few Protestants on Don John's galleys.

Lepanto symbolised the growing virility and confidence of Counter-Reformation Catholicism, and the story of the glorious triumph spread across Europe. Far away in Scotland, the precocious boy-king James VI penned a poem to celebrate the victory. The fact that it had been achieved by a grand Catholic coalition, and that the Protestant contribution had been minor, was not lost on Protestants who were concerned with politics and diplomacy.

On the other hand, the victory had cost much. The human sacrifice had been immense; and the months of planning, the sheer political and diplomatic effort that had gone into the assembling and holding together of the great Catholic coalition – all these had diverted the attention of Philip II and Pius V from the ongoing fight against Protestantism. The two men had cooperated well to create an extraordinary military alliance. Lepanto could in one sense be regarded as the high point of the Counter-Reformation; significantly, it was the Muslims, not the Protestants, who were defeated.

Meanwhile, in Western Europe, bloody wars were being fought between Catholics and Protestants, as we shall see in the next chapter.

CHAPTER 25

Dutch and
French Wars

ROM 1562 until almost the end of the century, France was
embroiled in horrendous religious turmoil. Paris, formerly
the most depraved city in Europe, now became the most dangerous
city, the scene of constant sectarian strife and murderous mayhem.
France was a Catholic country in 1562, but the Calvinist minority
(about two million, roughly 10 per cent of the population) was
significant, and growing. It was in this year that the country's
effective ruler, Catherine de Medici, the ferociously intelligent but
persistently devious Italian mother of the young King Charles IX,
tentatively allowed freedom of worship to Protestants – or Huguenots,
as they were known as in France – in their own homes.

The Calvinists were very active in France – particularly in the
south-west. They were effective in easing out Lutherans. Calvin's
printing presses in Geneva produced tracts and leaflets to be carried
over the border by eager emissaries. More than 200 pastors were
sent to France from Geneva in the late 1550s and early 1560s. Calvin
himself never explicitly endorsed absolute resistance to a legal ruler.
So, the Huguenots, in justifying armed resistance to the state, had
to make do with the tired device of insisting that their fight was
not with the legitimate monarch but with the monarch's treacherous
advisers.

Various senior figures in the French nobility were drawn to Calvinism, not only on religious grounds but also because Calvinism seemed to offer a means of liberating France: French patriots believed that both Madrid and Rome had too much influence in their country, with its constant convoluted dynastic struggles. Ironically, the region's civil wars – historians have identified eight separate wars between 1562 and 1598, but the country was really caught up in one continuous and enormously messy civil war – ensured that France's influence in the wider Europe was lessened, not enhanced.

The effective absence of France from European power politics meant that Spain was the dominant force, but under Philip II the Spaniards bankrupted themselves fighting wars against their own colonies in the Low Countries, against the English and, of course, against the Turks.

In 1562, near a little town called Vassy, fifty Huguenots worshipping in a barn were slaughtered by men under the command of the Duke of Guise, who then entered Paris as a triumphant hero. All over France, Catholic mobs went on the rampage. The Huguenots, fired up by Calvinist pastors from Geneva, and increasingly well organised, were not slow in fighting back, though they had to use guerrilla tactics; they were heavily outnumbered. But priests were murdered, and beautiful Catholic churches were sacked and vandalised – several thousand of them.

The nadir of the French religious wars came with one of the worst atrocities of the entire century, the infamous Massacre of St Bartholomew's Day in 1572. It had been arranged that, in Paris in August, Margaret of Valois, a leading Catholic, was to marry Henry of Navarre, a Protestant nobleman who was Bourbon (and was eventually to become King Henry IV of France). The 'mixed marriage', which was unlikely to be approved by the pope, had been promoted by Catherine de Medici, who thought that the religious and dynastic union which it would symbolise would suit her own interests and bring about a truce in the sporadic but intense hostilities that were sapping her son's kingdom.

The atmosphere in Paris prior to the wedding was charged. Catholic priests were openly urging the killing of heretics. A notorious curé called Vigor assured anyone who would listen to him – and many did – that God would punish anyone who stood by and allowed heresy to exist. He predicted 'torrents of blood' if the marriage took place, and he assured Parisians that this 'execrable coupling' was against God's will. Meanwhile, the price of food was rocketing upwards. Paris was on edge: the people were tense, frightened and looking for scapegoats.

The exact occasion of the massacre is a matter of confusion – which is not surprising, as Catherine was the supreme mistress of intrigue and deceit. One version has it that Catherine apparently could not resist the temptation to eliminate a Huguenot adventurer/statesman, Admiral Coligny (despite his title, he was a soldier and a politician rather than a sailor), who had been agitating for a war in the Netherlands in which the French would support the Dutch rebels. This was a crafty wheeze, for such a war would appeal to French anti-Spanish patriotism while simultaneously prosecuting a Protestant cause.

Catherine regarded him as an inveterate troublemaker (not without cause; he had tried to kidnap her son) and a threat to her overweening dynastic ambitions. She possibly thought that the ongoing celebrations after the wedding would divert attention from the killing. As it happened, her hired hitman, one Charles de Louviers, was not up to the job. He fired two shots but succeeded only in fracturing Coligny's forearm and wounding his elbow. Catherine changed tack and put on a sickening pretence of regret, but some of the Huguenot leaders who gathered at Coligny's residence demanded revenge.

It should be stressed that it is not absolutely certain that Catherine did employ de Louviers; he might have been an impressionable individual who had been fired up by priests like Vigor. Catherine's actions and motives were always difficult to disentangle; she was a serial liar, an inventive rewriter of history and one of the most duplicitous personages of the entire century – which is saying something.

It is also unclear whether the attack on Coligny was meant to start a full-scale attack on leading Huguenots who had gathered in Paris for the wedding. Calvinist propagandists have insisted that this was the case, but it seems more likely that the savagery that erupted was spontaneous. In any event, Catherine, who was now out of control, persuaded the royal council, and the puppet king, her son Charles, that, as Huguenot reprisals were inevitable, they might as well get their retaliation in first.

The bloodbath that followed this perverse and wicked decision was inexcusable in any context. Coligny was murdered by a Swiss servant of the Guise family, who slit his throat, decapitated the corpse and dangled the severed head from the nearest window for the edification of the Parisian populace. 'We've started well', the Duke of Guise declared. His thugs then trailed the mutilated corpse of Coligny through the streets. Coligny's testicles were ripped from his body and flung into the River Seine. In the Latin Quarter, where fifty years earlier the young Calvin had studied, the violence was hideous. It anticipated the bloodbath of the French Revolution. The streets of the Left Bank flowed with blood – but the carnage was one-sided. The Huguenots, taken by surprise and in a minority, could offer little organised resistance. Many were dragged from their beds, half-awake in that terrible dawn. They were slaughtered with a sadistic fury that is hard to understand.

One of the many serial murderers, Pezou, a butcher to trade, boasted that he personally slit the throats of several hundred Protestants in just a few hours and then flung each of the corpses into the Seine. The violence was perpetrated by neighbour on neighbour. No doubt, old hatreds and rivalries had been festering for years, and religious hatred was a convenient, if sick, excuse for long-dreamt-of reprisals. Even so, the bestial scenes were almost beyond either description or explanation. Well-established Huguenots like Mathurin Lassault, Catherine's personal jeweller, were killed alongside ordinary citizens. One such was one Madame le Doux, who was about to give birth to her twenty-first child. She was stabbed in the gut, and her half-born baby was left dying in the gutter.

Meanwhile, in the nearby English embassy, prominent figures such as Francis Walsingham, Walter Raleigh and Philip Sidney, guarded by the king of France's elite troops, could hear the constant screams. The killing was accompanied by looting and rape. Young King Charles laughed; he thought it was all a jape. When Philip II of Spain was told the news, he too – normally the most dour of men – laughed. He wrote to Catherine that the murder of Coligny was 'to the universal benefit of all Christendom' and was 'the best and most cheerful news'.

The Venetian senate sent their formal congratulations to Catherine. In Rome, Pope Gregory XIII, the successor to Pius V, had special medals struck to celebrate the massacre. On one side of the medal was his own portrait; on the other was an image of an angel watching over the murder of Coligny. A special Te Deum was sung.

The Counter-Reformation had proved a successful movement, but the triumphalism that followed the massacre was repellent. The Turks had been defeated at Lepanto the previous year in what was an honourable set-piece battle, fought according to the conventions, such as they were. The French Protestants had been defeated in a treacherous bloodbath which reflected ill on the march of revived Catholicism.

But defeated they were. In many other French towns and cities, there were copycat slaughters. In Lyons, 2,000 Protestants were killed in twenty-four hours. Altogether, in the space of less than a week, about 6,000 Parisian Protestants were killed, and in the rest of France the death toll gradually rose to about 20,000. The killings weakened the will of Calvinists in many parts of France, not least Paris itself. One Huguenot pastor, Sureau du Rosier, saw the massacre as evidence of 'God's indignation'. He thought that 'God detested and condemned the profession and exercise of our religion as if he wished to ruin this Church and favour the Roman'.

Later, du Rosier retracted, blaming his words on the devil – and his own weakness. But many other Protestants simply gave up. The Huguenots' collective will was broken by the savagery. Eventually, they did regroup and fight back, and the civil war lasted another twenty-six years. But there was now little doubt that France would remain a Catholic country. The killing sprees did not end until King Henry IV, with English and German support, issued the Edict of Nantes in 1598, granting conditional toleration to the Huguenots. Meanwhile, in the immediate aftermath of the massacre, Catherine de Medici was not contrite. She decided that all Protestants should be removed from public office. Coligny was posthumously, and quite ludicrously, tried for treason. His chateau at Chatillon was burned, and his property was seized by King Charles.

Later, King Charles himself was to die in mysterious circumstances; Catherine was reputed to have poisoned him. The Catholic League, led by the Duke of Guise, took control of Paris. When King Henry III eventually assumed power, he made little attempt to rule in a civilised or conciliatory way. He was a cruel degenerate and preferred to indulge in protracted homosexual orgies; he became known as the King of Sodom. He was the last of the Valois dynasty to rule France.

The massacres in Paris and elsewhere in France besmirched the name of French Catholicism for many decades. The city of Paris took almost as long to recover any kind of reputation as a civilised city. Throughout Europe, and not only in Protestant Europe, Paris became known as the city of Satan. On the other hand, it was now clear that Protestantism was not going to triumph in France as it had done in England and Scotland.

In England, the reaction to the Massacre of St Bartholomew's Day was one of horrified fury. Many people, somewhat irrationally, demanded as an immediate reprisal the death of Mary Queen of Scots, now imprisoned in their country. Mary did much harm during her life, but she can hardly be held responsible for the bloodbath in Paris. Yet the Bishop of London spoke for many when he told Cecil 'forthwith to cut off the Scottish Queen's head'.

Elizabeth, sage and canny as ever, would have none of it. She was determined to maintain positive relations with France, and she had not quashed rumours that she was to marry Charles IX's younger brother, the Duke of Alençon (even though she was twenty-one years older than the duke). Meanwhile, despite the wealth being plundered on a colossal scale in the Americas, despite the destructive and debilitating civil war within France, Spanish power was slowly declining. The sea victory of Lepanto was the high point of Philip II's long rule.

Apart from that, his reign was a series of disasters. Early on, there was the collapse of the Spanish–English alliance with the death of his wife Mary Tudor in 1558. The extended revolt in the Netherlands, which he simply could not crush, no matter how desperately he tried, was a persistent drain on his own energies and his coffers. And, of course, the defeat of the 'invincible' armada which he launched against England in 1588 was a humiliation which confirmed that Spain could not command the strategically crucial waters between England, France and the Netherlands. Indeed, one of Philip's most pressing problems was the growing sea power of England and the ability of Anglo–Dutch mini-fleets, manned by skilled Protestant sailors, to take control of the English Channel.

In 1566, Dutch Calvinists, who had been repressed by their Spanish overlords, suddenly came out into the open – quite literally, in huge open-air gatherings, attended by thousands, in the meadows near Antwerp. The great painter Pieter Breughel was on hand to record these extraordinary scenes. Sadly, the ferment of the gatherings descended, as so often at this time, into a diseased desire for destruction. Church after church, first in Antwerp itself, then in Ghent and its environs, was destroyed. Images were smashed, and much of great beauty was lost forever.

Against this background, the Dutch revolt, originally a series of minor rebellions against the Spanish colonialists, took on a more revolutionary tinge. The so-called Sea Beggars – skilled Calvinist sailors – controlled the coast, and they established a strong base in the northern territory of Holland. These men were quick, courageous and resilient. Even their soubriquet was a masterpiece of propaganda; originally contemptuously described as beggars by the Spaniards, they turned the term into a description of pride.

Slowly, they took over the inland towns as well as the ports, though their numbers were proportionally small. But disciplined Calvinist congregations of no more than a couple of hundred showed that they could control towns whose populations were measured in thousands.

William of Orange, better known at that time as William the Silent, took command of the revolt in the late 1560s, though he himself did not convert to Calvinism until 1573. Indeed, he was a somewhat elusive individual who managed to move glibly from Lutheranism to Catholicism and on to Calvinism – a peculiar progression. But he was a brave and effective leader. He founded the Dutch navy, which soon became even more impressive than the English one, and he was also noted for his personal belief in tolerance – which was fitting, as his own personal religious commitments were somewhat fluid. He was given to telling his men that, although they had been persecuted, this was no reason for them to persecute others. He was assassinated in 1584; his son Maurice was an even more effective soldier.

The orgy of iconoclasm and defiance in 1566 provoked Philip II – allegedly the most powerful ruler in the world – to attempt draconian suppression. He sent the Duke of Alva, his most formidable general, to the Low Countries with about 15,000 troops. Several thousand heretics were imprisoned and killed over the next few years. Many of these executions were sanctioned by Alva's infamous 'Council of Blood', yet the revolt was sustained. Indeed, the Calvinists seemed to be winning, and the heavy-handed Spaniards could not cope with the nimble guerrilla tactics of the Sea Beggars.

There was a terrible cost, not just in blood but also in prosperity. The Netherlands had been the most prosperous part of Europe. Now the flourishing economy, based on trade, was broken. Many Protestant refugees fled to England, as they already had from France. Many other Calvinists from the southern territories fled north. Eventually, in 1578, Philip had to send an even larger force to subdue the insurrection. But the Duke of Parma, even with 20,000 crack troops, failed, just as Alva had failed before him.

Many Englishmen, excited by the tenacity of the Protestant rebels in their fight against the undoubtedly brutal tactics of the Spaniards, crossed the water to aid the insurgents in a freelance capacity. Their queen steadfastly refused formally to support the rebellion until 1585, though she had for a time allowed her ports to be used by the Sea Beggars.

Elizabeth never had much sympathy with Calvinist rebels, even if her own realm's interests suggested that she should support them – and, when she convinced herself that they were little more than pirates (and she was probably correct), she declared that the English ports were out of bounds. Paradoxically, this actually gave the rebellion a fresh impetus, for the Beggars seized, with relative ease, the Dutch home port of Brill – and this dramatic development led to the Dutch rebellion becoming a full-scale national rising. A few months after the assassination of William the Silent, Elizabeth at last sent over an army, under the Earl of Leicester, to drive the Spanish out – much as she had sent an army and navy north to help the Scots drive out the French twenty-eight years earlier.

Eventually, a compromise was concluded in the early years of the new century: there was to be a Catholic south and a Protestant north, much on the lines of present-day Belgium and the Netherlands. The Counter-Reformation succeeded in France; it was only partially successful in the Low Countries.

PART 8

Progress?

CHAPTER 26

The Kirk
Reformed

HE Scottish Reformation was a revolution. First and foremost
a religious revolution, it was also a social revolution. It could
also be regarded as a political revolution; but this must be qualified,
as the lairds and aristocrats retained their political influence, and the
monarchy remained – and, in Scotland, unlike England, the monarchy
generally did more harm than good. It would have been a revolution
too far for Scotland to become a republic, but the disastrous personal
rule of Mary Queen of Scots undoubtedly held up the country's
progress. Mary refused to endorse the legislation of the Reformation
Parliament; even more ill-advisedly, she also refused to endorse
the Treaty of Edinburgh. To do so would have meant that she was
acknowledging Elizabeth as the legitimate queen of England.

For all that, Mary had seemed reasonably sure-footed at the start
of her troubled reign. She chose to rule in peripatetic style, moving
around Scotland with the confidence of a monarch who intended to
take charge. She allowed the new Reformation ministry a reasonable
financial settlement, and she let the first five superintendents of
the new Church each have the property of a bishop. She did not
intervene when priests who had celebrated the outlawed mass were
prosecuted. But a Catholic ruling a Protestant people had to show
sensitivity and good judgement – and Mary had neither.

The birth of her son James by her egregious husband Darnley in June 1566 was celebrated in spectacular style, not least in a Catholic baptism ceremony in Stirling. (Later, after his mother's enforced abdication, there was a less lavish Protestant crowning ceremony.) Before her abdication and her flight to England, Mary's rule had descended into all-too-predictable anarchy. When she placed herself at Elizabeth's mercy, she was understandably kept in captivity. Elizabeth supported Mary's many enemies in Scotland. The country was once again mired in civil war.

The first regent, the Earl of Moray, was assassinated in 1570. The second, young James VI's grandfather, the Earl of Lennox (father of Darnley), died after a fight at Stirling in 1571. The next, the Earl of Mar, also lasted just a year, but at least he died of natural causes. The fourth, the Anglophile Earl of Morton, whose family lands were in Angus, one of the early forcing grounds of Scottish Protestantism, was a comparative survivor. A hard, autocratic man, Morton had at least some political skill. He managed to last for six years.

During Morton's regency, and with his encouragement, young James was educated as a Protestant. The main teacher of the precocious child was George Buchanan, a formidable and austere intellectual who insisted on fierce discipline and subjected the boy-king to beatings. James did not forget; shortly after Buchanan died in 1582, James had all his books banned.

Buchanan may have been excessively stern, but he was a superb educator, teaching James many subjects in a way that unleashed the boy's considerable cerebral potential. James was priggish as well as bright, not dissimilar to the young King Edward VI in England twenty years earlier. Buchanan was balanced by the softer, more humane Peter Young, whose teaching was gentler, and who possibly had more long-term influence on James. He gathered 600 books – a considerable library for the time – for the edification of his royal charge.

Buchanan was one of the great intellectual exponents of the Scottish Reformation. He also, in his thinking, came close to outright republicanism. He had studied in Paris at the same time as John Calvin, and he was respected as a scholar across Europe. He was an early moderator of the General Assembly, a poet and a humanist of international repute. Originally sympathetic to Mary Queen of Scots, he turned against her after her marriage to Darnley and became one of her most eloquent and forceful detractors. When he taught young James, he had an unfortunate tendency to rail against his charge's mother.

He also expounded his view that rulers must be answerable to the ruled. Buchanan not only believed that resistance to rulers could be legitimate; more, he thought that the common good was a larger priority than the good of the ruler. This meant that a monarch could validly be deposed. It might seem surprising, and in some respects refreshing, that such a thinker should be teaching a boy-king – but James had the intellectual confidence to challenge Buchanan, and he certainly did not allow himself to be indoctrinated by his tutor.

In Scotland, the democratic impulse was now strong. South of the Border, Queen Elizabeth – who had of course intervened to allow the Scottish Reformation to happen – was furious with some of the revolutionary doctrines being propagated by preachers like Knox and the Englishman Goodman. She felt that they were acting and talking as if they were superior to their ruler, Queen Mary. At least Mary was the legitimate ruler; there was no such authority invested in the Scottish nobility, who still had far too much sway and tended to be reckless, selfish and sometimes wholly irresponsible. They swaggered around with their armed retinues. The interests of the wider kingdom were generally the very last of their considerations.

Morton, needless to say, had to resist many attempts to over-throw him. He was more effective and more far-sighted than most of the other magnates, although there was not much competition. He was a committed Anglophile and Protestant, a friend of Queen Elizabeth's senior minister Cecil, and no supporter of the imprisoned Queen Mary south of the Border. Morton moved round the country dispensing justice, if in a partisan manner, and trying to put on a show of firm governance. But his power base was in the east, and he never mastered the whole country. He could not control the aristocratic factionalism that still bedevilled Scotland. This was hardly the ideal soil for the young Protestant Church of Scotland to grow and fructify.

James VI eventually began to assert himself. Always possessed of a strong homosexual drive, he fell in love with a Catholic Frenchman, Esmé Stuart, who, from James's point of view, arrived on the scene almost miraculously and proceeded to smash the austerity of his court. Stuart was a smarmy figure, a man in his late thirties, married with four children, and a senior member of the French court. A cousin of the king, he had come to Scotland supposedly to attend to the family estates (he was a nephew of Regent Lennox who had been killed at Stirling in 1571, and was a descendant of James II).

As soon as he arrived in Scotland in 1579, the rumours started. He had brought with him a fortune in gold – from the French king, or perhaps the Guise family (to whom he was close), or maybe even the pope himself? Mary Queen of Scots was safely imprisoned south of the Border, but here was another troublemaker from France with the money and the cunning to corrupt yet further the Scottish nobility (were such a thing possible). Gossip had it that the man was a spy acting for the French government.

Such talk was ignored by James, who was now 13 and beginning to make regular public appearances. He found Esmé Stuart pleasantly different from George Buchanan and was soon manoeuvring to have his new friend made the Earl of Lennox. He also asked that Stuart should instruct himself with a view to becoming a Protestant. Stuart obliged and then proceeded, with James's besotted support, to install himself in a newly invented office: First Gentleman of the Chamber. He acquired further offices: he became Master of the King's Wardrobe, James's leading councillor – and Lord Chamberlain of Scotland. Thus, within a few months of his arrival in Scotland, Esmé Stuart became an earl, and a year later a duke, established himself as the controller of the young king's household and made himself, as far as the intelligent but impressionable young monarch was concerned, utterly indispensable.

Despite Lennox's much-trumpeted conversion to Protestantism, his behaviour – and, worse, that of his various French hangers-on – appalled the Kirk. Walter Balcanquhal, a fiery Edinburgh minister, preached aggressively against the French courtiers who were now polluting the king's household. He condemned the whoredom, the vanity, the adultery and the cruelty in the court. He told the Scottish nobility to reform their own behaviour and the king's house as well. This was strong stuff, worthy of Knox himself.

Balcanquhal was hauled before the king's council, whom he told, reasonably enough, that the council should not be the judge of doctrine. The trouble was that he had gone well beyond doctrine in his condemnation of the licentiousness of the sycophantic fops who now surrounded James. The matter was referred to the General Assembly, who endorsed Balcanquhal's stance.

Lennox and his most impressive acolyte, an adventurer of some style called Captain James Stewart, conspired to remove the regent from power. Morton was arrested and tried for his alleged part in the Darnley murder. He was executed in 1581 with a primitive form of guillotine – an unpleasant instance of the renewed French influence in Scotland.

Lennox and his entourage were lavishly rewarded by the king, who had increasingly resented Regent Morton. The Presbyterians among the nobility were alarmed by the growing influence of Lennox, and in 1582 a gang of them captured the king (with the approval of the General Assembly) and forced him to agree to the banishment of Lennox, who went back to France, where he soon died. Meanwhile, James managed to escape from his captors.

Esmé Stuart had only been in Scotland for three years, but this had been enough to indicate the weakness of the crown – and of the regency – and the divisions among the nobility. Against this torrid background, the localised work of the kirk sessions seemed to be taking place in another world.

Sadly, Scotland's nobility remained little more than a rabble. Some of them were thuggish; others were devious; yet more were a mixture of both. Scotland's Reformation would not have happened without noble support; but, in the years following 1560, the nobility gave an extended and appalling masterclass in how to drag a country back into turmoil as soon as stability beckoned.

Regent Morton had managed to give the country some equilibrium, but he also tried to draw back the growing influence of the nascent Kirk. He preferred the English model, where the crown had clear authority over the Church; and he contended for a system of royally appointed bishops.

The growing anarchy was exacerbated by the fact that, as early as the late 1560s, the powers of the great begetter of the Reformation, John Knox, were in decline. Knox had provided inspiration, invaluable leadership and consistent drive in the two crucial years of 1559 and 1560 when the Lords of the Congregation were delivering the Reformation but also squabbling among themselves. In the first years after the revolution, he remained by far the most impressive figure in Scotland – but he was growing tired.

In the late 1560s, he was a far less fierce and combative figure than the man who had hectored Queen Mary and applauded the murder of her 'secretary' Rizzio, or the man who had played a leading role in the trial of Jedburgh minister Paul Methven. (Methven was an outspoken preacher who was accused of adultery and tried in 1563. He was found guilty and excommunicated, but merely crossed the Border and became a minister in the Anglican Church.)

Knox was unable to abolish ecclesiastical patronage by lairds and noblemen. He was a fierce critic of his queen; he was less effective in challenging the authority of the Scottish nobility. His best work was now behind him – and, as he surveyed the state of Scotland, a decade after the revolution, he must have feared for the future. Professor James McEwen believed that the reformer who lived past his triumph would inevitably see a tarnishing of his vision, and be unhappy. He thought it would have been better if Knox had died in 1560, just after his great victory.

Although he preached at the coronation of James VI, Knox must have realised that his influence was waning rapidly. He was actually driven from Edinburgh by supporters of the exiled Mary in 1571, but returned in August 1572. His last public appearance came in November 1572, when he inducted the new minister of St Giles', James Lawson from Aberdeen. After this, his fine mind was no longer coherent; but, to the last, he defied the clichéd notion of him as the dour enemy of friendship and fun. When he was certain he was dying, he ordered a hogshead – which contained a huge amount of wine – to be brought up from his cellar, and he instructed his friends to continue drinking from it after his death.

People assembled outside his house. When a sympathetic friend inside asked him if he was in pain, some of the old fire returned, and Knox upbraided him, saying it was no pain that put an end to distress and anticipated eternal joy. He died during the night of 24 November 1572. His burial in St Giles' graveyard was attended by most of the nobility who had gathered to confirm Morton as the new regent. This graveyard, in which the greatest Scotsman was buried, was completely destroyed in 1633.

A statue of Knox by John Hutchinson stands in the quadrangle of New College, Edinburgh. It was under this statue that the moderator of the Kirk's General Assembly welcomed the pope to Edinburgh in 1982. A more spectacular monument to Knox, by Thomas Hamilton, is to be found in the Necropolis behind Glasgow Cathedral. It has been said that Knox has the best view over Scotland's biggest city. This is because his monument stands atop a 58-foot column, which itself stands at the top of the Necropolis hill. Knox, as he gazes out on 'the dear green place', is clad in a Geneva gown and is holding a Bible.

In the evening of his life, Knox could not summon the subtle but sinewy political skills required to steer the new Church through the complexities of Scotland in the immediate post-revolution era. The country remained encumbered with rapacious and violent men of high rank. Knox's real failure was that he was unable to subjugate them to any kind of authority, religious or civil. The country lacked a strong monarch and was once again subject to the capricious manoeuvring of a bunch of psychopathic lawless hoodlums, otherwise known as the Scottish nobility. Indeed, many of those hoodlums did not even pay token respect to the monarch but treated first Mary and then James with insolence and contempt.

Lord Eustace Percy, whose biography of Knox is generally gracious and kind (and much praised by Professor McEwen), wrote with unusual harshness of Knox in his final years. I prefer the verdict of Professor McEwen, which is that Knox coveted peace, but lived and died amid strife. He could not lead his people to the promised land that he could see so clearly. So, one of Knox's most eloquent academic admirers concluded that his life was, ultimately, a failure. In political and even religious terms, this is probably just; but Knox's long-term legacy, in the fields of education and democracy and social organisation, was superb.

On the other hand, in the years after his death, the leaders of Scotland seemed to be intent on returning it to the midden. The arrival of the oily adventurer Esmé Stuart, seven years after Knox's death, was to show just how fragile was the secular power structure. Luckily, the religious life of the nation had been renewed, and it was no longer dependent on the behaviour or the whim of the monarch. There was growing confusion about national power: who had it, and who could exercise it. The king? The nobility? The General Assembly of the Kirk? The king tried, without success, to rule his Church through bishops. The General Assembly had no assured constitutional role in the kingdom. The nobility behaved as the murderous, self-seeking wastrels they generally were. Yet, underneath all this, the new Church took root and grew.

Knox was the first dominant figure in the new Church of Scotland. The second was the great exponent of Presbyterianism, Andrew

Melville, a man who loathed the idea of bishops in the Kirk and worked with zeal to remove them. In this, Melville could hardly be said to be Knox's own idea of an ideal successor. Knox always resisted the Presbyterian system of ecclesiastical governance. On the other hand, Knox would have admired Melville's strength of purpose and spiritual fervour.

Like Regent Morton, Melville's roots were in Angus. He was educated in Montrose, St Andrews, Paris and Lausanne, and then flourished as a teacher himself in Geneva under Calvin's successor, Theodore Beza. He returned to Scotland in 1574 and worked as an academic – first in Glasgow, where he was principal of the university and introduced specialist teaching, and then in St Andrews, where he created an internationally respected school of Protestant theology. So, his early achievements in Scotland lay in developing and reforming university education.

He was elected moderator of the General Assembly in 1578 and again in 1582, 1587 and 1594. During these years, he emerged as a ferocious opponent of episcopacy. He led the committee which produced the *Second Book of Discipline*, which was less concerned than the first one with a utopian vision of a new Scotland. It concentrated on matters such as the royal supremacy (against) and the political autonomy of the General Assembly (for).

In 1584, Melville was so outspoken that he was sentenced to imprisonment at Blackness Castle by the River Forth. He fled to England; although he was able to return a year later, he found that King James VI was adamant that bishops should remain in the Kirk. To keep Melville quiet, James sent him off on a somewhat obscure mission to root out Jesuits in north-east Scotland. He was then allowed to return to St Andrews, but the king would not let him preach there. In the mid-1590s, Melville openly defied the king on the question of what he called 'the two kingdoms'. He believed wholeheartedly in the separation of ecclesiastical and secular jurisdiction.

James was determined to undermine his influence; Melville was banned from the General Assembly in Dundee in 1598 and again from the Assembly in Montrose in 1600. (James had cleverly won the power to determine the locus of the Assembly. An Assembly in a town such as Montrose was less likely to be truculent than an Assembly in the capital.) In 1602, Melville was confined to his college in St Andrews for publicly attacking corruption in the Kirk – and, in 1606, after the Union of the Crowns, King James summoned him to Hampton Court near London, then had him imprisoned in the Tower of London for four years. From 1611, he was exiled in France. He died in 1622.

Melville's zeal to remove episcopacy and to introduce a firm Presbyterian structure infuriated the king. James made it clear that he detested Presbyterianism. He preferred the ritual and the beauty he could find in Anglican services. When he was in his teens, and had embarked on his personal rule, he encouraged the Scottish Parliament to confirm the appointment of bishops. He believed that, through the bishops, he might control the young Church. James made it increasingly clear that he had no intention of being beholden to the national Kirk.

As he reached adulthood, James signalled that he saw himself as a clever political operator, determined to assert his political rule. Yet he never managed to destroy the presbyteries or the General Assembly, and never gained complete ascendancy over Melville. In the Scottish Parliament, he sought to control or even expunge the Presbyterian tendency in the Church. The authority of bishops was confirmed; the king was supreme in all affairs of the Kirk as well as the state. But power continued to swing one way, then the other. Just when James seemed to have gained complete control over his complex little kingdom, something happened to temper his authority.

James was physically weak and psychologically timid, though he did at times show signs of cerebral defiance and bravery. He was what is known in Scotland as a 'feartie'. He lamented the 'innumerable dangers' that surrounded him; he was all too conscious of ever-present threats to his safety. He was scared of strangers, of loud noises, of hectoring teachers. He remained a potential victim of violent, feuding noblemen who were ready, sometimes eager, for a coup d'état. His physical timidity was countered by a growing tendency to intellectual arrogance, but he lacked the personality and the character to subdue his appalling aristocrats.

It is to his credit that, as he grew into a man, if a singularly un-prepossessing one, he managed to gain at least some fitful control over his stormy realm and to give it something akin to stability. It is also noteworthy that he displayed none of the imperial, militaristic assertiveness of, say, James IV. In part, this was a function of his cowardly nature; it was also a pragmatic acceptance of the fact that Scotland was now an insignificant power in European terms.

The intervention of the English to secure the Scottish Reformation and drive out the French in 1560 had been to Scotland's benefit, but it also indicated with stark clarity the realities of international power. Too often in the past, Scotland had attempted war with other nations when it was incapable of prosecuting a successful military policy; now it was becoming, in most respects, reliant on England. Minor English incursions in the 1570s indicated that Scotland was almost a satellite of Queen Elizabeth's England. And Scotland's king's abiding ambition was to be king of England. To fulfil this, he did not need to go to war. All he had to do was wait.

From the English perspective, James reacted well to the execution of his mother in 1587 and the threat posed by the Spanish armada in the following year. As long as James wanted to succeed Elizabeth, he would remain loyal to her. In 1589, he married Anne, daughter of the Protestant Frederick II of Denmark. This marriage clearly posed no threat to England.

James still feared a major Catholic uprising in his own country. This was possible if not probable in the north. In such an event, he would obviously have to rely on Protestant support; and, whether he liked it or not, the Protestant leader was Melville. In 1592, Parliament restored some of the Kirk's former powers over itself, but the feuding between Melville and the king did not stop; rather, it intensified.

These disputes were essentially about whether the Kirk should exist independently of the crown. This was a major, protracted and debilitating conflict; but it is very important to remember that, despite it, two things were indubitable. First, Scotland was now well established as a Protestant nation. Second, at the local parish level, a new and pervasive religious culture, involving not just fresh ways of worship but also teaching and welfare and social discipline, was now firmly in place. In the long run, these grassroots developments were much more important than the governance of the Kirk at national level.

If Scotland was now Protestant, as it was, how could the king remain worried about a possible Catholic uprising? Part of the answer lay in his timid nature; he was a chronic worrier. But most of the answer lay in the sway of the Earl of Huntly, the powerful Catholic magnate in the north.

The Scottish Reformation had been accomplished in the midst of a revolt against a legitimate ruler; the English Reformation – and this was the key difference – was directed by the monarchy. The Scottish Reformation was despite the monarchy; the English Reformation was through the monarchy.

The Scottish Reformation, if not bloodless, was far less bloody than the English one. This was remarkable, because Scotland was a playground for murderous, lawless noblemen. Very slowly, towards the end of the century, King James began to assert some kind of control over them. And, in any case, their malign reach and their frivolous but brutal power-plays often did not extend down to the localised, reformed communities, where the work of the kirk sessions continued apace.

Context: Europe in 1600

By 1600, the limited success of Luther's Reformation was apparent in much of Europe. It had never made much impact in Spain or Italy; in many other countries, there had been steady progress, particularly in the second phase when Calvin's influence gave reform a much harder edge. But the forces of the Counter-Reformation, especially the redoubtable Jesuits, worked enormously hard – and successfully – to pull back much of southern Germany, as well as Poland, Hungary and significant parts of Switzerland. On the other hand, northern Germany and Scandinavia were to remain solidly Lutheran.

For many Germans, Luther had awakened a sense of national pride. At the same time, he had brought fragmentation and division – and this was true across much of Europe. Sixteenth-century Europeans could not live with diversity, or what we would today call multiculturalism. And there was still an expectation that those lower down the social order, such as peasants and servants, should accept the religion of their masters. Further, the Augsburg settlement of 1555 had been predicated on the understanding that subjects followed their princes. One of the paradoxes of the Reformation is that what had initially achieved freedom – to some extent political as well as religious freedom – became more and more associated with excessive discipline and control. Tolerance did not flourish in the Europe of 1600; divisions were hardening.

There were, however, one or two hopeful signs. In Poland in 1573, the nobility had issued the Warsaw Promulgation on religious freedom, which was intended to prevent bloodshed, imprisonment, exile or confiscation of goods as a result of religious differences. In France, the Edict of Nantes in 1598 formally sanctioned the observance of two religions in the same state – and a very important state at that. The Huguenots were to be allowed freedom of worship in various designated areas throughout France, with the principal exception of the city of Paris. These areas included the estates of Huguenot landowners. More significantly still, Protestant pastors were to be subsidised by public funds. The Huguenots were also permitted to maintain a number of garrisons. Yet the edict was intended as a temporary measure, and it reflected deadlock. There were not many Huguenots: they amounted to about 10 per cent of the French population. But they were resilient and aggressive, and they were not going to be suppressed.

In the early seventeenth century, an interesting Jesuit theoretician, Martin Becanus, was tentatively proposing that tolerance of heresy might be better than repression, because tolerance might in time encourage a stronger Catholicism. But the general trend was towards a narrow and rigid dogmatism. Most Calvinists and most Catholics claimed a monopoly of truth. Lutherans were perhaps a little more open-minded. But religious pluralism was not much apparent in the Europe of 1600. The best hope lay in the growing emphasis on the importance of education, which was in time (despite the efforts of many of the educators) likely to encourage dissent, open-mindedness and inquiry and even, eventually, widespread tolerance.

It could be argued that, by 1600, the Reformation had been most successful of all in Scotland, where, despite the self-serving antics of the turbulent nobility, the spiritual leadership of Knox had been so impressive. As for England, it was in 1600 clearly a Protestant country, but there was still a strong Catholic minority. Increasingly in England, Catholicism was identified with a direct threat to the security of the state.

In the mid-sixteenth century, England had been all over the place in religious terms, taking the *cuius regio, eius religio* notion codified in the Augsburg agreement of 1555 to absurd extremes. Henry VIII's personal Reformation was a peculiar mixture of cautious Protestantism and old-style Romanism; for the tyrannical king, its most important aspect was the fact that he led it. Under his son Edward VI, hardline Protestantism was in the ascendant; under Queen Mary, there was reversal to an angry Catholicism; and then, under the careful rule of Elizabeth, a kind of elegant compromise was reached. Her settlement was of course Protestant, though it was nothing like Protestant enough for the growing numbers of English Puritans. Yet these Puritans found it difficult to gain the political control they desired – and, in the coming century, on more than one occasion, Scottish Protestants were to come to the aid of their weaker brethren south of the Border.

The early Reformation, a vast and sustained protest against failing spiritual leadership, had challenged, among other things, clerical abuse, the cynical fantasy of indulgences and the sheer deceitful folly of much traditional piety. And yet, by the end of the sixteenth century, many Europeans, after decades of convulsion, discovered that they somehow preferred the old cycle of sin followed by forgiveness. They wanted to pray for the dead; they cherished the sensual appeal of shrines and beautiful liturgy; they enjoyed the release and public joy of regular religious festivals such as Christmas. At the same time, Protestantism was becoming more austere, more rigorous and ideologically intolerant. Monastic life had all but vanished in both Scotland and England.

Calvinists in France, the early Puritans in England, Presbyterians in Scotland – these folk were contemptuous of spectacle, sensual indulgence dressed up as religious activity, and clerical hierarchy. They were wholly uninterested in the glib provision of comfort or consolation. For them, religious doctrine was a hard-edged tool that had to be applied rigorously to every last detail of their daily lives. This was a tough and demanding religion, and it was not what Luther had envisaged. It owed much more to Calvin.

Against this religious background, the Western world was changing with mind-bending speed. The (somewhat fortuitous) defeat of the 'invincible' Spanish armada by the English, and Philip II's serial overspending, despite all his bullion from the cruelly colonised New World, and the protracted and debilitating war in the Low Countries – all these reduced imperial Spain to a husk of the power it should have been. The great political story of the latter part of the sixteenth century was the failure of Spain.

It is significant that the outstanding Spaniard of the sixteenth century, Ignatius Loyola, had devoted his life to the perfect service of the Catholic Church rather than to his country. The Protestant powers of England and the Netherlands – although the Dutch were not yet fully liberated at the turn of the century – were learning to deploy sea power, not just to destroy the ramshackle might of Spain but also to develop colonial enterprise across the world.

England and Scotland, after several centuries of conflict, were drawing much closer together, and the Reformation played a very important part in the new friendship. The Union of the Crowns in 1603 was an imperfect endorsement of this process. The king who now ruled both countries was an infuriating intellectual show-off, but he did evince a benign open-mindedness towards Catholicism. He had befriended the greatest Catholic magnate in Scotland, the Earl of Huntly. His first homosexual lover, the Duke of Lennox, had been a Catholic. His wife became a Catholic. His parents were both Catholics. So, although James professed to be a Calvinist, and had been educated by hardline Protestants, he had an understanding of and sentimental respect for Catholicism that marked him out as a man of great conciliatory potential. Unfortunately, he was unable to fulfil this potential.

The most powerful social, as well as religious, tendency in both Scotland and England was the inexorable rise of the Puritans. These people wanted to purify the Church beyond the wishes of the state. They believed in strict discipline, they became increasingly dissatisfied with the laxity of the Anglican Church, and some of them quit England for the Netherlands. Later, more of them were to quit England for America. But many others stayed, and they posed severe problems for the English state.

In Scotland, the Reformation that began in 1559 reached its high point with the National Covenant of 1638, signed by so many (and by some in blood). This was hardly a manifesto for religious tolerance; rather, it was a defiant religious assertion of national identity. Prompted by King Charles I's insensitive and completely unnecessary attempts to impose a new and much-disliked Prayer Book on the Scots, the covenant marked a high point of Scottish national unity and a stirring endorsement of the country's by now settled Presbyterian religion.

The actual document, which will be discussed in the next chapter, combined religious and political issues with careful craft. It made clear that defence of the true religion and defence of Scotland's national interests were one and the same thing.

CHAPTER 27

A Wise Queen, a Foolish King

THE Puritan movement was excoriated by Queen Elizabeth of England, the most effective and splendid monarch of the sixteenth century. Yet even she could do little about the Puritans; had she lived and reigned much longer, they might well have destroyed her.

As early as 1573, she had to issue a sternly worded proclamation 'against the despisers and breakers'. The tone of this angry document is evident in the very first sentence:

> The Queen's Majesty being right sorry to understand that the order of Common Prayer set forth by the common consent of the realm, and by authority of Parliament in the first year of her realm, wherein is nothing contained but the Scripture of God and that which is consonant unto it, is now of late by some men despised and spoken against, both by open preachings and writings, and of some bold and vain and curious men new and other rites found and frequented, whereupon contentions sects and disquietness doth arise among her people.

The proclamation then referred darkly to schism and divisions, and lambasted the 'negligency' of 'bishops and other magistrates'.

Elizabeth would sometimes complain that her father, Henry VIII, would never have tolerated the truculence and downright opposition to her rule that came from these increasingly confident Puritans. But then, Henry had been able to play off Catholic against Protestant; he would temper the influence of a Cromwell or a Cranmer by cynically encouraging, for a time, the likes of Stephen Gardiner or the Duke of Norfolk. And Henry was relaxed about executing anyone who crossed him – spouses, saints, leading statesmen, Catholics, Protestants, northern rebels. He indulged in semi-judicious murder with depressing regularity, whereas his daughter Elizabeth prayed to God, like the good woman she was, to allow her to govern with grace, with clemency and without bloodshed. And, if she did not quite manage that, at least she tried very hard.

In Elizabeth's reign, Catholics were steadily driven underground; events on the continent, notably the vile Massacre of St Bartholomew's Day, indicated that Catholicism could be a most dangerous and treacherous religion. Yet the majority of her Catholic subjects were loyal and decent folk, and they wished to have nothing to do with Jesuit campaigns for rebellion. In 1564, a religious survey, undertaken by her bishops for the Privy Council, indicated that 431 magistrates were wholly supportive of the Anglican settlement, 264 were neutral and only 157 were downright hostile.

A Catholic rising in the north, in 1569, started when a group of men entered Durham Cathedral, smashed the communion table, erected two altars, tore up the Bibles on display and tried to restore the mass. This was a kind of iconoclasm in reverse; smashing up religious furniture had more usually been the preserve of militant Protestants. As it happened, there was no mood for serious revolt. Only a few thousand joined the rebellion, and it quickly fizzled out. No serious battle was fought, and the ringleaders fled across the Border to Scotland, where they joined the remnants of Queen Mary's army. So, this was no second Pilgrimage of Grace.

Elizabeth was a kinder and more inclusive ruler than her father, and her instincts were never to crush trouble in a duplicitous and brutal manner. Her leniency and decency were most obvious in her continued failure to kill her treacherous cousin Mary Queen of Scots, which would have been the sensible course of action.

Elizabeth was never going to play the Puritans off against their enemies as her father would have done. She would not balance the occasional execution of a Puritan with the executions of Catholics, which would have been Henry's tactic. Her own instincts were towards high Anglicanism – not so far from the Anglo-Catholic leanings of her father. But she owed all to the arrangement that had been speedily thrashed out at the start of her reign, when the Catholic bishops had been routed and she had defiantly chosen to follow the Protestant course. After all, one of her earliest and most significant acts had been to send both her army and her navy north to support the Protestant rebels of Scotland.

In this, she had been encouraged by her great minister Cecil – and, indeed, it was Cecil who had driven her Protestant policies early on. Elizabeth's dislike of, and resistance to, militant Protestantism was much more than a matter of personal distaste. It was a matter of statecraft. This is what made her early intervention in Scotland at once so aberrant and so brave.

Time and time again, Elizabeth refused to follow the hard Protestant line – for instance, in refusing to support the heroic Dutch rebels who were defying their brutal Spanish overlords; in refusing to kill Mary Queen of Scots despite the constant pleas of almost all her advisers; or in refusing to intervene seriously in the protracted French religious wars to help the Huguenots, though she did send a little token aid over the water. Such decisions and interventions would have been highly popular; but she maintained her line for many years, though eventually the Dutch were supported in 1585, and Mary Queen of Scots was at last executed in 1587.

The case of Mary is salutary. For almost twenty years of her reign, Elizabeth had to tolerate the desperate danger represented by the most celebrated prisoner in her realm, a rival claimant to her throne, indeed a woman who had a very credible claim on her throne. Mary was not only a representative of the opposing faith but also one who was prepared to dabble in conspiracy, plotting and subversion. Mary was without doubt guilty of treason; she wanted to depose the woman upon whose mercy she had flung herself.

It was, then, hardly surprising that so many of those whom Elizabeth most trusted would constantly badger her to have Mary executed. The queen's delay was born of many emotions and instincts, not just her innate decency mentioned above. Also in the mix were her chronic indecision, fear, feminine solidarity, regal loyalty and, possibly above all, sentiment. For Elizabeth did have her sentimental side.

She was a complex and lonely woman, and the need to present a consistently tough and stern persona that was also feminine and glittering to the world no doubt produced inner turmoil. Occasional displays of peevishness and petulance which hurt those in her closest circle indicated terrible tensions. She would bicker bitterly with those who served her best and loved her most. Her courtiers, her maids and her advisers sometimes had to endure terrible tantrums and spiteful personal insults. But she did not behead those with whom she fell out.

So, it was almost miraculous that she finally steeled herself to sign Mary's death warrant. When Elizabeth at last did the deed, it was possibly the most popular single thing she ever did. Mary died, Elizabeth wept, and almost all her subjects rejoiced.

Two Oxford-educated Catholics, William Allen and Robert Parsons, represented a serious threat to Elizabeth. They worked with influential, well-placed and wealthy Spaniards. They also had many contacts in France and of course in Rome. As fears of a Spanish invasion grew, it became more dangerous to be a covert practising Catholic in Elizabeth's England. Allen (who was made a cardinal in 1587) and Parsons directed a small but well-organised resistance movement within England. Their chosen agents were Jesuits.

In 1574, Allen, from his base in northern France, sent three priests across the water. They were the first of many. They were hidden in secret 'priest holes', often in the great houses of the old Catholic nobility. Elizabeth had allowed her peers and nobles to remain Catholics as long as they were discreet about it. Less understanding was shown to the lower orders. Sir Francis Walsingham, Elizabeth's indefatigable spymaster, maintained an impressive network of agents and informers and even *agents provocateurs*. But even he could not hunt down every last Jesuit infiltrator. Those Jesuit priests who were captured were asked what came to be known as the Bloody Question: if the pope sends an invading army to England, would you support the pope – or the queen?

Two exceptional books, which I discuss in the bibliographical essay, provide the Jesuit side of this story. The first is the autobiography of a brave and resourceful Jesuit called John Gerard, who even managed to escape from the Tower of London. His Buchanesque account of his many adventures is a fine and exciting story which graphically recalls the horror of being a hunted man. The second, and even better, book is Evelyn Waugh's superb short biography of the most noble of the Jesuit infiltrators, Edmund Campion.

The Jesuit threat came to nothing, not least because of the eventual execution of Mary and, in the following year, the defeat of the Spanish invasion force. But the Elizabethan state found it necessary to execute a considerable number of Catholic priests: 131 between 1580 and Elizabeth's death in 1603.

The most fascinating aspect of religious life in England – and, to a much lesser extent, Scotland – towards the close of the century was that the main threat to the now well-established Protestant religion did not come from Catholics but from radical, even extreme, Protestants. This was, of course, to be the major theme of the history of England in the seventeenth century. England was very slowly breaking into the three-pronged Christianity which, after the convulsions of the seventeenth century, was to become settled: Anglicanism, Nonconformism and Catholicism. And yet, from the 1570s onwards, a careful observer of Elizabeth's England might have thought that Nonconformism would eventually win hands down.

One of the manifestations of the new Puritanism was the craze for 'prophesying'. At a prophesying meeting, a group of like-minded Puritans – laymen as well as clergy – would discuss a particular text of Scripture. The gatherings were democratic; all attending were encouraged to articulate their views and their interpretations. Several of the queen's bishops, and some senior members of her court, were sympathetic to these meetings. Edmund Grindal, the Archbishop of York, publicly supported them. It was therefore a surprise when, in 1575, Elizabeth appointed Grindal to succeed Matthew Parker as Archbishop of Canterbury. He was the outstanding candidate, but he was also notably tolerant of Puritanism.

In 1576, Elizabeth ordered her new senior archbishop to proscribe the prophesying. Grindal, bravely, said he could not do so without 'offending the majesty of God'. To compound this insolence, he added: 'I choose rather to offend your earthly Majesty than choose to offend God.' This was a crucial moment. Grindal was anticipating much that was to come. Even in the face of this defiance, the queen was reluctant to take action against the archbishop for fear of making the issue even more of a *cause célèbre* than it already was. Eventually, after a few months, she placed Grindal under house arrest at his palace and suspended him from all his duties. This infuriated several of her leading advisers, including her spymaster Walsingham, who regretted what he called, in an extraordinary phrase, 'this making war against God'. But Elizabeth insisted, in somewhat patronising fashion, that the prophesying had to be suppressed. She said she did not like 'the vulgar sort' attending discussions on points of divinity that were 'unmeet of unlearned people'.

Of course, the point was that, for a growing number of her subjects, discussion of the Bible was not about mere points of divinity; it was about their very lives and how to live them. The hardline English Puritans, like the militant Presbyterians north of the Border, wanted to apply their religious belief to absolutely everything. They did not believe in putting aside their religion when it was inconvenient. Grindal died in 1583. Elizabeth was careful to appoint as his successor John Whitgift, who disliked Puritans almost as much as she did.

Towards the end of her reign, the condition of the Anglican Church deteriorated as the Puritan tendency – the enemy within – intensified. There was growing anticlericalism, and the Anglican clergy looked back with regret to what they remembered, perhaps erroneously, as the respect given to and the privileges enjoyed by Catholic priests a couple of generations back. A clergyman in the East Riding, William Crawshaw, wrote that the ministry was now held in contempt. The Anglican Church had avoided one extremity and fallen into another. Too much dignity and authority had been stripped from the ministry. The clergy were regularly abused, both verbally and physically.

Elizabeth had to face down growing Puritan truculence in Parliament. In 1576, the Member for Barnstaple, Peter Wentworth, angrily criticised her for not giving her assent to earlier parliamentary bills calling for the death of Mary Queen of Scots. Wentworth said the queen had committed great faults – indeed, they were 'dangerous faults to herself and her state'. This was too much even for Parliament; Wentworth was sent to the Tower. After a few weeks, Elizabeth released him. But Wentworth, the brother-in-law of Walsingham, was an intelligent and articulate man, confident to the point of brashness, and he was not going to go away. He bombastically quoted from the Book of Job: 'I am the new wine which hath no vent and bursteth the vessels asunder.' Happy to indict both the monarch and her Parliament when it suited him, he represented a type that was to become much more prominent in the course of the next century: the assertive parliamentary Puritan.

Elizabeth was a consummate monarch – skilful, resolute (even if often given to indecisiveness) and canny. But, without doubt, the aggressive, sniping, impudent Puritans would have worn her down eventually. For her own sake, it was probably as well that she died in 1603, fading away 'as the most resplendent sun' England ever knew. Her two Stewart successors were devoid of her carefully promoted regal brilliance, and men of Wentworth's inclinations were to grow ever more forceful. It is not fanciful to see the first signs of the troubles that were to lead to civil war in these relatively minor episodes of the 1570s.

When James VI of Scotland was progressing south to assume his new role as James I of England, the first issue he had to address was religion. Before he had even reached London, religious trouble loomed. In Northamptonshire, he was greeted by a large group of ministers bearing a contentious document, the so-called Millenary Petition. This demanded substantial reform in the Anglican clergy and significant changes in the doctrinal settlement of the Elizabethan Church. James ignored advice that he should courteously accept the petition and then quietly forget about it. Instead, he convened a great conference of clerics at Hampton Court in 1604. He wanted to show them that he was a clever monarch, their equal – probably their superior – in learned and theological disputation.

James was an intelligent idiot. It did not seem to occur to him that he had totally failed to master the Church of Scotland. There was little reason to believe that he could master the Church of England. But he was delighted to give himself a stage on which he could interrogate Anglican bishops and display his biblical scholarship before an audience of supposedly admiring divines. While his learning impressed them, his crudeness appalled them. During an obscure discussion about whether midwives should have the right to baptise dying infants, he announced with typical crassness that he would rather his child were baptised by an ape than by a woman. (He possibly sincerely believed that some midwives were witches who stole babies.) The conference concluded with the new king accepting various reforms. In the short term, it seemed to have been an enormous success. But James had been playing with fire, and the conflagration was to consume his son, King Charles I.

James had been only too pleased to quit Scotland. His eighteen years of personal rule had seen him grapple diligently with his country's finances, but he could impose little authority on the country's barbarous and lawless aristocracy or its fiery Presbyterian clerics. He was a fusspot and a pedant. He displayed little anger or indignation at the execution of his mother by the English, because he was already looking forward eagerly to the day when he would be king of England.

James's performance at the Hampton Court conference was all too typical. He was an oddball among monarchs, timid and fearful physically, yet possessed of an overweening intellectual arrogance. It was as if he had been over-educated. He had never known his mother Mary or his father, the decadent poltroon Darnley. When he was still a little boy, he had been told that his mother had killed his father. Three of the four regents who ruled on his behalf when he was young suffered violent deaths. His godmother was Elizabeth of England, but James imbibed little of her guile or majesty.

He was by far the most literary monarch Scotland ever had, though in truth there was not much competition. He was always eager to pen pretentious works on kingship, emphasising his divinely ordained authority. Given that he could not control either his anarchic nobility or the disputatious and defiant national Kirk, these works seemed more designed to impress distant onlookers with his scholarship and brainpower than to be practical primers on how to rule effectively. His books were full of pretentious and silly misjudgements. For instance, in *Basilikon Doron* (1598), he condemned the Highlands of his own realm as being populated by two sorts of people. On the mainland, they were barbarous. On the islands, they were utterly barbarous.

Meanwhile, it was the Kirk rather than the king that did most to keep the kingdom in some kind of order through its national structure of kirk sessions and presbytery courts, which were more and more powerful, particularly in Lowland Scotland. Perhaps surprisingly, the effective imposition of Kirk discipline did not make the national Church unpopular. Quite the contrary.

In Scotland, Catholicism represented less of a danger to the state than it did in England; and, indeed, James had gone out of his way to ingratiate himself with the leading Catholic magnate, the Earl of Huntly, who notoriously murdered his northern rival, the Earl of Moray, in 1592. For this crime, James placed Huntly under house arrest – for a week. James knew perfectly well that Huntly was in regular correspondence with contacts in Spain, but this did not worry him. He liked Huntly and was also scared of him. James did declare himself worried about reputed Jesuit missions in the north of Scotland, and he sent Andrew Melville to track the Jesuits down and convert them (an unlikely task) – but this was probably just a ploy to divert the truculent churchman.

Another reason for James's tolerance of Huntly was that he was the enemy of the Earl of Bothwell (nephew of the maniac who had been the third husband of Mary Queen of Scots). Bothwell detested Huntly – and, as James was far more scared of Bothwell than he was of Huntly, it made sense, in James's eyes, to cultivate Huntly. The king actually convinced himself that Bothwell was a warlock. In his freebooting adventurism, Bothwell was worthy of his uncle. He was quite prepared to attack and kidnap the king.

If the Kirk provided discipline at local level, it found it more difficult to do so nationally. James was aware of his constitutional authority over both the General Assembly and the presbyteries, and he used his power to keep the Assembly out of Edinburgh and to fiddle with the timing of its meetings. He also tried to persuade the bishops to temper the influence of the Kirk locally.

The Kirk's distinguished leader, Andrew Melville, was prepared to hector James just as aggressively as Knox had when he harangued Queen Mary. In 1596, at Falkland Palace, Melville put James – whom he called 'God's silly vassal' – in his place by telling him explicitly that there were 'two kingdoms' in Scotland. First and foremost, before the kingdom of Scotland, there was the kingdom of Christ, whose subject James was. Of this kingdom, James was not a king, nor a lord, nor a head, but a mere member. This was splendid stuff – but Melville was eventually to pay for his insolence when James, as king of England, had him imprisoned in the Tower of London.

In 1589, James married Anne of Denmark, a relatively wealthy and stable Lutheran country. Anne brought with her a large dowry, which helped James in his constant efforts to improve the royal finances. At first, the marriage seems to have been reasonably happy, despite James's homosexual tendencies. Anne bore James seven children, the fourth of whom, Charles, was born in 1600. As king, he was eventually to become a menace to his subjects both north and south of the Border. In England, he openly defied his Parliament and waged war on his own people. He was eventually executed.

In the later years of her reign, Queen Elizabeth of England became worried that Anne was going to convert to Catholicism, and she wrote to Anne warning her of the dangers of papist counsellors. The rabble-rousing St Andrews minister David Black attacked both Anne and Elizabeth as the 'devil's bairns'. Black bitterly resented the reimposition of bishops in Scotland and believed that this was partly due to the influence of the English bishops, egged on by their queen. Anne eventually did formally convert to Catholicism, but only after her husband had moved south to become king of England.

James had far less trouble with Catholics than had Elizabeth. There was at least one serious plot involving the Earl of Huntly and other Catholic nobility (who comprised about a third of the total aristocracy; as in England, high-born Catholics were more likely to be tolerated by the state than the lower-born). Huntly and his old enemy Bothwell effected a kind of grisly reconciliation. Their alliance was potentially explosive.

James appealed to the Kirk for help; with splendid insouciance, he was told that ministers would pray for his kingship. James assembled a force led by the absurdly youthful Earl of Argyll, which met Huntly's men just north of Glenlivet. Some have described the engagement as little more than a skirmish; others reckon it was a full-scale battle. What is certain is that the Catholic horsemen were too strong for the Protestant infantry; Argyll's men were defeated, despite their superior numbers. But Huntly did not, for whatever reason, press home his advantage. Eventually, the rebellion evaporated; it was almost as if Huntly lost interest in it.

There were some nasty reprisals, including the burning of houses and farms belonging to the rebels. These episodes have often been regarded as mere footnotes in the history of Scotland, yet they point to the fact that the Scottish Reformation was not quite so bloodless as has sometimes been claimed. Bothwell fled abroad, but the king was loath to punish his friend Huntly, and indeed the earl renounced Catholicism and joined the Kirk a few years later. It could be said that the king's 'softly-softly' handling of the great magnate of the north had paid off.

The battle of Glenlivet was fought in bleak hill territory a few miles north of Tomintoul. It was in this area that a few Catholics later established a small clandestine seminary called Scalan, where Catholic priests were illegally trained. The moving story of this remote community has been well told by Dr John Watts in his book *Scalan: The Forbidden College.*

Well before the establishment of Scalan, efforts were made to destroy Catholicism once and for all. But, in parts of the north-east, and also in the northern and western Highlands, there was little organised Presbyterian missionary activity. On the other hand, there were hardly sufficient undercover Catholic priests to sustain the religion, and it is impressive that Catholic worship continued, as it somehow did. Scots colleges had been founded on the continent in Douai, Paris, Rome and Madrid – but not many Scottish priests returned home.

Occasionally, Irish priests came across the sea from the west, and there were little bursts of revival. Irish Franciscans are supposed to have baptised several thousand Scots in the remote north-east in the early decades of the seventeenth century. But, for proper Catholic worship to be maintained, permanent priests were needed, and they had to be trained. Acts of the Scottish Parliament made it illegal to send young men abroad for Catholic education. Few went, and fewer still came back.

James VI became obsessed with witchcraft. Not only did he believe that Bothwell was a warlock; he also persuaded himself that witches had whipped up the seastorm which had initially prevented his queen from arriving in Scotland. She eventually landed safely, but by this time James was almost unhinged. This malign obsession led to his writing an infamous short book, *Daemonologie* (1597), whose pernicious influence was to lead to a protracted witch-hunt in Scotland.

Earlier, John Knox had participated in a witchcraft trial at St Andrews. There was an unpleasant tradition of sporadic witch-hunting, but James's intervention gave the fitful persecution the stamp of royal imprimatur. Over the next 100 years or so, more than 1,000 victims – most of them women – were tortured and then killed.

In 1563, the Scottish Parliament had made the practising of witchcraft – or consulting a witch – a capital offence. It was not until 1590 that systematic persecution started in earnest. The persecution was encouraged by the king, a man who could be at once ridiculous and malevolent.

The moment James had awaited for so long came at last when Queen Elizabeth died, on 24 March 1603. The last of the Tudors left England infinitely more sophisticated – and stable – than the country which the first of the Tudors, Henry VII, had begun to rule 118 years earlier after a long period of disastrous civil war. But the most significant difference of all was that England now, just like Scotland to the north, had its own national Church. Henry, a pious and devoted believer in the universal Church, would have found this difficult, if not downright impossible, to comprehend. He would have been even more astounded that his granddaughter's truculent Parliament was demanding ever more religious change.

But both kingdoms were relatively stable. This may be seen in the smooth succession of James to the throne of England. James left his Scottish subjects with the promise that he would return every three years. (No doubt to the relief of many Scots, he came back only once.)

He was soon lecturing the English Parliament about the need for more than the mere union of the crowns; he wanted full integration of the two kingdoms, including, most controversially, one national Church. This was rejected by the English Parliament, while back in Scotland there was, if anything, even greater fear of loss of national religious identity.

The most spectacular episode during James's early rule in England was the so-called Gunpowder Plot of 1605. Robert Catesby and other Catholic rebels attempted to blow up the House of Lords on the opening day of the new session of Parliament, when James and Anne, and most of the peers and MPs, would be present. A man called Guy Fawkes was instructed to place a large amount of explosives in underground vaults prior to the planned explosion. Somehow, he managed to smuggle no fewer than thirty-six barrels of gunpowder along an underground passage.

The barrels were discovered on the night of 4 November. Catesby and several other conspirators were killed while resisting arrest; Fawkes and several others were captured and hanged. Before Fawkes died, he was enthusiastically tortured; and King James took a personal interest in the process. It has been suggested that some of James's advisers knew of the plot from the time of its inception and allowed it to run its course until the last minute in order to award themselves a colossal anti-Catholic propaganda coup. Whether that is true or not, there can be little doubt that the plot and its dramatic uncovering fuelled widespread anti-Catholic paranoia across James's England.

By the 1620s, the Scottish Kirk was moving swiftly down the narrow road of ever more rigorous Puritanism. For example, the celebration of Christmas was banned. Calvinist discipline, at kirk-session level, meant that the Scottish Church was far more influential in all aspects of daily life than was the case south of the Border. While this Scottish road was narrow, it was also very crowded. Many Scots – quite possibly the majority of Scots – were now fanatically devoted to their Calvinist religion. Indeed, to many in Scotland, the conduct of the official English Church now seemed little more than a betrayal of the Reformation.

At the same time, the Scots were well aware of, and largely supportive of, the growing Puritan dissent south of the Border. Eventually, the English and the Scots were to combine against their pig-headed monarch, Charles I. The fact that the two countries shared a monarch but little else meant that dislike of that sovereign's interference in religion was perhaps the only thing that could bring them together.

It had certainly suited the Scots to have an absentee monarch. But Charles's ignorance of Scotland proved disastrous. He had no feeling for what was going on in the north. A few years after he became king in 1625, he started meddling mischievously and offensively in Scotland's religious arrangements. He was playing with fire. If he did not desist, there could be only one result: all-out war. It was well understood by the Scots people that a king who would not defend the true religion, but would rather attack it, needed to be resisted.

The occasion of the great clash was Charles's stubborn attempt to inflict on the Scots a Prayer Book they did not want. The response climaxed in the production of the Scottish National Covenant of 1638, forensically drafted by Alexander Henderson, the leading minister of the day, and Sir Archibald Johnston, a precocious lawyer who was only 26 at the time. Johnston had intended to become a minister but then realised that he could not endure 'the burden of more souls than his own', so he settled for the law. In time, he became a kind of Chief Secretary to the Covenanters. Their document was quickly subscribed by the country's 'noblemen, barons, gentlemen, burgesses, ministers and commons'.

The Covenant was, and is, an enormously impressive document. It is less eloquent than the more celebrated but less complex Declaration of Arbroath, and some have found it dull and legalistic, even turgid. In parts, it is legalistic, necessarily so; but it is hardly dull or turgid. Indeed, it proved to be instantly popular and amazingly potent. Signed by the nobles and barons in Edinburgh's Greyfriars Church in February 1638, it was then copied and carried by horsemen all over the country, and everywhere (with the possible exception of the north-east) many people were desperate to sign it. No doubt, some who signed were 'persuaded' and others were perhaps compelled. But that cannot diminish the essential fact that this was overall a spontaneous and authentic display of national unity. The Scots were rallying round their beloved Kirk.

Of course, some who signed it (such was its essential ambiguity) believed that they were expressing their loyalty to their sovereign. Some who signed it would shortly be fighting for that very monarch against their brothers, the Covenanters. And the Covenant certainly claimed that the Scots were defending both the Presbyterian Church and their king. But most people understood that it was the Kirk, not the king, that really had to be defended. That was the core message of the document.

While the Covenant was careful not to undermine the king's authority explicitly, the implication was that his authority was conditional. If he did not protect the true religion, he would be in trouble. After all, the stability of the kingdom depended on the 'good behaviour' of the king. Charles I, like his father, was a fool. He could not read the significance of the document. With typical arrogant petulance, he dismissed it as impertinent and damnable. His emissary, the hapless Marquis of Hamilton, was despatched to Scotland to make the Scots think again. When he landed at Leith, he found himself in the midst of an incipient uprising. There were extraordinary scenes. Thirty nobles, around 600 ministers and about 20,000 ordinary folk gathered on Leith Links to make it clear, in a memorable demonstration of popular anger, that the Scots were determined to resist Charles unless he backed down.

The General Assembly, meeting in Glasgow later in 1638, was packed with Covenanters. The two distinguished architects of the Covenant were to the fore: the moderator was Henderson; the clerk was Johnston. Huge mobs surrounded Glasgow Cathedral so that the commissioners found it hard to enter the building. The king's representative, once again the luckless Marquis of Hamilton, tried to dissolve the Assembly; he was defied, and he had to quit in humiliation. The Assembly then proceeded to abolish bishops. Perhaps more than any Assembly before (and this was the first Assembly for twenty years) or since, it spoke for the Scottish nation.

I conclude this chapter by quoting a short extract from the Covenant (a long document). With its very Scottish mixture of cringe and defiance, of obsequiousness and threat, with its consistent and genuinely democratic concern to protect the national religion, it is an authentic masterpiece. Its words are almost quivering with suppressed tension. It could also be regarded, with validity, as an ambivalent document. It was certainly drafted with great sensitivity. It managed to profess loyalty to the monarch while at the same time giving him the most stark of warnings: behave, or else. It is at once subtle, threatening and inspirational.

> Neither do we fear the foul aspersions of rebellion, combination or what else our adversaries from their craft and malice would put upon us, seeing that what we do is so well warranted, and ariseth from an unfeigned desire to maintain the true worship of God, the majesty of our king, and the peace of the kingdom, for the common happiness of ourselves and posterity.

PART 9

Controversies

CHAPTER 28

A Failed Reformation?

Scala Santa

OME's cathedral is not, as some people think, St Peter's, but St John Lateran on the other side of town. Across the piazza from this fine church, there is an undistinguished building that houses the Scala Santa (the holy stairway). Supposedly, these are the stairs of Pontius Pilate's residence in Jerusalem, once ascended by Jesus and brought to Rome by Saint Helena, and now covered by wooden boards. Through the centuries, pilgrims have come from all over the world to ascend these stairs on their knees.

It was here that Luther, during his visit to Rome in 1510, allegedly fell to his knees and dutifully began the climb; about halfway up, or so the story goes, he suddenly stood up, turned around and made his way back down to the bottom. He wanted no more of this charade.

In the summer of 2007, I visited the Scala Santa with my wife. I admit that I went in a spirit of considerable scepticism. I thought I would react to the sight of the pilgrims ascending the stairs on their knees with doubt and detachment.

You can walk up steps on either side of the sacred staircase and then stand at the top, watching this extraordinary tide of humanity moving inexorably upwards as it flows gently towards you. The prostrate pilgrims, their faces consumed with faith and fervour, seem unaware of their surroundings or those observing them. It is as if some invisible force is gently hauling them upwards. Here are humans of all ages, from the very young to the very old, and apparently many races and many nationalities, more women than men, though plenty of men, many colours of skin – in short, here is a cross-section of the entire human family.

It is rare to see so much apparently sincere humility, so much negation of self. I was truly touched, almost in tears: what I witnessed seemed to me very moving. Although I venerate Luther, he also has the power to anger me (and so many other people too). Now I found myself thinking that the man was a fool to stand up and refuse to continue his ascent.

I watched one old nun with a very strong, almost masculine, leathery face, surrounded and almost crushed by younger, stronger pilgrims. As she at last reached the top, she rubbed her hands across the final step in a spirit of deep reverence. This surely, was a very Catholic kind of nobility. As a Protestant, I looked on, not in derision, but in awe. I was being reminded of just how strong the Catholic Church is. Of course, it would be absurd to suggest that this scene indicated that the Reformation had failed; but Protestants must surely understand the very powerful ongoing and global spiritual pull of the Catholic Church. Mumbo jumbo? I don't think so.

And, of course, Rome is crucial to the Catholic Church. Perhaps Jerusalem should in theory be the geographical focus of Christianity, but Rome has become the great spiritual nucleus: it is the Catholic Church's home. It is a hierarchical church, and here is the physical apex of the hierarchy. This is something that Protestantism utterly lacks. It has no Rome, no place to go and look around and accept that this is the centre of it all.

Of course, Luther and Calvin and Knox would say: all we need is the Bible and our faith. We don't need a beautifully adorned city of God here on earth. We don't need relics, we don't need images, we don't need popes or cardinals, we don't even need glorious churches and cathedrals, and we certainly don't need ancient steps that may or may not have been transported from the Middle East. And all that is ultimately true.

Yet the Catholic Church today represents Christian continuity in a way that does provide strength in a world that is changing very quickly, partly because of technology, at a speed which makes humanity confused and even afraid, having to adjust and readjust to constant change not just on a generational but on a yearly or even a weekly basis. In such a context, the old Church can certainly provide a kind of long-standing and ongoing reassurance. On the other hand, it could be the case that, in such an uncertain world, the fragmented, fissile and relatively young Protestant churches might yet be able to adapt to people's changing spiritual needs better than a venerable but ancient institution. And, of course, the likes of Calvin and Knox would no doubt tell me that spiritual needs do not change; they are constant.

About an hour's drive east of Rome, amid the beautiful Simbruini mountains, lies the little town of Subiaco. A mile or so beyond the town is a steep, narrow gorge – and here, built into the sheer side of Monte Taleo, is the Monastery of San Benedetto, built above the cavern where Saint Benedict, who established a tough and virile form of monasticism in the sixth century, spent much time in contemplation, with his meals being lowered to him by rope.

The monastery is now in effect a series of small chapels built into the rock, linked by steep stairs and little tunnels. There is a holy grotto, statues and splendid medieval frescoes. There is a painting of St Francis (the one saint truly admired by Protestants, or so I was told by a fellow visitor), completed in 1210 by an anonymous artist. There are various fine frescoes by Conxolus, a thirteenth-century artist.

Altogether, the monastery is a heady, almost overpowering place, full of shrines, collections of bones, wonderful artwork, and of course Benedict's cave. There are two lovely little gardens, the garden of the roses and the garden of the ravens. When we visited the monastery, it was very busy but not seriously overcrowded. Many of the visitors were clearly not from Italy; some were pilgrims who had come a great distance.

The impression I gained in this numinous place was more than anything one of continuity; much of the artwork on the ancient walls was painted many generations before the Reformation was even thought of. It is sometimes salutary to remember that, in terms of Christian history, the Reformation is still a very young movement.

Places of pilgrimage, symbols, images, grottoes and shrines – this is clearly not the stuff of Protestantism. Many of the early reformers would have dismissed much of what was on display in the spectacularly sited monastery as mere idolatry. And yet I return to the point I made earlier: people still feel the need to come from all over the world to touch and to see. Maybe, these days, they feel the need more than ever. Places of pilgrimage deserve respect.

As I reflected on the potency of these images and associations that pulled in pilgrims from across our planet, I wondered if there is a paradox; the young Reformation has become slightly out of time after making an enormous impact on the world over four centuries and more. The Reformation was built on the supremacy of Scripture. Luther said it is the Word of God that builds the Church.

The Word is everything

Now I sense that the image is regaining supremacy over the word. Certainly, reading and studying books sometimes seems in danger of becoming a minority interest as the electronic media gain cultural and educational hegemony. At the same time, images are recovering a power that may be transcending the impact of the printed word.

On the other hand, I well understand that the computer and the Internet have in a sense reinvented something of the primacy of words – but academics tell me that, while intelligent young people routinely expect to graze the Internet for information and intellectual succour, this is an alternative to devouring whole books. A religion that appeals directly to the senses and emphasises artwork, ritual, personality, celebrity, ceremony and symbolism seems in some ways more in keeping with the modern zeitgeist, the contemporary spiritual quest, than a religion that wants to keep pushing people back to the Bible, the Word itself.

An interesting development in modern Christianity is the rise of the Pentecostal movement. Pentecostals, Protestant as well as Catholic, are keen on language – but oral, not written, language. There is a lot of talking and less reading in this powerful movement. But it would be wrong to suggest that the early reformers ignored the spoken word. Of course they didn't. Calvin was a phenomenal preacher; he almost bludgeoned the citizenry of Geneva into a kind of spiritual submission with the force of his preaching – he delivered more than 250 sermons each year, including three on Sundays.

The Reformation was a great revolt against authority. The Catholic Church remains a hierarchical church, and authority is established in a direct line from the pope downwards. The Reformation was a fierce reaction against this line management, to use the modern jargon; it emphasised the primacy of the individual conscience. It wanted people to think for themselves rather than be told what to think by priests (who maybe didn't understand what the message was in the first place). Many of the reformers were also suspicious of people gaining comfort and consolation from artefacts, however gorgeous and enduring, created by artists.

One of the most striking – and impressive – aspects of the Reformation was its sheer demotic drive: a relatively small elite lost control over people because it no longer owned the means of communication. The Reformation bequeathed a new and liberating emphasis on education and universal – or near-universal – literacy. One thing that is not in doubt is that the Reformation was a political as well as a religious movement. The explosive rise of politicised Islam shows the world once again the enormous potency, and some might add danger, of the fusion of religion and politics. Protestantism might just be more suited to future political developments than Catholicism, though again I might be totally wrong.

But, if I wish to see the legacy of the Reformation in today's world, I find it in secular as much as religious achievement – in the rise of democracy, in the opening of minds, in the emphasis on education. I am, of course, not suggesting that Catholicism was or is inimical to these developments; but Protestantism drove them on with great force.

Meanwhile, the key to Protestantism is that it never had, and will not have, any centralised authority. It is the most devolved of religions; it always devolves right down to the individual, who, along with his or her co-believers, is supposed to be a priest – of a kind. The priesthood of all believers remains today as revolutionary a concept as it was in the sixteenth century. If ever a religion had the potential for speedy and unpredictable radicalisation, it was Protestantism – and this still applies.

This book has shown that, right from the start, Protestantism was not cohesive. It splintered and splintered and splintered again before it was even a generation old. What was perhaps a weakness in the past might just be a strength in tomorrow's world. But, on the purely religious measure, has Protestantism led enough people to God? Probably not, in Western Europe, anyway. This part of the world, where Protestantism began, is now largely secularised. From the start, Protestantism was divided about whether or not to work with the secular authorities. Nowadays, the secular authorities don't need to worry too much about Protestantism. They can safely ignore it. And they often do.

Protestantism played a huge role in ending the medieval world. It aided the rise of the early modern state. It had an enormous influence on the development of the USA, in the recent past the most powerful and influential country in the world (though probably not for much longer). But, if its mission was to evangelise, and to make the people truly Christian, not only in Europe but also across the globe, the verdict on its success or failure must be mixed. It has not failed, but it clearly has not succeeded either. This is not a despairing verdict; indeed, it gives today's Protestants both a challenge and an opportunity.

Meanwhile, I have presented Protestantism and Catholicism as separate entities. The two religions are no longer at war with each other; they are no longer enemies. Even when they were in effect at war, there was common ground. A feature of the sixteenth century is that there was no division in the gracious and noble way in which the martyrs met their deaths. Those who died so bravely died for their convictions, Protestant and Catholic alike, and they were certain that they died in the grace of their saviour who had already died for them, and that they were about to meet him. They had that in common.

But, of course, there were hatreds and fears; that is why there were martyrdoms. Even now, all the old hatreds have not totally vanished, as we are all too aware in the British Isles and elsewhere. On the other hand, I believe that this is one of the periods when the potential for genuine ecumenism is high. But I also believe that there cannot be meaningful ecumenism unless there is an understanding of the past, with all its bitter and furious divisions.

Finally, if Luther, Calvin and Knox arrived back in Wittenberg, Geneva and Edinburgh today, they would probably feel the need to start all over again. But then, that is probably what all Christians should be doing anyway – this day and every day.

CHAPTER 29

Three Contentious Matters

$\mathcal{J}$UST about everything connected with the Reformation was contentious in some respect, but here I wish to discuss three particularly controversial matters: the destruction and despoliation associated with the reformers; women and the Reformation; and Calvin and capitalism.

Destruction and despoliation

The dissolution of the English monasteries under Henry VIII in the 1530s was a disgraceful extended act of legalised vandalism and theft. It's true that Henry's great servant Thomas Cromwell, and those whom he employed to dissolve and strip the monasteries, were not motivated by purely religious ardour. Whether this makes their destructive and rapacious zeal better or worse is a moot point.

Parts of England, and Yorkshire in particular, still possess many ruins which testify to the glorious inheritance that was smashed away in four terrible years of state-sponsored destruction. A splendid guide to these picturesque and desperately sad ruins was written by a man I was privileged to know – Rev. Henry Thorold, who was both squire and parson of Marston, a large village a few miles south-east of Newark. In his *Collins Guide to the Ruined Abbeys of England, Wales and Scotland*, Thorold does not hold back. He describes the dissolution as disgraceful and distressing.

In the summer of 2006, friends who live in North Yorkshire took my wife and me to visit the ruins of Jervaulx Abbey. I found the place particularly moving – and it was while we wandered around the crumbling ancient stonework that I suddenly remembered the story of the Pilgrimage of Grace and decided to write this book. I soon found out that there were twenty-six monks at the monastery when it was suppressed. The last abbot, Adam Sedber, was executed for his part in the Pilgrimage. After the Pilgrimage had been brutally crushed, the lead and bells were quickly removed by Cromwell's agents. Most of the stone was plundered by local builders.

For a time, Jervaulx was used as a stud farm for royal horses. Then Henry VIII presented the Jervaulx estate to the Earl of Lennox as a tainted reward for supporting English interests in Scotland. Lennox's son Lord Darnley was one of the most grotesque personages in the entire colourful saga of Scottish history. When he was blown up at Kirk o' Field, was it a case of the sins of the fathers?

Enough still stands at Jervaulx, amid the flowers and the trees, to give an impression of what a magnificent building this must have been, even though it was not one of the larger abbeys. Henry Thorold states that the 'great thrill' about Jervaulx is that, because it remains private property, it has not been tidied up too much. The various preservationist organisations, which can be very officious, have not yet got their hands on it.

Thorold's anger is mild compared to that of Peter Galloway, a distinguished historian of Scotland's cathedrals. Galloway has been eloquent, and scathing, about the unfortunate effects of reforming zeal on Scotland's glorious medieval cathedrals. He has, in the context of the considerable vandalism and destruction that took place, wondered whether the downside of the Scottish Reformation did not, as far as cathedrals were concerned, outweigh the movement's various benefits.

On the other hand, Duncan Macmillan, in his magisterial *Scottish Art: 1460–2000*, while conceding the sadness of the wreck of Scotland's medieval past, reckons that it is difficult to form a balanced view. He writes that

> nothing has told so effectively against the reformers as their promotion of iconoclasm. Under the general label of Calvinism, because of their attack on what later centuries have come to regard as the very fabric of civilisation, the whole cause of Reform has been discredited and its central place in creating what is distinctive in the history of the modern West has been largely lost from view.

I can well understand the anger, although sometimes the destruction was not entirely due to the misguided zeal of reformers. Elgin Cathedral, which is perhaps the most beautiful of all Scottish ruins, was first attacked and partially destroyed by Alexander Stewart, the infamous Wolf of Badenoch, after he had been censured by the Bishop of Moray. Whatever the Wolf may or may not have been, he was clearly not a Protestant, as he lived in the fourteenth century.

Galloway's admonitions are perhaps most feelingly apprehended at Dunkeld Cathedral, whose actual ruins, while impressive, are less evocative than others. What makes Dunkeld very special is its exquisite situation at the edge of the little town, down the characterful but modest Cathedral Street. As you approach the building, you realise that these ruins are situated in glorious wooded parkland beside the fast-flowing splendour of the River Tay, here at its widest (upstream of Perth) and most beautiful, and near its confluence with the smaller River Braan. Telford's fine bridge over the river can be seen a short distance away.

What is particularly poignant about Dunkeld is that the 'village end', the choir and chancel, have been restored and reroofed and are now used as a Church of Scotland parish kirk. The attachment of this working kirk alongside the larger ruins makes for a most thought-provoking juxtaposition. The cathedral was desecrated in 1560, partly on the orders of the Lords of the Congregation. Beside the working kirk, there is a little museum in the chapter house, where there is candour about the scale of the vandalism: an information board refers to 'an orgy of destruction'.

Luther should not take too much responsibility for the destructive spree which swept Europe. His writings are so voluminous that they do contain contradictions, but in general he was cautiously in favour of ecclesiastical art. He was personally enthusiastic about the work of the great German painters Dürer and Lucas Cranach the Elder. Although Luther worked almost entirely through the spoken and written word, he was not averse to using images for propaganda purposes.

Cranach the Elder produced a remarkably elaborate and graphic coloured woodcut contrasting the numinous Luther and the false Antichrist (the pope, seen greedily counting his money). An even more vivid work of art by Lucas Cranach the Younger, the *Last Supper* (1566), presents various leading reformers as apostles at the table. Melanchthon is sitting next to Christ; Luther has a lesser place.

Calvin was much more severe than Luther. In his *Institutes*, he argues that giving any artistic form to God ends up with the human work being celebrated instead of God. He believed that God's majesty was far beyond the 'perception of the eye'. He thought there was a danger of believing in or trusting in some image in addition to, or even instead of, God.

There is perhaps a suggestion of patronising people here: Calvinists can do without visual images because they so well understand verbal images. There can be little doubt that visual images help many people to nurture an idea of God as a living reality in their lives. In England, Thomas Cranmer, the great guiding survivor of the English Reformation in all its twists and turns – until he was martyred in Queen Mary's reign – was surprisingly zealous in his attempts to ensure that all 'idolatry' was destroyed.

There is of course another side to all this. The Reformation was in part about cleansing, about stripping down to the bare essentials of religion. For me, the perfect physical manifestation of this spirit is to be found in the Grossmünster of Zurich, the mother church of the Swiss Reformation led by Zwingli and Bullinger. Situated in the centre of town, on a superb elevated site above the River Limmat, the twin-towered building shows how an aggressively austere and plain church, eschewing comfort or consolation, can yet be inspirational and powerfully numinous. Inside, the austerity somehow manages to transcend grimness, though there is definitely a certain frigidity of style. You are conscious of a lack of clutter – and also a lack of warmth. This is a fine church, and it is not joyless; but you can anticipate a religion of joylessness in it.

Much was stripped out of this church by Zwingli and his followers. Here, you sense the negative power of the Reformation, its revolutionary break with the past. To start again, you first have to jettison much. Another point is that, throughout the medieval period, there was enormous emphasis on what is now called visualisation. The reformers reacted against this, much preferring the word to the image. Indirectly, the Reformation thus contributed to the secularisation of modern art.

It has been argued that, when the Counter-Reformation got under way, the Roman Church began to lose its former role as the patron of great art. After all, the Renaissance popes and their legacy were not something to be proud of, despite the works of Michelangelo and Raphael. And, of course, one of the weapons of the Counter-Reformation was the Inquisition, which hardly encouraged free artistic expression.

But I think this view is erroneous. In the seventeenth century, the Counter-Reformation, as it progressed, developed a new house style, the Baroque. It is indisputable that the High Baroque appealed blatantly to the emotions and the senses. There is an element of defiance in it: the Protestants may destroy images and artwork, but people will not only continue to produce religious art – that art will be expressive, even flashy.

There was, for many years, a rather prissy Protestant distaste for the Baroque, whose greatest artist by far was the Neapolitan Gianlorenzo Bernini. His imprint is everywhere in Rome. No single artist has ever made more of an individual mark on a city than Bernini did on the eternal city with his glorious fountains, statues and churches. Physically, and perhaps in spirit also, Rome today owes more to the genius of Bernini than to any other single individual.

Bernini is too often associated with over-the-top flamboyance. Yet the most pleasing small religious building I have ever come across anywhere is his beautiful little church of St Andrew in Rome, situated near the Quirinale Palace. Although modest in size, if not conception, this church, with its exquisitely designed oval dome, somehow conveys the impression of being spacious and anything but cramping. Its impact is acutely spiritual; Bernini seems to be saying that God is not austere, God is not afraid of beauty.

Bernini had, for many years, an appalling reputation in Britain, especially in the nineteenth century. The worst culprit was the egregious John Ruskin, a puffed-up arbiter of artistic merit who ludicrously stated that it was impossible for false taste and base feeling to sink lower than they did in Bernini's art. Luckily, in the twentieth century, a more enlightened view at last took hold, partly because of the positive advocacy of Bernini by the distinguished English sculptor Henry Moore.

London is a great European city adorned with far less distinguished public art than Rome; but Westminster Abbey (which competes with the cathedral of St Paul as its most celebrated church) is an amazing building, with much history apparent. The abbey's crowning glory (literally) is reckoned to be the excessively elaborate Lady Chapel, which for me contrasts poorly with Bernini's church of St Andrew in Rome. The problem with the Lady Chapel is that it is absolutely crammed with regal claptrap. As we noted in Chapter 1, it was built by Henry VII as a monument to himself and his predecessor Henry VI. The work started in 1503, and the chapel, dedicated to the Blessed Virgin Mary, was finally consecrated in 1519.

It is very difficult to study the gilded effigies of Henry himself, and his queen, because of the grandiose grille designed by Pietro

Torrigiano, who allegedly arrived in England after fleeing from Italy, having broken Michelangelo's nose before he left. James VI and I, Henry's great-great-grandson, is also interred in Henry's tomb. In the chapel, several of James's homosexual lovers are commemorated. It also houses the extravagant tomb of Mary Queen of Scots, James's mother. The king had arranged for her remains to be brought to London from Peterborough, twenty-five years after she was beheaded.

Also buried here are Queen Elizabeth, the greatest of all English monarchs, who of course ordered the execution of Mary Queen of Scots, and Queen Mary – the 'Bloody Mary' who presided over so many Protestant martyrdoms. Queen Elizabeth's effigy is headed with a quite magnificent crown. But all this regalia is a little *de trop*.

So, while Westminster Abbey is undoubtedly magnificent in its own way, I prefer to reflect on England's history in a much more modest London church, situated obscurely in the Holborn area. This is St Ethelreda's, which is to be found halfway along a quiet cul-de-sac. The church is larger than it seems from the outside, and there is much notable history to be found within.

As early as the thirteenth century, this was a parish church. Then, for a while, it served as the chapel of the Spanish Ambassador to England. It became a Protestant church, being used among others by Welsh nonconformists, and then in the nineteenth century it reverted to Roman Catholicism. Today, it is the only pre-Reformation Catholic parish church that is still used for worship in London. There seems to be a genuine spirit of ecumenism in the building.

In it are to be found the statues of various martyrs, priests who were executed during the reign of Queen Elizabeth – a useful reminder of the way things swung this way and that in the London of the sixteenth century. There is also a statue of Margaret Ward, executed in 1588, the year of the armada, for assisting the escape of a Jesuit priest. Margaret and four of the other martyrs are saints. Underneath the actual church, there is a vast and intensely atmospheric crypt whose walls reputedly go back to the sixth century. In the Second

World War, many people took refuge here during the air raids of the Blitz.

Now the church is a beautiful and reposeful sanctuary from the bustle and busy self-importance of London. It possesses especially beautiful stained glass. Self-effacing and unsung compared to Westminster Abbey, it is for me a more pleasing and more spiritual place.

Women and the Reformation

Was the Reformation good for women? As a famous Scottish footballer might have said, maybe yes, maybe no. New opportunities were offered to women. Marriage and motherhood rapidly became more fashionable – and more spiritually pleasing – than celibacy. Yet the medieval convent and nunneries had provided both refuge and education. For those women who wished to avoid marriage and childbearing and general domestic drudgery and submission, convents were positive places. Also, the medieval Catholic Church venerated the Virgin Mary.

Was it better to be a minister's official wife than a priest's unofficial concubine? Probably, yes. There was certainly less odious hypocrisy. The priesthood of all believers, Luther's core belief, obviously included women as well as men. Luther himself married Catherine, a former nun. Yet women had no official role in the new Church. They certainly could not be ministers.

Luther, while on the one hand a beer-swilling and boorish peasant, was also a kind and sensitive man. He famously – for some, notoriously – said that 'marriage is not about sleeping with a woman; anyone can do that. It's about keeping house and bringing up children.' When Luther was imprisoned for his own safety in Wartburg Castle, he was close to a major breakdown. He was deeply, dangerously unhappy. He managed to get through the crisis by writing himself out of it; the torrent of magnificent work that flowed from his pen has no precedent in literary history. Nonetheless, Luther remained seriously unstable.

Three years later, all this changed with his marriage. Catherine made Luther happy – but did he make her happy? While Luther was a world genius, she was infinitely better than he was at the ordinary but not-to-be-underestimated business of day-to-day living. She had spent many years in a convent, but she was not too old to enjoy her 'liberation'. She was intelligent, with confidence in her own opinions (surely a necessary quality for any wife of Luther's), and was a capable manager. It is not patronising Catherine, just recording the reality, to say that she proved very good at the cooking and the gardening and the housekeeping and the stewardship of the family's finances.

Most of the many words that have been written about the marriage are from Martin's point of view; but Catherine, who bore Luther five children, does genuinely seem to have enjoyed married life with her larger-than-life husband. She was busy, enormously busy. As well as the children, Catherine's aunt and two of her nieces lived in the household. And visitors came in a flood, wanting to meet the most famous man in Europe. There was a lot of talk – there was always talk when Luther was around – and not a little buffoonery. It was a large, noisy, even rumbustious household. Catherine coped with it all admirably. She and Martin had not been wildly in love at first, but their fondness and companionship developed with parenthood into genuine love. Catherine was utterly inconsolable when he died.

Luther could undoubtedly empathise with women and their lot. He insisted that there should be schools for girls as well as boys (he most certainly did not believe in coeducation). He wrote that, over the years, the female sex had borne more severe and harsh punishments than men had. Yet, ultimately, Luther was a sexist who thought that a woman's place was in the home. Martin Bucer, one of the gentlest and most conciliatory of the reformers, was not a sexist. He was far ahead of his time in advocating divorce. It was to be a last resort, admittedly, but Bucer accepted that not all marriages were perfect; a woman (and indeed a man) could be trapped in marriage for all sorts of reasons.

The Anabaptists, radical as ever, allowed women great freedom – not least in preaching. A surprising number of Anabaptist women died as martyrs.

As for John Calvin – he hated excess, but he also disliked celibacy. He was a very strong advocate of marriage. He disapproved strongly of the 'imposition of perpetual celibacy on young women in the most ardent time of life'. He could not accept that young women should enter convents on a routine basis. He regarded motherhood, in a perhaps slightly patronising way, as a calling. His own children died young, but he was well aware of the joy that offspring could bring to a marriage. And, in theory anyway, he believed that the sexes were equal before God.

At the same time, he believed that a woman's place was in the home and that wives should be subordinate to their husbands. And, if he did not exactly believe in arranged marriages, he certainly thought that young people should not choose their own marriage partners.

Two of the most remarkable women of the sixteenth century were Queen Elizabeth of England and Teresa of Avila.

Elizabeth both played up and denied her sexuality, for reasons of statecraft. She was 13 when her father died. From then on, she was a potential bride in the context of European power politics. Matrimonial diplomatic alliances were commonplace in the sixteenth century. But Elizabeth was stubborn; she insisted that she wanted to live and die a virgin. Was this her genuine inclination, or the expression of her submission to the demands of policy and statecraft? She sometimes seemed to come close to marriage, but always shied away.

While she was happy to flirt with men, she apparently had both a physical and an emotional aversion to the idea of close relations with any specific man. She did not approve of the confused sexual career of Mary Queen of Scots. Was there an element of envy? Elizabeth was often very angry when her favourite maids, courtiers or servants married.

Perhaps her fear of marriage sprang emotionally from her personal history; her father had executed her mother, a lively and very sexy woman. His matrimonial record was despicable. And Elizabeth was a canny monarch. She realised that her potential as a bride was a crucial bargaining chip in the conduct of her foreign policy. Perhaps she became all too conscious of this and subsumed her own sexuality in the interests of the state she so magnificently led.

She knew she was a class act as a monarch, and maybe she made a hard and self-denying decision that, as queen, she would not let any man get in the way of her glorious rule. She presided over the long-lasting Anglican religious settlement, which prevented women from becoming clergy. Pope Sixtus V said, in an ambiguous phrase, that if only she were a Catholic, she would be dearly loved. He added, in patronising words that suggested that he really judged her as a man: 'How well she governs! She is only a woman, only mistress of half an island, and yet she makes herself feared by Spain, by France, by the Empire, by all.'

As for Teresa of Avila in Castile, she was 40, and settled in a Carmelite convent, when she experienced her most powerful vision of Christ. Her life changed immediately. She quit the orthodox Carmelites and founded her own order of barefooted Carmelites, dedicated to austerity and poverty. She created sixteen new convents across Spain. She wrote copiously; in this respect, she was almost the female equivalent of Luther. More deeply spiritual than Loyola, she was the conscience of the Counter-Reformation. Her female religious societies in Italy and Spain did much practical work for the poor; they also worked tirelessly to promote the spiritual life of women.

One Catholic intellectual, surveying her many achievements, amazingly argued that Teresa had actually ceased to be a woman and had been restored to the 'virile state'. She certainly encountered vicious sexism. Shortly before she died, a papal envoy, Father Felipe Sega, called her a disobedient and contumacious woman. Such nonsense seems amazing today – but, even in the more enlightened

Catholicism of the Counter-Reformation, Teresa was resented as well as admired. Happily, within a generation, she had been beatified.

Bernini's famous (some would still say infamous) statue of Teresa in a state of what appears to be sexual rather than religious ecstasy was privately commissioned by Cardinal Federico Cornaro. It is to be found in the Santa Maria Della Vittoria church in central Rome, not far from the railway station. It is arguably the most controversial statue in the entire world.

If Teresa and Elizabeth were in their very different ways exceptional women, justly celebrated ever since, then almost as much attention has been paid to the various wives of Henry VIII. Anne Boleyn, Elizabeth's mother, is perhaps the most famous; for me, the two most impressive were the first and the last. Catherine of Aragon was dignified and strong when she was subject to protracted public bullying and humiliation; Catherine Parr was not just a kind and sympathetic stepmother to Elizabeth but altogether a most civilised and sensible woman. It was good that she was able to outlive the old tyrant and marry for a fourth time.

John Knox is notorious for his 'blast' against the 'monstrous' rule of women – but we saw that this was directed (with little foresight) against 'Bloody' Mary Tudor, and he rapidly changed his tune when Elizabeth succeeded Mary. Knox himself was very much a ladies' man.

He was implicated in at least one notorious case of witch-hunting. Calvin himself had earlier quoted biblical sanction for witch-killing. This craze besmirched the Scottish reformed Church in the latter years of the sixteenth century and well on into the next one. It was enthusiastically encouraged by King James VI and I; but, long after he had moved to England, the Church of Scotland continued with the persecution. Sometimes, witch trials were accompanied by torture. The victims were usually poor innocent old women. It is difficult to explain this sustained wickedness.

Some have suggested that the Reformation, having expunged much of the fantasy and 'magic' that characterised the medieval practice of religion, needed to create a new, compensating focus for superstition, a new way of exorcising irrational fears. A group of readily available scapegoats was needed, and the most convenient victims were defenceless old women. But, whatever the underlying causes, this ghastly mini-pogrom is the worst stain by far on the early history of the Scottish Reformation.

Elsewhere in Europe, the Jesuits were the most zealous witch-hunters.

While there were no prominent female reformers in the early stages of the Reformation, Katherine Zell of Strasbourg should be mentioned because she insisted that singing – joyous singing – should be a key component of Christian services. Although Luther was a prodigious writer of hymns, other key reformers were more negative. Zwingli banned all music in worship, and Calvin confined it to the singing of psalms. Katherine Zell fought hard for the singing of hymns, not just biblical psalms, and even produced her own hymnal.

Calvin and capitalism

Before we study this controversy, it is important to understand that Calvin was not a fan of wealth or display. Quite the contrary. He did not approve of wealth, and he despised greed. He wrote that wealth led to, among other things, pride, scorn of God and cruelty. He considered it a 'major plague' that people had a lust for possessions. He even wrote that 'the rich are almost grieved if the sun shines on the poor'. He also believed that 'by its nature wealth does not prevent us from following God but human nature is so depraved, it is almost certain that those who are well off will choke on their riches'.

At the same time, he was careful not to condemn wealth absolutely: 'Riches by themselves and by their nature are not all to be condemned.' He understood the growing importance of mercan-tile capitalism: 'Venice or Antwerp could not be ruined without great injury to many nations.' He did, however, consistently condemn greed and people who thought they needed 'superfluous and excessively expensive luxuries'. Great men, those of importance in society, should be suspicious of their own greatness.

As for charity to the poor, there should not be reckless giving but a practical succouring. A man should not get so carried away by charitable enthusiasm that he would 'cheat his children or his household'. It was never right to impoverish your own family. So, while Calvin believed in giving and caring for the poor, he was realistic. Further, far from encouraging individualism, he definitely seems to have thought that community needs superseded the rights of the individual. He said it was 'improper' to neglect the common interest for the private interest.

All this, I think, suggests that his view combined common sense, Puritanism and a genuine concern for the poor. He pointed out that Christ had not 'glistened with the regalia of kings' but had rather been a humble workman. He also detested laziness and pointed out that 'we are born to work'. In the most sympathetic and helpful modern biography of Calvin that I have come across, Professor William Bouwsma of the University of California constantly emphasises Calvin's sheer practicality; he also concedes his ambivalence and inconsistency on economic and social matters.

The controversial German sociologist Max Weber argued, over 100 years ago, that the Protestant ethic, with its emphasis on predestination, was linked to the aggressive growth of capitalism. Calvin certainly believed in double predestination – all people were evil, but God has preordained the election of some to grace and others to eternal damnation – though he made less of this doctrine in his later years. For myself and many other Christians, it is a doctrine that seems difficult to reconcile with any notion of a just and benign God, though I have been told by at least one eminent historian of theology (the late Professor David Wright) that that is not the point. Defenders of Calvin's theology say that the doctrine is justified by scriptural texts; but then I recall that Calvin himself argued in another context:

'We are not to judge usury according to a few passages of Scripture'. If that is the case, why then should we accept double predestination on the basis of a few passages of Scripture?

Capitalism comes into the argument only indirectly. Calvin implied that the state of election – of having been preordained to salvation – could be evinced by being a member of Christ's body of faith. (For Calvin, this meant membership of a Calvinist congregation.) So, if someone belonged to a Calvinist church and steered clear of excommunication, he might well manage to convince himself that he was indeed one of the elect.

Cynics might then argue that, if you were thus assured of salvation, some human beings would ask: why bother with good works or indeed any kind of hard work, or even basic human decency? Max Weber's answer to this was that Calvinism produced in its adherents a need to prove their worth through conspicuous work and worldly status. From this, it was a short leap to suggest that Calvinists were likely to be notably successful in business and commerce. And, in parts of Europe, Calvinists undoubtedly were conspicuously good at trade, commerce and making money. Also, Calvin, unlike Luther (who had bitterly attacked the leading German banking family, the Fuggers), defended usury; and at least one Dutch Calvinist actually argued that usury was necessary to salvation – perhaps the most perverse argument spawned by the Reformation.

There is a case to be made that, in Calvinist Scotland, the opposite happened. A new spirit of social control and discipline was inaugurated. If anything, this militated against rather than for economic selfishness and a showy drive for individual success. Free enterprise and the kind of competitive market-driven ethic which leaves others behind were not typical of the new Scotland with its emphasis on collective social responsibility through the kirk sessions. Early Scottish Calvinism was marked just as much by social cohesion and communal concern as by aggressive economic self-aggrandisement.

It could, on the other hand, be argued that the Scottish Reformation's emphasis on education produced, in time, a driven and aspirational mentality in young Scots that certainly did not hinder them in pursuing business and commercial success. People had been given the chance to use their brains, and the Calvinistic ethos was less hierarchical than that of the old Church. This undoubtedly created a more fertile climate for individuals to 'make good', in the old Scottish phrase.

Ultimately, however, I suspect that the links between the growth of capitalism and religion should be interpreted in a totally different way. The Roman Church was, for many years, associated with excessive clericalism. There were simply far too many priests, many of whom were clearly lazy, corrupt and slovenly – and contributing little to society. Whatever these people were, they were not exemplars of the work ethic; and their sloppy sloth and subsidised lifestyles were offensive to many.

Furthermore, the senior clergy were often very rich, living off the Church's extensive landholdings and its large revenues and giving little in return. Indeed, in pre-Reformation Scotland, such clerics often flaunted their wealth and thus irritated lairds and secular landowners, who were sometimes their social rivals and competitors. For those who wanted to make their way in the world, displays of ill-gotten and glibly displayed clerical riches often seemed an affront. But this, I emphasise, is a description of a syndrome that was prevalent before the Counter-Reformation.

In Britain, the celebrated socialist historian R. H. Tawney wrote an enormously controversial and influential book that was partly intended to refute Weber. *Religion and the Rise of Capitalism* was first published in 1926 and was for many years a bestseller. Tawney argued, in somewhat lurid and emotive prose, that capitalism developed independently of Protestantism, although Protestantism may well have adapted to capitalism. But, in prosecuting this case, Tawney managed to attack both Protestantism and capitalism with gusto. There are many wonderful passages in Tawney's book, for example his eloquent attack on Henry VIII's dissolution of the monasteries. Tawney accused Protestants of idolising wealth.

The great Tudor historian Sir Geoffrey Elton reacted forcefully. He accused Tawney of undermining Protestant self-confidence and reviving Roman Catholicism. He even accused Tawney of contributing to the West's inclination to relinquish world leadership. These squabbles may seem somewhat arcane to the twenty-first-century mindset, but they were conducted with enormous passion and even venom. The residue lingers on.

I asked the Scottish writer and thinker Neal Ascherson to adjudicate on this argument. He told me that the most obvious impact of Calvinism on Scotland was a levelling tendency – a distrust of any individual who emerged above the collective.

> After all, the point about predestination is that, from the outside, you surely cannot know who the elect are. It's deceptive. People who are working hard and doing good things may be reprobate inside, untouched by grace. There is a generalised Scottish distrust of people who present themselves as leaders, in any field. Scotland is not about individualism. That is the big mistake many people, including Mrs Thatcher, make about the Scots. She thought the Scots venerated individualism.

Ascherson told me that Scottish society had for long emphasised the collective, primarily in religion but also in trade and commerce. He added that he understood that the received idea of Calvinist Scotland was that it celebrated tough, self-reliant individuals who, because they were assured of personal salvation, could therefore get away with rapacious self-interest and aggressive self-advancement. But, for him, the opposite was the case.

ENVOI

Calvin's Problematic Legacy

This envoi is a personal discussion of Calvin's influence on Scotland, so often attacked; and it ends with a subjective attempt to rescue both Calvin and Knox from their many Scottish detractors.

Was Calvin bad for Scotland? For several generations, it has been a cliché that his influence was and still is baneful. The radical Scottish writer and educationist, R. F. Mackenzie, a man whom I got to know after he had been fired from his job as headteacher of Summerhill Academy, Aberdeen, in 1974, had his own slant on the controversy.

In several long conversations I had with him, he surprised me with his virulence about the Scottish Reformation and about Calvin in particular. I argued that, while Knox was influenced by Calvin, he also developed and modified Calvinism. I asked: 'surely you cannot deny that Knox's educational legacy was superb?' I tried this tack once or twice, but to no avail. Mackenzie insisted that, from the publication of the *First Book of Discipline* onwards, Knox's sole intention was to use education – through the new parish schools – to dominate the minds of the young and to make them believe that the religious system that had been imposed on Scotland – 'imposed' was his word, as I remember well – was the only system that could possibly be tolerated.

I would counter by suggesting that most of the great reformers from Luther onwards wanted people to think for themselves, to read the Bible and to consider its message in their own minds. Again, Mackenzie would have none of it. There was only one message, one interpretation, allowed, and that was the message of Knox and Calvin. If you deviated it from it in any way, you were ostracised, you were in effect placed outside the community. Knox, following Calvin, was practising both social and intellectual control.

And this was comparatively mild compared to what he went on to say about Calvinism and capitalism. (This theme is discussed in Chapter 29; but I will just note here that Mackenzie insisted that capitalism was a product of Calvinism and that the indoctrination process was repeated, though now in an economic rather than a religious context. Far from being allowed or encouraged to think for themselves, claimed Mackenzie, young Scots were bludgeoned into thinking that capitalism was the only possible, the only permissible, economic system.)

Mackenzie was an intelligent and very well-read man. He rarely raised his voice; he spoke softly in the gentle Aberdeenshire accent he never lost, using many words of the Doric. Yet what he said was full of force and passion. I found it hard to have a dialogue with him on these matters. He was dogmatic and categorical. He was completely convinced that Calvin's influence on Scotland had been wholly malignant, and in this view he was speaking for many.

Now let us turn to a contemporary Scottish thinker, Dr Carol Craig. In 2003, her seminal book on *The Scots' Crisis of Confidence* was published. In it, she discussed the Calvinist legacy. Her thinking seems to me to be rather more subtle and complex on this matter than Mackenzie's (and I must emphasise that I mean that as no slight to a man I greatly admired; I was delighted when Mackenzie asked me to write the foreword to his book *The Unbowed Head*).

But let me quote what, for me, is a key passage from Craig's book:

Scotland's Calvinist past has bequeathed to contemporary Scots two potentially contradictory attitudes to authority, and they lead inevitably to tension. The first flows from the central Calvinist tenet of God's magnificence and mankind's abject state. This means that in comparison with the majesty of God even our noblest achievements are worthless. Calvin thus taught the Scots to feel humble and submissive and to obey unquestioningly their spiritual Lord and master. But alongside this essentially master/servant relationship the Scots were also encouraged to see themselves as equal to others in the eyes of God.... The Scottish Kirk is built on democratic foundations – in place of aristocracy, the Scots have elected bodies. What's more, to ensure that the Scottish people would never again be 'hoodwinked' by priests or clerics, the reformers ensured that the Scottish people, even the poor, were taught to read and understand the Bible for themselves. The Scots were thus encouraged to be somewhat sceptical and independent minded. And this spiritual independence of the individual parishioner is further encouraged by Presbyterianism's complete opposition to a priestly figure who acts as an intermediary between an individual and God. To this extent, every individual is equally in charge of his or her individual destiny.

That passage seems to me to be well balanced. Further, I reckon it is a concise, judicious and even brilliant summary of the case for and against Calvinism, insofar as Scotland is concerned. I showed it to one of contemporary Scotland's leading theologians and admirers of Calvin, Professor Andrew McGowan, and he said he thought it was excellent. The difference between Craig and Mackenzie – not that I am wishing to create an artificial gulf between them – is that Mackenzie was adamant that Calvin's influence had been utterly negative, while Craig concedes that there was tension between the good and bad aspects of the legacy.

And yet, before today's champions of Calvin decide to take up Carol Craig as one of theirs, I should add that I asked her to expand on her theme. She told me that she had given talks to literally thousands of people – and no Scot had yet challenged her assertion that, in Scotland, you are worthless until you prove you are worthwhile. If she asked people to discuss what they saw as barriers to confidence, they themselves came up with the idea that they felt compelled to prove their worth as individuals.

She added that this had no doubt been intensified in recent years by the consumer/celebrity culture, which was not exclusively Scottish; but Scots aged over 40 talked about feelings of worthlessness as inherent in the way they were brought up. Carol contended that this was part of 'our Calvinist legacy'. She also compared America's egalitarian values – the idea that we are all born equal and that anyone can become president, and the fact that Americans are strongly encouraged to prove their worth through activities – with the position in Scotland, which she regarded as much more complicated. Let me quote her again:

> In our egalitarian values, we say: Everyone is of equal worth, therefore no-one should think they are better than anyone else. This then leads to levelling down and encourages people to feel apprehensive about success in case they offend others and are ostracised. The confusion for us Scots is that we are encouraged to prove our worth but at the same time we hold back for fear of how we might be judged by others.

That seems to me a superb summation of the Scottish psyche; what I'm slightly sceptical about is the extent to which this stems from the work, teaching and influence of John Calvin, although I do not deny that Calvin was suspicious of ambition, which he regarded as the 'mother of many evils in society – and especially in the Church'.

On the other hand, if you study the last of John Knox's famous confrontations with Mary Queen of Scots (when he was combining his self-appointed role as prophet with his no-nonsense demotic confidence), you come to this wonderful and very revealing passage:

> *Queen*: What have you to do with my marriage? Or what are you within this commonwealth?
>
> *Knox*: A subject, madam, born within the same. And albeit I neither be earl, nor lord or baron within it, yet has God made me, how abject that I ever be in your eyes, a profitable member within the same. Yea, madam, to me it pertains no less to forewarn of such things as may hurt it, if I foresee them, than it does to any of the nobility.

In a way, this proves Carol Craig's point. Here, Knox is arguing at one and the same time for equality – he may not be an earl or a lord, but he can speak frankly to his monarch just the same – and for worth: he emphasises that he is a profitable member of the Scottish realm. This, of course, clearly implies that others are not profitable members. So, on the one hand, we have this egalitarian, demotic notion of all being equal, and at exactly the same time we have the idea that some are superior to others. At the same time, Knox was supremely confident, and he certainly did not hold back because he feared how others might judge him. So many tensions undoubtedly existed. Whether we can extrapolate from this that Scots have been burdened by a Calvinist inheritance that prevents them from having self-esteem is another matter entirely.

There has been, for many years in Scotland, a tendency to blame just about anything that goes wrong in society on Calvin. The late Professor David Wright of New College, Edinburgh University, told me that he would sometimes ask his students to go through the newspapers, seeing how many instances they could find of the adjective 'Calvinist' being used in a routinely pejorative and often absurd way. He was always amazed by how many they found without trying too hard.

I decided to play the game myself, on a weekend in the autumn of 2008. I went through the Saturday papers but could find no references to Calvin. But I struck lucky in the next day's *Sunday Herald*. An early page lead was a story about so-called 'doggers', and other people looking for casual sex with strangers, being driven out of the centre of Inverness 'to find partners in far-flung parks and woodland'. The prominent heading over the story was:

Calvinist attitudes blamed for surge in outdoor sex

The background was that the Scottish health minister had announced that Scotland needed to relax its attitude to sex if it was to reverse the rising number of HIV infections and teenage pregnancies. Following on from this: 'Sexual health workers expressed hopes that it would put an end to Calvinist attitudes that still held sway in parts of Scotland, mostly in the Highlands'.

Inverness in particular was experiencing 'a surge in outdoor sexual activity as what police termed old-fashioned attitudes were driving gay and straight people out of the town centre to find partners in far-flung areas'. The health minister, Shona Robison, was quoted as saying: 'The Highlands in general still have a strong Calvinistic steak, a prudish thing that sees sex as something that happens behind closed doors and drawn curtains'.

I sensed a certain contradiction here. The story seemed filled with indignation that 'Calvinist' attitudes were driving people looking for casual sexual encounters to places like Culloden battlefield, yet the health minister was suggesting that sex should not be regarded as something that had to take place behind closed doors and drawn curtains. Should this not have then meant that she was relaxed about sex taking place in the great outdoors, on battlefields or wherever? Or – heaven forfend – did she not want sex to take place either on battlefields or behind closed doors? I couldn't quite see where Calvin came into all this. I'm sure he would not have encouraged casual sexual encounters, whether behind drawn curtains or on battlefields – but then neither would goodness knows how many other people, not all of them without influence.

If we look at Scotland today, do we really see Calvin's influence everywhere? I hardly think so. Yet it has almost come to this: if you don't like something that is, or is not, going on in today's Scotland, then you just blame Calvin. Often, the complaints have something to do with sex. Of course, Calvin's attitudes were, by contemporary standards, strict. He insisted that sexual activity should only be permissible within marriage; and, despite Christ's leniency to the woman taken in adultery, he was fervent in his condemnation of adultery.

But he was more concerned to deal with greed and excessive wealth. He detested what he called 'the mad and insatiable lust for possessions'. He taught that wealth led to 'pride, pomp, scorn of God, cruelty and fraud', and further wealth led to people becoming brutalised. I am pretty certain that, if Calvin visited today's Scotland, he would be much more concerned by excessive consumerism, by people spending far more on themselves than they need and not giving to the poor and helping the weak, than he would be by the pervasive indulgence and promiscuity, for all that he would condemn those also.

It is not always realised that Calvin and Knox were consistently concerned with the condition of the poor, and improving it, far more than with promoting any kind of sexual repression. On the other hand, the kirk sessions in Knox's Scotland, once they swung into action, could and did sometimes take a repressive and prurient attitude to sexual matters, and that legacy may well have to some extent hampered sexual expression in Scotland over the years.

But this raises an exceptionally important question: if Knox and Calvin are to be blamed (I think unfairly) for the Scots being sexually repressed (which I certainly don't think they are now), then why on earth are Knox and Calvin not given the credit for their constant concern – well ahead of their time – with the welfare of the poor? You could validly argue that both of them were worried to the point of obsession about arrangements for poor relief, and with creating communities that looked after the weak, the poor and the inadequate, and that these priorities engaged them far more than anything to do with sex.

So, why do all those who so glibly attack them never praise them for what was so good and beneficial in their legacy? Is it just ignorance, or is it something more insidious? I asked the eminent historian and student of Protestantism, Professor Graham Walker, to comment on this pervasive tendency to blame Calvin and Calvinism for just about anything and everything that people object to in contemporary Scotland. He told me:

> I simply do not accept that Scotland's problems can be attributed to Calvin. There are very few Calvinists around today, and most certainly very few people who have any serious understanding and knowledge of his thinking. He is still misunderstood, and so-called Calvinist attitudes have become a mere caricature, a very tired cliché. I suppose it goes away back to the perception that Scotland was once a joyless country, and that people endured excessive control and punishment doled out by the kirk sessions. But there was also humour and joy in those times, as there is now, and you can find joy in Calvin's writing if you look for it. It is absolutely vital to remember that there was always a generous, socially concerned side to his thought.

At the same time, I would not argue that, by distorting the influence of Calvin on Scotland, people are taking part in any conscious assault on Protestantism. It is, of course, possible that what they say may contribute to the influence of Protestantism being further eroded.

But I think you have to look at other reasons for this. Above all, Calvin and Knox wanted people to study the Bible, and this is just not fashionable any more, partly because we live in what is more and more an anti-reading culture. For example, my colleagues and I see this increasingly in our students: they try to answer very complex questions in simple soundbites.

When I discussed the traducing of Calvin with the Scottish commentator George Rosie, he went further. He told me:

I just do not see the Scots as being in any way dour or repressed. I think this idea that we are dour and repressed, and that Calvin is somehow responsible for it, is nothing more than a daft stereotype. I go over the Border to Newcastle and London, and I don't see any difference in the way that people behave.

Professor Ian Campbell of Edinburgh University endorsed Rosie's point by telling me that he thought the view of Scots 'as glum and dour and unemotional and so on' amounted to 'a suite of characteristics' visited on Scots 'by people who just don't live here'. Further, he noted that, while 'Calvinism' had degenerated into a term of abuse, most of those who used it as such had never read a single word of all the millions that Calvin wrote.

But he did point out that, for many generations, the most influential person in many Scottish communities was the preacher. Much of Scottish intellectual life was influenced more than anything by 'great preachers in great pulpits'. And, while much of the preaching was about love, not darkness or predestination, no doubt some preachers might have ranted in a negative way. But it would be wrong, he insisted, to blame Calvin for that.

It is, of course, easy enough to present both Knox and Calvin as repressive. Knox talked about preachers being 'wondrous vehement' against 'avarice, oppression of the poor, excess, riotous cheer, banqueting, immoderate dancing and whoredom'. Significantly, in this catalogue of various targets for vehement preachers, it is avarice, oppression of the poor and excess that come at the head of the list.

Knox himself was quite relaxed about dancing, drinking in taverns and people generally enjoying themselves – these were not the same as riotous living and licentiousness. Of course, the kirk sessions practised social control and insisted on discipline and self-restraint; but they also looked after people. The word 'community' is so often used today that it has become almost meaningless. The kirk sessions did genuinely foster and nourish a sense of community.

And it is important to smash the myth that Calvin and Knox taught that godliness led to prosperity, or that affliction was a mark of God's disfavour. On the contrary; as the Scottish church historian Professor James McEwen was at pains to point out, they thought precisely the opposite.

In the realm of politics, Knox actually radicalised Calvin's teaching, going much further than Calvin in advocating popular resistance to tyrannical rulers. I find it perverse that someone who was relaxed about the prospect of ordinary people rising up against their repressive rulers – a revolutionary concept in his time – is himself so frequently associated with repression. Knox had no difficulty in linking religious freedom to political protest and political action. In Scotland, the national Kirk rapidly became a body equal in legal right and general standing with the secular state. As the late Professor David Wright insisted, Knox thought that God intended him to be not so much a scholar or a writer as a prophet, pointing the way forward. It seems to me that he pointed the way forward in a revolutionary manner.

Professor Andrew McGowan, in a paper written for the *European Journal of Theology*, notes that Calvin took up Luther's idea of the two kingdoms of Church and state but developed it – and then Knox developed it further. This then led to the position in Scotland where the national Kirk was in total charge of its own government, doctrine, worship and social administration, protected in this by the secular state but devoid of any control or interference by that state.

The implication of this was that religion should be a very public matter, something to be discussed and argued over every bit as much as the conduct of politics, not something to be hidden away in an almost furtive manner as if it were some dirty little secret. We must remember that Calvin and Knox were political innovators as well as religious and social innovators. And, while Knox in many areas went further than Calvin, they both emphasised, again and again, the democratic implications of their religious thought, even if they did not use the word 'democratic'.

Professor J. K. Cameron, in his introduction to the Saint Andrew Press edition of the *First Book of Discipline* (1972), was careful to note that all persons, all estates, were to be subject to social discipline: the rulers, the preachers and the poorest within the Kirk. He stressed that the congregational nature of the Kirk is repeatedly emphasised. 'In every part of the procedures outlined, the final word is always seen to be with the whole congregation; the fellowship of the congregations is jealously guarded. Neither minister nor elders are ever allowed to take the final decisions.' Here, once again, is the democratic, egalitarian principle which the detractors of Calvin and Knox seem so reluctant to acknowledge.

I started this chapter by citing the views – very critical of Calvin and Knox – of the visionary Scottish educational thinker R. F. Mackenzie, a man who was something of a prophet in his own way. To balance these, in particular on the subject of education, let me now turn to another Scottish luminary, the distinguished Scottish historian and commentator Paul Henderson Scott CMG. What follows is particularly significant, because Scott describes himself as a 'Presbyterian atheist'. He says: 'Like many nowadays, I am unable to accept the traditional views of any religion.' But he is broad-minded enough to continue:

> I am convinced that the Reformation in Scotland has been of great benefit to the country. There are two interconnected reasons for this.
> The first is the response of the reformers to the aspirations of the Scots towards social equality or democracy – in other words, to the sovereignty of the people expressed in the Declaration of Arbroath of

1320 and later developed by George Buchanan. In accordance with this ideal, the Scottish Reformation was initiated not by royal decree but by a popular rising. Its institutions, after lay patronage was abolished, became democratic at every level from the appointment of ministers by congregations to the various representative bodies up to the General Assembly, which was properly democratic several centuries before any Parliament.

The second point was the importance given to education, which was a necessary requirement of the first. You cannot have a genuine democracy without a population capable of understanding the issues involved. John Knox and his colleagues set out to achieve this with the proposals in the *First Book of Discipline*. They were so successful that Lord Macaulay was able to write in his *History of England*: 'It began to be evident that the common people of Scotland were superior in intelligence to the common people of any country in Europe'.

From this derived the strong demand for Scots for important positions in many European countries, the Scottish Enlightenment, and the remarkable contribution that Scots have made to the rest of the world in ideas and scientific discovery. Many visitors to Scotland have commented on its level of education. The English writer and savant Sydney Smith wrote from Edinburgh in 1798:

> The common people are extremely conversant with the Scriptures, are really not so much pupils as formidable critics to their preachers; many of them are well read in controversial divinity. They are perhaps in some points of view the most remarkable nation in the world, and no country can afford an example of so much order, morality, economy and knowledge among the lower classes of society.

In conclusion, I would concede that Calvin was a very complex thinker. I have tried not to ignore the repressive and harsh side of his teaching; without doubt, he advocated frugality, sobriety and self-control. He thought Protestants should spend much more time fasting. His 'perfect school of Christ', as Knox called Calvin's Geneva, was not an easy or a gentle school.

On the other hand, he always sought a kind of divine balance, in the home as much as anywhere. Thus, in domestic life, he believed that people should not be 'lavish' but neither should they be 'sordidly parsimonious'. In education, so important to him and to his colleague Knox, his approach, *pace* R. F. Mackenzie, was conciliatory and even anti-authoritarian. 'Those who take upon themselves responsibility for teaching and exhorting', Calvin wrote, 'should not sit above and prescribe.' Rather, the teachers should 'join with' the taught 'and walk with them as companions'.

Ultimately, I cannot see Calvin as anything other than a benign man – and a realistic one. For all his strictness, all his severity, all his austerity, this was a man who agonised empathetically and kindly about the human condition. While few human beings could drive themselves as hard as he drove himself, I believe he always remained on the side of the weaker members of the flock.

In many ways, the sixteenth century was a terrible century. In its tempestuous and violent course, Calvin stands out, among other things, as a good and constant pastor. And he himself thought that the pastor should seek a middle way between severity and softness. Some, he said, were always fulminating, forgetting their humanity; they showed no friendliness and exuded bitterness. Calvin wanted none of that. He never believed that sinners should be admonished without sympathy.

That is not how his critics and traducers, many of them so adamant and so vocal in Scotland, choose to remember him; but he needs to be rescued from such people. He wrote and preached a great deal, and he could contradict himself – but, for me, much of his teaching is informed by the noble and luminous quality of compassion.

He cared for people like you and me, as he put it: 'however much our wings drop and we limp along and sometimes even fall'.

Bibliographical Essay

THIS book is a personal interpretative survey of aspects of a momentous century of religious and political tumult in Western Europe. I have, however, benefited enormously from the work of academic historians, not all of whom write principally for each other. I have also benefited from the previous labours of those like myself who simply believe that the past is important and that we should think about it, enthuse about it where appropriate, and try to understand it.

I consulted many secondary sources – perhaps too many – as well as primary sources, so I shall invert the usual custom and list a selection of secondary sources first. But, before the list, I wish to discuss a few of the books that I found most rewarding.

The three most enjoyable books I read – if not the most useful – were Evelyn Waugh's exquisitely written little biography of the Jesuit martyr Edmund Campion; William Tyndale's utterly extraordinary work, first published in Antwerp in 1528, *The Obedience of a Christian Man*; and Professor Steven Ozment's *Protestants: The Birth of a Revolution*.

Waugh's book was published in 1935, when he was only 32 but had already established his reputation as a novelist. It was well received, though Waugh's historical accuracy was queried and his candid Catholic perspective did not please all reviewers. It is written with a zest and beauty that most historians can only dream of. It starts with a perfectly presented deathbed scene (that of Queen Elizabeth) and immediately moves on to an angry polemic against the Tudor legacy. It is that kind of book. It also features a positive portrait of Saint Pius V, the pope who excommunicated Queen Elizabeth – and even Waugh's most sympathetic biographer, Christopher Sykes, could not forgive him for this supposed misjudgement.

371

Waugh was writing not just as a committed Catholic but also as a contrarian. His elegant partisanship, and generally hostile perspective on Elizabethan England, make for a useful antidote to the continuing celebration of that queen and her era, something in which I personally am more than willing to indulge. At the end, Waugh presents a list of the books he found 'chiefly interesting and relevant'. He is careful to note that the list is not intended as either a display of industry or a guarantee of good faith. The same caveats apply to the list that follows these paragraphs.

A companion book to Waugh's biography is Philip Caraman's translation of John Gerard's almost Buchanesque account of his adventures as a covert priest in Elizabethan England.

The second book is in a sense a primary source, though I used the 2000 Penguin Classics edition, edited by David Daniell, of *The Obedience of a Christian Man* by the early English Protestant martyr William Tyndale. This is an eccentric (even for the sixteenth century) mixture of politics and religion, and in sum is perhaps more than anything a manifesto for the supremacy of the Bible and thus an attack on the papacy. It is also a rather hectoring guide to Christian living and a philosophical treatise on the nature of obedience. The style is not at all cohesive: Tyndale often wrote English prose that was sublime – and there are sublime passages in this book – but overall the quality of the prose is uneven.

The book received the dubious imprimatur of Henry VIII, who announced that it was a book all kings should read, although a few years later Henry wanted Tyndale dead. While quite short, *The Obedience of a Christian Man* is in places hard going, and it might seem perverse to commend it as 'enjoyable'. But I found that, as I persevered, I was well rewarded, and indeed later kept returning to the book with more and more pleasure. There is something almost hypnotic about it. It is possible that, more than any other single work, the book encapsulates the early spirit of the Reformation. It opens a window on the reforming mindset. It is combative, in places angry, in places serene – and, if I could choose just one book from that cerebrally tumultuous century that gives an insight into the thinking that revolutionised so many other people's thinking, this would be it.

On the other hand, if I had to choose one general commentary to the early years of the Reformation as a stimulating introduction to the period, I would cite my third choice, *Protestants: The Birth of a Revolution*, written by Professor Steven Ozment of Harvard University. From a perspective that is very favourable to the Reformation, Ozment consciously tries to revive interest in it as a great historical revolution; one of his main themes is that the Reformation was an assault on falsity, fantasy and illusion.

Luther, Calvin and Knox

Biographies of Luther abound; an excellent one is by the Cambridge historian Derek Wilson. It is particularly good on Luther's legacy. Of the other two listed below, John Todd's biography is straightforward and lucid; Heiko Oberman's is much more demanding, and useful in that it is written from an overtly German perspective.

Calvin has far fewer biographers. I found the discursive and themed biography by Professor William J. Bouwsma enormously helpful; it is more of a discussion of Calvin's theology and ideas than an orthodox biography. T. H. L. Parker, who wrote from the background of a man who served as both an academic theologian and an English country vicar, wrote a concise, straightforward and sympathetic biography. Less accessible, but brimming with ideas, is the biography by the French scholar Bernard Cottret.

John Knox was very well served by Roderick Graham in his book *John Knox – Democrat*, a dependable, solid, modern biography. Stewart Lamont's *The Sword-bearer* is much shorter. Lamont uses his own experiences as a Kirk minister to provide insights which other biographers may lack. Both of these works can be strongly commended, but my favourite biography of Knox is by Lord Eustace Percy, who among other things was the so-called Minister for Thought in Baldwin's government of the 1930s, and an early champion of constitutional devolution. His biography is graciously written and, for the most part, very sympathetic, although Percy rather turns on his subject towards the end. Professor James McEwen's *The Faith of John Knox* is not a biography but a series of superb lectures (originally delivered in New College, Edinburgh, in 1960) on aspects of Knox's thought and teaching. It starts with a crisp biographical essay.

Henry VII and Henry VIII

A classic modern life of Henry VII is by S. B. Chrimes; like its subject, the book is careful and dry. A more eccentric but exceptionally readable biography is by M. Van Cleave Alexander. But the best biography of Henry is generally reckoned to be the first, written by the savant Sir Francis Bacon in 1621 (see note below on primary sources).

There is a multiplicity of books about Henry VIII. David Starkey's biography *Henry: Virtuous Prince* focuses on the child and the young man – the years when he was indeed for the most part virtuous. There is little anticipation here of the wickedness to come. As you might expect, this is a stimulating and colourful book. Of the various other biographies I've read, that by Professor J. J. Scarisbrick, first published in 1969 and then comprehensively revised for the Yale edition in 1997, manages to be both magisterial and somewhat pained in tone.

Henry VIII's three children

There is a most readable and gently revisionist biography of Edward VI by Chris Skidmore. In *Bloody Mary*, the American biographer Carolly Erickson presents Mary Tudor as a courageous and resilient woman. Her book is crammed with fascinating detail that nevertheless sometimes gets in the way of the narrative. The biography by David Loades is slighter and more restrained in tone.

There are many books about Queen Elizabeth. I confess that my favourite remains the first I ever read, by Sir John Neale, published as long ago as 1934 and much reprinted and translated since then. Neale's style is at once scholarly, easy and urbane, but occasionally he lets his guard slip. At one point, while describing the thieving and plundering bravado of the queen's buccaneering sea captains, he simply splutters: 'The indiscipline, the irresponsibility, the venality of the age!'

A compact, lightly written and very engaging survey of all the Tudor monarchs by the Cambridge historian Richard Rex, simply called *The Tudors*, is a first-class introduction to this endlessly fascinating dynasty, intelligent and comprehensive in that it almost effortlessly ranges over much recent scholarship. At the same time, it is a delight to read.

Scottish monarchs

There is far less choice when it comes to biographies of the Scottish kings and queens, except of course for the ever-controversial Mary Queen of Scots. The kings James IV and James V are well served by the volumes in the Tuckwell Press series on the Stewarts, by Norman MacDougall and the late Jamie Cameron respectively. *The Cradle King: A Life of James VI and I* by Allan Stewart is a very full and richly detailed biography. As for Mary, the biography by Roderick Graham, listed below, presents a judicious and fair assessment, and a realistic one, though I think that even this book, despite its sceptical tone, is too sympathetic to a woman who was a liability to herself and a disaster both for Scotland and England.

Thomas Cromwell

The first Tudor textbook I read was Sir Geoffrey Elton's *England Under the Tudors*, first published back in 1955. It is listed below, but there must be a note of caution. This splendid book, ferociously readable, forceful and forensic in style, is, among much else, notable for its formidable championing of Thomas Cromwell as the architect of the new Tudor state and, indeed, as 'the most remarkable revolutionary in English history'.

I suspect that, for many years, many Tudor historians have been very conscious of Elton's and, through him, Cromwell's shadow. Certainly,

Elton does seem to have slightly overstated Cromwell's role. My view, after reflection over the years, is that Cromwell was a lawyer of genius and a brilliant user of Parliament, the man who more than anyone else laid the foundations for that institution's future sway and authority.

Yet he was essentially – like Wolsey before him – his master's servant. No monarch in the sixteenth century had a better servant, not even Elizabeth with Cecil – but a servant he was nonetheless. In recent years, the tendency has been for Henry's personal role in the English Reformation to be reaffirmed, to some extent at Cromwell's expense. In his thorough study, *The King's Reformation* (2005), Professor G. W. Bernard argues persuasively that Henry himself was the dominant and decisive influence in his own reformation.

Among other biographies, Diarmaid MacCulloch's long and scrupulous life of Thomas Cranmer must be mentioned. This huge book returned Cranmer, evangelical, statesman, liturgical genius, master of the English language and cautious hero, to where he belongs: at the very centre of the English Reformation.

A gorgeously written biography in the grand style is Richard Marius's moving biography of Thomas More, a splendid portrait of a complex and problematic Catholic martyr who perhaps should have been as influential as Cranmer, but wasn't.

The Scottish Reformation and its background

The book I have consulted most while writing this one is the *Dictionary of Scottish Church History and Theology*, a superbly comprehensive reference book published in 1993. There are many contributors, and the quality of the entries clearly varies, but this is a reference book that rapidly became indispensable for me. I had used it when working on my earlier book on the Church of Scotland, *Outside Verdict: An Old Kirk in a New Scotland* (Saint Andrew Press, 2002), and it was a genuine pleasure to return to it.

Alec Ryrie's study of *The Origins of the Scottish Reformation* is a densely textured but constantly stimulating analysis of the build-up to the climactic years of 1559 and 1560, which I found both challenging and instructive.

Jane Dawson's generalist introduction to this complex period of Scottish history, *Scotland Re-formed*, is an excellent book. I sense that catch-all general histories such as this are less fashionable than they once were. Professional historians will quibble about detail and emphasis, while general readers may prefer a straightforward 'grand narrative'. The challenge for Professor Dawson was compounded by the peculiarly complex and confused nature of Scottish history through most of the sixteenth century. I think she has provided a first-class guide to a period of near-anarchy as well as revolution.

Art

At least some discussion of art is called for in a book such as this, since so many of the reformers regarded it as crucial to expunge artwork from worship and from religious buildings. Although I understand the reasons for this, I believe that one of the most impressive aspects of the Counter-Reformation was its renewed emphasis on religious art that frankly appealed to the senses. Apart from anything else, this led to the recovery of Rome as Europe's most richly adorned city.

So, mentioned in my list are two quite magnificent art books. First, Charles Avery's appropriately sumptuous book on Bernini, the master of the high art of the Counter-Reformation, is very relevant in the context of the preceding paragraph. Even better is the splendid monograph by Batschmann and Griener on Hans Holbein the Younger. This is a beautifully produced book with a most intelligent text, and its many splendid plates give the reader the opportunity to study world-class portraiture of some of the players in our story, including Henry VIII himself, his son Edward, Anne of Cleves (thereby hangs a tale!), Sir Thomas More, Erasmus of Rotterdam and Francis I of France.

It was good to have Duncan Macmillan's always stimulating history of Scottish art to hand. His chapter on the Reformation period is a masterpiece in miniature.

List of the most useful books consulted

Alexander, M. Van Cleave, *The First of the Tudors* (Croom Helm, 1981).

Anson, Peter F., *The Catholic Church in Modern Scotland, 1560–1937* (Burns & Oates, 1937).

Avery, Charles, *Bernini, Genius of the Baroque* (Thames & Hudson, 1997).

Baghi, David and D. C. Steinmetz (eds), *Cambridge Companion to Reformation Theology* (Cambridge University Press, 2004).

Batschmann, Oskar and P. Griener, *Hans Holbein* (Reaktion, 1997).

Baumann, Michael (ed.), *Steps to Reconciliation: Reformed and Anabaptist Churches in Dialogue* (TVZ, 2007).

Beckingsdale, B. W., *Thomas Cromwell* (Macmillan, 1978).

Bernard, G. W., *The King's Reformation* (Yale University Press, 2005).

Bouwsma, William J., *John Calvin* (Oxford University Press, 1988).

Bowle, John, *A History of Europe* (Secker & Warburg, 1979).

Braddick, Michael, *God's Fury, England's Fire* (Allen Lane, 2008).

Burleigh, J. H. S., *A Church History of Scotland* (Hope Trust, 1988).

Cameron, Jamie, *James V* (Tuckwell Press, 1998).

Cameron, N. M. de S. (ed.), *Dictionary of Scottish Church History and Theology* (T&T Clark, 1993).

Caraman, Philip, SJ (trans.), *The Hunted Priest: The Autobiography of John Gerard* (Fontana, 1959).

Chadwick, Owen, *The Reformation* (Penguin, 1964).

Chrimes, S. B., *Henry VII* (Yale University Press, 1997).

Collinson, Patrick, *The Reformation: A History* (The Modern Library, New York, 2006).

Cottret, Bernard, *Calvin: A Biography* (T&T Clark, 2000).

Craig, Carol, *The Scots' Crisis of Confidence* (Big Thinking, 2003).

Daniell, David, *William Tyndale: A Biography* (Yale University Press, 1994).

d'Aubigne, J. H. M., *For God and His People: Zwingli and the Swiss Reformation* (BJU, 2000).

Dawson, Jane E. A., *Scotland Re-formed* (Edinburgh University Press, 2007).

Dickens, A. G., *The Counter-Reformation* (Thames & Hudson, 1992).

Donaldson, Gordon, *Church and Nation through Sixteen Centuries* (Scottish Academic Press, 1972).

Donaldson, Gordon, *The Faith of the Scots* (Batsford, 1990).

Donaldson, Gordon (with Robert S. Morpeth), *Who's Who in Scottish History* (Blackwell, 1973).

Duffy, Eamon, *Saints and Sinners: A History of the Popes* (Yale University Press, 1997).

Duffy, Eamon, *The Voices of Morebath* (Yale University Press, 2001).

Elliott, J. H., *Europe Divided, 1559–1598* (Collins, 1968).

Elton, G. R., *England Under the Tudors* (Methuen, 1955).

Elton, G. R., *Reformation Europe* (Collins, 1965).

Erickson, Carolly, *Bloody Mary: The Life of Mary Tudor* (Robson, 1995).

Ferguson, William, *The Identity of the Scottish Nation: An Historic Quest* (Edinburgh University Press, 1998).

Fernandez-Armesto, Felipe and Derek Wilson, *Reformation* (Bantam Press, 1996).

Galloway, Peter, *The Cathedrals of Scotland* (Scottish Cultural Press, 2000).

Graham, Roderick, *John Knox – Democrat* (Robert Hale, 2001).

Graham, Roderick, *An Accidental Tragedy: The Life of Mary Queen of Scots* (Birlinn, 2008).

Green, V. H. H., *Luther and the Reformation* (NEL, 1974).

Hall, D. and P. Lillbank (eds), *Theological Guide to Calvin's* Institutes (P. & R. Publishing, New Jersey, 2008).

Heinze, Rudolph, *Reform and Conflict 1350–1648* (Monarch Books, Oxford, 2006).

Hibbert, Christopher, *The Virgin Queen* (Viking, 1990).

Hughes, Philip, *A Short History of the Catholic Church* (Burns & Oates, 1974).

Hurstfield, Joel, *Freedom, Corruption and Government in Elizabethan England* (Cape, 1973).

Hurstfield, Joel and K. Haley (eds), *The Historical Association Book of the Tudors* (Sidgwick & Jackson, 1973).

Hussey, Andrew, *Paris: The Secret History* (Viking, 2006).

Hutchinson, Robert, *Thomas Cromwell* (Weidenfeld & Nicolson, 2007).

ATION

Kelly, Douglas F., *The Emergence of Liberty in the Modern World: The Influence of Calvin on Five Governments* (P. & R. Publishing, New Jersey, 2002).

Kernohan, R. D. (ed.), *The Realm of Reform: Presbyterianism and Calvinism in a Changing Scotland* (Handsel Press, 1999).

Kirk, James, *Patterns of Reform, Continuity and Change in the Reformation Kirk* (T&T Clark, 1981).

Kishlansky, Mark, *A Monarchy Transformed* (Allen Lane, 1986).

Knecht, R. J., *The Rise and Fall of Renaissance France* (Fontana Press, 1996).

Lamont, Stewart, *The Sword-bearer* (Hodder & Stoughton, 1991).

Loades, David, *Mary Tudor* (National Archives, 2006).

Loane, Sir Marcus, *Masters of the English Reformation* (Hodder & Stoughton, 1983).

Lynch, Michael, *Scotland: A New History* (Century, 1991).

MacCulloch, Diarmaid, *Thomas Cranmer* (Yale University Press, 1996).

MacCulloch, Diarmaid, *Reformation* (Allen Lane, 2003).

MacDougall, Norman, *James IV* (Tuckwell Press, 1997).

McEwen, James S., *The Faith of John Knox* (Lutterworth, 1961).

McGrath, Alister, *The Twilight of Atheism* (Rider, 2004).

McGrath, Alister, *Christianity's Dangerous Idea* (SPCK, 2007).

Macmillan, Duncan, *Scottish Art 1460–2000* (Mainstream, 2000).

McNeill, J. T., *The History and Character of Calvinism* (Oxford University Press, 1954).

Magnusson, Magnus, *Scotland: The Story of a Nation* (HarperCollins, 2000).

Marius, Richard, *Thomas More* (Dent, 1984).

Martines, Lauro, *Scourge and Fire: Savonarola and Renaissance Italy* (Pimlico, 2007).

Mason, R. A. (ed.), *John Knox and the British Reformation* (Ashgate, 1998).

Moorhouse, Geoffrey, *The Pilgrimage of Grace* (Phoenix, 2003).

Mullett, Michael, *The Catholic Reformation* (Routledge, 1999).

Myers, B. A., *Few Saints, Many Sinners: The Commissioners of the First General Assembly of the Kirk of Scotland* (Magdalen Chapel, 2002).

Neale, Sir John, *Queen Elizabeth* (Cape, 1934).

Neale, Sir John, *The Age of Catherine de Medici* (Cape, 1963).

Needham, N. R., *2000 Years of Christ's Power* (Grace Publications, 2004).

Oberman, Heiko A., *Luther* (Yale University Press, 1989).

Ozment, Steven, *Protestants: The Birth of a Revolution* (Fontana, 1993).

Parker, Geoffrey, *Philip II* (Hutchinson, 1979).

Parker, T. H. L., *John Calvin: A Biography* (Lion, 2006).

Percy, Lord Eustace, *John Knox* (Hodder & Stoughton, 1937).

Prebble, John, *The Lion in the North* (Penguin, 1973).

Rex, Richard, *The Tudors* (Tempus, 2006).

Ridley, Jasper, *The Statesman and the Fanatic* (Constable, 1982).

Ridley, Jasper, *Henry VIII* (Constable, 1984).

Ridley, Jasper, *Elizabeth I* (Constable, 1987).

Ritchie, Pamela E., *Mary of Guise in Scotland 1548–60* (Tuckwell Press, 2002).

Rosie, George, *Curious Scotland: Tales from a Hidden History* (Granta Books, 2004).

Ryrie, Alec, *The Origins of the Scottish Reformation* (Manchester University Press, 2006).

Scarisbrick, J. J., *Henry VIII* (Yale University Press, 1997).
Seymour, William, *Ordeal by Ambition* (Sidgwick & Jackson, 1972).
Skidmore, Chris, *Edward VI, The Lost King of England* (Weidenfeld & Nicolson, 2007).
Smith, Lacey B., *Henry VIII* (Cape, 1971).
Smout, T. C., *A History of the Scottish People, 1560–1830* (Fontana Press, 1998).
Starkey, David, *Henry: Virtuous Prince* (Harper Press, 2008).
Stewart, Allan, *The Cradle King: A Life of James VI and I* (Pimlico, 2004).
Tawney, R. H., *Religion and the Rise of Capitalism* (Penguin, 1961).
Thorold, Henry, *Collins Guide to the Ruined Abbeys of England, Wales and Scotland* (HarperCollins, 1993).
Todd, John M., *Luther: A Life* (Hamish Hamilton, 1982).
Todd, Margo, *The Culture of Protestantism in Early Modern Scotland* (Yale University Press, 2002).
Trevor-Roper, H. R., *Historical Essays* (Macmillan, 1963).
Tuchman, Barbara W., *The March of Folly* (Michael Joseph, 1984).
Watts, John, *Scalan: The Forbidden College* (Tuckwell Press, 1999).
Waugh, Evelyn, *Edmund Campion* (Penguin, 1957).
Wernham, R. B., *Before the Armada: The Growth of English Foreign Policy* (Cape, 1966).
Whale, J. S., *The Protestant Tradition* (Cambridge University Press, 1955).
Wilson, Derek, *Out of the Storm: The Life and Legacy of Martin Luther* (Hutchinson, 2007).

Other sources

An obvious key text for the Scottish Reformation is John Knox's *History*, self-serving and immodest as it may be. As William Ferguson points out in his study of Scottish identity (listed above), Knox showed little interest in the previous history of Christianity in Scotland and was in effect using his book to change the present and shape the future. But Knox's *History* is nothing if not vivid. It is written with great gusto, and occasionally (and intentionally) it is very funny. The edition I used was that edited by Dr William Croft Dickinson: *The History of the Reformation of Religion in Scotland by John Knox* (2 vols, Thomas Nelson, 1949). This contains the usual addenda, including *Patrick's Places* (a series of theses by Patrick Hamilton) and Foxe's account of George Wishart's martyrdom.

The Saint Andrew Press edition of the other crucial text, the *First Book of Discipline*, by Knox and the 'other five Johns', edited by Professor J. K. Cameron of St Andrews, is a book I have known for a long time, having reviewed it for the *Scotsman* when it was published in 1972. In many ways, I think this visionary blueprint is the crucial text of the Scottish Reformation.

The Scots Confession of 1560, translated into modern English by Rev. James Bulloch, was published by Saint Andrew Press in 1960 to mark the fourth centenary. I find this a less impressive work than the *First Book of Discipline*.

Rosemary Goring's *Scotland: The Autobiography* (Viking, 2007) is a marvellous compendium, quirky and accessible, of eyewitness accounts to various important and revealing episodes in Scottish history. The fifty or so pages that cover our period provide a marvellous taster that is bound to send the reader in search of other similar material.

I have frequently consulted, possibly with more interest and pleasure than I did as an undergraduate, two collections of documents I used then: S. R. Gardiner's *Constitutional Documents of the Puritan Revolution* (Clarendon Press, 1962) and G. W. Prothero's *Statutes and Constitutional Documents* (Clarendon Press, 1965). Supplementing Prothero is Claire Cross's selection of important documents, *The Royal Supremacy in the Elizabethan Church* (Allen & Unwin, 1969).

I have already mentioned the Penguin Classics edition of Tyndale's *The Obedience of a Christian Man*.

Luther's *95 Theses* are crisp and to the point. They are listed in full in many books, for example in Wilson's *Out of the Storm*, cited above.

Francis Bacon's *The History and Reign of King Henry VII* first appeared in 1622. Written in just fourteen weeks, it is possibly the finest biography in the English language. It emphasises Henry's pre-Reformation piety. An edition with a brief but pungent introduction by Brian Thompson was published by the Hesperus Press in 2007.

An up-to-date edition of *The Catechism of the Council of Trent*, originally edited by Saint Charles Borromeo and published by decree of Pope Saint Pius V, and much later translated into English by Dr Charles Callan and Dr John McHugh, was published by Tan Books of Illinois in 1982, more than 400 years after it first saw the light of day. This is the essential document of the Counter-Reformation. The twenty-eight-page introduction by Callan and McHugh is notably concise and clear.

Finally, and on a much lighter note, one of the great offbeat classics of our literature is John Aubrey's *Brief Lives*, a series of gossipy, acerbic and sometimes downright ridiculous biographical sketches. Although Aubrey's subjects were mostly figures of the seventeenth century, several characters from the previous century also appear, for example Bishop Bonner, William Cecil, Thomas Cromwell, Thomas More and Thomas Wolsey. The exceptionally brief entry on Cromwell manages to encapsulate condescension, snobbery, spite and malice aplenty in just two sentences. Aubrey died in 1697, leaving his eccentric masterpiece unpublished. My preferred edition is that edited by Richard Barber (Boydell Press, 1982).

Acknowledgements

IRST, I wish to thank the staff of the Highland Theological College – a constituent and degree-awarding part of the nascent University of the Highlands and Islands. The HTC did not exist twenty years ago; now it is a flourishing academic institution. Not least, it possesses a fine library, specialising in theology and church history, of more than 65,000 books. It is a most congenial place to work, and in particular I thank the librarian, Martin Cameron, for a succession of warm Highland welcomes and for help well beyond the call of duty.

In addition, I am grateful to Fraser Jackson, Fiona Cameron and Dr Nick Needham of the HTC – and, most of all, I'd like to acknowledge my very large debt to Rev. Professor Andrew McGowan, founding principal of the college, who is also visiting professor of Reformed Theology at Aberdeen University and a Church of Scotland minister in Inverness. For an incredibly busy man, Andrew has given his time – as well as his learning and his insights – most generously. I have benefited greatly from his consistent encouragement. In an earlier book, I embarrassed him by referring to a conversation we had in a pub; I shall now embarrass him again by saying that I particularly enjoyed discussing Calvin in his office over a large dram of Laphroaig.

It was also stimulating to discuss Calvinism and its impact on Scotland with two celebrated commentators on Scottish affairs, Neal Ascherson and George Rosie.

Along the way, I have at different stages been helped by Professor Nicholas Orme of Exeter University, Professor Graham Walker of Queen's University, Belfast and Professor Ian Campbell of Edinburgh University.

I was privileged to have two long and enormously useful conversations with that most distinguished scholar, Professor David Wright of New College,

Edinburgh University, shortly before he died in 2008. He unburdened himself of his learning with a light touch and a dry wit.

My old friend and colleague Stuart Trotter has lent me many books from his considerable personal library and also constantly provided me with something invaluable – a civilised and ever-patient Catholic perspective as I tested my many theories on him.

Ron Ferguson, Rosemary Goring and Peter Kearney at various junctures have been very supportive, probably more than they themselves realise.

I am most grateful to Dr Carol Craig, one of the most influential thinkers in contemporary Scotland, for giving me her views on Scotland's Calvinistic inheritance.

Still on Calvin, I had the interesting experience of discussing his physiognomy with the sculptor Allan Ross when he was working on a bust of the great man. This might surprise Allan, but his comments helped to mould my understanding of this most challenging of the reformers.

I have been lucky over the years to have enjoyed various chats – and sometimes arguments – about aspects of the Reformation and its impact with two learned and distinguished Church of Scotland ministers, the Very Rev. Dr Andrew McLellan and Rev. Brian McDowell. I owe them both a great deal.

The usual caveat applies: none of those mentioned above has any responsibility for any faults or misjudgements in this book. These are mine and mine alone.

Further afield, Antonio Rigillo and his Scottish wife Margaret have been wonderfully well-informed guides to Rome and its environs, as well as splendid hosts to my wife and myself. What I have seen in Rome in particular has been a useful counterpoint to some of my more bleak northern notions. This book is about the Counter-Reformation as well as the Reformation, and I hope I have been both positive and realistic about that remarkable movement.

In North Yorkshire, another couple who are old friends of ours, Ann and Jim Wilson of Sowerby, took us on a memorable visit to the moving ruins of Jervaulx Abbey by the River Ure. It was while we wandered through the evocative site of this great Cistercian house that I decided to write this book. I wish to thank them for their ever-generous hospitality.

Back in Scotland, I have often argued, in a friendly way, about our religious history with that formidable historian and, as he styles himself, 'Presbyterian atheist' Paul Henderson Scott CMG, and with his partner Laura Fiorentini. They too have been constantly stimulating and informative companions over many lunches and dinners.

Alan Taylor, editor of the *Scottish Review of Books*, kindly allowed me to use (in a modified version) my essay on Mary Queen of Scots that was published in the *SRB* in 2007.

At Saint Andrew Press, Richard Allen, Christine Causer and Jonny Gallant have been towers of strength and succour. Most of all, I wish to thank the head of publishing, Ann Crawford, and that most diligent of copy-editors, Ivor Normand. Only I know how much I owe them.

And my wife Julie has been gracious and patient as she had to live not just with me, which no doubt is bad enough, but also with Luther, Calvin, Knox, Loyola and Melville, not to mention Zwingli, Savonarola, Teresa of Avila, Gasparo Contarini, Theodore Beza, Catherine Parr and goodness knows who else, which is more than anyone deserves. But she has always been a generous sounding board for my sometimes confused enthusiasms and concerns.

I'd like to conclude by thanking those who, many years ago, first nurtured my interest in history and my understanding that the past is important, if not my understanding of the past – a very different matter. At Aberdeen Grammar School, initial interest was stirred by Norman King, an eccentric teacher once described in the *Aberdeen Press & Journal* as the poor man's Humphrey Bogart. Well, Bogie he wasn't, but he was a good teacher. At Fettes College, Edinburgh, I was privileged to be introduced to the Reformation by an even more eccentric history teacher, a splendid Irishman called Paddy Croker.

At Oxford, my main tutors were Harry Pitt in modern history and Professor James Campbell in medieval history. These two pillars of Worcester College were civilised, scholarly and rigorous guides to the past. I was taught Tudor history by a doughty don of the old school, Lady Rosalind Clay. I also remember with pleasure the occasionally irreverent, if not irreverend, lectures of Rev. Dr V. H. H. Green of Lincoln College, yet another eccentric historian (I later learned that he was the model for Le Carré's George Smiley).

And, finally, I recall the redoubtable Dr F. D. Price of Keble College, whose lectures on constitutional history made that supposedly arid subject surprisingly entertaining. I record with special and heartfelt gratitude his almost excessive enthusiasm for the Scottish Covenant of 1638. Those who claim that the teaching of history at Oxford University ignores Scotland are, in my experience, simply wrong. Mind you, I greatly enjoyed bringing up the subject of Scotland in tutorials whenever the opportunity arose, and sometimes even when it didn't.

Text Acknowledgements

Harry Reid and Saint Andrew Press are grateful to the following authors, their executors and publishers for permission to include brief extracts from the works listed below in this book.

Eamon Duffy, *The Voices of Morebath*, Yale University Press, 2001.

Roderick Graham, *An Accidental Tragedy: The Life of Mary Queen of Scots*, Birlinn, 2008.

Rev. Stewart Lamont, *The Sword-bearer*, Hodder & Stoughton, 1991.

Duncan Macmillan, *Scottish Art 1460–2000*, Mainstream, 2000.

Lord Eustace Percy, *John Knox*, Hodder & Stoughton, 1937.

John Prebble, *The Lion in the North: A Personal View of Scotland's History*, Penguin, 1973.

Pamela E. Ritchie, *Mary of Guise in Scotland 1548–60*, Tuckwell Press, 2002.

George Rosie, *Curious Scotland: Tales from a Hidden History*, Granta Books, 2004.

David Starkey, *Henry, Virtuous Prince*, reprinted by permission of HarperCollins Publishers Ltd. (Copyright David Starkey, 2008.)

Index

Acheson, Robert, 179
Alençon, Duke of, 289
Alesius, Alexander, 75
Alexander VI, Pope, 26, 29
Allen, William, 316–17
Alva, Fernando Alvarez de Toledo, Duke, 290
Anabaptists, xlv, 127–30, 350
Anglicanism, 239, 351
  and Puritans, 310, 315, 317–19, 327
  see also Church of England
Anne of Cleves, 100–1, 103, 213
Anne of Denmark, 305, 310, 323, 326
anticlericalism, 32, 36–7
  in England, 82, 109, 206, 319
  in Germany, 58
  in Scotland, 74–5, 76
Antony of Navarre, 150
aristocracy, English
  and Church lands, 62, 116
  old Catholic, 317
aristocracy, French, 192–3, 284
aristocracy, Scottish
  and Charles I, 328
  and James VI and I, 298, 300, 305–6, 321, 323
  and Knox, 176, 184, 300–2
  and Lutheranism, 76–7, 162
  and Mary of Guise, 175, 177, 179–80, 225, 228–30, 231
  and Mary Queen of Scots, 256–7, 259, 297

Armstrong, Johnny, 160
Arran, James Hamilton, 1st Earl, 34
Arran, James Hamilton, 2nd Earl, 165–6, 172, 175
Arthur, Prince, 7, 21, 63, 68
Ascherson, Neal, 357
Aske, Robert, 93–7
Augsburg, and Luther, 50–3
Augsburg Confession, 191
Augsburg settlement (1555), 191–2, 307, 308
Auld Alliance *see* Scotland, and France
austerity
  and Calvin, 135, 143, 370
  and Catholicism, 351
  and Protestantism, 267, 309
  and Scottish Reformation, 246
  and Swiss Reformation, 131, 143, 154, 344–5
  see also destruction
authority
  biblical, 6, 30, 51, 87, 121–2
  and monarchy, xxxvii, 85, 104, 192–3, 283, 297, 321, 328, 367
  papal, 30, 51–2, 64–6, 70, 82, 102, 125, 243, 275, 337
  and reformers, xl

Bacon, Sir Francis, 4, 15
Balcanquhal, Walter, 299
Balzac, Honoré de, 146
Baroque art, 345–6

Caithir c2005 lorma's Brownie pack
Tyndale on preaching 56